THE COMPLETE
——— BOOK OF ———
GARDENING

THE COMPLETE
BOOK OF
GARDENING

A Comprehensive Guide to Planting, Growing, and Maintaining Your Garden

Klaas T. Noordhuis

BARNES
&NOBLE
BOOKS
NEW YORK

This edition published by Barnes & Noble, Inc.
by arrangement with Michael Friedman Publishing Group, Inc.

1998 Barnes & Noble Books

ISBN 0-7607-1086-4

M 10 9 8 7 6 5 4 3 2 1

Art Director: Jeff Batzli
Designer: Beverly Bergman

This edition, originally published as *Tuinieren Het Hele Jaar*, is authorized and published
under license granted by Rebo Productions b.v. (©1993)

Color separations by Fine Arts Repro House Co., Ltd.
Printed in China by Leefung-Asco Printers Ltd.

CONTENTS

Introduction

The love of people for their gardens is unchanging. What does seem to change often in gardening is taste. Styles develop, then may disappear, only to return later in a somewhat different form. With all of gardening history to look back on, gardeners today enjoy the richest opportunities.

Certainly the number of available plants has increased over the course of time. For instance, we have more species of plants at our disposal today than we did some six hundred years ago. But it is not simply the number of plants or the species used that defines a garden style; just as important is the way in which a garden is conceived and designed as a whole.

Some Historical Notes

We know that ancient Babylonian, Egyptian, Greek, and Roman societies designed their gardens with care. Although the plants grown in those gardens were for the most part "useful," rather than purely ornamental, plants, the aesthetics of design gave these gardens characteristic form. In western Europe, the first recorded gardens designed in a particular fashion were those maintained by monasteries, during the Middle Ages. Typically these gardens, enclosed by small hedges, were laid out in squares and planted with an eye to symmetry. Symmetrical planting was typical of the Renaissance garden of about 1600, too, but by this time many of the useful plants were replaced by ornamental ones chosen for their appearance alone. The selection of ornamental plants to be had was limited to those that thrived locally, with the occasional addition of a choice specimen brought from afar.

The usual Renaissance garden consisted of square or rectangular sections divided by paths of uniform width; there was no main path. The garden was detached from any neighboring structure and consequently, the squares could lie on any axis in relation to nearby buildings. It was between 1600 and 1750, in the baroque period, that a clear connection between building and garden developed. For the first time they together formed a beautiful unity; a broadened central axis led through the garden to a midpoint of the symmetrical building nearby. The garden sections were right-angled and symmetrical at two sides. The garden enhanced the shape of the building, as they were very much in harmony.

Only a few of the Renaissance gardens in Europe have been restored: Villandry (France), part of Herrenhausen Hannover (Germany), and the Prinsentuin in Groningen (the Netherlands). Wooden pavilions can nearly always be found there. In your own garden today, you can achieve a similarly charming effect with new materials.

A rococo garden seat. The slight asymmetry allowed in the garden during this period can also be found in the central ornament of this garden seat. This can be seen clearly in the detail.

Gradually, the baroque period merged into the rococo. The rococo style, where elaborate ornamentation was paramount, was applied between 1725 and 1775. The rococo garden doesn't rely on the strict formalism of one central axis, but makes use of from three to five, depending on the size of the garden. The sections separated by pathways were similar to those of the baroque period, the difference being that a slight asymmetry was allowed.

The French Revolution (1789) was not only a political turning point, but a turning point in the art of gardening, too. Severely styled gardens disappeared, and the preference was for everything to look natural—so much so that smoking volcanoes were constructed, dead trees were planted, and even molehills were imitated. Artificial grottos and ruins were built.

Botanists brought new plants with them from their voyages, and great sums were paid for the ownership of really exceptional plants. The phenomenon "tulipo mania" is well known: Enormous sums were paid for single tulip bulbs. This speculative market involved other species that are common now, too, but were rare and costly then. For such plants, owners of country estates built orangeries, the forerunners of the "glass palaces" of the nineteenth century.

In late-eighteenth-century England, the landscape style developed, wherein a garden was ideally to look

When viewed from the garden, the surrounding landscape appeared to be an extension of the garden. The walls that fenced off the garden from goats, cows, and sheep, could not be seen from the garden.

more or less like natural landscape. Winding paths, hills, and vistas were designed to overlook and incorporate surrounding countryside. The formal, straight-sided ponds of the baroque period were changed into naturalistic ponds. A typical characteristic of this period is that, from one vantage point, the beginning and end of paths and ponds can't be seen. If money were plentiful, an island with a grove of trees was often constructed near one end of a pond, creating the impression of a body of water of much greater length.

In order to interweave garden and landscape, ha-has were constructed: sunken walls, which could not be seen from the garden, but which prevented livestock from the nearby meadows from entering. (This fencing system is applied only in zoos nowadays.)

Laying out gardens was a luxury only the rich could afford until the middle of the nineteenth century, when residential gardens began to be seen. The landscape gardens were immense, but lacked privacy and intimacy, and the reaction to this was the cottage style. Cottage gardens were small, sometimes symmetrical and enclosed by hedges. Cottage gardens are actually based on farm

Back to the nineteenth century with salvia, Canna indica, *and New Zealand flax. Winding paths and a border of grass around the flower bed are typical of this period.*

gardens; they were colorful with perennial plants. Near country houses, several smaller gardens might be laid out, each with its own atmosphere, with interesting little vistas through hedges to enclosed "rooms," the sun rooms. Garden "border" plantings with perennials were, and often still are, very bright. During this century they have been refined by various designers. Borders may be laid out meticulously for certain color effects, inspired by such great examples as that of Sissinghurst in Kent, England, which was designed by the author Vita Sackville-West.

Today, there is great variety in residential garden design. It is important to bear in mind that the care and maintenance available should determine the size and sort of garden to be created. A grass lawn and flower beds call for considerable manual labor, so take into

This concrete pineapple is the symbol of prosperity and fertility. In just a few years, the concrete will be covered by algae and mosses. Do not paint these ornaments, and do not clean them, either. Left alone, they acquire a lovely weathered appearance.

A striped tulip typical of those popular in the seventeenth and eighteenth centuries.

account that good design planning can allow for some of the maintenance to be done mechanically. At the moment, symmetry, straight lines, and trimmed plantings are in vogue. The question for today's gardeners, though, when creating a new garden, is not what is in style, but rather, how they can realize a very pleasing design that can be maintained comfortably.

Learning from History

Creating a new garden in an "old" garden style is most successful when the nearby buildings are contemporary with or share elements of that style. This asks a lot, for the purist will want to borrow not only the characteristics, but also the materials, from the period concerned. A stickler for detail would not want to use nineteenth-century plants in an eighteenth-century garden. However, it may be preferable and easier to apply several pleasing characteristics of an old style and create a modern garden using modern materials. Truly old landscape materials are not only expensive, but they may not be found without a long search. Victorian brick

Old tools find a place again in contemporary gardens. These rhubarb pots were set over the young rhubarb plants (the pots do not have bottoms), so that the plants grew faster, as the pots retain heat. In addition, the stems of rhubarb grown this way are softer, and the rhubarb is redder. Here and there, one can again find these old pots used in kitchen gardens.

and antique garden gates can be hard to come by. Instead, use new building and accent materials, and let the design and plants you choose express the style. Take your home into consideration when planning your garden; if, for many months of the year, you will only see your garden from indoors, take this into account in your design.

Planting

Before you plant your garden, you must give some thought to what is permissible with respect to your neighbors, as well as to your housing association, landlord, or any other authorities. It is prudent to respect the law, and the standards of the environment. Your neighbors, with whom you may get along well, might move one day and their successors might take another view of your garden. So, plant with an eye to the future. Plant trees at a distance of at least 6 feet (2m) from your property line, shrubs 3 feet (1m) and hedges 1½ feet (0.5m). Consultation beforehand with the neighbors is always a good thing, and it is certainly a necessity if a planting is contemplated to follow along the boundary between two properties. A joint boundary planting can be an advantage to both garden owners: It saves space and money. Naturally, you must then both agree on the choice of plants, as well as the maintenance of the planting. Should the shrubs be trimmed at waist height, or would trees that quickly grow to a height of 13 feet (4m) be a better choice?

If you and your neighbor can't come to a comfortable agreement, fencing situated just on the perimeter of your grounds is the best solution. At street-corners and crossroads it is often inadvisable to locate high plantings, for reasons of traffic safety. Choose lower-growing shrubs and hedges here. Municipalities often loan or sell strips of property on the condition that no trees be planted, as they would interfere with cables or pipes. However inconvenient the rules may be, you must abide by them. Make certain you know of any regulations applying to your property.

It may be that certain plant species are restricted in your area because of diseases. One contagious disease is fire blight, which affects fruit trees, hawthorn, cotoneaster, and firethorn. Dutch elm disease has spread throughout North America and Europe, killing countless elm trees and drastically changing the landscape. The American bird cherry is restricted in parts of Europe for another reason; it is so vigorous as to be a pest, spreading from gardens to the wild where it crowds out native plants. In parts of the United States, the rampant spreader loosestrife has overtaken large

A trimmed hedge (here, Buxus) contributes to the neat, restful look of this garden. Imagine that quantities of flowers are blooming along the path. The fanciful shapes of the flowers would be balanced by the severity of the hedge. Without the flowers, the Buxus soon looks a bit boring.

portions of wild meadow and roadside. It is always wise to check whether any plants are discouraged in your area.

Plant Names

You will encounter them again and again in any book on gardens and houseplants: Latin names. This is not surprising in itself, for most disciplines have their own language and jargon. For aviators, English is the medium of communication; in the diplomatic world, French is still widely used, and the medical world assigns Latin names to many diseases and ailments. But the existence of various common names for the same plant makes it difficult to discuss plants accurately. The Swedish botanist Linnaeus (Karl Von Linne) proposed in 1753 a system of plant nomenclature, in which every plant is precisely and uniquely identified by two words: The first word is the name of the plant's genus and the second, the name of the species. This is called binary nomenclature. Because botanical names are in Latin, they are italicized. Let's look at the example, *Plantago major*.

This Renaissance garden was drawn by A. Vredeman de Vries. The drawing was published after 1587. During this period, the garden is typically divided into square sections, in the center of which is planted a tree. The hedges are trimmed in the shape of arbors (covered walks). There is no clear correspondence between the shape of the garden and that of the building.

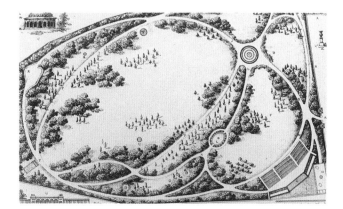

In early landscape gardens, the paths had no ends, so that visitors to the garden could wander around as long as they pleased.

A romantic garden seat: the cast-iron legs of this garden seat are fashioned in the shape of branches. Bridge railings and garden fences were often constructed in concrete during the Romantic period to resemble branches. They could often not be distinguished from the real thing when grown over with moss after a few years.

"*Plantago*" is the generic name, always capitalized, and "*major*" is the specific name, lowercased. This plant, *Plantago major*, is a naturally occurring species. When the same plant originates or is cultivated in a nursery, it is called a "cultivated variety" (or often "cultivar" or "variety"). The cultivar name is always capitalized and set off by single quotation marks, thus *Plantago major* 'Rosularis'. Here, "'Rosularis'" tells us the plant in question is a certain cultivated variety, or cultivar, of *Plantago major*. Sometimes, small differences between plants of the same species may occur in nature, due to different growing conditions. These plants may be described as varieties of the species, and here again the name is given in Latin, lowercase. One advantage of

botanical binary nomenclature is we can see immediately whether we are dealing with a naturally occurring plant or a cultivated plant. Another advantage of binary nomenclature is that there can be no mistaking one plant for another when they—confusingly—share the same common name, as many do. In horticultural circles only the scientific names are used.

Owing to new insights, it is sometimes necessary to change plant names. Basically, the first assigned binary name of the plant in question is kept. Infrequently, it is discovered that one plant has been assigned more than one Latin name under the Linnaean system. Even if the more recent name(s) is very commonly used, it is dropped. Unfortunately, nurserymen do not always adhere to the new terminology: *Azalea mollis* has been called *Rhododendron japonicum* for fifty years. The name *Poinsettia* is not scientific either: The name should be *Euphorbia* (Christmas flower). This can make for confusion.

When purchasing plants, it is of great importance to give the correct name. Just "prunus" is not enough. This is the generic name of a small shrub, as well as of a large tree. *Prunus laurocerasus* is considerably more clear than "prunus"; it means cherry laurel. But there are different cherry laurels, varying from a height of 6 inches (40cm) to 13 feet (4m)! *Prunus laurocerasus* 'Rotundifolia' is truly clear: an evergreen, nonflowering shrub with large glossy leaves, sensitive to wind, and suitable as a hedge in a sheltered area. When you read the last description, you can see it is impossible to render such a description in our own language with such economy. It will also be clear to you that, when it comes time to order a plant, the substitution of a species "that comes close" can play havoc with your plans. If you wanted a fast-growing, tall hedge to fence something off, such as *Prunus laurocerasus* 'Rotundifolia', the beautiful flowering shrub *Prunus laurocerasus* 'Otto Luyken', which is quite short, would be useless to you.

1 The Garden Design

It is said of vacations that the joy of planning one rivals the pleasure of the vacation itself, and this can be said of gardening, too. The design stage, a time when anything is still possible, is creative and exciting. Use this time well, for the consequences will determine the look of your garden for a long time.

For many years in England, it has been the custom of numerous private gardens to be open periodically for public viewing. Increasingly in many countries today, one can find organized excursions that visit such gardens. Visiting other gardens is an excellent way for gardeners at all levels of expertise to gather useful information and become inspired. Enthusiastic gardeners love to show their gardens to people who share their interest. It's an exciting way to pass along advice and exchange experiences. For the beginner, visiting other people's gardens is a good way of finding out what sort of garden best suits you. And the more gardens you see, the better you can judge which ideas you might adopt for your own garden.

Don't forget to include botanical gardens, arboreta, public gardens, and parks in your research. Many botanic gardens provide the plants with nameplates, so you can actually jot down the names of those that interest you in order to plant them in your own garden later. And many botanic institutions sell guidebooks that provide helpful information on specific plantings and specimens.

Fortunately, today's gardeners have an excellent resource: the nurserymen who search far and wide for a spectacular variety of plants. Often they eagerly seek out a color or growth habit of a certain plant that is just a shade different from the existing selection. The large and evolving supply of nursery plants makes it possible for gardeners to create unusual, and changing, combinations. It can also mean that the favorite plants of some gardeners disappear from nursery stock offerings, in preference for new introductions.

Small, specialized nurseries and plant suppliers are thriving. Nurserymen who specialize in peonies, hostas, herbs, fruit trees, vines, roses, bulbs, and rock-garden plants, among others, are not difficult to find nowadays.

A rigid pattern, such as used in the Renaissance, can be filled with flowers or vegetables. The success of such a design depends on the strength of the basic pattern. The filling-in can be done with all sorts of plants, according to one's own taste and ideas (Villandry, France).

Because many nurseries will ship plants great distances, gardeners need not rely only on the local nursery or garden center anymore.

Another source of garden plants is the garden warehouse, or garden supermarket. Due to the scale of such firms and the great number of plants they have for sale, they may be able to offer plants at a cheaper price than a smaller nursery can. You may see many plants for sale in full bloom at a garden warehouse; although they may look very attractive, don't be tempted to buy only blooming plants. After all, you'll want your garden to look nice throughout the year.

"New" developments occur in the world of gardening all the time, and inventions come and go with great–and predictable–frequency. Today's garden trends will fade, overshadowed by the appealing trends to come tomorrow. City dwellers feel increasingly estranged from nature, freeways criss-cross through once-wild land, and where there once were meadows, industry now mushrooms. People have begun to miss the beauty of nature more acutely than ever, and so home gardens are on the rise.

Form and Content

There is a growing gulf between professional garden designers, who concern themselves chiefly with the form

The rondeau at Sissinghurst, Vita Sackville-West's garden. The garden is divided into garden rooms. From the tower this garden is an interesting sight. This style of gardening is slowly but surely coming into fashion again.

of the design and know little or nothing about the plants themselves, and ecologists or plantsmen, people who are more or less expert on plants, their needs and habitats. The most artful gardens certainly need some skill and creativity when it comes to giving the garden form, but they also call for knowledge of plants. A garden designer who knows much about both subjects can design a garden that offers variety. A successful garden is designed to be compatible with the demands of the owner, the appearance of the building or buildings, and the rest of the surroundings. It

---

TIP

Some beginning gardeners cannot wait to get their hands dirty. Others are worried about "making mistakes," and procrastinate. There is no better way to learn about gardening than to garden; doing is learning. You should, however, make the most of the experiences of other gardeners, perhaps the beginning gardener's greatest resource for advice and reassurance.

keep—before you buy a plant or even pick up a shovel. Then make a list of any features you wish to add. Finally, cross off your list anything that is truly unrealistic; don't forget financial considerations. This will make it much easier for you to determine the final contents of your design. It does make a difference whether you plan to change the layout or the contents of an existing garden or whether you are going to design

Bamboo, ornamental grass, gravel, and concrete slabs are the only ingredients of this garden. The owner certainly has little maintenance work to do.

This summer house dates from 1920. The garden furniture is from the same period. Most working people can enjoy the sun for only a short time at the end of the day. This chair basks in the last rays of the sun.

is the compatibility that gives each garden its own character. Gardens rarely stand alone; some correspondence is usually necessary between building and garden, and garden and surroundings. More and more often we see that landscape architects are involved in the total design, that is, structure *and* landscape, as early as in the design phase of a building. This is the ideal situation, which makes for the most successfully integrated results. Many building architects (fortunately, there are exceptions) design a structure as though it were going to exist in isolation, without considering the surroundings, an unfortunate situation. When that happens, the landscape architect faces a difficult task: to bring the new structure and the surrounding landscape into harmony by skillful planting and hardscape design.

Practical Considerations

Note any unique characteristics of your garden, or the area you wish to turn into a garden, and make a sort of inventory of existing features you wish to (or must)

a completely new garden. Completely new gardens are most often an option only in new housing developments, as it is rare that any other kind of site is empty of some plant or landscape feature that would require consideration. No two sites are precisely alike, and so no two landscape solutions will be identical, either. Even so, this can work nicely to your advantage, offering you inspiration for design and features that might otherwise never have come your way.

A Design for an Existing Garden

First, note what you wish to leave standing where it stands. Don't concern yourself about where the lawn currently is, or where you want it to be just yet. You may be looking forward to a more or less complete design

There is much choice in the area of flagstones, stones, and other paving materials. Do not use more than two kinds of paving for one terrace. Too many colors in one terrace makes for a restless effect, so that any harmony with the surrounding plants or landscape is disturbed.

One large statue or an eye-catching planted container add more to a garden than many small vases or ornaments. Do take a chance on one relatively major purchase for the garden–the effect will most likely be splendid.

overhaul, and if that is the case, existing lawn is of but little consequence. Consider the trees. Poplars and willows, for example, grow very fast and are not suitable for small gardens. They are inexpensive at the outset, but cutting them down after twenty-five years is expensive and frequently cannot be done without damage to the rest of the garden. Consider carefully whether you really wish to remove any of your trees. And bear in mind that many trees take a long time to mature; will you be around to enjoy the trees you are thinking about planting now as replacements? We might well wonder whether we have the right to cut down a tree that is older than we ourselves are. We cannot remove lightly what our predecessors planted and nurtured years ago. An existing tree can often be designed around.

One reason to cut down a tree, in spite of these considerations, is when it is in the way of another tree, or is sickly and would be dangerous if it were to fall over. A tree with a crown so large it endangers nearby trees should be cut down ("thinned") for the sake of the other trees, so that they can develop better. Sometimes it is possible to take a less drastic step; for example, cutting off a heavy branch may be sufficient to give enough light to the surrounding trees and garden, restoring to the situation some balance for years to come without resorting to cutting the tree down entirely.

Don't wait too long to prune your trees when they need it. You risk crowding your valuable trees so that their beautiful shape is lost. So many trees fall victim to land development and the building of highways that their population has decreased alarmingly. Wherever you have the opportunity to plant a tree, do yourself (and the neighborhood) a favor, and do so. Trees combat air pollution in their way, and screen noise pollution; they provide sanctuary for many creatures, and contribute to our comfort and well-being in so many ways.

The First Design

First things first. Now that you have made up a "wish list" of those things you want in your garden, and you are quite certain that those things can be reasonably achieved, try to imagine what life would be like with the garden of your dreams. How is your future, and the future of any family members, likely to change the demands made on your garden in the years to come? Think about what it will be like caring for this garden. Will you be able

A newly designed garden with a distinctive shape. Whether you choose round, square, or free-form shapes, always take a window or door of the house *as a point of departure for your design. Unfortunately, the axis shown here is not centered in front of the window.*

If you choose a "round garden," you must follow through the curves around the side of the house.

to meet its maintenance needs? Can you manage it alone, and if not, what sort of assistance will you require? If water supply is an issue, would this garden suffer unduly from drought? Designing and laying out your garden are only part of the job ahead of you. That preparation, however complicated it might seem now, isn't much work in comparison to the time you will spend maintaining your garden. The years ahead are the very reason it is so important to plan carefully at the outset. It is difficult not to think about all the plants you want, but do try to imagine there are no plants in your garden. Now you must try to decide on the contours of your new garden. To help you, make a drawing to scale.

You don't need to be a talented artist to make a good garden plan. Use a scale of 1:100, or ready-made graph paper. Measure the perimeter of the garden carefully and draw in your house to scale; don't forget to indicate the windows and doors. Make several copies of this drawing, so the whole family can start filling in. Once again, forget about the plants; they come later. Now you can ask yourself questions about what you want. Because your answers to these questions are probably not simple or completely decisive, it is important to take some time to think about your design. One such question, which at first seems simple to answer, is:

Where shall we build the terrace?
• Consider that a terrace in the shade is very pleasant on hot summer days.
• You have bought the house because you liked the look of it. Consequently, the terrace should be situated

where it looks toward the house.
• A sandbox for the children should be near the terrace. Children do not like to play in a sandbox that is too far from the rest of the company, and their parents like to have them where they can keep an eye on them.
• Later, this sandbox can be made into a small pond, so take that into account now.
• A swing painted the color of the house doesn't clash and need not be hidden at the back of the garden. The swing can be incorporated into your garden design in an attractive manner and can even become a graceful element. And for the swing the same goes as for the sandbox: Parents and children like to keep an eye on each other. Therefore, near a terrace, room for a swing should

If you do not get around to changing an existing garden extensively, a temporary filling-in with annuals and *some tubs and pots full of flowers is one solution. Result: a wild but still cultivated garden.*

Anybody can shape a tree. You can trim many species of trees and shrubs into cubes, globes, pyramids, or disks. Once you have started trimming, you must stick to your decision.

be taken into account.

Each part of the garden should to be analyzed in this way, to help you determine what is important to you. The same goes for a kitchen or vegetable garden. It does not have to be large, and it can be accommodated into virtually any plan. Don't think about exactly what you want to plant just yet, until you finalize the layout of the different parts of your garden.

If you want paths, plan them to be relatively broad; 3 feet (1m) wide is really not too wide, even for a very small garden. On your drawing you can visualize elements of your design even better than in reality; if the proportions seem appropriate in the drawing, they will seem so in reality. It is not for nothing that the design of a garden begins with a drawing. Working on your garden plan will help you develop a better sense of proportion.

One of the things that should be decided early on is whether you want to incorporate flagstones or other paving materials in your design. The size of larger paving materials can in part determine the width of paths and the size of a terrace. Flagstones are commonly available in the sizes 8 inches square (20cm), 12 inches square (30cm), 16 inches square (40cm), 19 inches square (50cm), and about 16 by 24 inches (40 by 60cm).

Determine whether the ground in the garden slopes down to one side. A garden that rises at the back visually appears smaller. Usually a slight downward slope toward the back is preferable. A level garden is the most restful to the eye. Note variations in grade on your drawing wherever an area more than a third of the garden in size is significantly higher or lower than the rest. In the case of gardens smaller than 100 square yards (about 100 sq m), changes in the grade are not advisable as they make the garden seem smaller than it really is. Sand is needed to form a base for any paving (you will often need considerable amounts of sand), and this may raise the elevation of your paved area by 2 inches (5cm).

Drainage

For wet gardens, you will probably want to take steps to improve the drainage. (An advantage to land that is naturally very wet is that it is ideal if you wish to build a

A garden with a large barometer and a simple paving of gravel. Because the surfacing is unobtrusive, the plants and the furniture show to advantage.

pond or a marsh garden; only under very wet circumstances you should consider designing one of these, because marshy conditions are difficult to create artificially.) Find out whether there is an existing drainage possibility on or very near the site in question, a ditch or a sewer, for instance. See to it that the drainage pipe lies in the ground as level as possible, with a slight downward slope. Remember to place the pipe above the highest winter water level, for otherwise the garden will fill with water at that time. As a rule, pipes will draw water from a surface area of no less than 18 feet (6m), so that one pipe through the length of the garden is ample for a small garden. Soil conditions can vary greatly even in a single neighborhood, and that includes drainage. But it pays to consult someone knowledgeable about the conditions in your area. Other gardeners, farmers, even excavation workers may know something about the soil where you plan to garden if they are familiar with the area. They may be able to tell you, for instance, if the area is predominantly heavy clay, so drainage is poor, and what you might be able to do to increase the porousness. For most private gardens, drainage pipe with a coil casing is easiest, and it doesn't require that sand or gravel be brought in; the piping can be put in the ground right away.

Where to Plant

People seem, generally speaking, to be of one of two minds. Either they want a garden that is beautiful when enjoyed from outdoors, or they want a garden that is beautiful when viewed from indoors. There is no question

Pergolas can be welded from lengths of metal pipe. A pergola in the garden creates the illusion of depth. The actual distance between the photographer and the veranda is only 48 feet (15m)!

A terrace in the shade. On a hot day it is nice not to have to sit in the sun, so be sure to reserve a place for a terrace or just a seat in the shade when planning your garden. In this photograph, a few trees and vines offer reprieve from the sun.

that your new garden can be both. Where should the most important views be in your new garden? Perhaps you would like the garden to look beautiful chiefly when admired from a public street. If you work at home and receive clients there, for instance, this consideration is not unimportant. Naturally, it is also possible that you want the garden to look nice from the house. On rainy days and (depending on where you live) during the entire winter, you will see the garden only from the house, and then it functions as a sort of extension of the living room. You might take the window from which the garden is best enjoyed as a starting point in creating your design. A kitchen window, for example, is one such vantage point, or a bedroom with a terrace door, or a living room or family room.

Think about your privacy with respect to the neighbors. Determine where you want hedges, fences, or walls. Exactly what your barrier is to consist of, be it a wooden fence or a hedge, isn't important at this point.

Tree trunk sections should be treated with preservative or they will soon rot when wet.

Remember that wood becomes extremely slippery, especially in the shade!

In this phase, just decide on the height and width of the barrier, and the effect you wish to achieve. Hedges do not always have to run strictly along the property line; a portion of the hedge that turns inward offers the added interest of some hidden corners, naturally adding variety to the design.

Take a ruler and draw dotted lines of the directions from which the garden will be viewed most. These identify your lines of sight, and the principle views. This will show you which part of the garden ought to remain "open," to maintain the illusion of space. When you have determined the viewing directions, you can go on to determine other fixed points. Review your wish list of the garden elements you long to incorporate: pond, sandbox, greenhouse, paths, collapsible washline, garden shed, children's garden, pergola, carport, shady

terrace, statuary, garden seat, bicycle stand, lighting, arbor, a large tree, a dog run (or even a rabbit hutch), flagpole, large pots, compost bin, and so on. Do you want formal flower beds, a vegetable garden? Determine the best locations now. You can increase the illusion of depth by placing something tall in the foreground of the principle view. This might be a few pillars with vines or climbing roses, any ivy-covered trellis, or a few narrow trees that won't block much light. Remember: A garden that slopes upward toward the back seems smaller than a level garden or one that slopes slightly downward toward the back. A slight slope away from the house is an advantage in another way, too, for then water flows away from the house rather than settling in around the foundations where it can result in considerable dammage.

Paths

When the basic form of your garden is decided, it isn't necessary to install a pond or a pergola immediately; in fact, it is easier on the pocketbook to spread the costs out over a period of time. However, the laying of any paths ought to be finished before you start planting. Grass paths are the cheapest to lay out, but their edges need much maintenance to look truly neat. This applies to gravel paths as well. (Gravel has another disadvantage, too: Children can hardly resist the temptation to throw the gravel about.) Cheap paving stones can be combined with small stones and pebbles; the pavement is not expensive, and is pleasant to look at. Using small stones by themselves is not only expensive as a purchase; the laying of them is costly. The paver you choose always determines the exact height of the pavement in connection with the drainage. If the pavement lies just a

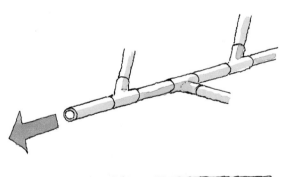

Lay pipe without casing on a layer of sand, and cover with peat soil; the peat soil prevents the holes in the pipe from silting up. Then, fill in the trench again. If there is no existing drainage ditch or sewer available to you, you can dig a gravel drainage pit yourself. Increase the drainage potential of the pipe by laying side connections.

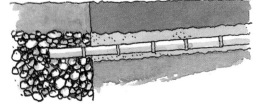

bit higher or lower than the existing ground, any plants that have just been planted are already in the way because the ground needs to be filled up a bit or dug off. If that is the case, it is better to postpone the planting until the next season.

Firewood stacked in the old-fashioned manner is an attractive ornamental element in the garden. You needn't hide the firewood out of sight.

TIP

Cut flowers outside the house

Bouquets of flowers have always been picked for bringing indoors. Now that the garden has become an extension of the living room—many living rooms have French doors to the terrace—it is also nice to make bouquets for the garden. These bouquets can look a little wilder, an effect that can be achieved with large bunches of dill, rhubarb, and cabbage leaves, and produce from pumpkin to cucumber. Particularly shady spots are suitable for such bouquets, as the bouquet won't wilt as quickly as in full sun; indoors as well as outdoors, strong sunlight takes a toll on cut flowers. The bouquet need not be expensive; an armful of cow parsley, Queen Anne's lace, and buttercups in a large vase next to the front door welcomes your guests heartily. If you place the vase somewhere where it can be seen from the house, it can be enjoyed both indoors and out.

Ponds

When it comes to ponds, there are great differences in mechanics and price. You can choose a fiberglass, plastic, or rubber liner, an earth-bottom pond, concrete sprayed over steel mesh, or concrete blocks. For the real do-it-yourselfer, a concrete pond is recommended. See page 47 for a discussion of these options.

Lawn

A handsome part of many an attractive garden is lawn. Portions of your garden about which you are undecided can be "grassed over" for the time being. If and when you change your mind later, you can convert the lawn as you wish at no great cost. For a discussion of sods and grasses, refer to information on lawns, in chapter 3.

Trees and Shrubs

Next to the house, a large tree can affect much of the design picture for your garden. A large, established (and probably expensive) tree is a significant landscape feature. For a location at the back of the garden, where the overall picture of house and garden is experienced infrequently, a smaller, cheaper tree is recommended. Trees well on their way to maturity give the garden the appearance of permanence. The amount of privacy you want to have also plays a decisive role in your choice of plants and other materials. Larger plants will appeal to those who wish to sit in their gardens in complete privacy. Trees and shrubs offer visual privacy, of course, but also help screen out unwelcome noise. You should know that large plants have a longer period of growth arrest when they are transplanted, so the initial advantage of planting a larger, more expensive shrub or tree for early impact has that drawback after a few years. In the long run, you may do better installing a younger, smaller tree or shrub. Although plants represent only a small part of the costs of a garden, you can save much by starting with smaller-size plants, without affecting the end result. Advice from nurserymen can be of great value, but take what they say with a grain of salt—they still want to sell their merchandise. Often their advice is a bit biased. You must decide for yourself what you want, and be able to insist on a smaller plant when making your purchases.

The Collapsible Washline

Choose a sunny place in a breezy location for this, for then your laundry will dry quickly and be out of the garden

One long edging planted with only one kind of plant is a tranquil sight. Red and purple impatiens lag in growth behind the pale pink and white ones.

An old cooking pot spilling over with flowers is nice in the garden. Be careful: Too many pots and baskets give the garden a cluttered look.

before you know it. Accessibility is important; you won't want to trudge out to a far corner of the garden every time there is washing to hang on the line. A collapsible washline above the middle of the terrace is less than practical; naturally, you'll want to sit there yourself during good drying weather. Find a place out of sight of the living room (or wherever else people tend to congregate in your home) for hanging out the wash. It is better to use small drying racks in small gardens, where a collapsible washline would severely limit other design possibilities. You don't want wash day to take over the garden entirely.

A Sandbox for Children

The sandbox must be built in a place where you can keep an eye on the children. It is as important that the children be able to see their parents; otherwise they will not enjoy their play. Locate the sandbox in a warm place away from drafts. It would be ideal to build the sandbox in a spot where, years later, you'd like a pond or a large flower tub. Children grow faster than you think! Plant a tree for some shade if one is not nearby. Sandboxes are nicer if there is a ledge to sit on; not only is it more comfortable for the children playing in it, but it may mean less sand brought into the house. A stone sandbox could sport a wooden plank or two for seating. Build the sandbox high enough so that rainwater will run out easily. Fill it with sand that

The construction is time-consuming, but the maintenance is simple in a garden with many boulders, *planking and flagstones, slow-growing evergreens, and ornamental grasses.*

is not too fine. Sharp masonry sand is best; when it is wet it will dry rapidly. A lid is a practical addition (especially if there are cats nearby—a lid is the only way of ensuring that your sandbox does not quickly turn into a litter box).

Garden Lighting

Garden lighting is especially recommended for small gardens onto which the living room (or other sitting room) looks out; it "enlarges" the room. Another con-

In the case of a healthy tree, a bark wound heals in a few years. Nevertheless, avoid harm by not transporting young trees home in the trunk of the car without first tying burlap around the tree trunk for protection.

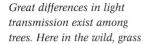

Great differences in light transmission exist among trees. Here in the wild, grass *still grows well under birches, but not under beeches and chestnuts.*

pump in a pond must operate continuously, even if the pond lighting is switched off.

Electric underground cable has an iron casing that cannot easily be cut through by accident with a spade. Nevertheless, the cable must be buried at a depth of 2 feet (60cm). That way, you will never be bothered by the cables when you do normal garden work. Still, it is a good idea to make a drawing of where the cables are buried, because it won't be long before you have forgotten the exact location. (You may *think* you'll remember, but it is almost certain you won't.) This is information you will want to pass on to the next inhabitants of your home.

For your garden lighting you can use a transformer, but safety is sufficiently guaranteed with an earth leakage circuit breaker. Always go to a professional with your electrical plans; if necessary he or she can give you advice and steer you from dangerous or costly mistakes. It is critical that for outdoor use only watertight electrical fittings be used. This also goes for the lighting in a greenhouse, where fittings should be at least splashproof, although, because of the high humidity, fittings that are entirely watertight are better. Here in a greenhouse, a permanent electric outlet is a good idea if you plan to use heating cables for warming seed flats. Light in the garden can add drama. It can heighten desirable effects and notable features and ornaments, but it can also result in overkill. The entire garden needn't be lit from every angle. Try to spotlight various areas of the garden selectively. You want a soft effect, not the impersonal illumination of a baseball stadium. To use outdoor lighting to make your home more secure, illuminate doorways and their approaches, and the plantings around vulnerable first-floor windows. (For lighting the doorsteps themselves, you may prefer to install motion-activated lights. Some of these are

siderable advantage of garden lighting is that it may deter possible burglars. Most intruders are leery of approaching a well-lighted building; light makes it seem less certain that no one is at home, and it is more difficult to avoid detection in bright light than under cover of darkness. (This is true of gravel, too—just as light is an optical deterrent, gravel is an acoustic deterrent. The fact is that burglaries tend not to be committed in bright light and with much crunching.) Lighting for the front door is necessary. Not really necessary, but convenient, is lighting for garden steps, the area near a pond, summer house, garden shed, or greenhouse. You must decide as you work on your garden plan where you will need permanent electric power and what can be switched from the house. The

It is easy to set up a bamboo trellis. The morello trees that have just been planted have been pruned and fastened— carefully—to the trellis.

Wooden garden furniture left outdoors year-round needs a roof in the winter and sometimes even in the summer. A veranda offers shelter from the wind, and it protects the furniture. Note the "wind hatch" that can be opened in the event of a severe storm, to prevent wind setup.

so sensitive that a pet or other small creature can trigger the light, so you will want to investigate the options available.)

Steps in the Garden

Sometimes differences in grade should be minimized or eliminated. Sometimes, though, they present an opportunity to add interesting features to the garden. You can work around a slope by constructing steps or by a sloping path. A sloping pathway looks best and is easier to travel if the degree of slope is less than 6 inches (15cm). It is usually wise to install lighting by any steps, preferably close to the ground.

As with paths, steps should be constructed to seem a bit too wide at first. Later, when surrounding plants have grown and filled in, you will see that the steps don't look too broad anymore. In the beginning of living with a young garden, you must put up with a few disproportions for perhaps a couple of years; after all, a garden needs time to grow.

Concrete steps call for a foundation. A foundation that will reach under the frostline in the ground averages 2 feet (60cm). For simple steps, you can use mortar (or concrete mortar) to affix smallish stones in the concrete. When freezing weather arrives, the steps will then "come up" or heave in one piece and should not sustain any damage. Most beginning gardeners don't realize how simply steps can be made of concrete. Use a mixture with a good amount of chalk, so the steps will have a nice green look to them after no more than a year–they will actually look old. An occasional sprinkling of buttermilk will stimulate the growth of algae on new concrete.

If you lay brick in fierce sunshine or keen wind, you

must cover the newly laid steps with plastic sheeting or damp burlap for a few days to allow the concrete to cure, otherwise the desiccation will proceed faster than it ought. Railway ties, or crossties, have long been employed as edging for flower beds and borders, and as steps. Crosstie steps that are laid in the shadow of the house or under trees become extremely slippery with the growth of algae or moss, and this can be hazardous. In full sun as well, crossties should be kept up in order to prevent them from becoming slippery. They are safer to use as edging for level areas. If you build your own, treat the wood with environment-friendly stain. Creosote, the preservative frequently used in treating the wood for industrial use, is cheaper, but it will burn nearby plants and they will shrivel.

Steps may be entirely rustic, rather casual, or formal; old-fashioned–looking or contemporary; and elaborate or simple in the extreme. Whatever the aesthetic effect you hope for, your steps must be sturdy and safe–that is

A small garden statue in a large garden will stand out more if a plate of glass is placed behind it. The statue is almost "framed."

the priority. Consider who will be the primary users of the garden steps. Is a handrail necessary? Should the treads be somewhat deeper than those of ordinary stairways, to accomodate the needs of people who are less than steady on their feet? Will the building materials you are planning to use provide traction adequate to your needs in all kinds of weather? Give some thought to how the building materials you want to use will look as part of your whole garden picture, and with your home.

A Flagpole

If it is placed well, a flagpole can be a harmonious element of the garden design. Consider locating it by the side of the house, in line with a straight hedge, or perhaps in the middle of the lawn.

The size of a flagpole is determined by the size of the house. A pole of 25 feet (8m) will suit a large house, and a pole of 15 feet (5m) is sufficient for a small house. A mast that is too large will overwhelm your garden, and

An old garden gate can be suspended simply from two   *wooden posts. The effect is surprisingly nice.*

A colorful element in the garden can sometimes replace flowering plants. Admittedly, it takes courage to paint a pergola or garden furniture   *bright red. Do adjust the color scheme of the flowers to the color of the paint, or they will not be able to stand the competition.*

one that is too small looks awkward.

Standard flagpoles are white, but you can paint the pole in colors harmonious with the house. Once again, take the surrounding plants into consideration. Small, immature trees will grow tall before you know it! A flag ought to be able to flutter freely; branches may damage the flag. (Always wind the rope around the pole one turn; a flapping rope frightens birds and is bothersome to the neighbors.)

There are some patriotic souls who want to share their pride with their neighbors, and they choose to erect a flagpole. There are other reasons for having a flagpole,

too. Some people collect decorative flags for the sheer beauty of them. There are sailing enthusiasts who run nautical flags up flagpoles that serve as land-locked "masts," a fanciful decoration that celebrates a beloved pasttime. And for those with a keen interest in weather and the natural world, there are windsocks that indicate the direction and strength of prevailing winds. Whatever your inclination, keep the sizes of the flag and pole in proportion; a flag that is too large looks silly.

Types of Gardens

In this book, there is a distinction between the "town" or "city" garden and "natural" gardens, which can be of numerous different types. The reason for a separate discussion of the city garden is the fact that in the city, a garden must contend with factors that don't affect

---

TIP

Winter housing

Some nurserymen make some of their greenhouse space available to people who do not know what to do with their tub plants over winter. If the "rental" cost seems reasonable to you, make arrangements to give your larger plants a vacation. See to it that your plants are clearly marked with your name and address if you are going to send them away to overwinter elsewhere. Always write your identifying information in soft pencil, which remains legible the longest under humid conditions; a sturdy wax pencil is a valuable addition to your stash of garden tools.

suburban or country gardens, such as tall surrounding buildings, and more limiting city regulations. Of course, you are free to pick and choose aspects characteristic of different types of gardens to use in your garden. Such factors as soil conditions and the amount of light and shade will to some extent determine the direction your planning takes. But if you are planning a city garden, you can certainly plant heather there. In a ground-cover garden, the addition of a pond from a water garden would be handsome. Here is a short inventory of garden types. You can borrow freely from them in creating the garden that suits you best. Cost and how fast you want your garden to be full-grown will be factors in your decision making.

City Gardens

City gardens make quite different demands on a design than gardens that lie in the middle of the countryside. It may seem difficult to create something nice on a severely limited piece of ground, surrounded by other houses and tall buildings to boot, but it is possible. The typical feel of a city garden is that it is an additional room to the house. Surrounding buildings even provide the garden with a milder climate, sheltering it from strong winds and perhaps a punishing sun. If you make much of your little piece of property, your city garden can give far more pleasure per inch than a huge garden in the country.

Plan colors and flowering times before you plant. A purple or violet rhododendron would have harmonized better with the yellow iris. The yellow iris always flowers in the first week of June. If you like pink or red rhododendrons, buy those that flower early. When flowering is spaced throughout the season, you can enjoy color longer.

Often it seems a city garden is more enjoyable than any other because it is possible to sit outdoors in greater shelter, and because the contrast between the bustle of town and the tranquillity of the garden is so great.

As a rule, the walls of surrounding buildings give off so much warmth in the evenings that even then the gardens are warm enough to sit in for at least a few moments. However, many city gardens are quite hot during the daytime, so you should consider arranging for some shade, whether by constructing awnings or roof

---

TIP

Plants for deep shade

Asarum europaeum, Convallaria majalis, Fragaria vesca, Geranium phaeum, Glechoma hederacea, Lamiastrum galeobdolon, Lamium orvala

extensions, a pergola, or planting a tree. Shade is appreciated by many delightful plants. A city garden is not only a green oasis in town for you, but it also offers a pleasant shelter for birds who, it seems, are not bothered by city noise. As always, begin working with your garden "wish list" by first examining the site you've got, and all the opportunities (and restrictions) it offers. This step is the key to what you will be able to achieve. Is the soil deep and workable, or are sections of the site taken up with rock? Does most of the area appear to be moist and in partial sun, or will much of your garden lie in sandy shade?

Shade Plants

There can be much shade in the city garden due to high walls, the obstruction of tall buildings, and often also trees, but it is wrong to think that this only limits your options. Many plants that thrive in sun like some shade, too, although it means that they will produce smaller flowers. Shade is a bit more difficult for evergreens. On

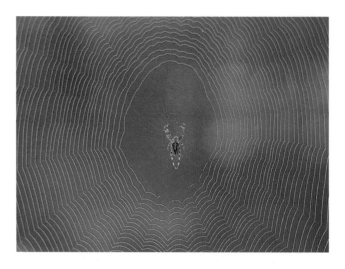

Give a moment's thought to the fauna that live in the garden. Cobwebs are really splendid when bedewed.

Snails are much less harmful than slugs. They often eat algae off of bark. Of all places, it is nice to encourage snails in a small city garden; the colors of their shells can be very pretty.

the other hand, where foliage is the primary attraction, as it is in many shady gardens, beautiful leaf shapes and colors can produce charming effects in city gardens. Species of maple, many vines, and small bulbous plants add the necessary tension. Many plants that thrive in acid soils are also shade-loving plants. A separate corner or border with some extra peat moss is an ideal growing place for this group of plants. Shady spots are pleasing to lots of forest plants, such as Solomon's seal, lily of the valley, and wood anemone. And if your city garden already

contains a homely shed lean-to, while it may not exactly win a beauty contest now, you can let it be overgrown in a jiffy with a fast-growing vine such as *Clematis vitalba*, or a glorious climbing rose–a wonderful way to cover an eyesore and store your garden equipment at the same time.

Many plants are demanding when it comes to sun or shade. In other words, you have to comply with their growth requirements for them to perform for you at their best. This means that for the city garden that has no shade, it is better to postpone planting shade plants for a year, until your new trees and shrubs grow enough to cast some shade on the ground. This is particularly important for ferns (with the exception of royal ferns and *Pterium aquilinum*).

Half-shade plants can often perform well in the sun if given enough water. It is easier to select plants that will be happy in your soil type than to try to alter the soil type to please the plants. But even soil that is perfectly suitable for the plants that you wish to plant there should be cultivated.

Prepare your soil so that it is nice and friable by adding well-rotted manure, compost, and sharp sand (sometimes called "builder's sand"). Plants growing in a shady spot in lime-rich soil can grow very fast indeed. Do a little research before you buy such plants; very rapid growth has the disadvantage of requiring pruning after as little as two years, depending on the plant.

For vines, you can attach wires to walls, the sides of buildings, and even to structural overhangs so your climbers can grow upward seemingly of their own accord.

Do consider their maintenance when choosing these plants, and whether you will be able to reach the plant easily for pruning or training once it has grown as you hope it will. Choose climbers that pull themselves up vertical surfaces by means of clinging to them (for instance, ivy or woodbine), rather than by twining around supports you provide for them if you think you won't be able to reach the plant to maintain it once it has grown a bit. When you grow vines, you add a vertical dimension that makes a small garden seem larger.

Natural Gardens

Natural gardens can be very pretty, but you must realize that the beauty of wild nature cannot really be imitated. Countless seemingly insignificant environmental factors determine whether a plant will grow well (or at all) in a certain place in the wild. These factors, in combination

Even in the middle of a city, the garden pond attracts several kinds of insects, such as this dragonfly—a bonus you probably had not considered when first designing your garden.

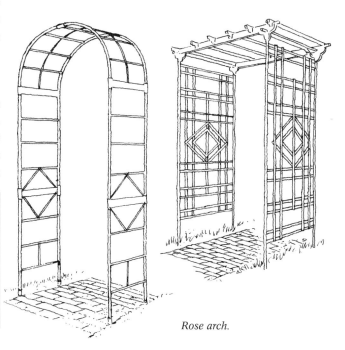

Rose arch.

TIP

Rose arches

If you have a bare section of wall, you might put a rose arch against it, and plant it around the base with honeysuckle, which climbs quickly and stays green. A vine-covered rose arch makes a lovely recess in which to set a statue.

with the available amounts of sunlight and water, soil type, the amount of wind and the direction from which it tends to come, and whatever animal life is nearby, mean that there is endless variety to wild plant communities. A garden is purely culture, a sort of addition to nature. Imitation of naturally occurring plant communities is more difficult than you might think. Creating a balanced plant community can take years of work, and the hand of the gardener can usually be seen. There are lots of types of naturalistic gardens to choose from:

> ground-cover garden
> heather garden
> perennial garden
> botanical (or "native") garden
> flower meadow
> marsh garden
> rock garden

Gardens that include many plants indigenous to the area look more "natural." At a time when the head gardeners of the great stately homes in England labored to create highly manicured and artificial gardens, William Robinson wrote the book *The Wild Garden* (1870). The romance of more naturalistic gardens found an audience. And, after garden designer Gertrude Jekyll had set a good example, the use of wild plants increased, and since then there have been enthusiastic fanciers of wild and "native" gardens.

There is a difference between a natural-looking garden and a nature garden. In a nature garden, a natural plant community comes into being by itself. Man's interference is usually confined to the encouragement of the environment, and pruning and mowing once the plant community is established. Nature gardens can be a source of annoyance to the neighbors, who fear huge amounts of weed seeds self-sowing in their own gardens. This can indeed happen in the first few years. After all, lots of pretty "weeds" are the pioneers that first grow in bare soil. Grass seed never really inconveniences gardens, either.

It is not very easy to create a nature garden. However, if you move to a house where the garden has been neglected for a very long time, you already have a head start. If you want to continue in that direction, don't spade the garden, but simply remove or prune such dominating plants as brambles and elders, and the natural variety of the community will increase in a very short time. Not only will the number of different plants

Standard fruit trees are suitable for almost every garden. They allow a good amount of light to filter through.

increase, but you will also encourage insects, such as butterflies, and frogs and toads. Here in the nature garden, snails turn out to be only useful creatures, taking charge of dying plants.

For the greatest variety of plants in a nature garden, some differentiation in the types of soil is necessary. Determine the quality of the soil you have, and alter the composition in areas by working in some sharp sand or garden peat as needed. You can work old building rubble deep into the ground of one section to create a dry environment if you like.

For the natural garden, select carefully those plants that will thrive in the soil, groundwater level, and sun and shade you can offer them. With a natural garden, perhaps more than with any other garden, you need at least some basic knowledge of the plants in your garden. Many natural species have small flowers; you will have to be particularly careful in choosing where you put plants so they show to best advantage. Work the soil well, and create low-lying and higher areas. Put in different types of soil as you wish, and immediately plant any trees you may want for shade. The soil in your nature garden will be richer and poorer in different areas. Chemical fertilizers wash away easily, so you will want to add natural soil amendments. Keep the highest parts "poor." The lower portions of the garden will become rich by themselves as nutrients in the soil leach from high to low ground with the rain.

Experience helps gardeners develop a sense of good plant combinations and quantities. How can you know which plants fare best in large groups? Which species would be nice repeated as solitary plants throughout the garden? Skill doesn't come from a horticultural education, but from keen observation, both in nature and man-made gardens. When you set out to observe a plant, observe its natural environment, too. For example, you may not know much about a certain plant, but if you notice that it grows near where rhododendrons thrive, you can assume that the plant likes acidity and relative humidity. Good habits of observation will help you learn to make successful combinations and to make the most of each part of the garden. You will soon notice that a dry spot in the shade is the most difficult spot to fill in. Perhaps it should not go without saying that, whether your interest is in fostering a nature garden or creating a natural garden, you and your garden environment are better off without the introduction of pesticides and herbicides. The same is true of chemical fertilizers; in most cases it is preferable to work in organic soil amendments that improve the tilth of the soil, its general condition, at the same time as they adjust the pH or nutrient content. Think of yourself as the temporary guardian of your garden; you want to pass it along in better condition than it was when you "received" it.

The Flower Meadow

Cultivated flower meadows may be annual or perennial. The annual meadow, typically planted with poppy, cornflower, chamomile, and quaking grass, must be sown each year. Most suitable for this type of meadow is poor, sandy soil. Among your meadow of "quiet" plants you might sprinkle the occasional, more exotic plant, such as annual lupines, and *Escholzia*, *Rudbeckia*, and violets.

If you mow your meadow every year and subsequently remove the grass, the soil will become impoverished.

Clearly, a meadow is a very informal sort of garden, not compatible with just any type of house, and not suitable for the site of just any property. In the right spot, the appeal is undeniable–think of Monet's poppy meadows. You can buy ready-made seed mixtures for sowing your meadow. These commercial mixtures are specially formulated for clay or sandy soil. Owing to its early flowering, the "perennial" meadow is more interesting. The annuals, naturally, come up at the same time. A word to the wise: There is no such thing as an instant, perfect garden in a can.

You can plant bulbs such as fritillaria, snowdrop, and anemone there to excellent effect. The *Gagea lutea* and *Primula japonica* may be suitable for wet spots. Mowing of flower meadows should be done only after the plants have gone to seed. After mowing, the meadow looks dry and yellow at first (this has its own appeal, to the romantic). Leave the mown grass lying for a few days. Dry grass weighs less and is therefore easier to move, and it will also keep the sun from burning the sods if you leave it for a while. Don't let the dry grass lie there *too* long, though, or it will kill what's underneath it by depriving it of sunlight. Any seed that is not yet ripe will have a chance of ripening quickly and spreading while the mown grass lies on the ground. The flower meadow is hardly an "instant garden."

Commercial annual meadow flower mixtures contain mostly poppy, cornflower, chamomile, and such grains as oats and wheat. If you use an annual mixture to plant your meadow, you'll have to spade and sow again each year to get this sea of flowers.

The Ground-Cover Garden

Before a ground-cover garden is laid out, the area to be planted should rest for a year, during which all roots and weeds have been exterminated rigorously. Couch grass and goutweed must be removed especially thoroughly, as it is much more difficult to eradicate these plants later on when they are more established. The ground-cover garden must be weeded by hand (a cultivator risks damaging the close-set ground-cover plants) and, in this way, ground-cover gardens are no less toilsome than other types of gardens. The ground-cover garden style can give the garden a natural look, and it is not very difficult to create such a garden. If you put in accent plants in large clusters, a certain measure of the restfulness created by your ground-cover carpet will remain. You can vary the landscape by planting solitary trees and shrubs, by highlighting areas with striking perennials, and by extending the season of bloom with bulbs.

What makes a ground-cover garden particularly easy is that the ground does not need to be leveled before planting. This is true of any paths you wish to include, "paved" with tree bark or wood chips. The rolling effect of changes in grade are enhanced by the thick growth of a healthy ground-cover carpet. The laying out of this garden is easy. Again, this type of garden is not suitable for really lazy people, as it calls for maintenance work no less than any other type of garden. But, the *look* is one of deceptive nonchalance.

Ground covers are often perennials, and they may or

Rigid and natural in contrast: With plantings of low-growing sempervivum and sedum in several hues, the stones show up well.

may not be evergreen. There are ground-cover roses. Scrambling vines can be used as ground covers. Short, dense shrubs are also appropriate, as are low-growing conifers. Plants that are good ground covers have one thing in common: Their growth is so dense that it is difficult for weeds to compete with them.

Great variety is possible in the ground-cover garden. Some perennials prefer shade, while roses and shrubs thrive in sunlight. The plantings you select may be wildly diverse, yet unified by a ground-cover tapestry.

For a ground-cover garden, large areas must be planted with one species. It is nice to supplement the ground covers with bulbs and individual shrubs, as a garden of only ground covers looks bare.

The Heather Garden

Heather gardens grow well only in sandy and peaty soils. Of course, it is possible, with considerable effort, to make clay soils suitable for a heather garden. You do that by making the soil more acid. Still, after all your hard work to alter the soil and get the heather to thrive, your garden will look somewhat out of place in the surrounding landscape. Heather gardens look very attractive in the first few years, but you will eventually have to learn how to prune and "rejuvenate" the heather. Plant calluna in drier soil, erica in more damp soil. Some species of grass, such as *Deschampsia flexuosa*, thrive on drier ground,

It is difficult to combine the bright colors of these poppies with softer colors in the perennial border.

and others such as *Molinia caerulea* can endure damp circumstances. Crowberry may be planted in the wettest soil; this plant covers great stretches of ground and can withstand shade well, too. (It does not flower, however.) To plant only heathers and conifers would be a bit monotonous. Small-flowered ground covers and perennials add a pretty touch to the varied heather garden, as do deciduous shrubs that lose their leaves and conifers.

Determine the degree of acidity of your soil before you plant a heather garden. A heather garden is absolutely unsuitable for soil that is rich in lime. A simple pH test can be conducted with a kit from your local garden center. You can easily find out whether there is lime in the soil with the aid of a few drops of hydrochloric acid (HCl).Take care when handling this, as it is very caustic.

The more the acid fizzes, the more chalk (lime) you have in your soil.

The Perennial Garden

If you want a garden without a lot of lawn, plant your garden with perennials. You will need to plan for a good number of paths to give you access to all the corners of the garden. Planting many different perennials one after the next gives the garden a restless jumbled look; repeat plants sporadically through the garden so they look as though they are meant to be there, not there by mere accident. To create a restful feeling in a garden of many different kinds of plants, make the paths wide enough and plant a border of one kind of plant along them. This border plant should preferably be an evergreen. You will also achieve a fine effect by planting several large areas with just one species of low-growing perennial, which will act as a ground cover, helping to "knit" the garden together.

Perennials require maintenance, but if you spread it out over time it is manageable. After all, even a lawn must be mowed each week, and mowing cannot be postponed. When you do a little maintenance every day, the total job seems much less daunting.

Children cannot play in a perennial garden. You might plan for large terraces for play, but that will hardly make a game of football possible. A separate play area is the solution for the lover of perennial gardens. A variation of the perennial garden is the botanical, or native, garden. The difference between the botanical garden and the perennial garden is that the former contains only indigenous plants.

Perennials

Perennials are herbaceous plants that die back in autumn and come up again in spring. Some will thrive for several years, while others may continue to grow in your garden for five or ten years, or longer. You need a combination of several species of perennials in your garden to have flowers in bloom during the entire growing season. Most perennials do not flower longer than eight weeks. Early-flowering and late-flowering kinds offer an almost unlimited choice of color. The larger the garden, the more kinds of perennials you can plant. Repeating groups

Page 37:
Many kinds of perennials, in many colors. Despite the great number of species, the calming green of the Taxus *provides the necessary relief.*

of one species in a few places throughout the garden gives a more restful effect.

It is difficult to say how many plants must be planted per square yard (or meter), because the garden itself and its surroundings have quite an impact on this. An average of five plants could be used in your general figuring if you are considering perennials of middling size, but there are many exceptions. Of small alpine plants you would need far more, but a single gunnera plant takes up several square yards on its own.

You must not think of flowering only in the summer. With some planning, your garden can provide interest (if not precisely flowering) the whole year round. Some perennials are evergreens and, although most of these do not flower exuberantly, they provide interest in the garden when nothing is in bloom. Year-round interest is important if you do not want a cheerless garden in the winter. Plants that develop attractive seedpods, or that have curiously sculptural shapes when their leaves have dropped, or that will catch and hold the snow as it falls in winter all have some visual merit to offer. So, when buying perennials, don't think only of the flower; the plant must be attractive when it is not flowering. Some perennials look dreary later in the summer, when you still sit out in the garden quite a lot. The solution is simple: Such plants as these must have other plants growing in front of them as a screen, which will carry on in an attractive way.

The Border

When one thinks of perennials, one thinks of borders. The border came into fashion at the beginning of this century; famous garden designers who earned a reputation through their work with borders are Gertrude Jekyll, Vita Sackville-West, and Mien Ruys. A border is an area that lies between a hedge or a fence and a path or lawn, and that is planted with perennials, and sometimes

Even glass can be functional in the garden, especially in combination with water.

complemented by roses. The ideal location for a border is on the longitudinal axis of your house, so that you can view the length of the border. This is an ideal arrangement, as the perennial border consists of portions in flower at different times. If such a border is viewed crosswise, those sections not in flower would be too obvious. Place plants that grow tall at the back of the border and low-growing plants toward the front. Plant medium-high plants between them, not in a rigid, rising line, but dispersed a bit through the depth of the border. The often-heard advice to use an odd number of plants of any kind is nonsense. After all, in one or two years, the numbers of plants will have increased so the numbers originally planted cannot be counted anymore. Also, some plants grow faster than others.

The old-fashioned flowers so popular today will grow in almost any type of soil. Unusually delicate plants need more attention; you can mix sharp sand with compost or clay with sand and peat or compost, as needed. Wet soil can be drained. Frost damage to perennials tends to

Grouping boulders well is very difficult. Do not build them into a great tower, or scatter them like marbles, either. Irregular grouping gives a natural effect.

occur in soil that is too wet. A dry plant can endure much more cold. Plants that are sensitive to frost often survive when kept out of the wind. It is not just the cold, but a combination of cold and wind, that makes plants that cannot absorb water in very cold weather wither. Wait before planting the fussiest plants until the windbreaks and hedges of the new garden have grown enough to give some shelter.

The Rock Garden

It looks easier than it actually is to use stones and rocks in a garden. You want a happy medium between impressive piles like megaliths, and sporadic pebble scatterings. The best rock gardens are irregular and the stones don't look "placed," but rather natural. You will have to experiment, moving stones and rocks here and there, then stepping back some distance to observe the effect of the arrangement. Well-designed rock gardens look both natural and artistic. Often, leftover corners of the garden are reserved for the rock garden. "Corners," because it is really very difficult to integrate a rock garden

You can still make something nice out of rubble and roofing tiles. Never bury trash: Remove it or use it.

TIP

A rock garden in a flower box

If you have a generous paved area in full sun, you can create an alpine garden in a large window box, an old feeding trough, or other large, rather shallow container. For your miniature garden you might choose several of these suitable rock garden plants:

Primula	Aubrieta
Saxifraga	Campanula (low-growing species)
Sedum	Arabis
Sempervivum	Alyssum
Cyclamen (wild)	

---

in close proximity to, say, an annual bed or perennial border.

When you choose rocks for your garden, you must think about proportion: Large surfaces need large boulders and large plants. When you start a rock garden, you naturally place the bottom stones first. Boulders must be submerged to such a depth that they cannot move if you lean on them while weeding or when you walk on them. They should not be positioned so shallowly that they appear to be sitting unnaturally on the surface of the ground. A few large boulders have more effect than many small ones once the plants are fully grown.

A rock garden must be located in an open, sunny spot—not near a high wall or under trees, but somehow out of the wind. Evergreen shrubs can form an effective windbreak that is in harmony with the look of a rock garden. Rock gardens feature alpine plants. If you think about the natural habitat of alpine plants, you will understand why your rock garden will be most likely to please you if it can get as much sun as a mountainside.

A water feature in the rock garden can be very attractive and naturalistic. You can sink a pond at several levels. For a garden that strives to approach nature as much as possible, it is important that the water appear to be where it is naturally. Natural ponds would be found only at the deepest point of your garden. When we create a pond at a higher level, we need to be able to suggest to the viewer that the water has a natural source, a more complicated process. As the surface area of a body of water increases, the water evaporates more quickly. You will need to fill up a broad, shallow pool more often than a narrow, deep one.

2 Laying Out the Garden

The possibilities and limitations of the piece of ground that will become your garden play an important role in the design of your garden. Even though you may think you have given these full consideration, there will almost certainly be things you have overlooked or that you could not have anticipated.

This needn't pose a problem; gardening almost always involves choosing from among different possible solutions. Keep in mind though, what you are sure you want, and what you do not want. The cost of plant material is only a relatively small part of the cost of gardening, but you can save quite nicely by starting with smaller plants. This doesn't alter the end result, because plants will grow larger anyway.

The white garden of Sissinghurst (England) is world-famous. Here you see white flowers elegantly combined with gray-leaved plants. Remember that gray-leaved plants tend to prefer dry soil. (The gray appearance is caused by tiny hairs on the leaves, which help prevent dehydration.)

Rust spots on a Prunus *leaf. Many diseases are particularly noticeable in autumn.*

The spittlebug causes this wet muck, which is not harmful and can be washed away with a jet of water.

Annuals and Biennials

Not every garden owner is also a garden enthusiast. If you belong to the latter group, you can derive great pleasure from sowing annuals and biennials. We recommend that other people, who have less time for their gardens, buy plants at a nursery or garden center.

With a little help from parents, children can also become interested in gardening, but don't require too much from them—failures can thoroughly spoil any fun in gardening. That is why you must not let children select the seed for their garden all by themselves; they are likely to choose seeds of flowers that look beautiful but may be inappropriate or very complicated to grow and care for. Seeds with which children should have great success are listed in chapter 15. It is important to involve children in the layout of the garden; after all, they will determine the future of our garden culture, and they will have to keep up our work.

Generally speaking, you buy annuals in May or the beginning of June. Unlike annuals, biennials grow only a rosette of leaves in the first year and flower in the second year. The best time to buy biennials is in August and September. Unfortunately, many people don't visit garden centers at that time, so we most often see biennials used by parks and public gardens. Put a note on your calendar to remind yourself to go to the garden center at the right time later on.

It is safe to plant annuals in spring after all danger of

This part of the garden, with no more than five fast-growing species of plants, looks full-grown after only two years. In the foreground is Acaena buchananii, *backed by* Alchemilla mollis *and hosta. A* Buxus *shrub and taxus hedge complete this composition.*

frost is past. Even though it may be mild earlier outdoors, you must resist the temptation to plant those beautiful colors in your garden too early. Even a good garden center starts selling these plants much too early, owing to the great demand, and they may or may not caution you to be careful of night frost.

Flower boxes can be planted earlier, as long as you are prepared to carry them inside at night when it threatens to become really cold.

"Bedding plants" is what annuals often used to be called, because they were planted out in beds. Now that their range of use has increased considerably, we prefer to call them annuals. Annuals are excellent in combination with roses, shrubs, and perennials. For instance, you can let an attention-getting annual grow through a conifer. Flower boxes and hanging baskets are eminently suitable for annuals. The nice thing about annuals is that you can try out a new combination each year. For the north side of the house, impatiens and lobelia are very suitable. For low windowsills, standing geraniums are the prettiest; for bright contrast, red is often the color of choice, but pink and white geraniums may look

---

TIP

The mature heights of plants in your garden can vary a good deal from the heights given in books or indicated on the packets of seed. Height and size depend on the type of soil and the location. Plants will always be smaller in poor soil, larger in rich soil. Plant growth is also strongly affected by fertilizer use. Temperature plays a role, too; a plant on the south side of the house will grow faster than the same plant on the north side. If you are troubled by a plant that doesn't seem to be a vigorous grower, you should ask yourself a number of questions: Is the plant being crowded by its neighbors? Does it have to compete too hard for sunlight and water?

Keep landscape views open where possible.

best with the garden. Hanging geraniums grow most profusely. (Actually, we must speak of the window-box geranium as *Pelargonium*, to avoid confusing it with the true garden geranium that we see in the perennial border.)

Almost all annuals like full sun, but some of them will also grow reasonably well in partial and even full shade. For the north side of the house, and in city gardens that receive sun for only brief periods, these plants are very suitable:

Begonia semperflorens
Datura stramonium
Impatiens
Lobelia erinus
Lunaria annua
Mimulus guttatus

Solomon's seal and sweet-scented woodruff are suitable for shade gardens.

Myosotis
Nicotiana
Polygonum capitatum
Tagetes tenuifolia

The Correct Soil for Containers

Plants in containers need even better care than plants in the ground. Use new potting mixture each year, and do not forget to apply extra fertilizer in the summer. Never use soil from the garden to pot your plant. It is a great temptation to do this, especially if you have forgotten to buy potting mixture when buying plants. Potting mixture retains water and fertilizer better so the plants grow well, and it is sterile. Make it a habit to fertilize your container plants outdoors with the "indoor" plant fertilizer at the same time you fertilize the indoor plants. Adding the correct fertilizer encourages good plant growth. Potting mixture contains garden peat and peat humus. In itself this artificial substrate is too acidic; that is why lime is added to

Rhubarb can be attractive in ornamental gardens. The red stems of these plants (they match the color of the door) cannot be seen here.

Large areas planted with a single species of plant give the small garden a restful air.

A broad path leading straight from the door into the garden invites you to take a walk.

correct the pH so it is suitable for most plants. Special substrates are available for anthuriums, cacti, and ferns. This soil mixture retains water very well, so it is particularly appropriate for containers; the medium requires water less frequently, and plants are less likely to dry out. Another advantage of a commercially prepared mixture is that it contains virtually no weed seeds.

Ornamental Shrubs

Some ornamental shrubs grow fast and others grow slowly. So don't arrange the plants you have just bought by the heights they have at the moment, but look at the growth that is expected after five years. You need some imagination for this, but it is absolutely necessary for the success of your garden plan. Shrubs are available at very different stages at the nursery. The potentilla you buy is almost full-grown, while a *Hibiscus syriacus* is sold when it is small and needs a few years to grow to maturity. Not only is the height at maturity a factor to consider, but the rate of growth is important, too. It is nice to have a large

English hanging baskets

If you have ever been to England, you undoubtedly are acquainted with the containers of flowers that hang from many buildings. These baskets are not filled in the same way as a hanging flowerpot. The open-mesh wire basket is planted from all sides.

You will need:
Wire basket, diameter 12–14 inches (30–35 cm)
Peat moss, a large handful
10 quarts (liters) of potting mixture
20 to 24 plants

Procedure:
Hang the basket over a work table. Place some peat moss on the bottom of the basket and plant three plants right through the mesh. Put more peat moss around the sides and fill the center of the basket with potting mixture. Position twelve plants all around the basket through the mesh. Round off the top of the mixture, plant it with five plants, and finish with a little peat moss. The globe will now be quite heavy. Hang it from a sturdy hook, away from drafts, because hanging baskets dry out rapidly. You must water the basket every day.

Plants for the hanging basket:
• Ferns
      Davallia
• Vines
      Hedera helix (ivy)
      Ampelopsis brevipedunculata 'Variegata'
• Perennials
      Campanula garganica
      Campanula poscharskyana
      Lysimachia nummularia
      Alchemilla mollis
• Annuals
      Impatiens (busy Lizzy)
      Fuchsia
      Helichrysum petiolatum
      Lobelia
      Felicia
      Petunia
      Asparagus sprengeri
      Tolmiea

In early spring, the basket can be filled with violets in combination with ivy. Variations on the hanging basket for the kitchen garden might include, for example, thyme and strawberries.

If you prune Forsythia intermedia *'Spectabilis' well, you can achieve this effect— although probably on a less spectacular scale than at this nursery.*

plant at the outset, but the fast growth may compete too much with, or overwhelm, other plants, so that a considerable amount of cutting back would be necessary—that costs time and energy. The seeming disadvantage of small plants, that they require patience, becomes an advantage with respect to maintenance later on. Do not plant shrubs you know will grow very large in places that ultimately will be too cramped, thinking you will trim them later. Trimming is meant to help the shrub develop well on its own so that it will flower abundantly. Shortening a shrub because it has become too tall is the opposite of trimming.

If you discover that a shrub is growing in the wrong place only at a later stage, it is wise to dig it up and move it in order to make room for a plant that is suitable for the site. During the first few years, shrubs newly planted behind a border of perennials are not in proportion to the plants in the border, as many perennials become full-grown in the first year and shrubs take years to grow. That is to be expected; just be patient.

Most shrubs flower in spring and lose their leaves in autumn or winter. It takes planning to create a varied

The sloe, Prunus spinosa, *flowers richly if it is not trimmed.*

shrub border where evergreen shrubs, variegated or red-leaved shrubs, and flowering shrubs create year-round interest. It is important to choose your plants with forethought and not be tempted by an impulse, for instance, when a particular shrub that flowers beautifully catches your eye. You can possess a collection of nice shrubs, but you want to give the garden variety–of color, leaf shape, plant shape, and so on.

As a rule, slow-growing shrubs are expensive, and faster-growing shrubs are cheaper. Have patience, and don't try to achieve your desired result with large shrubs immediately. Larger shrubs experience more of a setback in growth when you plant them out, so in fact the difference in size when bought is caught up in no more than two years. Place larger shrubs in locations where you need them for reasons of privacy; there they are at home and very useful. Finally, when selecting shrubs for specific places in your garden and around your home, consider the relationship of the scale of the mature plant to its surroundings.

Pruning and Trimming

Some shrubs should not be trimmed (e.g., skimmia), some only very little (hibiscus), and others moderately (aucuba and lilac). Jasmine must always be trimmed considerably. Buddleia may be cut to 1½ feet (0.5m) above the ground. It may be necessary to completely cut down shrubs that

have been neglected for a long time, but this is a step of last resort. Forsythia is often difficult to trim because of its very irregular way of growing–beginning gardeners are baffled about how to approach the task, and what to cut. Do not plant this shrub in front of other garden attractions as it flowers before the other shrubs even leaf out. It is a fine accent near the back of a large border, as a specimen plant elsewhere, and in groups toward the property lines.

TIP		
Shrubs that attract butterflies		
	Color	Flowering period
Buddleia (butterfly bush)	all	September
Crataegus (hawthorn)	white	May
Lavandula (lavender)	blue	June–August
Ligustrum (privet)	white	June–July
Prunus laurocerasus (cherry laurel)	white	May
Prunus spinosa (sloe)	white	April–May
Rubus (blackberry bush)	white	various
Syringa (lilac)	white/blue/violet	various
Viburnum opulus	white	June

Which Shrub in Which Location?

When designing your garden, it is good to remember a few facts concerning the shrubs:

Shrubs that cannot bear lime include: *Andromeda, Arctostaphylos, Azalea, Calluna, Clethra, Cornus canadensis, Daboecia, Empetrum, Erica* (except for *E. carnea*), *Fothergilla, Gaultheria, Kalmia, Ledum, Vaccinium,* dwarf conifers (except for *Pinus*), *Hortensia, Acer palmatum, Cytisus scoparius.*

Shrubs that need lime include: *Aralia, Berberis, Buddleia, Daphne, Ligustrum, Rhus, Ribes, Spiraea.*

Shrubs that withstand wind and so are suitable for balconies and roof gardens include: serviceberry, hazel, *Elaeagnus, Eunonymus, Ligustrum,* several kinds of prunes, wild roses, elders, and *Viburnum opulus.*

Ferns

Ferns do especially well in shady gardens. There is always shade at the north side of the house, and tree cover can provide shade too. There is a difference between the two types of shade, however: Trees take much water from the soil in summer, so that there is too little water left for the ferns.

Humus retains water better. Before planting ferns, you can add humus by putting wood chips and decaying leaves on the ground, and give them time to rot. Never discard fallen leaves, but let them prove their worth to you. In winter leaves insulate the ground, keeping it warmer longer, and they keep the soil surface damp.

Ferns that are easy garden plants include:
Adiantum pedatum (Venus' hair), 16 inches (40cm), evergreen

Asplenium, 6 inches (15cm)
Athyrium filix-femina (female fern), 30 inches (75cm)
Blechnum spicant (hard fern), 16 inches (40cm), evergreen
Dryopteris filix-mas (male fern), 30 inches (75cm)
Matteuccia struthiopteris, 30 inches (75cm)
Osmunda regalis (royal fern), 30 inches (75cm), evergreen
Phyllitis scolopendrium (tongue fern), 16 inches (40cm), evergreen
Polypodium vulgare, 19 inches (50cm), evergreen
Polystichum aculeatum, 9 inches (25cm), evergreen
Polystichum setiferum, 16 inches (40cm), evergreen
Pteridium aquilinum, 5 feet (1.5cm)

When all perennials have died back in the winter, hedges provide important framework for the garden. Evergreen hedges are especially striking then.

TIP

Plants in a garden wall

For a romantic accent, consider planting a garden wall with a tumble of colorful flowers. Certain plants thrive in a garden wall, in shade, or in half shade, if several conditions are met. When you build a wall for planting, use a little Portland cement, and much chalk and sharp (builder's) sand. Leave some access for plants to root in the ground by the base of retaining walls, so they will thrive. Select plants according to the sun exposure they will receive.

Suitable ferns are: *Asplenium adiantum nigrum,* wall rue, *Saxifraga, Asplenium viride, Cystopteris filix-fragilis, Gymnocarpium robertianum,* and tongue fern.

Other plants that will feel at home there are: *Cheiranthus cheiri* (wallflower), *Corydalis lutea* (yellow fumitory), *Cymbalaria muralis* (mother-of-thousands), and *Chelidonium majus* (greater celandine).

The shorter ferns are also suitable for the rock garden, provided it does not lie in the bright afternoon sun. Make a soil mixture of sharp sand, leaf mold, and peat moss, and do not fertilize too much. Do not cut off the old leaves until spring arrives; the dead leaves protect the plant over winter. In addition, rimed fern leaves are a lovely sight in wintertime!

Water Gardens

People are always fascinated by water. It is also a special experience to see plants beautifully mirrored on the water's surface, and to watch the insects attracted by this environment. Furthermore, many would say a water garden is not complete until it is home to frogs and fish living in it; these animals are a pleasure in themselves,

although they require a certain measure of maintenance. And it is fascinating for children to observe what happens with the tadpoles, how certain insects "walk" on the water, and how fish behave: For them, as for us all, water gardens are not only amusing; they are also marvelously instructive.

Water Garden Design

Water is almost indispensable in a garden. Splashing water is pleasant to listen to, but it can also mute other sounds of the environment; splashing water in a noisy environment—whether there is nearby traffic or construction, for example—is not just beautiful, but also functional. However, you must consider the disadvantages of a water garden. It needs a reasonable amount of maintenance. Even a shallow pond can be dangerous to small children under the age of three. It is easy to build your water garden in the wrong spot. Do not sink a large pond right in front of the living-room window, for example, if you do not like rain; a rainy day seems all the wetter when you see drops falling into water all day long.

But now that we have looked at what can go wrong, let's note that for the rest, they give a lot of pleasure for a long time.

Some evergreen ferns are such excellent ground covers that they don't give weeds a chance. They also look pretty.

The Materials

Choose carefully among the many materials from which water gardens are made today. Ten water gardens, all made of different materials, were sunk for the Floriade exhibition in the Amstelpark in Amsterdam. During the exhibition it turned out that nine of them needed repairs—and these water gardens had been sunk by experts! This shows that a well-considered plan and utmost precision are needed for the successful installation of a water garden.

The different materials vary greatly in price and quality. Water gardens can be made with plastic sheeting, synthetic tanks, concrete, plastic, clay, and zinc. Finally, if the groundwater level does not fluctuate too much, a natural pond is a nice option. For this, a water level that stays more or less the same is essential; a dried-up pond is unappealing. Among other things, your choice of pool material (sheet lining, concrete, and so forth) may be affected by whatever edging you wish to apply. It is difficult to lay an edge of tiles around a pool lined with plastic sheeting if the sides have not been reinforced with

A shallow spot in the pond is used by birds to bathe. Black-   *birds and thrushes especially make happy use of this.*

you will detect it instantly. Note that pipes for electricity and perhaps water pipes must be laid before the pool is in place. The water supply can come from the roof, or the drainage that goes to the sewer or into a drainage ditch.

Some water gardens simply beg for a work of art in the middle. This can be the ideal place for a fragile piece of art, as children and pets cannot reach it. However, it is important that whatever supports are needed be fixed so they are stormproof. A pool with plastic sheeting wouldn't be suitable for a statue; you need a hard base for this. You also need a hard base for any stepping stones. These sorts of things will influence your choice of materials for the pool. If you construct a sheeting-lined pool, you must place a few large paving stones in the middle of the pool (under the sheeting).

These turtles can hibernate outdoors in the water garden. The pond depth must be at least 24 inches (60cm), and the pond bottom must contain   *sufficient organic substance for the turtles. Keep a hole open in the ice on the pond surface in winter.*

Try to get some small green frogs or tadpoles from a water garden enthusiast. When the   *sun shines, the frogs will sit in a row at the edge of the water.*

wood or concrete. Complete information on how to sink a lined pool or ready-made tank can be obtained at almost any garden center that sells these materials. The manner in which you use the material is as outlined by the manufacturer. You can even rent a video that shows you how; inquire about this when buying your materials, or at a "do-it-yourself" video store. Follow the instructions precisely. A pool is like a level: If it slopes,

The choice of materials not only influences what ornamental features you may want, such as stepping stones, but also the kinds of plants that you wish to plant in or next to the pool. Reeds and bamboo may damage plastic sheeting.

Sheeting

There are several kinds of sheeting, most of which are slowly disintegrated by ultraviolet light. Ask an expert at a local water garden center whether he can recommend one that can withstand sunlight. It may seem attractive to buy agricultural plastic sheeting, which is much cheaper. You must not, because it is thinner and may start tearing spontaneously after a few years, particularly in places that get sunlight. Choose sheeting that is specifically created for the job. Other possible causes of damage to the sheeting are small, sharp stones that lie under the sheeting, and playing children who might poke sticks into it. Good water-garden sheeting comes in two thicknesses: 0.5mm and 1mm. Because it is difficult to fold the stiff material, it is better to construct pools with complicated shapes of the thinner sheeting. For large pools of more than 30 feet (100m), the thinner sheeting is recommended as well. This has to do with the costs, but also the weight. Sheeting for such a large pool will weigh more than 300 pounds (150kg)!

Use wooden planking only in sunny places. In shade, they soon become slippery because of the growth of algae, especially if they are near water.

In cases with changing water levels, it may be better to choose the liner method when building your water garden. The water level should be reasonably constant in a natural pond.

When a pool is sunk, some folds in the sheeting will always result. That does not matter, as the weight of the water will flatten them over time. Plan to leave an extra 8 inches (20cm) at the edges for finishing. Once the pool is one-third full of water, the sheeting cannot be shifted as the weight of the water will make it too heavy. That is why the sheeting must be placed well beforehand, so no tension will develop when it is filled. Special acrylic cloth can protect the underside of the sheeting from sharp stones and any other projections.

Concrete Pools

The construction of a concrete pool is much more work than a lined pool. If you want paving right to the edge of the pool, you will need strong sidings, an advantage of the concrete pool. Concrete edging has a taut outline that can be quite pleasing to look at, especially if the surroundings suggest that the pond is not natural anyway. Owing to the damp environment, the concrete edge will soon be overgrown with algae and, after that, mosses.

A concrete pool must be reinforced by iron. Constructing a reinforcement of accordion netting is easiest for the do-it-yourselfer. The netting can be folded. With a concrete pond, you must keep in mind that the water must be changed after a few months before the plants and animals can be introduced; a new concrete water garden is not an instant habitat for creatures.

This pond liner has not been concealed well. Not only does this spoil the illusion of a natural pond, but the sun hastens the disintegration of the liner. The liner plastic contains a compound that prevents hardening, and thus tearing, and it is this softening agent that makes the plastic sensitive to the sun's rays.

Location and Finishing

First determine a location for your water garden. If this ground is higher in comparison with the rest of the environment, a natural edge is out of place, because you can see directly that it is not a natural pond anyway. Here, an edge finished with wood, tiles, or concrete is more logical. To encourage natural plant growth, the location of the pond must receive some sunlight, but the sun must not shine there all day.

A wood-sided pool, which gives the water a dark, almost black surface in which surrounding plants are mirrored, can be very beautiful. Nevertheless, water plants do not feel at home in such a pool. Of course, in a new garden it is not always possible to create a shady place for the pool immediately. But do not despair—your new garden plants will grow soon and then this problem will be solved. However, it is better to wait a year longer

Never put reeds in a lined water garden. The sharp roots will grow straight through the lining, especially in the folds.

TIP

Concrete vats

It is possible to raise water plants in concrete vats on the terrace. Because surface water takes on the temperature of the surrounding air, it is even possible to cultivate tropical and subtropical water plants in this fashion; for this, the vats—each with a broad surface area, and relatively shallow—must be placed in a sunny location. The lotus flower looks nicest on a terrace, but *Salvinia*, *Pistia stratiotes*, and *Eichhornia* are excellent too. Concrete vats are inexpensive, and by arranging several on a sunny terrace you create a special kind of water garden, one that you can rearrange with little difficulty as the mood suits you.

A fast grower, Pistia stratiotes *can be enjoyed throughout a warm summer in a water garden.*

before you put fish in your pool. It takes some time before a natural balance has developed. You can help by throwing a bucket of ditch water (from a clear ditch) into your pool.

Edge Finishing for Natural-Looking Pools

Always allow for the fact that, owing to evaporation, the water level might drop somewhat in your pool, making the lining visible. You can buy a kind of synthetic netting that can be placed over the pool edge and that will hold the soil in place. With this netting it is possible for grass to grow up to the water on top of the sheeting. Ground-cover plants can also grow in this; it is best to plant evergreen ground covers so that the sheeting remains out of sight during the winter months, too.

Suitable evergreen plants for pool edges include:
Hedera helix
Waldsteinia ternata and *W. geoides*
Cardamine trifolia
Cotula squalida and *C. pyrethrifolia*
Ajuga reptans
Asarum europaeum
Campanula portenschlagiana
Pachysandra terminalis

Bricks of peat are often used to finish the edges of pools. See to it that the bricks touch the water, so that they do not dry out. They must not touch the surrounding ground, for then they will siphon the water from the pool into the nearby soil. The pool will partly empty, and the surrounding ground will become too damp.

A final touch of edging hides pond liner.

An Italian garden in Greenwich, England. The severe formality of the pool *and its surroundings is in harmony with the contemporary gardens.*

The Relationship between Surface and Depth

Imagine a pool in the shape of a well: small of circumference and deep. The water in it stays cool. Imagine another pool shaped more like a puddle of water on the street, broad and shallow. On a sunny day, the temperature of the water can rise considerably, to 104°F (40°C). Clearly, there must be some balance between the surface area of the pool and the average depth, so that the water is neither too cold nor too hot. In the case of good ready-made pools, the manufacturer has already taken care of this. When planning your water garden, consider the following information: Per yard (meter) of surface area, the water volume in the pool can vary between 80 and 160 gallons (300 and 600l). In the case of a pool with a flat bottom, this comes to a depth from 12 to 24 inches (30 to 60cm). The shallower the pool, the more important it is that it not lie right out in full sun. Pools in which fish and water lilies hibernate must have a deeper area that provides cooler temperatures. For small pools, 24 inches (60cm) is sufficient; for larger pools, up to 30 inches (75cm) is better. Take into account the needs of your plants and fish.

Pool Soil

Ready-made pool soil that has been specially formulated for water plants can be bought at nurseries and garden centers. The mixture contains a high proportion of clay, so that it doesn't directly mix and go into solution, and the water cannot become muddied. You must never use potting mixture for your water garden: It floats and muddies the water immediately. Special mixtures developed especially for water gardens will stay where you put them. Too much organic material adds so much nitrogen to the water that algae growth develops later, and that calls for cleaning or biological controls. So take care to keep fertilizer out of the water. If you fertilize your lawn, you will be fertilizing your pool, too, as rain will cause runoff.

Don't plant a water garden too densely, for after a few years you won't be able to see *the water. The reflection is one of the most attractive aspects of a pond.*

A rococo pond: symmetry at two sides, a variety of stylized shapes, few flowers, but still a restful garden. This look would be nice in a small garden too.

Water Plants

Water plants are sold when they are very small, and people who are starting their first water garden tend to buy many–many different kinds of plants and many individuals of the same species. When the water plants grow to maturity, the surface of the water should be partly visible; you don't want it completely covered in plants. It gives a more peaceful effect, and beautiful cloudscapes (or a clear blue sky) will be reflected on the water's surface. There are water plants that grow horizontally (floating plants) and water plants that grow vertically. You want a pleasing balance of the two. The first year after planting, your water garden should have grown quite a bit and look quite good. Of course, it can be added to if so desired.

Cloudy water is the biggest problem in a pool. This may come about because there are too few underwater plants, the suppliers of oxygen. Another cause may be fish turning over the bottom. For more information, turn to page 57.

Too much algae is a great nuisance in a pool. Fortunately, water snails eat algae and other waste that has been deposited on the water plants and the edges of the pond. And there are water fleas to eat the excess floating algae. So, if the water becomes cloudy during the summer, ask your local pet shop, garden center, or water garden specialist about how to obtain these helpful

The white water lily is suitable only for large water gardens. Don't choose your water plants by color only, but consider the size of the full-grown plant. A suitable water lily can be found for any water garden.

creatures. Or, you can seek them out in the wild. In a ditch, and by choice at a spot where old wood sticks into the water (for example, pilings or bridge supports), there are always many water fleas. The water teems with these little animals that move by fits and starts. You can catch

Salamanders take to water only in spring. During the summer they live under stones or in other damp areas. If you pick up a salamander by the tail, it will drop its tail and leave it between your fingers while it scurries away. In spring, the speckled belly of the male turns bright orange.

The best place for a water garden is in half shade. If there are no trees in the area where you want your water garden, you can create shade quickly by constructing a *pergola around or over the pool. Any of several vines will produce the desired shade within a year, and the pergola adds dimension to the garden.*

Planting Time for Water Plants

Water plants start active growth when the water is warmed by a strengthening sun. In spring, in many areas about mid-May, the plants look green again, and sales at garden centers get going. When annual plants are sold in spring, and danger of frost is past, the time has also come to put water plants in the water garden. Transport your new plants from the nursery or garden center to their new home in a plastic bag, as dehydration can occur faster than you think.

Digging Up

We often see a hill next to a pool. Although planting it will give a nice atmosphere, and the combination of a pool and a hill make a pretty picture, it will be immediately clear to the beholder that the soil from the pool has been used for the hill. This is not desirable; it is better to use the soil dug from your pool a bit farther away, and then preferably to give whatever you build from it a completely different size and shape than the pool.

many in a short time, using a fine mesh fish net from the pet store or aquarium shop. Once you have moved a number of them into your pool, the algae can clear up in no more than one day.

Too much fish food in the water can also cause clouding. It is best to feed your fish a little at a time regularly, providing just as much food as the fish will eat all at once, as excess food will drop to the bottom and cloud the water. Floating fish food won't sink right away, and it allows you to enjoy the sight of your pets as they come to the surface to feed. As the temperature drops in autumn, the fish eat less, and in the winter you do not have to feed them at all. Your aim is to provide a biological balance in your pool. Don't put too many fish in the pool right away. Buy several fish (remember, at least eight weeks after the pool is built), and wait and see how the balance develops.

Water in a Japanese garden can be given direction by means of paving (Botanical Garden, Bremen, Germany). Sometimes the stones are laid overlapping like roof tiles, creating a wave effect.

A water garden in a greenhouse increases the humidity. Because most prefabricated pools are larger than a greenhouse door, the pool must be installed in the greenhouse before it is completed. (Actually, you build the greenhouse around the pond.) The water will remain warmer if an insulating layer is installed in the ground first.

A water garden must be absolutely level. Even a tiny bit out of plumb, and the liner will be visible at one side.

Plan in advance for a shallow area to grow marsh plants or others that prefer not to stand in deep water. In the case of this concrete pond, it is possible to grow certain plants in the water in baskets. In that way, you can easily fish them out of the water if necessary.

This water garden can be turned conveniently into a sandbox or a flower bed one day. During construction, make sure that the pool and the edges are completely level.

Brown frogs mating near the spawn of a toad. There is always something to see in the water garden.

The sinking of a new pool will bring considerable chaos to an existing garden, not just at the work site where the pool is under construction, but also in those places where the surplus soil has to go. Find a good destination for this soil; you certainly needn't have it carted away, but can use it to advantage. Variations in garden levels can give the garden extra dimension, so you can think of the challenge of "disposing" of the soil from the excavation as opportunity for your garden. This may be your chance to create some subtle changes in grade in a small area, or enrich a spot with poor, thin topsoil.

Pools and Small Children

The little ones always find water attractive. If you have small children, you must realize that there are hardly adequate means to keep them away from the water. Before building a pool, be sure you understand any legal restrictions or requirements that may apply to you. A fence often does not look quite right, and children often perceive it as only an extra challenge, something to climb over. One good measure to ward off danger is to stretch thick accordion netting just under the water surface from the water's edge at least a yard (meter) into the pool. Plants such as water lilies will still be able to grow toward the middle of the pool. Or, you can postpone your water garden until the children are older. If you

build a sandbox where a future water garden is planned, you can convert it to a pool later. Children prefer playing in a sandbox near their parents, so this solution is reasonable if you have planned a water garden near your terrace, for example. Take the time now to consider carefully all the safety implications of constructing a water garden or an ornamental pool.

Fish

It is difficult to give a rule for the right number of fish for a pool. The first requirement of fish is oxygen. When the pool is new, it isn't biologically balanced yet, and the water doesn't contain much oxygen. You cannot introduce fish until about eight weeks have passed, when the newly installed plants have grown somewhat. You must also take into account the size your fish will reach in your pool. Once you have stocked the pool well with plants and you are sure you have given the fish the correct food in the right amounts, if you still see the fish come to the surface to gasp for oxygen, you know you will have to buy a device to increase the oxygen in the water. Some mechanical pool filters are

A water garden must be kept up so that part of the water is always visible.

Oxygen in the Pool

A shortage of oxygen can be remedied by mechanical means. An oxygenating apparatus can be connected in the house and the oxygen conducted to the pond through a pipe. (If you dig a trench for this, you can lay a second pipe for the electricity to run a water pump for drainage, a fountain, or a filter at the same time.) An oxygen apparatus is inexpensive and will keep the pond partly free from ice in the winter, and transport oxygen under the ice. When there is ice on the pool, you must hack a hole through it and remove a bucket of water, so that a layer of air forms under the rest of the ice. This layer of air provides some insulation, so that the pool will freeze less deeply. Always keep a hole clear in the ice.

Cloudy Water

The causes of clouding in a pool include: not enough plants, too many fish, too much fertilizer, water that is too warm, excessive fish food. Your goal is to create a biological balance, such as is to be found in natural bodies of water. A discoloration may occur in spring and autumn, but that is not serious. However, too much sun quickly uses organic material and nutrients in the water to create an explosion of algae: The balance is disturbed. Prevent this by adding more oxygenating plants, and monitor any means by which fertilizer may be getting into the pool. Add a few buckets of water from a clear, natural ditch, preferably water containing many water fleas, and add them to your pool; it will be as clean as a whistle in two days. Fish may eat the water fleas quickly, so you might have to repeat this treatment.

equipped with aerators. Individual aerating devices are sold separately, too. If the fish are suffering, quick action should be taken. Adding more oxygenating plants to your water-garden community will achieve the same effect in the long run—but perhaps not swiftly enough for your fish.

Fish may be carnivores or plant-eaters. Carnivores will eat young fish, so that your fish population will not have a chance to multiply. Perch, pike, and eel are less than suitable not only because they are carnivorous, but also because they turn up the bottom so much that the pool is cloudy. Rock bass are very suitable for the naturalistic pond. They are rather shy fish that you will see only if you sit quietly by the water for a while. For this reason, many water gardeners choose koi, fish that don't make heavy demands, and can be found in splendid colors (orange, red and white, or any mixture of these). These fish may have beautiful fins. Koi can become very tame indeed. They are handsome pets, and with patience, they can be trained to accept food from your fingers, or to appear when you clap your hands (they anticipate feeding time). However, they are an easy prey for herons and other predators. (Plastic herons that are supposed to frighten away their own sort are not effective. The real herons do not recognize the plastic birds as herons—you can see that by the way they calmly stand next to them! In nature, herons never stand together.) Herons are so bold (even in small city gardens in some areas) that coarse-meshed netting to protect your fish is often not effective. If raccoons, herons, or other predators are likely in your area, you must be prepared to watch out for your fish—and to replace your stock as needed.

The water garden environment is rich in activity—here, the birth of a dragonfly. Even in the middle of a city you can expect all sorts of water-loving creatures to make a beeline for your pond.

Snails can help purify the water. They eat the algae that grow on the sides of the pool and from the surface of water plants. The larger pond snail, however, will eat your water plants, too, which may be okay if you have enough plants. In new ponds, excessive algal growth almost always appears. This problem will usually solve itself in time. As your water plants grow, they will gradually cast shade over the water surface, making it uninhabitable for algae. If all else fails, look for a commercial preparation designed to kill algae, but leave fish and other plants unharmed, and use it strictly according to the manufacturer's instructions.

Diseases and Pests

If you open a specialized book on water gardening of about twenty-five years ago, you will see mention of many chemical controls. Today we have a different approach. Always bear in mind that the biological balance of your water garden is very delicate and easily disturbed by chemical and other remedies. For that matter, this applies equally to natural habitats; the plant growth in a nutrient-poor moorland pool can become completely upset by the contamination of one empty fertilizer bag. Good maintenance right from the start helps keep the fish and plants healthy, and will to a great extent keep pests and fungi outside the garden community.

A terrace above the water. The vertical palisade wall blends in well with the tree trunks. In the foreground: Iris × germanica.

If you live near a pond frequented by ducks, your water garden may have some visitors. A flock of ducks can ruin a water garden completely within an hour, eating everything in sight. Wire mesh around the garden will probably help.

Herons, as mentioned previously, venture into built-up areas more and more, and can be found in towns too. Your fish can be protected by means of a net, but this is not a pretty sight. Another solution is a pergola built over and around the pond. This provides the pond with the necessary half shade, and it disturbs the fly-in and escape route of the herons, and that of ducks, too. Ducks and herons are most active hunters in the early morning, so simply chasing them away is inconvenient and sometimes impossible.

Plants around the Pool

When it comes to edging, there is a great difference between natural and artificial ponds. Natural ponds have a fluctuating water level; the water level of artificial ponds remains constant, and the shore plants stay dry. Actually, in that sense they are not really "shore" plants, for they

If you do not have room for a water garden, you can construct a fountain in a large flower planter. The planter could sit on the ground or be embedded in the ground.

might just as well be growing elsewhere in the garden. Still, they enhance the atmosphere of the water garden. A few examples of useful plants for a naturalistic edging are: brunnera, gunnera (for extremely large ponds), *Hemerocallis*, hosta, and *Rodgersia. Ligularia, Lythrum* spp., and *Lythrum salicaria* can manage on dry land, although they really are marsh plants.

Water Plants

Water plantings are an interplay of horizontal and vertical lines, connected by the reflection of the blue atmosphere above. A minimum of two thirds of the water surface must remain visible when the plants are full-grown. Particularly in the nineteenth century, pools were designed in such a way that the house was reflected in them, giving the picture of garden and house unity. If this is your aim, too, duckweed and any other large, obstructing plants must be removed regularly.

In smaller gardens it is easy to reflect part of the house on the surface of the water. Tall-growing plants framing the reflection on opposite sides can make this very effective. A water lily may be a pearl in the water, but in the case of a small reflecting pool, it is out of place and disturbs the reflection. A large-flowered water lily will take up a large area of the water's surface.

When planning a water-garden planting, consider the great difference between geometric and landscape shapes. For a baroque pond with a severe outline, an appropriate planting might be one that is perfectly symmetrical. With a natural pond shape, use plants and arrangements that look a bit wilder. Your choice of pool

An elongated, winding water garden suggests a brook. All sorts of exciting water and marsh plants are suitable for a pond of this shape.

style determines a certain atmosphere; once that is established, you can see whether certain plants fit in. Select both vertically and horizontally growing plants; a nice balance between them will render a beautiful composition. Because water plants are always very small when you buy them and grow rather large in just one year, after only two years you will have to prune them. Start pruning when you see your plants need it; in any case, before the surface of the water has been overgrown. Water plants are often shipped from suppliers accompanied by some duckweed, which can be removed with a fine rake (for a very small pool, a kitchen sieve is also suitable). If the pool is overgrown with duckweed, ultraviolet light in the sun's rays is prevented from reaching the water and the oxygen needed by the underwater plants and the fish will diminish. If the water garden is overrun by duckweed, the water will become black and smell foul. The fish, unable to breathe, will die.

Hedge bindweed (Calystegia sepium), *as its common name suggests, is a weed that grows particularly well in hedges, and it is difficult to remove. As soon as it sends up shoots in spring, pick them off, and* *continue diligently. With luck, you will have rid yourself of this weed after just one season. Against the mesh of chicken wire, for example, this rampant weed can look rather nice.*

Hedges

Many plants make suitable hedges, which is why it is a pity that many people think only of *Berberis* and conifers when they want to plant a hedge. Almost all shrubby plants can be trimmed into a desired shape. Plant a hedge of a different sort than that of your neighbors, and your garden will catch the eye and offer welcome variety. Visitors coming to your home for the second time will no longer look for the number of your house, but for your hedge; it will be distinctive. Although the selection to choose from is considerable, take care if you must avoid shrubs that are sensitive to frost. *Cupressocyparis leylandii* is planted quite a bit today; it grows rapidly, but is sensitive to cold weather. With a hedge, it is wise not to put all your eggs in one basket; don't install many plants of one kind that are not hardy.

Should the hedge be evergreen or not? How high must it be? Must it grow slowly, or would a fast-growing hedge be better? Are flowers or berries wanted? Are thorns acceptable, or desired? It is easy to fashion a hedge from many kinds of shrubs. *Ribes alpinum* is nice for a low hedge, and *Ribes sanguineum* for a taller one. If you like, you can let the shrubs grow separate from one another. Trees, such as beech, maple, alder, lime, holly, hawthorn, and elm, can be trimmed into hedges as well. To stay in form, the trees must be trimmed with hedge clippers at least once a year. Poplars are the most time-consuming tree for hedging; each winter all the branches must be cut back to the trunk with pruning shears. Hedges that grow slowly need to be trimmed only once

Hedges of hornbeam (Carpinus betulus).

Taxus baccata *'Fastigiata'*.

High hedges were created with hornbeam (Carpinus betulus) in the garden of Herrenhausen, *Hannover, Germany. A majestic entry archway can be made from this hedge plant.*

a year; fast-growing hedges can stand several trimmings a year. Growing a tall hedge quickly means a lot of work in the future.

If you plan to live in the same house for a long time, choose a slow-growing hedge, as it will give the most satisfaction over the long term because it requires less maintenance, and after a rather quiet start, it will give you just as much pleasure. In that case, a privet hedge, for example, is out of the question. Naturally, cost plays a role. Slow-growing plants are more expensive, but you can partly compensate for the extra cost by buying smaller plants. In order to make the choice easier, we can divide hedge plants into groups.

Evergreen, fast-growing
Prunus laurocerasus 'Rotundifolia', up to 10 feet (3m)
Ligustrum ovalifolium, up to 8 feet (2.50m)
Thuja, up to 13 feet (4m)
Taxus × *media* 'Hicksii', up to 8 feet (2.50m)
Lonicera nitida, up to 6½ feet (2m)

Evergreen, moderately fast-growing
Prunus laurocerasus 'Caucasica', up to 10 feet (3m)

Pyracantha, up to 8 feet (2.50m)
Aucuba japonica, up to 8 feet (2.50m)
Berberis julianae, up to 8 feet (2.50m)
Escallonia, up to 6½ feet (2m)
Bamboo, several kinds, up to 13 feet (4m)

Evergreen, slow-growing
Taxus baccata, up to 13 feet (4m)
Ilex aquifolium, up to 11½ feet (3.50m)
Mahonia aquifolium, up to 5 feet (1.50m)
Elaeagnus pungens, up to 6½ feet (2m)
Pieris japonica, up to 5 feet (1.50m)
Buxus sempervirens, up to 5 feet (1.50m), depending on
   the species
Viburnum tinus, up to 8 feet (2.50m)

Deciduous, very fast-growing
Acer campestre (hedge maple), up to 10 feet (3m)
Salix (willow), up to 10 feet (3m)
*Alnus glutinos*a (alder), up to 10 feet (3m)
Populus nigra 'Italica' (Lombardy poplar), 19½ feet (6m)
   and more
Tilia (lime tree), up to 10 feet (3m)

These hedges are recommended if you do not object to maintenance. The poplar is the most time-consuming, as every winter the branches must be cut back to the main trunk. The result is a knotty trunk that looks graceful.

Deciduous, fast-growing
Hypericum androsaemum, up to 3 feet (1m)
Symphoricarpos, up to 5 feet (1.50m)
Carpinus betulus, up to 13 feet (4m)
Crataegus, up to 10 feet (3m)
Ligustrum vulgare, up to 6½ feet (2m)
Elaeagnus angustifolius, up to 11½ feet (3.50m)
Sambucus nigra, up to 11½ feet (3.50m)

Buxus *lends itself to many purposes. Trimmed globes provide edging here, but a few in the border also can produce a splendid effect.*

Deciduous, slow-growing
Fagus sylvatica, up to 13 feet (4m)
Cornus mas, up to 10 feet (3m)
Euonymus alata, up to 8 feet (2.50m)
Spiraea, the higher kinds, up to 8 feet (2.50m) (grow
   moderately fast)

Tall flowering hedges
Ribes, up to 6½ feet (2m)
Rhododendron, different per species
   shrub roses, up to 8 feet (2.50m)
Fuchsia magellanica, up to 6½ feet (2m)
Berberis darwinii, up to 6½ feet (2m)
Escallonia, up to 6½ feet (2m)
Pieris japonica, up to 5 feet (1.50m)

A hedge does not have to be monotonous. Introduce projecting or indented planes, or undulating tops. You can create all sorts of features with many hedge plants; one popular favorite is a recess for a garden seat.

The sloe, Prunus spinosa, *is an impenetrable shrub ideal for a bird sanctuary. Even before the leaves have formed, this shrub is laden with white flowers. At a distance, it looks much like the hawthorn, but the flowers appear a month earlier, and there is a difference in the color of the berries, too.*

Short flowering hedges

Spiraea japonica, up to 2 feet (0.75m)
Potentilla fruticosa, up to 3 feet (1m)
Hypericum androsaemum, up to 3 feet (1m)
Rosa nitida, up to 2 feet (0.75m)
Hydrangea, up to 5 feet (1.50m)
Spiraea × *bumalda* 'Froebelii', up to 5 feet (1.50m)
Spiraea × *bumalda* 'Anthony Waterer', up to 3 feet (1m)
Lavandula, up to 2 feet (0.75m)
Skimmia japonica, 4 feet (1.25m)
Prunus laurocerasus 'Otto Luyken', up to 3 feet (1m)

The short, flowering hedges can be trimmed severely, but you may let them grow as they like, taking into account that they will become a bit broader.

Hedges that must be cut to the ground each year
Rosa rugosa
Hypericum androsaemum
Lavandula

Trimming Hedges

Trimming hedges is not as difficult as it looks. You can see exactly up to where a hedge has been trimmed the previous time, if it has been well maintained. Trim only to the old wood. If the hedge has not been cut straight, you can place bamboo sticks in the hedge and stretch a string or wire between them; the guy wire used by construction workers is suitable. Use the string as your guide while trimming. Stretch the string or wire taut and completely level. If the ground is sloping, it is advisable to trim the hedge level, and let it go downhill step by step instead of following the grade of the slope. It will sometimes happen that a hedge is neglected for many years. In that case, cut back the stems to the desired height; almost all species will sprout well again

Carpinus betulus (hawthorn) is suitable for a small garden, as long as it is trimmed each year. Left alone, the hawthorn grows to a height of 65 feet (20m). It is not an evergreen, but because many of the dead leaves tend to stay on the plant, it maintains a look of reasonably dense foliage.

For this type of hedge, the hawthorn and the sloe are very suitable. In the south of England one can see such impenetrable hedges everywhere, and they are used to keep livestock penned in. Note how the stems have been sawed from the top. One disadvantage to this method: Water can collect in the incision and encourage rot.

(exceptions: *Chamaecyparus, Thuja,* and birch). When a beech hedge is cut back severely there is a risk of sunburn, so trim prudently to maintain attractive, healthy foliage.

An "English" Hedge

Primitive peoples used thornbushes to keep livestock inside a sort of corral. For an impenetrable hedge, whether for cattle or people, use hawthorn, sloe, some species of roses, or berberis. It will take a few years before

If the stems are cut in this way, from the bottom, they cannot hold water. This method is therefore preferred as it does not encourage rot.

Dare to let a hedge grow in a smaller garden. A wall of green can enhance the perception of depth and create intriguing little corners partly hidden from sight.

Page 65:
End result if you let the hornbeam (Carpinus betulus) grow: The bottom is bare. Trim it at least twice a year. Once a hedge has been neglected, it will never become really dense again, so good maintenance cannot be postponed.

the plants grow tall enough to act as a barrier, so it will be necessary to supplement the developing hedge with temporary fencing if your aim is to keep something either "in" or "out." If you let this type of hedge grow freely, it will bloom profusely.

Laying

The full-grown hedge can be made more impenetrable using the technique known as laying. Make partial cuts or saw incisions in the stems, then bend the stems gently to the ground, all in the same direction—into the hedge. (In order to make the stems accessible, the hedge must be thinned out a bit first, enough so that you have room to work.) After bending the stems, position stakes in the hedge, and weave the branches horizontally, using the stems and stakes to hold them in place. The result is a hedge that is absolutely impenetrable. This type of hedge must be trimmed every three to four years.

Bulbous and Tuberous Plants

Most gardeners cannot imagine a garden without bulbs. Especially in spring, when there is not yet a leaf to be seen on the trees, the garden needs some color. Bulbs are a gorgeous solution, bursting into bloom in shades of blues, lavenders, purples, yellows, golds, and more. How

Anemone blanda *'White Splendor'* is one of the strongest anemones for underplanting.

TIP

Carnivorous plants

Few carnivorous plants are suitable for growing in the garden. The sundew (genus *Drosera*) can sometimes be found in educational botanical gardens. An insect such as a butterfly is attracted by the plant's flowers, but then is trapped by the sticky drops on the leaves. The butterfly will decay slowly, providing the plant with a steady source of nitrogen.

pleasing it is to see some life in the garden as soon as the snow has melted. It proves that nature has not sat still over winter. There is quite a lot of confusion over the terms "bulb," "tuber," and "rootstock," and they are often used mistakenly. We all know that a potato is a tuber, and so is the dahlia. The crocus is less obviously a tuber, as is the gladiolus.

The difference between a bulb and a tuber is that a bulb consists of layers, and a tuber (think of the potato) is uniform throughout. The crocus looks like a bulb, but if you cut it in half you will see that it has only one outside layer. In addition to bulbs and tubers, there are several "bulbous plants" that have a rootstock, such as *Anemone nemorosa* (wood anemone). We speak of "noses" or "pips" with *Convallaria majalis* (lily of the valley). These are sprouting buds on which there are roots. In this chapter, we will use only the word "bulbs" for the sake of convenience.

Planting Bulbs

Early spring is the time when everybody longs for fresh green growth and color in the garden. The flowering time for bulbs for most areas is from February through May, so most gardeners have four months to enjoy them. There are summer- and autumn-flowering bulbs, too. When you buy bulbs, determine the flowering

The "Pickwick" crocus. Large-flowered crocuses do not spread reliably. Increase their numbers yourself by sowing the pollinated seedbuds.

time; you will enjoy your bulbs most if you plant varieties that will flower consecutively for as long as possible over the bulb season. You can hardly make a mistake concerning color combinations, as few other

The Crocus tommasinianus *spreads best, but the larger* C. tommasinianus *'Ruby Giant' also spreads. Pick the seedbuds in May and spread them throughout the lawn immediately.*

plants are flowering at that time. Bulbs that flower later in the season tend to be larger and taller-growing, but by then the perennials have also started to grow. Planning bulbs for late spring/early summer becomes a little more complicated because the entire garden is coming to life. You will find perennials that combine well with bulbs, creating beautiful combinations that make the most of both kinds of plants. Plant bulbs in groups, never singly. For small bulbs, plant them in groups of about ten in an area as large as a saucer. Place early-flowering bulbs near to the house so that they are visible from indoors. After all, you will not often walk through your garden in the cold, early-spring months.

The smaller bulbs feel at home under old trees, an environment that is damp in the winter and in spring, but when the leaves on the trees start growing again (and evaporation increases and the ground becomes dry), the bulbs die back again. Snowdrops and crocuses especially like dry ground in the summer. Winter aconite shows its preference for clay by spreading wholesale.

Many popular spring-flowering bulbs traveled from countries around the Mediterranean Sea and Germany as early as the sixteenth century. These plants are often found near country estates, castles, cemeteries, and old farms. They thrive in soil rich in humus. Among others, this group includes:

Galanthus nivalis	*Eranthus hyemalis*
Galanthus elwesii	*Scilla hispanica*
Crocus tommasinanus	*Scilla siberica*

These bulbs reproduce not only vegetatively (by producing young bulbs off the "mother" bulbs), but also by spreading–that is. by multiplying. Many of these plants grow in woods in rich clay soil with an upper layer that is rich in humus. Most of the bulbs thrive in all kinds of soil, but the winter aconite grows only in clay; there are a few exceptions to the rule.

Fertilizing Bulbs

In contrast to the preferences of other plants, it is best to fertilize bulbs in autumn, when they have begun growing already and need the nutrients most. Supplemental fertilizing in early spring will help them to return to the summer resting period in good health. Usually the fertilizing that is ordinarily carried out in the garden is sufficient for bulbs.

The South Side of the House

Against the south side, where it is sheltered and where the sun is reflected by the wall, a microclimate is created

Muscari *'Blue Spike'*, Narcissus poeticus, *and* snowdrops that are past *flowering run wild beautifully. It is best to plant them together in large groups.*

that makes it possible for some species to thrive there better than elsewhere in the garden. In addition, this side of the house often gets the most attention because it is nicer for you to work in, too, and because you can enjoy the milder temperatures there early in the season. One condition must be met for the planting of bulbs here, however: The location must not be too damp in the summer.

Choosing Bulbs

Plant bulbs among perennials. The old-fashioned *Fritillaria imperialis* (fritillary) in red, orange, or yellow is spectacular. *Fritillaria persica* looks a bit somber with its brown-purple flowers, but can be very nice in combination with other flowering perennials. Some special irises are *Iris magnifica* and *I. bucharica*. *Leucojum autumnale*

Anemone nemorosa is not a bulbous plant, but has small rootstocks that enable the plant to spread rapidly in soil that is rich with humus.

TIP

Hang birdhouses where they won't be baked by bright afternoon sun, and with the entrance facing away from prevailing winds. This will go a long way toward making a birdhouse a comfortable home. The kinds of birds atttracted to a birdhouse depends not only on the shape of the house, but also on the size of the entrance. You can choose which birds you'd like to invite into your garden.

is suitable for light soil and bright sun. You can try *Nerine bowdenii* in a very warm location; its flowers are often sold as cut flowers. *Sternbergia lutea* is a small, yellow, autumn-flowering bulb. Some bulbs that flower in summer are *Zephyranthes* and *Tigridia*.

Bulbs for the Rock Garden

Many small bulbs are suitable for the rock garden.

Excluding tulips, hyacinths, and large-flowered narcissi, there are loads of bulbs ideal for the rock garden's many different microclimates. The south side on top of a slope is dry and warm; the north side at the bottom is damp and cooler. Plants are very sensitive to these differences, which in turn make a great difference in flowering times. These seemingly incidental botanical preferences can help you achieve a succession of bloom.

If you want flowering bulbs to make a showing very early, plant the earliest-flowering bulbs on the south side. You might try this with *Iris reticulata* and *I. danfordiae*, for instance, two irises that can flower through the snow. The winter aconite (*Eranthis hyemalis*) can do this, too, but it likes heavy clay; it is pointless to try out this tuber in sand.

Spreading is possible and makes for a pretty effect. You can let nature take its course, as many bulbs will multiply. Irises are best planted together; narcissi can be planted separately or together. Always adhere to the rule that bulbs are planted at a depth that is twice the height of the bulb. An exception: Snowdrops can be planted deeper to prevent them from drying out in the summer.

Potted Bulbs

It is a lot of work to cultivate bulbs in pots, but if you have little room and much time, it is very rewarding. You can actually bring the bulbs near you to enjoy them close at hand. (Photographers take note: Photographing at close range in the right light is easier, and you have your choice of background.) For most species it is best to buy new bulbs each year for potting, and then plant them in the garden after they have flowered, where they may perform again the following year. Bulbs for indoor culture must be prepared in a cool place—"precooled." There are glasses made specifically for holding a single crocus bulb; they are much the shape of hyacinth glasses, but smaller. Unfortunately, the glasses are very difficult to find, if the crocus size is at all available. The ready-made hyacinth "glasses" that are today made of plastic are unsuitable. They simply fall over when the heavy flower comes into bloom. The glasses are much sturdier, and a good deal more attractive.

It is handy to bury tulips and hyacinths in the garden in large pots (at least five plants together). You can leave them there, or remove the pots to grace a bare spot in the garden at about the time they start flowering. If you bury several pots at the south side of your house and several at the north side, you will have a spread in flowering time, due to the great differences in temperature.

Wild rabbits prefer grass and herbs. They cause enormous damage during freezing weather when there is nothing for them to eat but bark. You may be tempted to offer them food to keep them away from bark, but that may invite even more rabbits into your garden.

How to Increase Bulbs

You usually buy bulbs in the autumn, but if there are already large clumps of narcissi, snowdrops, and crocuses in the garden, it is a good idea to dig them up and to separate them in February, when the bulbs must start coming above ground. Be very careful to keep a lot of soil clinging to the roots to protect them, as the plants will not grow more roots if they are damaged. Bulbs do not have side roots; only the tip of the main root can drink in water. Plant back one third of the clump in the old spot and divide the rest into about ten small clumps, tearing them apart gently with your fingers. The clumps can be dug up and planted again directly after the green foliage has died back. Place a stick to mark them as early as when they are in flower, for the green foliage will be gone sooner than

you think (and then you will not be able to find your bulbs again). Plant the bulbs directly where you wish them to grow. They will increase quickly, so you can repeat this division after no longer than two years. In this way, the number of bulbs will virtually double each year.

It is possible to replant all bulbs that flower in spring directly, except for the tulip and the hyacinth. It is better to store them in a cool, dry place, and plant them again in September. Increase hyacinth bulbs as follows: Before replanting the bulb, make a few incisions in the shape of a cross or a star in the bottom of the bulb with a sharp, sterilized utility knife. Young bulbs will form on the outside of the incisions. After three years, you will have new, flowering hyacinths. When you have dug up the tulips in June or July, you must let them dry for fourteen days. After that, remove the old, shriveled bulb, loosen the young bulbs, and take off the dirty, loose outer layer, known as the "tunic." This is called "peeling." Now store the bulbs in a cool, dry, dark, well-ventilated place until September; good air circulation reduces the chance of infection with molds.

Sowing Bulbous Plants

If the soil is suitable (a clay soil), some bulbs can be sown. Extract the seed from *Crocus tomasinianus*, winter aconite, *Scilla siberica*, cyclamen, and corydalis when it is ripe and sow it in the prepared spot immediately. You can just scatter the seed on the ground.

After the incisions are made in the hyacinth bulb, young bulbs form on the outside of the incisions. Use a very sharp, sterilized utility knife.

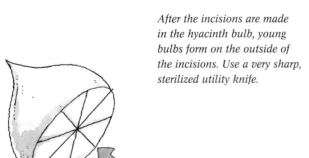

You may be surprised to see that the seed will come up in totally unexpected places. Therefore, sow in several locations. It does, however, take a few years before these bulb seeds start flowering (usually three), but you will be well rewarded for your patience. For very large gardens, this is the best way of increasing your stock because you would otherwise need immense quantities of bulbs, and sowing seed saves not only money, but the time and effort of digging. This method is suitable only for places that are not weeded.

Autumn Bulbs

Some bulbs start flowering the moment the trees drop their leaves. Both the supply and planting times are September. Because not many people visit a garden center then, these bulbs find their outlet through specialized bulb merchants and nurserymen, for the most part. Species such as *Colchicum* (autumn crocus), bulbocodium, and winter-hardy cyclamen are a few autumn-flowering species. The green of *Colchicum* comes up in spring, and can grow as tall as 20 inches (50cm); the flower appears on a bare stalk in autumn. The foliage is quite decorative. Be sure not to disturb it, as it is producing food for the bulb. All autumn-flowering bulbous plants are suitable for naturalizing—that is, increasing in naturally wild settings on their own.

Ornithogalum umbellatum, *does not flower well when*
ordinary star-of-Bethlehem, *planted in a shady spot.*

Bulb Diseases and Pests

As a rule, small bulbous plants do not suffer from diseases. As for pests, only voles can do great damage. As voles make use of moles' burrows, you need to discourage moles as well. Although the mole never eats roots or bulbs, it can greatly damage the garden in other ways. The greatest damage to bulbs is caused by mice, and especially voles, that venture above ground only at night. Their presence can be detected by holes in the ground. Voles are herbivores. The best pest control for mice and voles consists of mowing grass and weedy spots around the garden. Tall grass offers good shelter to mice. The embankments of ditches and roadsides are often mowed only once a year—not enough to control voles. In short: The well-maintained garden will have far less trouble with these little pests than a garden in a wilder state.

Tulips and hyacinths can be infected by viruses and molds. Plants infected with a virus must be removed ruthlessly because there is no remedy, and because of the danger of spreading, you mustn't keep them in hopes that they'll improve. For molds, there are several remedies; it is best to ask for information from the bulb supplier. Healthy bulbs that have been planted in a place that is not too damp rarely experience problems. Exceptions are *Fritillaria*, *Leucojum*, and *Camassia*; they require a damp environment. Consequently, it is best to plant these bulbs right after you buy them, so they don't dry out. If that isn't possible, store them in damp potting mixture temporarily.

When to Buy Bulbs

To achieve a blooming spring, you buy bulbs in October and November. The autumn-flowering species such as the autumn crocus must be bought in August or September. Bulbs will not do as a Christmas present (at least, not when they're intended for the garden).

The autumn-flowering species are greatly underused. This is a pity, for November is a month in which hardly anything flowers in the garden, in frost-free areas. If you plant autumn crocuses among the spring crocuses, that spot will flower twice. Make a note to buy autumn crocus at the end of August.

The summer-flowerers such as dahlias and gladioli can be planted in early May, when the soil is reliably warm. You don't want them to poke up through the ground when night frost can still be expected; that would most likely kill them. Most temperate locations are frost-

Brick laid lengthwise lengthens the path visually. A gradual transition from path to lawn is created here by fanning out.

Weeds on the lawn have a positive side. White daisies, yellow dandelions, or blue speedwells are a temporary enrichment of the garden.

free after May 15. This is important, as the summer-flowering bulbs cannot bear frost at all, unlike the spring-flowering bulbs. If the ground is still very wet at the beginning of May, it is better to wait a little before you start planting; the bulbs may rot in cold, wet soil. Remember not to work the soil when wet, as you can ruin its structure.

The Right Place for the Right Bulb

Before you start planting bulbs you must consider where you should plant them. Magazines and packaging look so tempting that many people tend to buy a bit of everything—but if you come home with bulbs for which you do not have a proper place, it is not worth the money spent. Bulbs should fit in with the atmosphere of the surroundings. A marsh area calls for different bulbs than a woodsy spot in the garden. Tall tulips, perfect for a flower bed, are not suitable under trees; that is where the tiniest of the bulbs look most appropriate. Autumn-flowering bulbs would be useless planted among tall perennials, which would effectively obscure them even when not in bloom. Take a good look at the descriptions

on the bulb packaging, or in catalogs. You need an idea of what the mature plant will look like, and its needs in the garden. A thoughtful choice will guarantee the best results.

Dandelions are lovely on the lawn as long as they are flowering. However, their seed will spread everywhere, and the heads are ugly after flowering. It is easy to remove dandelions with a sharp knife.

Bulbs in the Lawn

A sprinkling of bulbs in the lawn can be enchanting. If you want to have a perfectly smooth lawn, though, this is less appealing because mowing the grass must be delayed until the bulbs finish flowering and their foliage has died back. Long after the bulbs have finished blooming, the foliage is generating food to be stored in the bulb; if the foliage is removed too soon, it deprives the bulb of food. A good sod may experience a lot of damage from late mowing.

The most suitable bulbs for this are those that do not have to be dug up again. In clay soil, some bulbs will even multiply, providing you with a lawn full of flowers in no more than a few years. (This only applies to clay, which dries sufficiently in the summer.) Some bulbs suitable for lawns reproduce reasonably quickly in a vegetative (not by means of seed) manner. *Crocus, Eranthis, Scilla, Leucojum, Fritillaria* (damp lawn), *Galanthus,* and *Narcissus* can be planted in the lawn. Other botanical species look better in the border, chiefly because the green foliage dies back late.

TIP

Solitary plants

If a lawn is relatively large, and a simple, ornamental planting is wanted, a few solitary plants can be installed. When you draw attention to a solitary plant or a planting all of one type, it is known as a "specimen" planting. The following plants are suitable:

Acanthus

Aruncus sylvester

Ornamental grasses

Cortaderia

Filipendula rubra 'Venusta Magnifica'

Gunnera

Hemerocallis

Kniphofia

Ligularia

Bamboo

Yucca

Trees

In most cases when a tree is cut down prematurely, it is because the tree has grown too large for its location, or because the garden is too small for the tree. Think carefully before choosing a tree–you want the right tree for the location, and it is a shame to cut one down due to lack of forethought. There are very narrow, tall trees ("fastigiate") that will scarcely bother you with shade. There are splendid full-branched specimens with which you can give structure to the garden. You can choose trees with very open crowns so that many plants will grow under them. Consider the downside of any tree you are seriously thinking about acquiring, too. Take into account falling fruit, roots that lift nearby pavement, and the attraction of bothersome insects. All trees drop their leaves, but small leaves are less of a nuisance than large leaves.

The following information may be of help to you in determining which tree will suit you. The large selection of trees to pick from does not mean that every one that interests you can always be obtained. Ordering the tree you want in advance is often a necessity in order to avoid disappointment, and to take advantage of the best

If you wish a young birch to grow into a sturdy tree, you must cut back the side branches, leaving one clearly defined main trunk. For a straight trunk on this tree, the left "crown" of the plant must be removed now.

planting time. In spring, the most popular trees are already sold out at nurseries. You can frequently place your order in the summer for delivery in autumn, and you may be glad you planned ahead. It is said that a tree planted in November must grow; a tree planted in April might grow. In other words, the chances of renewal are much less in the spring than in the autumn. As many factors that cannot be influenced by nurserymen play a role, those experts cannot solve every possible difficulty you may encounter, and they cannot be held responsible for trees that fail to thrive. See to it yourself that the planting time and the growth conditions are right. After all, your tree is your investment. Some kinds of trees are supplied with root balls, evergreens among them, as well as trees that strike root with difficulty. Most trees do not need a root ball, however. Fruit trees, for instance, do not seem to need a root ball.

Selection Criteria

Trees of a size such as that of chestnut, oak, and beech are appropriate for very large gardens, parks, and panoramic landscapes. Somewhat smaller trees such as birch, alder, and maple are excellent for medium-size gardens. A third category of smaller trees includes the fruit trees, hawthorn, holly, ornamental pear tree, and bird cherry. Several Japanese bird cherries also belong to this group, suitable for small gardens.

When you buy a tree, you must take into account the width and the density of the crown. Do you hope to grow other plants under the tree? Will the tree at maturity cast desirable shade? Large-leaved trees and shrubs have more sound-damping effect than trees and shrubs with

The larch is not often planted, unfortunately. It does not flower, but its beautiful young shoots in spring and the golden ones in autumn are a very ornamental feature of this needle-losing conifer. Its rapidity of growth is only surpassed by that wonder tree, Metasequoia glyptostroboides.

The cypress (Chamaecyparis lawsoniana) *looks pretty at the nursery. This pointy little conifer reaches a height of 82 feet (25m). As a hedge* *this cypress is unsuitable, although some nurserymen recommend it for hedging, because it is easy to cultivate.*

depth now. Put a tree pole, a stake to give the new tree support, in before planting. It is handiest to make a hole with a drill, so that the pole stands firm. Stakes about 8 feet (2.50m) tall are a good size. Situate the tree pole on the windward side of the tree, and take care to attach the wide strap in a figure eight between the tree and the pole, so that the trunk won't slide or rub against the pole later on.

Conifers

The conifers make up only a small portion of trees suitable for gardens. Conifers are fine when combined with other plants. When they stand by themselves, they are not very exciting. They don't flower, nor do they change appearance with the change of seasons; conifers always look more or less the same. When you see that pretty little conifer with a nice shape at the nursery, you must not forget that the plant will grow and won't stay that shape for long. You would like it to remain small, so you ask the wrong questions at the nursery: "It won't grow too large, will it?" The salesman, who does not want to disappoint his customer, will play up to you somewhat, if unintentionally. Pose your questions in such a way that the salesman cannot deduce your preference concerning height, width, type of soil, sun or shade, and so forth. It is better to ask, "How tall will this plant become?" or "Does this tree do best in sun or shade?" and not: "Will it thrive in sunlight?" This way, you will get unprejudiced answers. A popular misconception is that conifers need

small leaves, so the screening of environmental noise such as that of passing traffic can play a role in the choice of a tree. Trees that flower are lovely, but their fruit sometimes causes trouble: chestnuts cluttering the terrace and berries that stain carpets when they travel into the house on the soles of your shoes. The pods of locust trees must be raked and collected when they fall in great numbers. Roots of some poplar species grow under and actually lift up pavement, so never plant poplars near paved paths.

Planting

It is important to dig a large enough planting hole, larger than the root system of the tree. This way the soil around the roots will be nice and loose later, and it will be easier for the roots to make their way out into the surrounding soil. The soil dug from the planting hole can be enriched before it is put back into the hole. The color of the trunk of your new tree will show you how deep it was planted at the nursery; you must plant it at the same

Ground covers under trees: an easy garden.

hardly any maintenance. The maintenance starts with the planting. Plant with care, and you give your tree the best possible start.

Planting Conifers

The planting hole must be a good deal larger than the root ball. Conifers need loose, acid soil. This can be achieved by adding peat moss to the soil, if it is needed; a soil analysis is a good idea. Soils that are very rich in chalk are unadvisable for conifers. The planting hole must be large so the soil can remain loose around

When planting a hedge, you must dig a trench. Dig up and loosen the soil at the bottom well. Dig your trench with one straight side, and place the privet plants against this side.

the roots that will form; this makes for a better distribution of peat moss around the root ball, too, if you want to add some directly to the planting hole.

Pruning and Trimming

Pruning can be done as early as February. Cutting back to the bare wood should be done only with taxus. Other conifers will remain bare if you cut them back too far. Taxus must be pruned twice a year, *Thuja* and others no more than four times a year.

Conifer Hedges

Taxus × media 'Hicksii', which is much cultivated and is relatively cheap, is not especially suitable for a hedge in many areas; owing to the verticality of the branches, the plant will be pulled apart by a heavy layer of snow. *Chamaecyparis* (cypress) is also quite unsuitable for a hedge. This conifer is difficult to prune, and it cannot

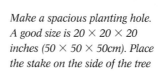

Make a spacious planting hole. A good size is 20 × 20 × 20 inches (50 × 50 × 50cm). Place the stake on the side of the tree that will get the most wind. Do not give the newly planted tree water until you have finished with digging and planting.

withstand wind. As it grows, the underside receives less light and soon becomes bare. (However, it is eminently suitable as a solitary tree if the groundwater level is not too high.) *Thuja* can bear much more humidity. The *Chamaecyparus* will grow much wider than the *C. l.* 'Columnaris'. Anyway, the blue color of these conifers can be intrusive in the landscape, so you must apply it selectively. The ordinary *Thuja occidentalis* is cultivated less and less. This plant is sown, and that is why there are great differences in the manner of growth between one plant and another. Another disadvantage is that this species becomes bronze-colored in the winter; it looks like it is dying. *Thuja plicata* remains fresh and green. There are several varieties of *T. occidentalis* that are very suitable for a hedge. A good nursery or garden center can advise you. Just as with *Thuja, Taxus baccata* is also sown. The differences in growth reveal themselves in the shape of "flames." The "marbled" hedge is an effect that develops when one plant grows faster and narrower than the next. (A little variation in color occurs, too.) Because

When the taxus has grown into a cylinder shape, it will add a calming note to this garden of different shapes.

of this, the hedge, although it may be trimmed into a severely formal shape, does not look dull, as it probably would with *T. media* 'Hicksii', which is "slipped." When all the slips come from the same plant, they grow into plants identical in shape. The branches grow vertically so that the plant is damaged by heavy snow. Conifer hedges are often planted because people think that they need little maintenance. This is not true. The more they are trimmed, the more dense they become, and this of course is desirable. A conifer hedge once neglected cannot be severely cut back, and must be replaced by a new hedge.

In small gardens, conifers are often placed in the border, where they add variety. If the hedge is not cared for on one side, the entire hedge will be lost eventually. That is why it is important to make good arrangements with the neighbors.

Taxus grows less fast then *Thuja*. The disadvantage of having no privacy in the first years of a young hedge is compensated by less maintenance later. In general, the slow growers need less trimming. *Pinus mugo*, a pine, stays relatively short and does not have to be trimmed at all.

Taxus baccata grows slowly. It has been used in gardens since antiquity, and applied in hedges since the

Larch in early spring, just before budding.

next to a young tree at the nursery, this conifer would hardly ever be sold anymore. When you see a beautiful full-grown conifer in your neighborhood, you can ask the owner for a cutting that you can take to the garden center, where an expert can tell you exactly which plant it is from. The best thing to do is to look up the correct Latin name, so confusion is avoided in your pursuit of precisely the same plant. If you desire many conifers in your garden, it is a good idea to visit a botanical garden or a garden that is maintained by professional gardeners. There you can write down all the botanical names of plants you admire, as all the plants in such gardens should be identified with nameplates. This is an excellent way to "shop" for plants. Try to see the conifers you like as full-grown plants, so that you can more easily imagine their appearance at maturity and how much space they would take up in your garden in the future.

Renaissance. This taxus is very suitable for a location in the shade. Because of slow growth, this is one of the most expensive of hedges. If you have time, however, you can start with young plants, seedlings that are two or three years old. It takes a few more years to achieve the hedge you want, but the price is much better.

Solitary Conifers

Think about the place where you want to plant a conifer, and how large a tree you want. The size it will be in three years is not as important as the size it will reach in twenty years. There is an enormous selection to choose from and there is a suitable conifer for every spot. The cedar is a good example of the importance of planning ahead. This sweet little conifer (about 3 feet [1m] tall when you buy it), will grow to 98 feet (30m) tall—and very wide. Still, most cedars are planted in gardens no bigger than 33 feet (10m) square, where they are out of proportion when mature. The fast-growing conifers become much larger than the more expensive dwarf conifers. Replacement in the future is much more expensive than having to plant only once. When planting conifers, it is necessary to keep sufficient distance between the trees. Of course, this looks rather bare the first few years. Filling the gaps with annuals is a possibility, but it is better to fill the garden with ground covers and low-growing perennials; it does not matter that they will be overgrown later by the trees. They look attractive and you will be less irritated by weeds. When you buy a tree, you must pay attention to height at maturity and growth rate, and not to the appearance of the plant at the moment of purchase. The conifer that is sold most as a specimen tree is *Chamaecyparis lawsoniana*. This tree is very attractive when you buy it, but if a full-grown specimen were placed

Bonsai Conifers

Dwarf conifers in pots are sometimes sold as bonsai trees. Because a human hand has scarcely touched such plants to give them the shape they have when sold, these plants

The grand orangeries of old are very suitable for art exhibitions. Orangery in Herrenhausen, Germany.

Japanese garden (Floriade 1992, Amsterdam). Traditional planking used to be made of natural stone or wood. Concrete slabs are *an excellent replacement, creating a contrast between artificial and natural elements.*

have nothing to do with bonsai. Especially often, *Chamaecyparis obtusa* 'Nana Gracilis' is sold in pots as "bonsai" for prices that far surpass the market price of an ordinary garden plant. Still, many conifers are suitable for flower boxes and pots. Design a combination of tall- and low-growing conifers with conifers that will drape over the side of the container. In the summer they can be supplemented by annuals or low-growing perennials. All dwarf forms are appropriate for containers. Conifers that grow large can be used, too, as long as they are trimmed several times during the growing season so that they stay compact. Do not fill the pots with ordinary potting mixture, but with a mixture rich in peat, which is more acid. If you are unsure of which potting mixture to buy, just ask a professional at your local garden center for advice.

Conifers in an Existing Garden

Sometimes a conifer will seem to have grown too large for a garden, and you are inclined to cut it down. Before you do, look to see if you can prune it substantially. By removing the bottom branches (called "limbing up") and thinning out the crown, you may be able to create a nice shape. After this treatment, it will be another two years before the conifer regains its natural shape and requires attention again. Perennials can be planted around the trunk, in a circle, for a pretty accent.

Heeling In

Plants on order do not always arrive when you are ready to plant them. Perhaps the planting location is too wet, for example. In cases such as these, you must temporarily store the plants. Dig a shallow trench, and set the roots or root balls of the plants in at a slant, so they are supported by the ground. To prevent mold, do not place them too close to one another. In a shaded, sheltered spot, make a trench for heeling in. You have no way of knowing how long the plants will have to stay there. At nurseries, plants are heeled in first in autumn. Then the plants will strike root more easily in spring. If a delivery arrives when the ground is frozen, you must unpack the plants immediately and store them in plastic in a cool, sheltered place, such as the garage. Outdoors, heeled-in plants do not suffer from frost, but indoors those whose roots are protected with only a little soil must be kept in a frost-free spot. Important: Frost on bare roots is fatal.

3 Garden Maintenance

Garden maintenance is a catchall expression for the most varied sorts of activities that are part of gardening. It includes pruning, which must be done in the correct manner and at the right time. It includes fertilizing, for which you need to know what type of soil you have. It includes sowing and propagating plants. It includes recognizing diseases and pests in time to deal with them. You cannot do all of this with your bare hands. You need equipment, and the correct equipment is very important.

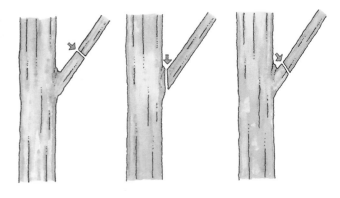

"hatrack"   too flush   correct

sawing wounds that are very conspicuous, say, along a much-traveled path or near a terrace. What hasn't changed is that branches should be cut in the correct manner with pruning equipment that is not only clean, but also sharp.

For this, use only equipment that is specifically meant for pruning. Do not use a carpenter's saw; it isn't good for the saw or the tree. With heavy branches, it is best to cut the branch partly through from the bottom, 1½ feet (0.5m) from the trunk, and then to cut it down from the top. After that, remove the stump near the trunk, which is easier to do cleanly now that it isn't heavy, and you won't run the risk of tearing the tree. As you can see from the drawing, the branch must not be sawed off too near the trunk, for you could damage the trunk. The

Pruning

Recently, theories on the maintenance of trees, and especially pruning, have changed considerably. Today, using concrete to fill up hollow trees is absolutely unthinkable. The use of various substances to paint on wounds is thought to be less critical then formerly, although some camouflaging "liquid bandage" is still recommended for those

The first four drawings show you how not to prune: the branches have been pruned too near the node or in the wrong direction. The last branch has been pruned

correctly: both the direction and the distance to the node are right. The position of the pruning shears shows you how to prune correctly.

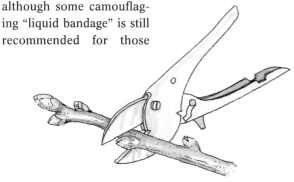

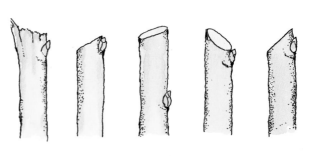

Remove suckers at the base. For this you need to dig some soil away first.

the next. With long neglect, pruning must be more drastic, usually at the expense of flowering. It is better to prune species that are sensitive to frost in springtime. Some shrubs are an exception to ordinary pruning: *Prunus triloba* is completely cut back to just above the place where it was grafted immediately after flowering. The result: a kind of small-scale "pollard willow" in appearance. The stem grows thicker so the flowering branches show up splendidly.

Grapes

Grapes must be pruned before mid-February. Because grapes start into growth very early in the year, the plant will "bleed" if it is pruned late, and this cannot be stopped. Maples may not be pruned between March 1 and July 1 for the same reason.

collar of the branch—this is the edge of bark between branch and trunk—must remain intact. You must aim for a wound as small as possible, as near as possible to the trunk.

When to Prune

There is a difference between winter pruning and summer pruning. You may prune year-round except in the late spring, when the juices of the plant get going. However, in summer it is more difficult to see what should be pruned. That is why pruning for thinning out must be done in the winter, when trees and shrubs have lost their leaves. There are shrubs that flower on the current year's growth (such as potentilla), and shrubs that bloom on last year's wood (such as forsythia). One of the myths in the gardening world is that there is a considerable difference in the pruning of these two groups of plants: There is no difference.

With yearly pruning, you don't need to cut away very much, so that the flowering is hardly affected. You can prune early-flowering and late-flowering shrubs at the same time. After all, a professional gardener cannot keep returning time and time again to prune one shrub after

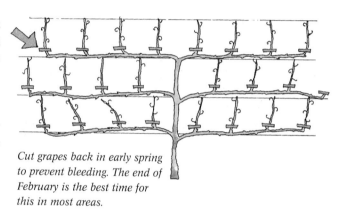

Cut grapes back in early spring to prevent bleeding. The end of February is the best time for this in most areas.

An elegant herb garden laced with little hedges does not need to be rich in flowers. A variety of foliage colors can give a nice effect.

Pinching to remove side buds. This will allow the terminal bud to develop better and produce a larger flower.

The shape of the sunken garden is repeated in the taxus hedge. Many sunken gardens were constructed at the beginning of this century.

Taxus baccata *'Fastigiata Aurea' is a slow-growing evergreen.*

Currants

A currant bush in healthy growth will yield more fruit, but for that it should be pruned once a year. Pruning results in a pleasing habit for the bush, too. Leave four to six main branches, and see to it that enough light can reach into the bush. Lateral branches will start growing again soon after pruning, so the bush will look thicker again. You can begin pruning as soon as the fruit has been picked, but a disadvantage of pruning at this time is that it is still difficult to see which branches ought to be removed. It is better to limit yourself to winter pruning. First cut away branches that rub together, and branches that grow haphazardly through the bush. For a handsome bush, you can also cut off awkward branches that stick out horizontally. Leave the small lateral branches that will bear fruit. This method of pruning is suitable for white, red, and black currants. The gooseberry can be pruned in the same way. Pruning really doesn't influence the height of the bush. The black currant grows tallest, the gooseberry grows shortest. Always consider the mature sizes of bushes before planting; it would be a pity to lose a bush because it was too tall.

Buddleia

Cut off all the branches to 1½ feet (0.5m) from the ground each year. Such treatment may seem drastic, but it yields good results. This is best done in March to April, once freezing weather has passed, and this way of pruning gives the most beautiful flowering. During the growing season, the still-herblike branches must be cut back to three eyes (buds).

Roses

Roses that are sensitive to frost, including all ordinary tea roses and polyantha roses, are pruned after all danger of frost. Pruning them earlier may put the cut branches in danger of freezing. You will find more detailed information on the pruning of roses in chapter 5.

Shrubs That Flower on the Current Year's Growth

Shrubs that flower on annual wood, such as *Potentilla*, *Spiraea × bumalda*, and *Hypericum*, may be cut all the way to the ground, but it is better to thin out only half of them. You should prune not only at the sides, but throughout the plant. If you prune half of the plant each year, it will be completely rejuvenated after two years, while something of the plant remains to enjoy after each pruning. After all, a bare garden is not the intention of pruning. Of course, you can also cut back one third of the branches, so that the shrub will be completely rejuvenated in three years. If you do not prune these shrubs enough, the flowering will be seriously reduced. It is necessary to fertilize in spring. Professionals prefer cutting back the entire shrub to the ground, as this is a faster method than thinning it out from the center, twig by twig. What professional gardeners do is not always the best for a beautiful home garden, but they must think economically. Do not always take the professional gardener as an

Most kinds of hedge shrubs can be trimmed to any height.

Note the taller columns at both sides of the entrance.

example. There is no question, however, that you ought to work on this group of plants consistently for years of good flower production, as well as an attractive shape.

If there is an old shed or other structure in the garden that needs to be pulled down, it would be intriguing to see whether part of the walls can

be used in the new garden design. Here, the severely trimmed hedges enhance the rectangular shapes.

A combination of Buxus *hedges and taxus gives this park in Oxford a pleasing green richness.*

Pruning Trees

Pruning may be done for several reasons: to increase flowering, or to create a more beautiful shape. The latter is usually the reason in ornamental gardens. Even for fruit trees, the shape of the tree is probably more important than the amount of fruit it will bear.

"Pruning is growing," as the saying goes. And indeed, there is better growth and flowering if the pruning is done well. Never prune more than one third of the crown branches, or the relationship between the roots and branches will be disturbed. If the root system is too large for the branches, the tree feels the impulse to grow too strongly and may send up sucker branches that grow vertically up through the crown. Especially in the case of hawthorns and fruit trees, these branches are very visible. Take them off at the base. If two branches rub together, one of them must be pruned away; the look is more pleasing, and severely chafed branches are prone to infection. Taking off the bottom branches to create a trunk is not very difficult. At least two thirds of the tree

Trees are not pruned to make them smaller or shorter, but to give the crown more light. The tree grows and flowers better if light reaches the branches equally.

should consist of crown. You can saw off one branch higher each year, so that the balance between trunk and crown is not disturbed.

Trees do not always have to be pruned in the winter. Nevertheless, it is easier for the amateur to do it then. In situations where the main branch divides into two, low on the tree, the branches that should be pruned are more visible in wintertime. Take off the branch that is most at an angle, to encourage the tree to develop a uniform crown in the future. Dead branches naturally must always be removed from the tree. It is easy to determine whether a branch is dead. Remove a small piece of bark with a sharp knife. If the tissue right under the bark is green, the branch is alive. Brown, tough tissue means that it is dead. Sometimes an entire tree may die. (Think of the romantic, naturalistic period in gardening history, when dead trees were left standing.) In some cases, letting a dead tree stand looks attractive, but you must continually

The Renaissance garden is well suited for small-scale plantings. If you use a small-leaved Buxus, *the hedges can be kept very short.*

evaluate whether it poses a hazard. The dead bark is soon populated by insects, and attracts birds. Woodpeckers love pecking dead wood. In addition, beautiful toadstools will start growing on it. If, after years, a dead tree seems in danger of falling, you can cut it down, and leave it where it lies, if you like. The tree will remain damp, and moss will begin to grow on it.

Training Trees

Trained trees develop many twigs that grow vertically. The crowns, which are pruned level, should have a lateral branch that grows every 11 to 15 inches (30 to 40cm).

These lateral branches are fixed with wires. In early spring, all lateral branches growing more or less vertically can be pruned back to two eyes. Pruning every year will promote the density of the crown. If you leave off pruning, the lateral branches that grow sideways will become too heavy.

Trained trees need much work. When the lateral branches have grown, they must be fastened on again. The branches grow faster than you think, and then the wire grows into the bark—not a healthy situation. Loosening the wires each year is a solution to prevent pinching off. After about eight years the branches will be strong enough on their own, and the wires (or bamboo sticks, if you prefer) can be removed. Tree stakes must be removed in time, too. Unfortunately, it happens all too often that the trunk is pinched off by the tree belt; the stake that was put there with the best of intentions has killed the tree because of negligence.

Topiary

Numerous shrubs are eminently suitable for trimming into shapes. Many gardens have hedges that fence them off. These hedges can also be trimmed into different shapes; they can be made shorter, narrower, crenellated, with shelves, or curved alcoves perfect for sheltering garden seats. Topiary can give us all kinds of fantasy

Taxus and Buxus *can be trimmed into all sorts of shapes. These figures are made from taxus.*

shapes. There have been chairs, peacocks, bears, vases, ships, and doves made of taxus and *Buxus*. The art of topiary has almost been lost, but in recent years it has been making a comeback, thanks to the increased interest in formal gardens. In England the great variety of topiary is without peer. Trains, hunting scenes, pyramids, and spheres adorn the English garden in many sizes.

Suitable plants for trimming into shapes are:

Thuja plicata
Taxus baccata
Buxus sempervirens
Ilex crenata
Ilex aquifolium
Taxus cuspidata 'Aurea'

Shaping Tips

For curved shapes, construct the form you want of chicken wire, and give it additional support with stronger wire. Let the plant grow within this "cage" and trim off any growth that sticks out through the mesh. Pyramid and cube shapes are simpler than this: Position bamboo sticks over the plant to outline the shape you desire. All the

When pruning a hedge, keep in mind that it needs sufficient light at the bottom, so the base must be broader.

plants recommended for this technique grow extremely slowly. That is best; otherwise the topiary would lose its shape too quickly. However, you will need patience. It takes many years (depending on the size you wish to have) before the rabbit or peacock you are working on is full grown. Then, of course, you will have many years to enjoy your handiwork; slow growth becomes your ally.

Pruning Calendar

Consult this pruning calendar. You can prune your shrubs at different times, but it really is preferable to prune them all at once. That way you will not forget one, which would be undesirable because yearly pruning is absolutely necessary, and they will grow at relatively constant rates.

January	fruit trees (if there is no frost)
February	almost all shrubs that do not flower in early spring; grapes
March	all roses, except for standard roses and tree roses
April	plants sensitive to frost, such as *Caryopteris* and *Ceanothus*; heather that flowers in winter; fuchsia; evergreen shrubs
May	viburnums that flower in spring
June	some roses; lilacs
July	branches that hang over paths may always be pruned
August	standard roses and tree roses (thinning out); *Clematis montana*; lavender
September	long shoots of fruit trees, on which the end bud has already formed
October	dead wood, which can be seen readily now
November	fruit trees and shrubs
December	almost all shrubs (if there is no frost); watch out for the exceptions!

If your garden is maintained by a professional, it is probably impractical to schedule repeat visits, or it may not be financially worthwhile to schedule a visit to prune only a few shrubs. When planning your garden, ask yourself whether you or a professional will maintain the garden.

Prune Prunus laurocerasus *with pruning shears. Large leaves that are half cut off look odd.*

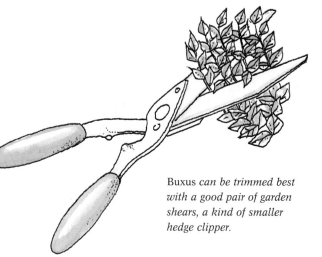

Buxus *can be trimmed best with a good pair of garden shears, a kind of smaller hedge clipper.*

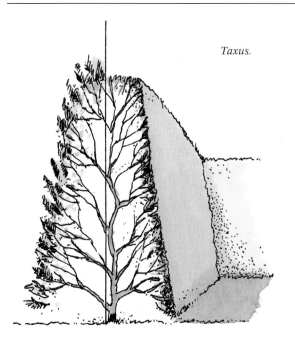

Taxus.

important. In a garden, slow-acting fertilizer with a relatively high potassium level is more suitable. Cattle breeders would sooner recommend cow manure, so give some critical thought to the advice you get. Impartial advice is best.

Compost

Reserve a certain place in the garden for a compost heap. In nature, leaves fall to the ground, decay, and return nutrients to the soil. Leaves falling around the base of the tree they grew on benefit that tree. Healthy soil contains many microorganisms such as molds, and worms. The garden is not natural, though; we tidy everything. However, we can try to follow nature's good example. Pile garden waste and organic vegetable waste on a compost heap hidden from view. It is handy to choose a spot not far from the house, because you may make several trips there a week, even if the weather conditions are less than ideal. In autumn, distribute your

---

TIP

Late-flowering shrubs

In order to have a flowering garden in autumn, you must use perennials. What is less well known is that numerous shrubs flower late in the year, too.

Among these are:

> *Hibiscus*
>
> *Perovskia*
>
> *Ceanothus*
>
> *Celastrus* as a shrub
>
> Tea roses
>
> *Hypericum*
>
> *Magnolia grandiflora* (sensitive to frost)
>
> *Fuchsia magellanica*
>
> *Abelia*
>
> *Lespedeza thunbergii*
>
> *Aralia*

In addition, many currant bushes will add color (and birds!) to the garden.

To speed up the composting process, garden waste can be shredded in a compost grinder. The grinder has two openings for loading: one for garden waste and one for twigs up to an inch (2.5cm) thick. It is easier to set up an orderly compost heap with neat sides with shredded garden waste.

Fertilizing

There are many different opinions on fertilizer—how much, how often, with what, when. Farmers are very knowledgeable on the subject. In arable farming, a high yield can be achieved when nitrogenous manuring is given with a liberal hand. A high yield is unnecessary in the ornamental garden. In a garden, we desire strong plants that flower well and have a healthy green color. In the ornamental garden, seed production is not

decayed compost throughout the garden. This way you create a natural cycle. You'll be able to work soil more easily because of the increased organic content. In wet weather you will not see as many puddles, and when it is dry, water will be retained better in the soil. Compost is also a natural insulation layer when applied to the ground surface before the onset of winter.

Worms are attracted to compost as it provides them with food; a compost heap will increase your worm population. They dig tunnels through the soil, aerating it as they travel, and plants grow better with well-aerated soil. Rainwater drains quickly through worm tunnels, too. If sufficient compost is used, supplemental fertilizing may not be necessary. For large gardens large, loosely piled compost heaps are sufficient; for smaller gardens you can get by with a low fencing of thick wire mesh, or stones. In the city garden, plastic compost bins are ideal. It is best to turn over the compost heap each month to accelerate the composting process. You can leave the heap alone for a year; the composting process will take longer, but takes very little effort. Why burden society with extra waste, and deprive your garden of black gold?

Making compost

For the city garden, fertilizing with only compost is enough if you process all your kitchen waste. Almost all organic leftovers (no meats, please) from the kitchen, as well as ashes from the fireplace qualify for the compost heap. The compost heap can be sited

Good fertilizing results in a good harvest.

somewhere in half shade where it is a bit humid, but do not place it on ground that is very wet, as oxygen is needed for bacteria and molds do their composting jobs well. With a suitable ratio between humidity and oxygen, the temperature in the heap will become so high because of decay that any weed seeds will lose their germinative capacity.

Several kinds of compost bins can be bought, with a wide range in price, for small gardens. If the composting goes well, you will not be bothered by smell or vermin.

Liquid Fertilizer

If you come to live in a house where the garden has not been fertilized in years, you can quickly remedy the deficiency with liquid fertilizer that is specially meant for fertilizing leaves. A plant can absorb nutrients through its leaves, in addition to its roots. To prevent burning the leaves, you must use the correct dosage, and do not spray in bright sunlight, in order to avoid scorching the leaves. The ready-made fertilizers are complete, and make up for any deficiencies of manganese, iron, and other trace elements. It is best to atomize the fertilizer so that all the leaves of the plant can be treated. Absorption by the leaves takes place very quickly, in contrast to absorption by the roots.

Inorganic Fertilizers

Fertilizers formulated to treat specific deficiencies are best applied following a soil analysis. Take specific measures only once you have determined the precise nature of the problem.

Chicken Manure

Chicken manure is rich in nutrients, but as garden fertilizer it has a disadvantage: It is so high in nitrogen that it can easily burn the plants. Use the manure in limited amounts only after it has become well rotted. Muck out the chicken coop regularly and save the manure for two years; after that, the risk of burning has been reduced enormously. Work the well-rotted manure into the soil, if you like, to reduce the concentration.

Stable Manure

The use of stable manure is not always ideal. The manure must be matured. Manure that is rich in straw is not recommended, as straw binds nitrogen, so that a temporary deficiency of nitrogen can develop. This problem could be solved again by adding extra nitrogen, but a soil analysis beforehand is imperative. Stable manure contains a high count of weed seeds; the

inevitable consequence is much weeding. We recommend stable manure only for roses, although the nutritional value of cow manure is much lower than is often thought. A considerable amount of well-rotted stable manure in autumn can provide good winter protection for roses. Still, it is much easier to use artificial fertilizer granules. This means less effort in transport, less time, it does not cause weeds, and there isn't undesirable straw in the garden.

If you want to apply horse manure, you must first get a tetanus injection at the doctor's, especially if you will work with your hands in the soil later. Horse manure is quickly decomposed by microorganisms, a reaction that releases much heat. Cucumbers and other vegetables thrive in a raised bed where the soil has been enriched with horse manure.

Peat Moss

Peat humus and peat moss may not be considered to be fertilizers, but they do act as such indirectly. In poor, sandy soil, water, and nutrients are retained much better if there is a layer of humus. Heavy clay becomes more workable, especially in very wet or very dry periods, if peat is worked in. These products increase the degree of acidity (they decrease the pH value; low pH equals a high level of acidity). That is why you must not use too much

Every vegetable gardener knows that fertilizing is an important factor for a good harvest of fruit and vegetables.

Fertilizing is just as important in a flower garden to grow beautiful, healthy plants.

peat moss or peat humus as an additive to sandy soil for plants that do not like acid. You may be considerably more generous with them in clay. It is very important to know the degree of acidity beforehand, and a soil analysis will help you here.

Diseases and Pests

We do not have to go into detail concerning diseases and pests. Before trying to fight disease, it is better to remove the diseased plants and figure out the cause of the problem. Consider the disease to be a warning: The cause is to be found in the environment of the diseased plant.

You can ask yourself several questions to trace the possible cause of the disease:
- Is the drainage good (are there leaking pipes)?
- Is the composition of the soil suitable?
- Does the plant get the sun exposure it prefers?

Before you buy a plant, learn its preferences. The right location is the basis for healthy growth. Snails prefer to eat unhealthy or sick plants; of course, a young lettuce

Do not let grass grow tall right next to the kitchen or vegetable garden. Many snails will creep into the garden in the evening.

plant that still looks weak looks unhealthy to a snail, too, so the presence of snails is not always completely decisive about the health of your plants.

Elements that seem to have nothing to do with plant diseases need more attention than the disease of the plant itself. One of these elements is the contribution of worms. They turn over the soil, thus creating a better structure and giving plant roots more room. (Drainage is quicker, too.) Do not try to fight ants, either; they eliminate plant lice and small caterpillars and do not cause damage themselves. The usefulness of the ladybug is well known. Many people think that toads, which have a marked leaning toward damp places, are less than pleasant.

Bud gall on a Quercus rubra. *Gall can be found on all parts of the tree; there are root galls, trunk galls, branch galls, fruit galls, stamen galls, leaf galls, and, as the photograph shows, bud galls.*

Nevertheless, you should protect the toad, never mind his appearance; toads live on snails, wood lice, and other insects, without doing any mischief themselves. Do not let weeds and grass grow up at the foot of trees, especially fruit trees. Tall grass provides a hiding place for vermin, which can cause much damage, especially to bulbs and the roots of fruit trees. Apart from the aid you receive from several kinds of insects, it is important to prune and fertilize well. This is the best you can do to ensure healthy plants, and any use of pesticides can then be held to a minimum.

There is not much we can do about some diseases, and they may also have nothing to do with the location of a plant. Dutch elm disease is caused by a fungus transmitted to the tree by one of two insects. This disease is difficult to control, and because it is so easily carried from one elm to the next, do not plant elms, unless you are prepared to protect them from feeding beetles, and are watchful that the fungus does not spread from the root system of one tree to the next—not easy tasks. These are such extreme measures that it is best not to plant them for now. When all field elms disappear in a few years, the disease will probably subside, and we can take the risk

again with new elms. There are many almost-resistant

> ### TIP
>
> **Biological control of caterpillars on cabbage plants**
> The cabbage worm, which transforms into the cabbage white butterfly, need not become a terrible pest if you check the undersides of the leaves for eggs regularly. Just crush them when you see them. You can plant tomatoes and sage next to the cabbages, a sometime-deterrent as the butterflies do not like these plants. Put pots of peppermint next to the cabbages when it is butterfly season and they will stay away.

varieties available today, which is an encouraging development.

Fire blight is a disease that tends to strike plants of the rose family. Pears, cotoneasters, firethorn, and an important figure in the landscape, the hawthorn, suffer much. If you wish to plant a hawthorn hedge, it is best to mix it with *Acer campestre*. The leaves of this plant are similar to those of the hawthorn, and *Acer*

Page 91:
Gall on the underside of an oak leaf. When it is young, the gall is bright red; later it will become brown. Here, you can clearly see the different stages of development of the gall.

These egg-shaped gall are on the veins of the leaf. Inside lives the white gallfly larva, Mikioli fagi.

campestre can be nicely trimmed as a hedge. If you plant them alternately, the whole hedge will not be lost if the hawthorns die. Mostly older elms and poplars suffer from wetwood, or slime flux. Because lots of dead branches are an unseemly sight, plant with moderation.

Rose diseases will be discussed separately.

Handling Pesticides

When it comes to chemical treatments, take curative and not preventive measures. If we take only curative measures, as in treating aphids on a plant, we know for sure that it is necessary. We do not know this with preventive measures. You may see chemicals sold as "plant protection products," but they are probably simply pesticides. For weed control, the herbicide dosage can be much less than the directions on the package instruct, if the outside temperature is correct when you use it. Some products need a rain-free period of six hours, others twenty-four hours.

In the morning, when there is dew on the plants, a much higher concentration is necessary because the dew dilutes the dosage. It is better to spray in the evening; burning your plants with toxic chemicals is almost ruled out then. There tends to be less wind in the evening, so you can put more pressure on the spray, so that the pesticide is atomized; that way the distribution will be much better, and you can do with less. You must be careful not to disturb the environment with too much chemical pest control. Read the instructions well before you use the product. Be sure to wear gloves and protective clothing if it is recommended. Pesticides must be stored in a closed cupboard,

inaccessible to children, and safe from freezing temperatures. If an accident occurs, you must go to a doctor immediately, taking the packaging with you as the toxicological group is always mentioned on it. You can see why pouring one chemical into another bottle or package is absolutely unthinkable, because you must be certain of the chemicals you are using, and the manufacturer's cautionary information must be right at hand.

Is This Plant Still Alive?

In the summer it is easy to see that a plant is dying if its leaves start wilting. With some wilting diseases (for instance, with clematis) the infected plant can grow up from the ground again. In spring, everyone is curious to see whether a shrub will bud again. Some shrubs only do this in late spring, among them *Campsis*. Shrubs that have just been planted bud much

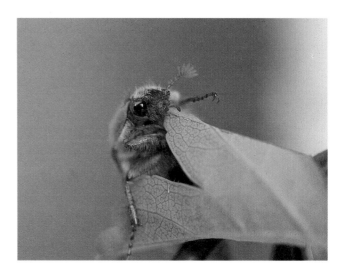

The May beetle is a feared visitor to gardens.

later; sometimes you will have to be patient until August for flowers. There is only one thing you can do: wait.

By scratching your nail along the bark of a young twig, you can see whether there is a green layer under the bark. If the tissue there is brown, the twig is dead. Try again at the bottom of the shrub. In this way you can quickly check whether a plant has sustained frost damage, even after a severe winter. But even then, you ought to wait and see. Most plants can start sprouting from the ground again, and the time each plant takes to do this differs.

Weeds

Weeds are by definition all the plants you do not want in your garden. Plants some people have a fondness for are called weeds by others. Most people consider the so-called field weeds to be undesirable. Weeds can be divided into annuals, biennials, and perennials.

Weed Control

Weed by hand between your perennial plants, especially during the first few years after planting. Do it late in the year for once, so that you can start with a "clean" spring.

Wise gardeners check their plants regularly for insect damage.

If you are careful of the bulbous plants, you can weed between shrubs with a hoe. If you use the hoe in very dry weather, the uprooted weeds will dry out immediately. Then you need not rake them out. When the conditions are humid, each weed has to be meticulously raked away, as the roots will take root again quickly. If you do not have time for an all-out weeding session, you can at least see to it that certain plants do not reproduce, by picking off flowers and seedpods from (among others) garden

Ants milk plant lice as though they were tiny cows.

Some pests seek out one particular host plant where they make themselves at home.

The caterpillar of the emperor moth.

that you are unintentionally reproducing the weeds. Potatoes are often planted in larger gardens, one year before the actual garden planting begins, as a weed discourager. Because potato plants are tall and grow densely, weeds are smothered under them, even the most stubborn ones. (A dividend: Potato plants produce pretty, delicate blossoms.) Remember: One year's vacation from weeding means ten years of weeds. This seems a bit exaggerated, but it is basically true. (But you needn't give up a summer vacation; remove all the weeds you can just before leaving home, and repeat this immediately after your vacation.) No one enjoys weeding, but if you are proactive, you'll save time in the long run.

Ecological Management

To let nature have its way completely leads to chaos in a garden. Some supervision is always necessary. Your carefully planned variety will disappear if vigorous plants, especially root weeds, are allowed to do their own thing and run roughshod over the community you hoped to achieve. Vigorous plants must be curbed regularly so they don't eliminate the plants nearby from competing for sun, water, and nutrients. And although small amounts of weeds can be nice, seedpods must be removed to prevent that plant from overgrowing the entire garden.

balsam, cow parsley, hogweed, dandelion, and stinging nettle. Of the root weeds, goutweed and couch grass are great tormentors, but a cultured plant such as the Chinese lantern plant can become very troublesome, too. Still, you need not be too worried. With some discipline and great regularity, weeds can be removed fast without resorting to chemical means. Weed the soil surface with a hoe each week. In small gardens and between perennials, pick them by hand each week.

Poppies growing wild. Because it reproduces so fast, the poppy can be looked upon as a weed at times.

Within the period of one summer, you will be completely rid of them if you have started in early spring and have not skipped a week. People often try to pull the roots from the soil, but that is often a frustrated effort. Little pieces nearly always remain, with the result

This thistle may be a weed, but it does have a beautiful flower.

Garden Equipment

Good garden equipment is essential, not only for the starting of a garden, but also for its maintenance. Some equipment is not too expensive; other pieces are a considerable investment. To help you make up a list of

The yellow sow thistles with hollow stems are annual weeds. The purple thistles are biennial.

Equisetum (horsetail) breaks off easily at the joint if tugged. In damp soil, you must remove the underground portions of this parasitic plant to eradicate it.

Impatiens glandulifera *spreads so rapidly that many garden owners consider it a pest. Unwanted seedlings can be weeded out easily. Children find the plant curious–a tap against the flower causes the seed to shoot out with considerable velocity.*

the equipment you'll need, it is worthwhile to list the characteristics of your garden before you buy anything. Otherwise, you may come home with a lawn mower that is totally unsuitable for your needs.

Lawn Mowers
There are three main types: the cage mower, the rotary mower (among which is the hover mower), and the bar mower. The last is meant for tall grass, on shoulders, for instance, and is used in ecological gardens. Both other mowers are sold as electric lawn mowers and gasoline-driven machines (two-stroke or four-stroke). Lawn mowers can be bought with two different kinds of professional advice: from the garden specialist, who is concerned with your particular garden conditions and wants to sell you a correspondingly appropriate machine; or from the hardware store merchant, who bases his lawn

mower recommendation on reliability, the quality of the motor, and whether the machine can be repaired easily. Unknown makes, bargains or not, sometimes run into difficulties in service and supply of parts later on. Base your choice on the sort of lawn you have and the frequency with which you want to mow it. Then, you decide whether you want a gasoline mower or an electric mower, a rotary mower or a cage mower, and whether you prefer to walk or to push, or whether a machine that drives itself is the best option. Ask your friends whether they are happy with the machines they have.

Electric Mowers

Electric mowers are suitable for lawns with few trees. Lawns far from the house, the location of your power supply, are awkward because of the long cord that is needed. An earth leakage circuit breaker is necessary for safety. You can buy separate safety switches especially for lawn mowers. The motors themselves are protected against overheating. If a machine automatically switches off often, the grass may be too tall and the machine must be set higher. Except for sharpening the blade, there is hardly any maintenance to be done, an advantage for those not mechanically inclined.

A separate sweeper collects up the mowed grass. The mowed grass can be left on the lawn to dry for several hours before it is collected, so that it will weigh much less.

Manual lawn mowers come in several widths. They are suitable for lawns up to about 400 square feet (300 sq m).

Gasoline Mowers

Two-stroke motors need lubrication. Four-stroke motors have a crank chamber. The two-stroke motor does not have a crank chamber; the fuel also lubricates the motor, and the oil does not need changing.

These machines can mow very steep inclines. They can be placed on their sides for cleaning, which is convenient. The disadvantage is that older machines often have trouble starting; they are less suitable for people who are not strong. Buy a two-stroke only if you have to mow many inclines or along ditches or ponds. The hover mowers, although the mowing result is less good, are also very suitable for this.

Four-stroke motors run on pure gasoline. The crank chamber contains oil for lubrication. This means that the machine should not be tilted too much when you clean it. Consequently, this type also is unsuitable for steep inclines. An advantage: It starts easily and the plugs do not get dirty often. Always check the oil and change it whenever necessary. If they are well tuned, these mowers make little noise.

The following types can be bought both in the electric version (also battery-powered) and with two-stroke or four-stroke motors.

Bar Mowers

Suitable for inclines, orchards, and lawns with a nineteenth-century appearance. Meant only for taller grass, the flat-cutting blades cut off, but do not shred, the grass, so the grass can be converted into hay or fed directly to animals. This machine is absolutely unsuitable for the maintenance of beautiful lawns. You can buy it only in the gasoline version.

Hover Mowers

Especially good for edges of ditches, inclines, or when there are many shrubs under which the grass must be mowed. The more difficult starting of the two-stroke motor as well as the inferior mowing result must be put up with in exchange for these pluses. Height adjustment is done by moving the blade on separate rings, an action that cannot be done at a moment's notice. Do not let children mow with it. Tether the machine with a rope if there is a risk of slipping down an incline. Wear heavy shoes when using this machine.

Cage Mowers

If you desire a good-looking lawn and want to catch the grass as it is mowed, the cage mower is ideal. The machine has to be meticulously cleaned after use and is suitable only for very level lawns. During vacation the mowing must be arranged for; tall grass is not mowed well and the machine runs aground in it. With the cage mower you can make lovely lanes in the lawn by mowing backward and forward continually and not going around (the well-known lanes of soccer fields).

This electric hover mower has a mowing width of about a foot (30cm), and so is suitable for small lawns with an incline. The mowing result is not as good as that of a blade cage mower.

In short: This is the mower for neat lawns of garden owners who can summon the discipline that this machine requires.

Rotary Mowers

A rotary mower does not give as good results as the cage mower. It is suitable for ordinary lawns where the grass is not mulched or gathered, although attachments are options with most of these machines. If you want the grass to be caught, buy a machine with a fixed bin at the back. With bins at the sides, the machine will mow crookedly on soft ground owing to the weight of the mowed grass when the grass bin fills up. Separate bags are inconvenient to empty. The rotary mower is the most popular machine.

General

Machines can be bought in different widths. Buy a width that suits your garden. Considering how long you think it will take you to mow your lawn will help you determine a convenient width. (One hour's mowing a week can be a pleasant activity, three hours of mowing is a drag.) Depending on their width, manual mowers are suitable for lawns up to 820 feet (250m).

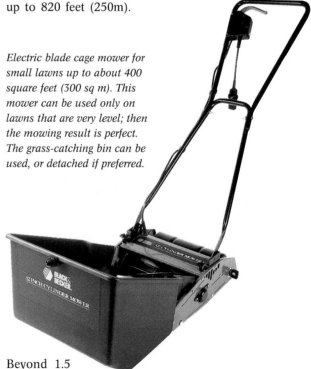

Electric blade cage mower for small lawns up to about 400 square feet (300 sq m). This mower can be used only on lawns that are very level; then the mowing result is perfect. The grass-catching bin can be used, or detached if preferred.

Beyond 1.5 miles (2.5km), motor mowers on which you can sit or garden tractors are handy. Lawn mowers are dangerous things. Do not let children handle them. Always check whether the blades are still before touching the machine to examine or clean it. The manual mowers are also cage

A rotary mower with a catching bin at the back that drives itself. Bins that are attached to the sides have the disadvantage that the machine will sit less level as the bin fills up. On the other hand, it is more difficult to remove a bin from under the push handle.

mowers. People often think that the machine blades are "dull," but usually this is because the machine has not been adjusted well. Old machines should make a singing sound. The bottom blade and the cage blade must be barely touching. To check the machine, carefully set it

An electric rotary mower for a small lawn. Always check whether the height can be easily adjusted before you buy a mower. With this machine, the wheels must be unscrewed.

upside down and check whether a sturdy piece of paper can be cut with a smooth edge. The blades probably are dull if the paper tears. If the paper slips between the blades, the machine is too loosely adjusted. Experiment, adjusting until the machine "sings." In practice, well-known makes do not always provide the best quality—a critical eye is indispensable. In late summer, lawn mowers are often on sale. This may seem attractive, but let your lawn indicate which machine you need, and not just the price or whatever leftovers they still have in the shop at that moment.

Once you have bought a machine, always have the blades sharpened by a professional. If the blades are not "balanced" after sharpening, the machine starts to vibrate and becomes more sensitive to abrasion.

Manual Equipment

To facilitate your garden work, there is an abundant selection of equipment in all sizes, types, and price brackets. Handling equipment is different for each gardener. Some basic equipment is necessary for every garden. Look through the list that follows, and note what you are missing. You needn't buy many tools, but they should be of good quality; such purchases pay for themselves over and over again.

Garden Rake

It is nice to own two rakes: a narrow one, for working between perennials, and a broad one for paths and shrubs. Rake handles are always narrow and a bit springy, so that they are pleasant to work with. If you put a rake away temporarily, make it a habit to place it with the teeth downward.

Leaf Rake

In practice, the light bamboo rake is the most suitable for raking mowed grass. A broad metal rake with long teeth is suitable for raking leaves, and is also good for raking fine gravel. It can be employed for cleaning out ditches as well.

Spade

For digging soil and turning it over, for digging up shrubs and perennials, the garden spade is the most suitable tool. See to it that the spade is sharp. Never use a spade as a lever while digging up plants; the handle can't take the stress. Clean the spade after digging. If the blade is rusty, digging will be much more strenuous than cleaning it would have been in the first place. For lazy gardeners, there are expensive stainless steel spades that can be left outdoors.

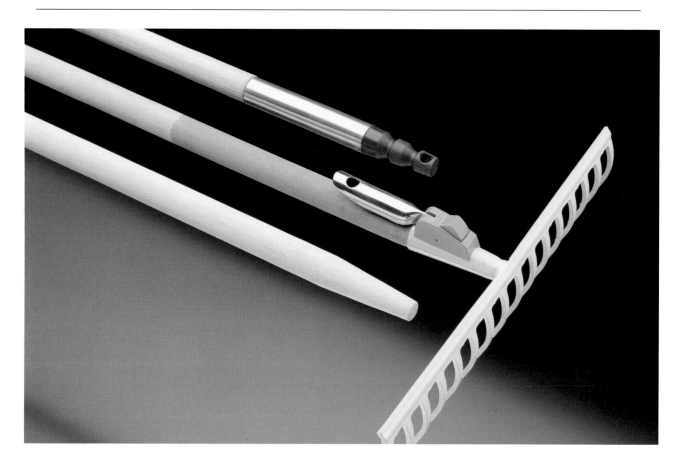

Shovel

The garden shovel is much cheaper than a spade. It is meant for shoveling sand and garden waste. It is not suitable for ground work. The handles are available in different lengths. It is a good idea to try various models to see which feels best before you buy one.

Hoe

The push hoe, the wooden type, is most common and for sale in two designs: welded and forged. The latter is more expensive, but lasts much longer. Always see to it that the hoe is sharp and free of rust. New hoes from the shop are always blunt and must be sharpened first. If you always keep your hoe sharp, you will facilitate your work.

This separate leaf rake can be attached to any handle. The rake and the handle are both rather heavy. Many people are much happier with the bamboo leaf rake. Although it wears out sooner, you'll wear out two for the price of one metal leaf rake.

There are several coupling systems for equipment intended to save storage space. The separate parts are easier to hang up. You will need more than one handle, as different pieces of equipment are used more or less at the same time with most gardening activities.

Cultivator

The cultivator is made in a three-forked and a five-forked model on a long handle, long enough to allow you to work standing upright. The first is meant for use in heavy soil. With a straight back, you can quickly loosen the soil so that sprouting weeds wither. It is ideal equipment to keep a garden free of weeds. You must use the cultivator when there are no weeds yet and the work still seems meaningless. In the long run, you perform a little work now in order to avoid a lot of work later on.

The first purchase for every garden: a sturdy spade.

Grass Cutter

Long-handled shears, the so-called English garden shears, work best. With these, you can cut edges with a straight back. You want a straight edge along the lawn. Wrong usage has caused these shears to fall into disuse. Success is easy if you know how to use them. The edges of the lawn should be cut twice each year.

To use this tool properly, keep your left hand still and cut only with the right hand. If you go to the trouble to practice a bit, the shears will be highly satisfactory. Smaller shears tire you out quickly, and therefore make you less efficient, but they are adequate for small lawns.

Hedge Clippers

Good manual hedge clippers are faster than an electric hedge trimmer. Think about the time it takes to unroll and roll up the cord. Cleaning hedge clippers is also no more than a moment's work. Clipping straight is an art that cannot be learned from a book. If necessary, step back from the hedge now and then to gauge how you are doing; you'll be able to see whether you are heading off on a slant, and will be able to correct it. While clipping, you must not look at the spot you are clipping, but straight along the hedge, a bit farther on, to keep an eye on the long straight line. If the hedge is already quite straight, you can see how far to cut by the old wood; use that as your guide. For *Buxus* and taxus that are cut into particular shapes, there are the so-called palm shears, a smaller tool than the hedge clipper, which allows for easier, and more successful, mobility.

Small Equipment

Plant shovels are for sale in several widths; the narrow

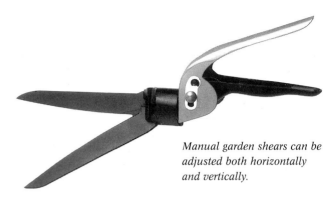

Manual garden shears can be adjusted both horizontally and vertically.

ones are better if there are many bulbs in the ground. While planting, you will do less damage with a narrow shovel. Every gardener has a different approach: one gardener rather likes to use a hoe for weeding, another gardener prefers a hand fork, a three-pronged fork, or a

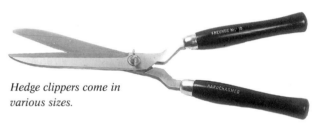

Hedge clippers come in various sizes.

small cultivator. You must find out for yourself what suits you best. Manual equipment is often difficult to locate when it has been left out in the garden, especially equipment with green handles. Orange or red is more visible, and will help you keep track of your equipment. Lawn mowers can be damaged by hand tools lying invisible on the lawn.

High-Pressure Sprayer

You can use a high-pressure sprayer for controlling weeds, and spraying plants, to wash off alga growth on the house or

These manual shears have a rechargeable battery. They are suitable for clipping grass edging along a wall, for example. The edge of grass lawn along a border is easier to cut with long-handled shears, so that you can do the work while standing up.

Do not buy electric hedge clippers without some thought. With a small hedge, unrolling and rolling up the cord is more work than the clipping itself. Cleaning electric hedge clippers also takes up much more time.

terrace, and for leaf fertilizing with liquid fertilizer. It is important to clean it after use. Do this immediately, for afterward you will have forgotten what substance you used last time. You must not spray when there is wind, for then you can't control the fall of the spray. When the pressure is adjusted lower, the sprayer will release larger drops that do not travel as far. The atomization is better with higher pressure, so that plants can be treated in their entirety. You must always wash your hands after using chemical substances.

Wheelbarrow

The wheelbarrow lets you carry in one load what might otherwise take four or five trips. You can choose from several models. Wheelbarrows such as are used by construction workers are best, sturdy, well balanced, and often with a square lip. Store the wheelbarrow upright when putting it away, so it will take up less space.

Pruning Shears

Even amateurs would do well to buy a professional model of pruning shear; you can find models specially for left-handed use. With good shears, pruning becomes a pleasure, and well-made shears are less likely to wrench or tear the branches being pruned. The so-called anvil shears with a cutting blade are less suitable for thicker branches.

Pruning Saw

A curved pruning saw is ideal for pruning shrubs or thin tree branches. Do not buy a saw with a plastic handle, as you will often prune when it is cold, and then the plastic can break easily under the stress of vigorous use.

Tree Pruner

This is a long-handled pruner, sometimes with double leverage, with a wooden or aluminum handle. Together with pruning shears and a pruning saw, the tree pruner is indispensable for pruning.

You can buy hedge clippers in all sorts of models. It is not a bad idea to first ask friends about the type they like and why they like it.

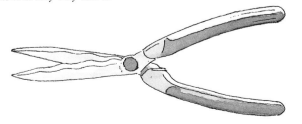

Garden Hose and Watering Can

Hoses are cumbersome to stow away, so the shorter the hose, the less bothersome it is. Good couplings facilitate fast coupling. A reel extends the life span of a good garden hose. It is best to coil your garden hose loosely after each use, and always drain it thoroughly if freezing weather is expected. Watering cans can be had in metal or plastic, in sizes from very small to enormous. For beds that have just been seeded, there are accessories such as "roses," which allow the water to fall in a fine, gentle spray so the newly sown seeds do not wash out of the soil.

Tree pruner with anvil.

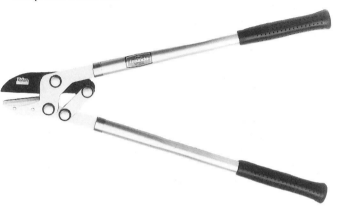

Binding Material

You must always keep some binding material—garden twine, strips of cloth, and so on—with your garden equipment. Tying up a plant often cannot be postponed while you rummage for materials. Raffia and several kinds of garden wire are very useful. This is one area where your enthusiasm for recycling and finding uses for odds and ends really comes in handy. For tying plants in such a way that the binding really can't be seen, it doesn't matter whether your choice of material

A reel extends the life span of your garden hose. Buy a garden hose in a length that you will really use. It is pointless to buy a hose that is too long—you will only make more work for yourself.

is camouflaged or obvious. The one thing you must be mindful of is that the tie doesn't chafe or cut into the plant in any way; damage to branches, stems, and so on weakens the plant, and invites trouble.

Sods must be set at sufficient height to mow over the edge.

The Lawn

Laying out a lawn requires much preparation. Preparation of the soil must be thorough. If a lawn is also to be used as a walkway, a "grass path," steps to improve drainage are often necessary. After intensive spadework, choose the kind of grass seed you want. Sod is an alternative to seed that you should consider.

Sod or Sowing

When to use sod and when to sow? This depends on several factors. The time of year in which you wish to sow is important. The ideal time for sowing is July to August, but you can sow between mid-April and mid-October in most areas. You need not buy sod during the ideal sowing season. You will achieve the same result either way, in short order. For small gardens up to 82 feet (25m), it is better to lay sod. For larger gardens it depends on

whether you want an instant lawn; do children or dogs need to be able to play on the lawn immediately? In that case, lay sod. If there are many cats in the neighborhood that will enjoy paying a visit to your garden and can destroy grass seed in doing so, sod is to be recommended, too. In short: The choice between sod or sowing depends on the time of year, the surface area to be made, and, finally, what you are willing to pay. Sod is more expensive; you pay for the convenience of an "instant lawn." After no more than a few months, you can't see any difference between a sown or sodded lawn.

Preparation for Sowing

The preparation is the same for sowing and for laying sod. First you need to spade the soil well and let it rest for a few days. Then level the soil with a rake and roll it. When you buy seed or sod, you can usually borrow or rent a

A cage mower gives the best mowing results. You can tell that this type of mower has been used because of the stripes it leaves in the lawn.

Sod is delivered on pallets. When the weather is warm, overheating can develop in the stacked sods within a few hours. If you cannot lay the sod immediately, it is best to separate the rolls. If you let them lie for more than two days, they must also be rolled out.

roller at the garden center. At home, fill the roller with water. It is easier to work with a roller that is completely full. You can immediately feel whether the surface to be sown is already level enough by the movement of the roller. A level lawn is important because it makes mowing easier, safer, and more efficient. You can be sure that the extra effort you put into establishing your lawn will be amply compensated later. Raking level sometimes entails moving some soil. If you get down on your knees and look along the ground, it is easy to see where soil is lacking in places and where some has to be removed.

Professionals rake at least three times, rolling between each raking. After rolling for the last time, it is time to

A shaded border with grass paths. Always retain a few vistas.

sow. Do this in the evening when there is little wind. If you must sow in a wind, you'll need to use a seed drill (a small sowing machine): Figure about 2 pounds (1kg) of seed per 430 square feet (40 sq m) of land. Save some seed for supplementary sowing later on. Additional seed is useful if some patches remain sparse after most of the grass has come up, and for those times when soil under your lawn must be excavated.

After sowing, you must rake the seed in carefully. If you roll once more now, the soil will dry out less rapidly, and this will improve the germination of the seed. Weed seed comes up more quickly than grass seed, unfortunately. You can buy one of several products to control these weeds, but although the weeds are an eyesore for those who prefer an immaculate lawn right away, they will disappear completely after the grass has been mowed twice. Daisies and speedwell are perennial weeds and won't appear right away in your new lawn. They can be fought individually–cut them out with a utility knife–or chemically if they cover the entire lawn. Always think twice, though, before resorting to chemical herbicides; manual eradication is the wiser course.

TIP

Flagstones

Many of us want a professional to do the paving. From experience he knows where to begin and to which side the water must drain off. It is best to lay flagstones yourself when they are used as steps in a border or on a lawn. Make only those paths that won't be used in all weather conditions from flagstones, as they become extremely slippery because of algae growth, especially in the shade.

Laying flagstones

Stretch a string to mark the sides of the future path, indicating the height it is to be. The stones must either lie level or follow the slope of the terrain. If the slope is too steep, the stones must be laid level, and steps constructed instead. One problem with this stone is that the thickness of the flags is not uniform. Put a 4-inch (10cm) layer of sand under the stones. This will give you enough leeway to adjust the height of the stones. If you remove some sand under the center of any stone it will not wobble.

Flagstones in the lawn must be at the same height as the surrounding lawn; hence, they must lie lower than the top of the grass. That way you can mow over them, and it saves cutting the edges. Overgrowing grass must be trimmed away regularly.

poorer the soil, the more variety you will see in the plants. Because the entire lawn must be raked off after mowing, a flower meadow is just as much work as a traditional lawn. There are lovely periods during which the lawn looks as though it is blooming, but also long, dull periods. Do inquire of your neighbors, if they live close by, whether they will be happy with your informal "lawn."

Moss often grows on the lawn in the shade and in damp spots. Sometimes it is possible to remove the grass and keep a carpet of moss. This project calls for extra work to get started, but once the moss is established, mowing becomes a thing of the past. Set foot on it only for maintenance when strictly necessary, for it is quite fragile.

The Flowering Lawn

You can achieve a sort of wildflower lawn by mowing it only a few times each year. It looks unsightly if you walk through it, so some paths should be constructed. The first time you mow is mid-June, when the main flowering of the plants has ended. The hay must be raked off entirely; we call this making the soil poor. Mid-September is the second time you mow. You may not use fertilizers on this lawn. If this is a completely new lawn, you can sow it with grasses that do not form thatch, and with a flower mixture consisting both of annuals and biennials. The

Never let a path form the boundary between border and lawn. Repeat the grass on one side or repeat a few perennials on the other. A path is more inviting if it goes through or between something.

Daffodil meadow in the Wisley gardens in London. This blooming lawn can't be mowed very early—not until the green foliage of the daffodils has died back.

TIP

Shrubs with golden and yellow leaves

- *Alnus incana* 'Aurea'
- *Aucuba japonica* 'Variegata'
- *Berberis thunbergii* 'Aurea'
- *Chamaecyparis obtusa* 'Crippsii'
- *Cornus alba* 'Aurea'
- *Corylus avellana* 'Aurea'
- *Euonymus japonica* 'Ovatus Aurens'
- *Gleditsia triacanthos* 'Sunburst'
- *Ilex aquifolium* 'Flavescens'
- *Laburnum anagyroides* 'Aureum'
- *Robinia pseudoacacia* 'Frisia'
- *Ligustrum ovalifolium* 'Vicaryi'
- *Philadephus coronarius* 'Aureus'
- *Ribes alpinum* 'Aureum'
- *Sambucus canadensis* 'Aurea'
- *Taxus baccata* 'Standishii'
- *Thuja occidentalis* 'Rheingold'
- *Viburnum opulus* 'Aureum'
- *Weigela* 'Looymansii Aurea'

Sowing

The seed of one species comes up quickly, while another species may take three or four weeks. Germinative power is important. The rate of germination has to do with the age of the seed and how it was stored. Always buy fresh seed, and store it in a cool, dry place. Some perennials are so-called cold-germinators (anemones, for instance). Annuals germinate best at a temperature of above 50°F (10°C). A good degree of humidity is also important for germination. In early spring, when the atmospheric humidity is low, it is wise to place an old sheet or a burlap sack over the seedbed so the soil will dry out less rapidly. (Obviously, this covering must be removed directly after germination.)

Sowing Outdoors

Seeds of the castor-oil plant (*Ricinus communis*) weigh about 1 gram apiece, while 1 gram contains more than 50,000 begonia seeds. Consequently, the sowing of these species is very different. The general rule is that the seeds are sown as deep as they are thick. Very fine seed is sown on the soil surface, and then you scatter some fine sharp sand on top. After that, gently press it down. Larger seeds can best be sown in a layer of potting mixture that has been put on top of the garden soil. If

Great Dixter, the famous garden of Christopher Lloyd, author of garden books.

Lloyd has terraced his lawns at many different levels.

the soil is pressed down firmly after sowing, it will retain more water. Soil must never be allowed to dry out during germination; if it does, the seed will not germinate. When the seedling plants come up, they must be thinned out. Beginners always sow too thickly,

Many seeds need a cold period to germinate. We call this "stratification." Under

natural conditions, the weather sees to this process.

For children ,it is fun to let a chestnut germinate. Put the chestnuts in the refrigerator for a few weeks, and they will soon germinate.

Sowing under Glass

You can usually sow in a cold frame outdoors as of the end of March. Annuals started in a cold frame will flower earlier. Work peat and sharp sand into the soil before you sow. When the seedlings have come up, you must open the cold frame at least a bit to air them during the day when there is sun; called "hardening" or "seasoning," this will help them begin to acclimate. When there is a chance of night frost, the frame must be covered for insulation. After a few weeks the young plants can be planted out. If you like, you can sow directly into peat pots. Sow more than one seed to a pot, as it is unlikely all will germinate. You must check the cold frame every day: in the morning, to protect it against too much sun or air circulation, and in the evening, to close it and protect it against possible night frost.

Sowing in a Greenhouse

Lucky gardeners with greenhouses can start sowing in February. (For that matter, you can start sowing earlier in a cold frame furnished with an electric heating cable.) You can achieve the same on a windowsill in the living room.

Do remember that in April the plants must be placed outdoors during the day. Water the plants only in the morning and during the daytime. Because temperatures drop at night, the humidity rises, and evening watering encourages condensation on the plants, leaving them susceptible to fungus diseases. In spring, the humidity is low; in summer, it is much higher (of course, this depends to some extent on where you live, too). If your

but experienced gardeners need to thin out the new plants, too. Seedlings do not fare well when they must struggle to compete for light and moisture, and when crowded together they are prone to disease. They need good air circulation. You must do this in time, for otherwise the plants will grow "leggy," and run a greater risk of damping-off, a fungus disease. By mid-April, when the soil has warmed and there is no danger of frost, you can start sowing outdoors.

When the beechnuts have fallen, the husks remain on the tree for a while. The long pointed bud, a recognizable feature of the beech bough, has already formed again.

greenhouse is floored in tiles, check to see whether they are dry in the morning; if so, you know you need to water the plants.

Diseases Affecting Annuals

As increasing numbers of resistant varieties are cultivated, annual plant diseases appear less and less. The fungus diseases mentioned in this chapter concern only young plants that have just been sown. If you have problems, the cause is most often soil that is too damp, or the wrong

Nigella damascena. *Pink and white varieties of this plant can also be grown. The seed heads are attractive in dried flower arrangements.*

Tropaeolum *(garden nasturtium) is usually sold as mixed seed, but if you try you can find seed of only the* red or yellow variety. Garden nasturtium is a rewarding plant for children to grow.*

location (in too much shade, for instance). Rather than attack the problem by spraying, try to change the condition of the soil and the location–if not this year, then next year.

Children's Gardening

For childish enthusiasm, it is disastrous to meet with failure the first time children garden, so some supervision can be helpful. The choice of seeds is important. Some seeds can hardly fail, and the list below does not include poisonous plants. All these seeds can be sown directly outdoors between mid-April and mid-May, depending on the variety and on the location of your garden. These plants are recommended for adults who are sowing for the first time, too:

Borago officinalis
Calendula officinalis (marigold)
Centaurea cyanus (cornflower)
Clarkia elegans
Cosmos bipinnatus
Eschscholzia californica (California poppy)

Eschscholzia is native to dry plains and central Chile. It is one of the easiest of plants to grow, one that can be sown by children with satisfying results. Think of the location it prefers in nature when sowing: dry and sunny.

Helipterum roseum
Impatiens balsamina
Lathyrus odoratus (sweet pea)
Nigella damascena
Papaver rhoeas (poppy)
Phacelia tanacetifolia
Portulaca grandiflora
Tropaeolum (nasturtium)
Zea mays (corn)

All hues can be tried with this list of plants, and they are not difficult to sow. Sowing in rows is simplest. That way, weeds are easily recognized—good experience from

Pistil of the tulip. If the pollination is successful, the seeds will ripen in June.

new gardeners. Most plants are difficult to plant out; just thinning the seedlings is sufficient.

Other Propagation Methods

Slipping (or taking cuttings), division, and layering are convenient ways of propagating ornamental plants. This can also be done by grafting and budding, a method that has been in use since the Middle Ages, but which needs some experience. Unlike sowing, this is vegetative reproduction. When we sow we get new individuals that are different from their parents. With the other methods of propagation, we reproduce the same individual, and end up with a uniform bunch of plants. When you propagate by taking cuttings, for

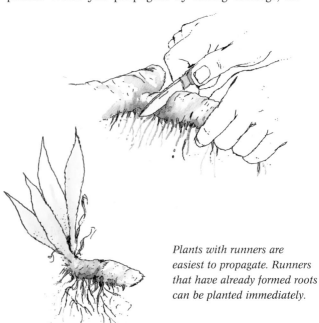

Plants with runners are easiest to propagate. Runners that have already formed roots can be planted immediately.

instance, all the slips come from a single plant; so actually, the young plants are still the same plant and will grow to look identical under the same growing conditions.

You can propagate a great many plants by division, taking cuttings, layering, and so forth. Find out whether the plant you want to propagate has not been grafted onto a rootstock. With a lilac, for instance, it is possible to cut off the shoots from the ground and to transplant them, but only rootstock shoots come out of the ground. The rootstock plant flowers with pale blue loose flowers, not as pleasing as the grafted lilac. Nurserymen typically graft lilacs; that is one reason why lilacs cost about five times as much as, say, the *Ribes* shrub. *Ribes* can simply be slipped and layered. If you want to plant a long hedge, layering is a worthwhile method. There is a difference of two growth seasons between the plant you bought at the

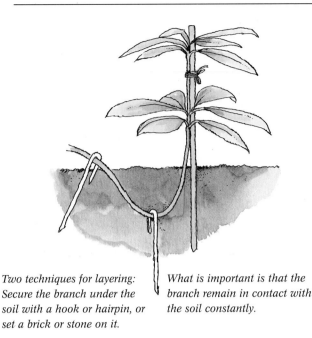

Two techniques for layering: Secure the branch under the soil with a hook or hairpin, or set a brick or stone on it.

What is important is that the branch remain in contact with the soil constantly.

nursery, and the one you have taken as a cutting, and rooted and grown yourself.

Buy a small number of plants at the nursery, and try your hand at propagation. As a rule, the cheapest plants are the easiest to reproduce yourself. Not only will you save considerably by doing this, but it is fun.

Slipping or Taking Cuttings: General Guidelines

Slips are cuttings removed from the plant to be propagated, about 6 inches (15cm) long. Strip off the leaves and halve the remaining leaves. This causes evaporation to decrease. After all, there are no roots to take in water yet, and the plant must conserve moisture. Your slips, or cuttings, should be rooted in sandy soil; try potting mixture to which you've added sharp sand. You can buy different kinds of hormone powder that will encourage the cutting to put out roots. (You can also use talcum powder for its antiseptic effect.) Dip the slip in a little saucer of hormone powder, and tap it softly to shake off any excess powder; put it directly into the soil and firm it gently. End shoots seem to give the best results.

Houseplant cuttings need not always be taken from a stem. *Streptocarpus*, African violet, and begonia are among those that can be propagated very successfully by leaf cuttings.

Buxus

You need a great many *Buxus* plants for a hedge. You will save a lot of money if you propagate *Buxus* yourself. However, you must take into account that *Buxus* cuttings take time, two years before they can be planted outdoors in their final location.

When you take *Buxus* cuttings, it is very important to remember which plant they came from, as there may be considerable differences among plants. Especially if you want to use the plants for a formal hedge, a uniform appearance is required. If that is the case, the cuttings must all be taken from the same mother plant. Put them in a soil mixture of leaf mold and sharp sand. A shady spot is preferable, as the slips will be less likely to dry out there. You can take cuttings in spring, and in August and September. It takes a year for them to take root. After a year, the plants can be planted out in a nursery bed, and after another year they can be transplanted to their final location. Not many people know that these tiny plants can grow into huge shrubs with thick trunks. A mature height of some 13 feet (4m) can be achieved if their cultural needs are met.

Division

Most perennials and some shrubs (botanical roses, sorbaria, and others) can be divided, as can some bulbs such as snowdrops and crocuses. Carefully dig up the

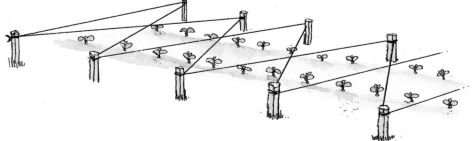

To deter birds, you can stretch black string over the nursery bed.

To prevent evaporation, you can encourage cuttings that have difficulty taking root by covering the pot with a plastic bag, loosely secured.

whole root system (as much as possible) out of the soil and try to pull it apart with your hands. If this does not work, you can divide the plant with a sharp knife, or tease pieces of really large plants apart using two pitchforks, placed back to back and pulled apart with a sort of teasing motion. If the roots are undamaged, the plant can perhaps be divided once more if there is enough of it. Perennial borders must be cut out in this manner every three years, so that plants that have become too large are returned to their proper proportions again. Whenever

you are dividing plants is a good opportunity to improve the soil with compost, well-rotted manure, or other organic fertilizer.

Air Layering

This method is usually applied to houseplants on which the bottom has become bare, but it can also be applied to some kinds of shrubs. The area where you want the plant to grow new roots must be scored somewhat with a knife. Apply some hormone powder to this place. Subsequently, bind some peat moss around the damaged area, and keep the moss quite damp. Cover the moss-covered area with plastic fastened at the top and at the bottom. After about a month, sufficient roots will have developed above the damaged place so that you can pot the "slip."

Layering

Layering is a simple method that works well with shrubs. In the case of rhododendrons, this is the best method for amateurs. Nurserymen propagate these plants by cuttings, but they enjoy the advantages of greenhouses with automatic watering systems. Consider a shrub that has branches that hang down and actually lie on the ground. It is enough to lay a spadeful of sharp sand on a branch,

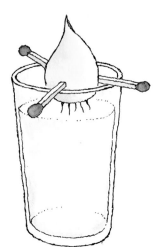

An avocado pit lends itself to experimentation that will interest children. Make three holes in the pit with a screwdriver or scissors, and stick matches or toothpicks into the holes. Suspend the pit over a glass of water with the blunt side downward. The pit will grow roots and can then be planted.

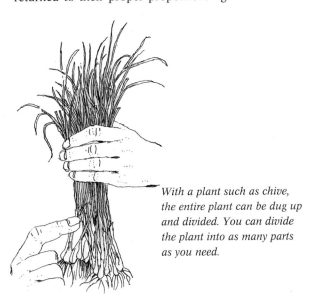

With a plant such as chive, the entire plant can be dug up and divided. You can divide the plant into as many parts as you need.

to weigh it down, and hold it on the ground. Where the branch is in permanent contact with the ground, new roots will grow.

In the case of other shrubs, the branches must be bowed gently down. For this you can use wire or a stick, so that the branch cannot spring back up. After a year, when there are enough roots, you cut the young plant off from the parent plant, and can transplant it wherever you like.

Other Methods

Nurserymen often make use of other methods of propagation, too. Lilac and hibiscus are grafted. Roses and fruit trees are often budded. Grafting is the most difficult method of reproduction for an amateur, and for the enthusiast who wants to try it, consulting a book on the subject is recommended. (You can investigate whether horticulture classes are available near where you live, if you are so inclined. Learning to perform this procedure is greatly facilitated by in-person demonstration.) Grafted plants are much more expensive than sown plants or plants raised from cuttings. That is because grafting is a labor-intensive procedure, and many attempts fail even when it is done by professionals. The basic principle of grafting is that one plant is surgically joined to the trunk of another plant. The rootstock is usually a wild variety of the cultivar that is grafted onto it. Grafting is a way to grow larger flowers and better fruit onto a more vigorous rootstock.

In grafting roses, the fact that underground shoots are effectively prevented also plays a role. Pay attention to the fact that rootstocks of garden shrubs still send up shoots. This is called suckering, and these volunteer shoots, the "suckers," are not desirable. Cut them off at ground level as soon as you notice them, for otherwise they will continue to grow at the expense of the grafted plant.

Cultivated lilacs are grafted onto wild lilac rootstocks that would grow pale blue flowers if they were allowed to flower; take care that the shoots growing under the lilac are removed, as they will produce inferior flowers if left to grow.

Phacaelia is one of the plants most appealing to bees. It can be sown directly where you want it. Not only is it a rewarding plant for children to sow, but the bees that are drawn to it will supply hours of fascination.

TIP

Shrubs with pendant branches

Small weeping trees reach a certain height, depending on where they have been grafted. That height remains the same; only the branches grow, and they grow downward. The plants remain more or less as tall as when purchased; they can grow a bit broader. A few examples:

Caragana arborescens 'Pendula'
Corylus avellana 'Pendula'
Cotoneaster hybr. 'Pendulus'
Laburnum alpinum 'Pendulum'
Morus alba 'Pendula'
Salix caprea 'Pendula'
Salix purpurea 'Pendula'

These plants are all very suitable for growing in pots. Plant in a pot with a broad bottom that will allow adequate room for the root ball (otherwise the tree will soon drop its leaves). Do consider planting two of the same kind, to give your garden the restful charm that comes with symmetrical accents. You could place two pots at the sides of a gate or flanking a garden seat, for instance. It would create an elegant effect to mark off a square or rectangle by placing four pots at the "corners." And what more inviting way to draw attention to the start of a garden path than by setting a graceful, weeping tree on either side of the entrance?

4 Notable Types of Plants and Their Applications

Who hasn't admired a house that was beautifully covered with ivy? Vines, which serve beautifully as hanging plants in many cases, can add variety and dimension to any garden.

A completely different group to consider is poisonous plants. You can grow them in your garden safely only if you know how poisonous they are, and the manner in which they are toxic. It is prudent to have some knowledge of poisonous plants. In addition to these interesting groups, we'll discuss tub—also known as container—plants, biblical plants, and rock garden plants in this chapter. A variety of different types of plants contributes to a rich effect.

Using bark shavings to surface a path is an inexpensive and beautiful solution in a natural-looking garden. A few tree trunks can serve as garden seats. In such a garden, a dead tree overgrown with a climber is a romantic note.

Vines and Climbers

There are many different kinds of climbing plants. This group is often erroneously called "ivy," but that name applies only to members of the genus *Hedera*, which we can enjoy both in the garden and as a houseplant. Vines and climbers as a group include many different sorts of plants. You can determine which climber would be a nice addition to your garden if you know a bit more about these horticultural gymnasts, which offer you lush foliage, colorful bloom, and seasonal drama.

When we see walls, we think of climbers. This Carpinus betulus *'Fastigiata' has been planted directly against the wall, and will be full-grown in two years.*

Shrubs for Walls

We call anything that can grow up a wall a climber, but climbing roses are an exception. Although we call them "climbing," they must be given support. The firethorn, the large-flowered magnolia, and *Ceanothus* are examples of trained shrubs, shrubs that grow well in the garden without support, as ordinary shrubs, but with support they "climb."

Unfortunately, there are quite a few misunderstandings about climbers. You may hear that climbers damage walls (even crawl through walls), that spiders live

Magnolia grandiflora.

in them, that walls covered with vines are always damp, that mice crawl up along them, that they grow under the roof and cause damage, and so on.

These misconceptions come about because of the confusion between "climber" and "ivy." Climber is a general name for all kinds of climbers, but the name "ivy" is very specific. Ivy can indeed affect walls if they are constructed with soft cement (rich in lime). That is why only older houses are damaged by ivy. But people used to plant ivy to grow on houses because it added insulation. Rainwater drips from the pointed leaves away from the side of the house, so it remains relatively dry. This applies not only to ivy, but to many other climbers.

Climbers grow upward using one of several techniques. There are clingers, grabbers that pull up by themselves if they have a wire or other very thin support around which they can wrap themselves; and trained plants, that find their way up with the aid of a gardener. Furthermore, there are also several shrubs that can be planted against walls, then gently fastened to the wall in a few places as they grow, giving the impression that they are "climbing." Whatever growing conditions your garden has to offer, whether you want to add vertical dimension to your garden or simply screen an eyesore or an unattractive view, there is a climber ideally suited to your needs.

TIP

A birdbath can be bought in any of many models, and may sit on a pedestal or, like the flat dish shown here, sit directly on the ground. Birds do not distinguish between a birdbath designed specially for them and any old dish.

This structure, which will shade the garden seat, is a suitable support for rambler roses, or wisteria. Pergolas and other constructions can be welded from thin or thick pipe.

Training

Bamboo

Bamboo is especially suitable for training such fruit trees as cherry, apricot, and peach. Buy bamboo stakes 9 feet (2.7m) long. Place two stakes upright at opposite sides of the tree, a total of about 8 feet (2m) apart. Fasten five or six bamboo stakes horizontally to this. Only the standing stakes must be fastened to the wall. Now it is simple to train the tree. Cut away all the tree branches that grow forward and backward out of the plane of the wall, and bend as necessary the branches that grow sideways into a horizontal position within that plane. When side shoots grow, they should be cut back to two eyes; this pruning can be done any time during the growing season.

TIP

Climber support

Support must be in place before the plant is planted. Climbers grow faster than you think, and once they are off and running it is often too late to add fastenings. In addition to this, the growing plant may be damaged if the support concerned needs work later.

Planting

Devote several hours to the planting of a climber; it will reward you later with better and faster growth, better flowering (if applicable), and greater resistance to diseases and pests. It is important, especially if you want a densely foliaged climber, to plant it at the right side of the house; a climber can be found for any side of the house. Contrary to what you might think, it is not the northern exposure but the southern exposure that poses the most problems. There you run the greatest chance that the leaves will be sunburned.

Wire

Wires can be stretched along a wall both vertically and horizontally. Screw hooks with eyes create the points that define (and hold) the grid of wires. The screw hooks must be made of copper. (If they are made of iron, you will find ugly rust stains along the walls, which is very annoying if they are plastered.) If you need a drill to pull the hooks into the wall, keep a vacuum cleaner handy, particularly if you are drilling into a white wall; stone dust is difficult to remove from the wall. The wire may be of green plastic-coated wire or, preferably, stainless steel wire.

Stretch wires horizontally for trained shrubs and fruit trees. Vertical wires are suitable for training roses and clematis, and, of course, for creepers such as honeysuckle and *Aristolochia*. An advantage of wire is that the plants

Wisteria sinensis starts flowering before the leaves appear. Prune the long shoots each year, as this promotes flowering.

can be taken down and fastened quickly again when the walls need painting.

Climbing frames

Ready-made climbing frames can be bought. Unfortunately, the climbing frame you are likely to find will be too small for the climber you have probably envisioned—perhaps not when the plant is young, but certainly when it has started to grow fast. So it may be better to make it yourself. Fasten some wooden slats horizontally to the wall, the highest one to the height you wish your climber to grow. Because the back of the slats will rot, you must paint the slats with a wood preservative before you use them. You may then want to paint them the same color as your house. Nail small slats, also painted with preservative first, vertically about 2 ½ to 3 inches (10 to 12cm) apart. You can tailor your climbing frame to the size of your house. These slats are suitable for training fruit, especially grapes, as well as for other climbers and creepers. Because there is a small space between the slats and the wall, the plants can grow around them.

Other Fastening Techniques

Climbers can be "fastened" to vertical surfaces with so-called clematis hooks, nails with small lips. You must

Fire thorns may be laden with red, orange, or yellow berries–   *until the blackbirds discover them.*

hammer in new nails every time the plant has grown enough to need training or support. You must go about it using these nails in a disciplined way. The plants grow fast, and you can soon fall behind.

It can happen that, when you have been away on vacation, your climber has grown to such an extent that the branches cannot or can hardly be disentangled, and then of course they can't be secured to the wall. The result

The flowering of ivy is not spectacular.

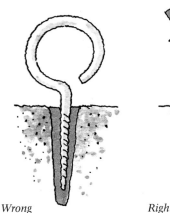

Wrong

Right

Do not choose screws with eyes that are too large. It is the wire that is meant to pass through the eyes, not the plant itself. Watch over your growing climber. It is easy for a new

shoot to make its way through the eye of a hook, and when this branch grows thicker, it will be strangled by the metal around it.

is a top-heavy climber and, because the nails aren't strong enough to support the weight, the entire plant comes tumbling down. Many gardeners find it preferable to construct a reliable support first and only then plant the climber.

Drainpipes

Drainpipes are often ugly. Climbers, in this case creepers, cannot wind around that thick pipe. Here it becomes a question of stretching a wire up behind the pipe. You can simply fasten it to the pipe supports that are there anyway. The height of the pipe and the side of the house determine which climber can grow there. You must paint the drainpipe before you plant the climber. In winter, when the leaves have fallen, the pipe will be visible again. In this case, you are painting for color and not for maintenance, as with wood. The plant won't damage the pipe.

TIP

Not all climbers are clingers or twiners. For vines and climbers requiring assistance, you must attach plant supports to the wall. For this, use copper, or stainless steel bolts or eyescrews. Galvanized steel will rust later, and rust stains look shabby on a white wall. For this reason, don't use ordinary nails, either. You want the mechanics of your support system to be as discreet as possible.

In many cases, bare fences lend themselves to climbers. This simple little fence will be

totally transformed when it is painted white and overgrown with rambler roses.

It is easy to construct a wooden frame yourself. Here is an espaliered–trained with its branches extending

horizontally in one plane– peach that can easily be cultivated in a small garden.

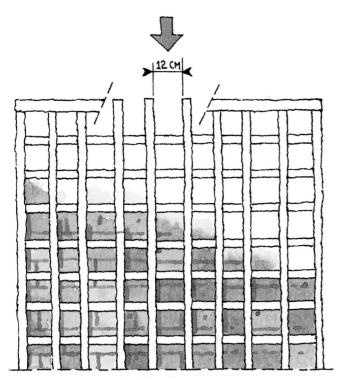

It is easy to construct climbing frames out of thin slats. See to it that there is some room between the wall and the climbing frame, or else the plant won't be able to get behind it.

Pergolas

Pergolas covered with climbers look gloriously romantic, but the plants meant to cover them often fail, usually because pruning and supporting the plants don't take place with sufficient regularity. Climbers must be regularly maintained during the growing season, particularly from June through September. With climbers that are still young, this is a job that needs to be done every week. Just cut off all shoots that stick out perpendicular to the direction of growth, even if the plant is still very small. You must secure the top shoots frequently. Once the plants have reached the top of the structure, they gain a better hold on their own and from then on require little looking after.

If you are delinquent in your maintenance, a tangled knot of

You can propagate Hedera helix *by cutting off shoots of young branches and sticking them into the ground immediately; at least 80 percent will take root. You can also put the shoots in a glass jar filled with water. If you wish, the jar can stay outdoors.*

TIP

Climbers are strong growers. The small plant will soon reach impressive proportions if it is well looked after. For instance, *Wisteria* easily reaches a height of roughly 10 feet (3m) after the first year, and after two or three years it can grow to 20 to 26 feet (6 to 8m) with ease. The support needed by a *Wisteria* of this size is often not provided. In due course, another climber, *Celastrus*, also grows into a heavy plant that needs a reasonably thick steel cable. It is wise to provide strong support before planting. In the beginning, a thick cable for a small plant will look odd, but this disadvantage is certainly outweighed by the future advantage of a secure climber.

Honeysuckle (Lonicera caprifolium) *naturally grows at the edge of woods. We usually think of walls and pergolas when we think of climbers, but you can train a climber to grow up into an old tree. Shade agrees with this plant.*

branches will form at a height of about 6 feet (1.8m). The top of your pergola, which should have enjoyed such pretty views from under the branches of the climber, will remain bare and uncovered, as the newer branches and shoots grow back over and through themselves. It does not take up much time to keep up with young climbers, but it does have to be done—often. Once your climber reaches maturity, it will look after itself for the most part.

"Self-adhesive Climbers"

It is not wise to let clinging climbers grow up plaster walls. It may happen that the climbers will come down together

Ready-made pergolas are constructed simply of brown wood. When overgrown by deciduous plants, such as hops, the wood is visible

during the entire winter. You may want to paint the pergola the color of your house, in that case.

Rounded slats look attractive on a pergola. You can fasten them in all kinds of ways.

with the plasterwork if there are strong winds. Replastering the wall would be a dreadful nuisance. It is better to stretch wires over plasterwork, simple for structural maintenance, as you can always detach the wires. When it comes to the truly independent clingers, those climbers that pull themselves over a surface by means of minature suction cups, it is best not to plant them where they will cover a surface that requires any sort of maintenance–unless you don't mind cutting the clinger down.

Clematis montana.

Where to Plant Climbers

The following plants are suitable for different exposures:

Clinging plants
N   *Hedera helix*
E   *Parthenocissus*
W   *Parthenocissus*
S   *Campsis*

Shrubs that climb with support
N   *Prunus* (trained morello), *Hydrangea*
E   *Forsythia suspensa*
W   *Magnolia grandiflora*
S   *Ceanothus* 'Gloire de Versailles'

Plants that need support
N   Some species rambler roses
E   *Pyracantha*
W   *Camellia*
S   *Vitis*

Creepers
(Support with wires and frame)
N   *Aristolochia*
E   *Lonicera*
W   *Polygonum*
S   *Actinidia, Wisteria*

Clematis *'Nelly Moser'*.

Evergreen climbers
N   *Hedera helix*
E   *Pyracantha, Akebia*
W   *Magnolia grandiflora, Jasminum beesianum*
S   *Lonicera japonica*

Remember that climbers need much attention the first two years after planting. They must be checked often during the growing season and, where necessary, secured again each week. If you give them the attention they require, you certainly will not be disappointed.

Clematis

Clematis is one of the most popular garden plants, and it is the climber that is sold most. Entire books have been written on this plant. Do not consider only color when you select a clematis, but think about the location you have to offer it. There are clematis with somewhat varying culture requirements. Clematis can be divided roughly into three groups. The differences between the groups are expressed mostly in the method of pruning.

Group 1

These clematis do not need to be pruned, and may grow very tall. This group includes *Clematis montana* (up to 49 feet/15m), *C. alpina,* and *C. macropetala.*

Group 2

The clematis belonging to group 2 must be pruned. They flower on last year's growth and therefore, if pruned back completely, will not flower again for a year. This group includes *C.* 'Nelly Moser' and *C.* 'The President', two extremely popular clematis varieties.

Group 3

Clematis belonging to group 3 must be annually pruned back to 1½ feet (0.5m) above the ground. This group includes *C.* × *jackmanii* and *C.* 'Ville de Lyon'. These late-bloomers flower on current growth. They do not reach great heights due to yearly pruning. A low wall is a fetching support for these plants.

Vita Sackville-West was celebrated for allowing roses to climb through fruit trees. Clematis, too, is eminently suitable for training on trees, provided the trees aren't too large. Oak and the beech are unsuitable for this, because of their size and also because their foliage is too dense to let sufficient light through for the climbers. Birches, ornamental cherries, some maple trees, and especially

Clematis vitalba.

fruit trees can be recommended. Several clematis of the species *viticella*, such as *C.* 'Abundance', *C.* 'Minuet', *C.* 'Royal Velours', and *C.* 'Etoile Violette' grow well through large conifers. Taking root in the dry ground around conifers is difficult; the soil in the large planting hole dug for the clematis must be replaced with good soil, and the plant must be watered regularly. Even then, it may take one or two seasons before it starts to grow well, but then the result will be staggering.

Clematis alpina and *C. macropetala* are very suitable for growing through roses. Don't neglect to take the color of the roses into account; although the first flowering of the clematis is earlier than the flowering of the rose, they may flower simultaneously later on, and it would be a shame if the colors clashed or were so close that the clematis went unnoticed. You want a distinct contrast in color, to draw the eye to the planting scheme.

There are also perennial clematis that do not climb, growing 2 to 5 feet (60cm to 1.5m) tall. The best-known are *Clematis heracleifolia*, *C.* × *jouiniana* 'Mrs. Robert Brydon', *C. recta*, and *C. integrifolia*. You may not often see them, as they are generally available from specialized nurseries, and can be ordered through a number of catalogs. They are suitable for low fences, and for perennial borders, too. You can let clematis hang over a wall, the flowers spilling like a waterfall.

Clematis grows best against an east-facing or a west-facing wall. Always protect the roots from the heat of strong sunlight by planting a small shrub in front of your clematis, or placing decorative stone over the roots. This will not only ensure that the roots remain cooler, but it will slow moisture loss due to evaporation, too. A roofing tile over the roots would be sufficient to start the young plant off correctly. The leaves can suffer

from sunburn if the plant is grown against a south-facing wall. The wildly flowering *Clematis vitalba* can make itself at home on a north-facing exposure, but it will take two years before it flowers. Always fasten a climbing frame or training wires before you plant. This is forgotten all too often, so that probably half of the plants sold do not develop the beauty that the buyer expected.

Diseases

Various diseases can affect the clematis. Of these, the wilting disease that is caused by the fungus *Ascochyta clematidina* is the most serious and it is almost unavoidable–sooner or later you will be confronted by it. One day you notice a wilted leaf, and within a week the entire plant has wilted. Naturally occurring clematis varieties are less quickly affected. It is almost impossible to prevent. Do not site a new plant in the same place another clematis was infected until the soil has been disinfected (with formaldehyde, for instance). Treatment with benlate every two weeks may produce good results. Do not grieve too much if something goes wrong. Much can go awry with plants such as roses, dahlias, and even potatoes, too, but that is simply the way it is when you handle living material.

Fertilizing

To keep clematis healthy, fertilize it with a layer of well-rotted stable manure or compost in early spring. The fertilizer you apply can be the same one you use for roses. The plant likes having a thick layer of mulch over its roots. Clematis can grow both in soil that is rich in lime and soil that is rich in acid. It is not necessary to add lime or peat, but the plant will appreciate sufficient humus. If you add a layer of organic material, about 2 inches (5cm) each year, it will stimulate the plants considerably.

Toxic Plants

The concern about poisonous plants is often rather unwarranted. When a plant with toxic characteristics is sited judiciously, the danger is lessened. We should not completely ignore the disadvantages of this group of plants. Gardeners—especially parents of small children—need to know exactly what is in their garden; toddlers put everything in their mouths, particularly if the color is interesting. Foxglove, although extremely poisonous, is for some reason not very appealing to children, but the berries of *Taxus* (of which only the pip, or seed, is poisonous), are a danger, and the plant does not belong in a garden with children. Only parts of some plants are very poisonous, while other parts are edible. The leaf of

Datura stramonium.

the rhubarb is poisonous, while the stem is not at all poisonous, and is often cooked and eaten.

This book will describe the plant and its garden application; botanical descriptions will be found in other reference books, as will toxicologic descriptions. Specific guides to poisonous plants are published for those very interested in the subject. The plants mentioned below are those that pose considerable danger. Instruct children never to put any part of an unknown house- or garden plant in their mouths, and that they must be cautious, as some plants

Never eat many unripe tomatoes. Strange as it may sound, the unripe tomato *contains solanine, which in considerable quantity is toxic.*

cause uncomfortable—and even serious—reactions when touched. If you suspect a child has ingested or come into contact with one of the following plants, it is wise to call a doctor. But children are not the only vulnerable ones; animals are sensitive to certain poisonous plants, too. That is why we do not recommend feeding animals with pruning waste from gardens, however economical that might seem. Garden plants that may be dangerous to animals are mentioned here. Houseplants, for instance, *Dieffenbachia*, are not on the list; tub plants, such as oleander, are.

The selection of tub plants commercially available changes quickly because they are so popular, so that it is possible that some plants of interest to you do not appear on this list. *Aconitum napellus*: All parts of this plant are poisonous, even the nectar in the flower. The poison can be absorbed through the skin from the leaves; children must not pick the leaves.

Aristolochia durior: This climber is very poisonous. Fortunately, none of its parts looks appealing to eat.

Arum maculatum (wake robin) and *A. italicum* (Italian arum): The berries of this plant are poisonous; the other parts cause skin irritation.

Cicuta virosa (water hemlock): This plant, with rare exceptions, is virtually never grown in home gardens. The sap is extremely poisonous, especially in the rootstock. Danger threatens whenever a garden pond is cleaned, and parts of weeded plants are set aside for later collection. Never handle these plants without the protection of gloves. Call for medical assistance if you are concerned about exposure to toxins.

The cup of poison from which Socrates drank contained the·sap of this plant, and the result is well known.

Colchicum autumnale (autumn crocus): All parts are very poisonous. The flower strongly resembles a crocus, but the foliage that appears in spring months ahead of the flower, does not.

Convallaria majalis (lily of the valley): Here is a fine example of a common, even sweetly homely, garden favorite that is toxic. At least one fatal accident involving this plant is known: a child that drank water from a vase that had contained these flowers. Animals do not forage these plants, but the poison remains in

The plum is not poisonous, but the pits certainly are, particularly if several are eaten at once.

Atropa belladonna (belladonna): All parts of the plant are poisonous. The berries look like cherries; eating only a few berries is fatal.

Brugmansia stramonia: All parts are poisonous, especially the unripe fruit and the seeds.

Arum italicum. *The orange-red seedpods are the most beautiful aspect of this plant in late summer. The flower is less notable.*

Colchicum autumnale *flowers in September. Take into account that the leaves attain a height of 20 inches (50cm).*

plants that are dried, and animals have been known to eat these.

Daphne mezereum (mezereon): The mezereon has very poisonous berries. Just a few can be fatal to a child. Although the berry color is very attractive, the taste is

Digitalis purpurea.

dreadful and a child most likely would not want to eat a second berry, fortunately; even so, do not plant this in a garden children visit.

Digitalis purpurea (foxglove): Foxglove is a biennial plant that grows naturally in transitional woodland areas. The foliage and seeds are very poisonous. Accidents seldom occur with this plant, as it does not look appealing to eat and tastes bitter.

Euphorbia (snow-on-the-mountain): This also includes such weeds as milkweed, and the houseplants crown of thorns and poinsettia. The milky sap irritates the skin, and is particularly dangerous to the eye, which requires immediate medical attention upon exposure.

Ginkgo (biloba): The seedpod of this plant causes skin irritation; the fruit is not toxic, in spite of the repulsive odor it gives off when crushed.

Hedera helix (English ivy): Animals that eat it are unaffected by the poison. The berries are poisonous to humans, if eaten in great quantity. The branches of climbing hedera flower up out of harm's reach. Only the

shrub ivy *Hedera helix* 'Arborescens' has flowering branches that are near the ground, where the berries can be reached by children; do not select this variety for a garden frequented by children.

Helleborus niger (Christmas rose): All parts of the plant are poisonous. Other *Helleborus* varieties are poisonous, too.

Heracleum mantegazzianum (giant hogweed): Never plant this where children play. The sap in the stem and leaves cause red blotches on the skin, and can even cause open wounds. Warning: Wear gloves and long sleeves when pulling up this plant. Greater irritation can develop when affected skin is exposed to bright sunlight. Gardeners with callused hands are not so quickly affected by the sap. However, when your skin starts to feel irritated, you are too late to prevent a reaction. (*Dictamnus* and *Ruta* [rue] have the same effect.)

Hyacinthus (hyacinth): Severe itching may occur with repeated handling of the bulbs, as they have a dusting of sharply pointed crystals. It is a good idea to wear gloves when planting a number of them.

Hyocyamus niger (henbane): This annual or biennial herb is not used much. The roots pose the greatest danger, as they resemble parsnip and horseradish. Henbane belongs to the *Solanaceae* family (as do potatoes).

Hedera helix.

The flower of hogweed. The plant has the characteristics of a weed; once you have it in the garden, it pops up everywhere. The dried flowers of hogweed are very beautiful, though.

Laburnum anagyroides (laburnum): The deadly dose lies between ten and thirty seeds. Although the green pods do not look very attractive, this is a plant to be watched when children are about. The plant is not immediately dangerous to dogs and cats. Do not plant it too near a pond, as fish can be affected by the pods.

Lantana camara: Lantana is a tub plant often enjoyed in gardens in warmer regions. The unripe fruit is very poisonous. It looks green and attractive. Avoid sun exposure after you have touched this plant.

Lycopersicon lycopersicum (tomato): This plant belongs to the potato family, too (*Solanaceae*) and contains solanine, though in small amounts. Do not eat too many green (unripe) tomatoes.

Nerium oleander (oleander): Almost all parts of the oleander are poisonous. Even when the plants are dried, the poison remains. Eating one leaf can be fatal. Cases of poisoning have been reported throughout history, both with humans and animals. Always keep the plant out of reach of small children. This applies to fallen leaves and flowers, too.

Ornithogalum (star-of-Bethlehem): The bulbs are poisonous. Touching the sap causes skin irritation.

Paris quadrifolia (herb Paris): All parts of the plant are poisonous, especially the rootstock and berries. The berries are especially dangerous, as they resemble the blueberry.

Phytolacca americana: All parts of the plant are poisonous, especially the fruit when unripe. The sap of the ripe fruit can cause a burning sensation to the skin.

Polygonatum (Solomon's seal): This plant contains the same poison as *Convallaria*.

Prunus dulcis (bitter almond): This plant is not widely planted. The seed in the pits of the peach, prune, apricot, and cherry also contain amygdaline. One seed is not dangerous, but a few could certainly cause poisoning symptoms.

Rheum palmatum (ornamental rhubarb): The stems of our vegetable, the rhubarb, are delicious, but the leaves are poisonous. This also applies to ornamental rhubarb.

Rhododendron

This shrub is especially poisonous to animals. Be careful with pruning waste!

Ricinus communis (castor oil plant): This annual has seeds that are extremely poisonous. They look like attractively speckled beans. Keep them away from

Polygonatum odoratum.

Plant rhododendrons and azaleas in places where cattle from a neighboring meadow cannot get at them.

nnot do without this plant, it is best to ... so that no seeds will form. This is one of the mo... plants, and poisoning warrants immediate medical attention.

Solanum dulcamara (bittersweet): In nature, this plant grows mostly on banks and in other damp places. In the past few years, *Solarum dulcamara* 'Variegata' has been sold as a climber. The unripe berries are very poisonous.

Solanum nigrum (deadly nightshade): This is a well-known weed from the kitchen garden. The unripe green berries are especially poisonous. In New Zealand, the Maoris eat the leaves as a vegetable and make jam out of the berries; imitation of this behavior is strongly discouraged.

Solanum tuberosum (potato): All parts of the plant are poisonous, except the ripe tuber when growing or away from sunlight. Solanine is the poisonous substance found in all plants of the potato family. Green tubers (that have had considerable exposure to light) and the berries are extremely poisonous.

Taxus baccata: All parts except for the flesh of the fruit are poisonous. The seed within the fruit is extremely dangerous.

Never plant taxus where animals might eat them. Fewer than one hundred needles contain enough poison to be fatal to humans. The attractive fruit is most dangerous to children. This applies to *Taxus media* 'Hicksii' in particular, which

Who would have thought that parts of our beloved vegetable rhubarb contain poison?

produces much fruit. By far, the most garden-plant poisonings occur with taxus. Consider carefully whether it is wise for you to plant taxus in your garden.

The ornamental rhubarb, Rheum palmatum, *has large pointed leaves. It flowers* *just like ordinary rhubarb, and the leaves are just as poisonous.*

Viburnum opulus (guelder rose): Large amounts of the ripe berries are dangerous to children. This plant is one of the best additions to the bird shrubbery, so plant it away from the reach of children and where birds can enjoy them.

Vincetoxicum: Although this plant is seldom found in home gardens, it is increasingly seen in botanical gardens. All parts are poisonous.

Viscum album (mistletoe or bird lime): The berries and leaves are poisonous. The white berries are not very appealing. Mistletoe grows in trees and parasitically on trunks of trees. It tends to grow in spots too high for children to reach. When making seasonal decorations for your home with this plant, place it where little fingers won't be able to touch it.

Wisteria sinensis and *W. floribunda* (wisteria): Although wisteria is poisonous, it doesn't pose great danger. It is unwise to let it grow over a pond, as the fallen leaves are dangerous to fish.

Tub Plants

Large tubs planted with orange trees were one of the glories of baroque gardens. At English stately homes, one often sees tubs in which *Agapanthus* is planted, and in landscape gardens wooden tubs planted with green or variegated agaves are handsome accents. The old-fashioned fuchsia, clivia, and agapanthus were put outdoors in the old days. Today, when so many home gardens have a paved terrace, the use of tub plants has grown. The problem with our modern houses, though, is that they can be less than suitable for this group of plants: Central heating makes indoor air drier. We keep our houses warmer today than they ever could be in the past. When indoor heating was much less efficient, not all the rooms in a house were used in cold weather; some rooms were used only for entertaining and were never heated when unoccupied. These rooms were ideal for keeping tub plants over winter. You can use the guest room for this if it does not get a lot of sun. Tub plants shouldn't remain indoors throughout the year, nor should they be left outdoors in the winter. Some kinds can endure just a few degrees of frost. Tub plants are not really houseplants, nor are they garden plants. They deserve special consideration.

When selecting a tub plant, the first thing to do is to see what wintering options your home offers. Who does not dream of a greenhouse, a conservatory, or an orangery? Unfortunately, few of us can make those dreams come true. But fortunately, tub plants can be kept without a greenhouse, conservatory, or orangery. What you need is a cool, frost-free spot. The degree of cold will help determine the plant you choose.

A cool room that receives some light, or a basement or a (frost-free) garage that is dark may be what you have to work with. If all you have is a cold area where temperatures reach freezing, you can grow plants that are winter-hardy in frostproof pots, dishes, and tubs.

Pots and Tubs

All sorts of attractive pots are available, most manufactured in warmer climates. That is why earthenware pots are often not frostproof. That isn't a problem for the plants that will be indoors in winter anyway. Never use a pot with a narrow opening at the top; it will be difficult to transplant the plant later. Always

Page 127: Solanum dulcamara, *bittersweet, or woody night-shade. This plant can be found both in nature, in damp* *places, and in gardens, where we mostly see the variegated* S. dulcamara *'Variegata'.*

Never feed pruning waste from rhododendrons to animals. The poisonous substances are often present even in the dried plant!

TIP

Plants for bird lovers

It is difficult to find sturdy plants that will draw, and stand up to, birds. Where there are many birds the plants can suffer; the birds leave their droppings on them, peck at them, and often eat the buds, so that plant growth is impeded. Consider buying full-grown plants, preferably evergreens that are not poisonous to birds and that grow particularly fast. If you choose to build a proper cage aviary, put a few extra plants next to it, so that you can exchange them when necessary.

Fast-growing and evergreen plants:
> *Prunus laurocerasus* 'Rotundifolia'
> *Thuja occidentalis* and *T. plicata*

Fast-growing deciduous plants:
> *Elaeagnus angustifolia*
> *Cornus sericea*
> *Sambucus nigra*

Moderately fast-growing plants:
> *Elaeagnus pungens* 'Maculata'
> *Cotoneaster salicifolius*
> *Juniperus virginiana*
> *Amelanchier lamarckii*

If nothing will grow in the aviary, you can plant a fast-growing nontoxic climber just outside the cage.

Weeds that most aviary birds find delicious:

Brassica (cabbage)	leaves, seeds
Convolvulus (convolvulus)	plant
Capsella bursa-pastores (shepherd's purse)	seeds
Centaurea (cornflower)	seeds
Chenopodium (goosefoot)	leaves, seeds
Cichorium intybus (endive)	seeds
Cirsium (thistle)	seeds
Helianthus annuus (sunflower)	seeds
Heracleum (hogweed)	plant, seeds
Lathyrus pratensis	seeds
Plantago major	seedbuds
Poaceae (grass family)	seeds
Polygonum (knotgrass)	plant
Senecio (groundsel)	seeds
Stellaria media (chickweed)	plant
Taraxacum (dandelion)	plant
Trifolium (clover)	seeds
Urtica dioica (stinging nettle)	plant
Viola (violet)	seeds

buy pots with a large hole in the bottom; if there is no hole, you have to make a hole yourself, easy to do with a small masonry drill. Ornamental pots – "cachepots" without drainage holes—are useless in the garden, as they fill up with water. That is also why flower saucers are inadvisable outdoors.

Only use a pot with a broad bottom for a windy location, not only because a pot with a small base is likelier to tip over, but because the potted plant acts as a windbreaker. For containers that must stay outdoors over winter, it is best to employ wooden tubs or thick-walled hand-fired earthenware pots. Make sure that water can drain away from the bottom of the container—this lessens the chance that the pot will freeze.

The drainage holes of pots placed in the border soon silt up. You can prevent this problem by sinking a can under the hole of each pot, first removing the top and the bottom of the can to fashion a cylinder. This cylinder, or ring, will hold the bottom of the pot above the soil so that it will drain properly.

Wintering

About mid-October in temperate climates is the time for bringing tub plants in. Prune the plants and clean the pots (there are often snails on the bottom of the pots). Bring the plants indoors when the leaves are dry. Put any

A canna needs the same treatment as a dahlia. The winter temperature certainly must not drop below 50°F (10°C). Cannas are suitable for large flower beds and flower boxes or for large flower tubs.

evergreens nearest to the window; the deciduous plants do not need light during the winter months. If the windows are closed all the time, mold and insect problems can develop; good air circulation is important.

The ideal wintering temperature of most plants lies between 40° to 50° F. (5° to 10° C). The plants can be put outdoors again usually by mid-April, after all danger of

An agave will not easily flower in a tub. In a large tub, it might flower after many years; the flower stalk may grow no less than 10 feet (3m) tall.

The Cycas revoluta, *a palm plant, can withstand frost* *when it is older. This plant has just grown a new crown.*

frost. Do remember that they must be placed in the shade during the first few days of their return outdoors. Even though it is early in the season, they are vulnerable to sunburn. It is wise to keep an eye on the weather forecast in the first few weeks, as you must protect the plants from frost at night. Close to the house, because the walls give

Fuchsias can be bought in vir- *pink, white, and violet hues* *tually thousands of colors: red,* *can be had in all combinations.*

off radiant heat at night, plants enjoy a warmer environment, and the chance of frost damage is less. It tends to be less cold under trees, too.

The Wintering Place

If the only spot for wintering-over plants is one that gets no daylight, many bulbous and tuberous plants are suitable for you to grow in pots: *Agapanthus*, *Ismene*, *Zephyranthes*, *Vallota*, *Canna*, *Amaryllis*, *Crinum*, *Eucomis*, and *Galtonia*.

If you do not have any wintering place at all, only those plants that can stay outdoors in their pots and withstand severe frost are options. Remember that evergreens cannot endure morning sunlight after night frost in spring. Some varieties are: *Buxus sempervirens*, *Arum italicum* and *A. maculatum*, *Campanula portenschlagiana*, *Hosta*, *Yucca flaccida*, *Allium karataviense*, and *Aucuba japonica*. Plants that can withstand some frost, but should be moved to the garage or cold frame when there is severe frost, are: *Passiflora*, *Lavandula*, rosemary, laurel, *Phormium tenax*, some *Buddleia*, *Hebe* varieties, *Cupressus* varieties, camellia, and *Poncirus trifoliata*.

All other plants from the "tub plant" group need a cool, absolutely frost-free space with sufficient light and humidity. Note that humidity decreases greatly when it

Clivia can stay outside in the summer very well, although it needs a spot in the shade.

freezes. The cooler plants are, the less water they require. A weekly check is recommended.

Small Grafted Trees and Climbers

You may have longed to flank your front door with a few small grafted trees, but the price of such horticultural ornaments is high. Cultivated trees are expensive, and what's more, if you buy them, you will miss the fun of doing it yourself. Start out with a pot that is far too large;

Jacobinia.

the plants will grow faster, and when they are large they will be less likely to fall over, as a heavy pot will act as a sturdy anchor with a low center of gravity.

Suitable plants for this use include: *Abutilon,* bougainvillea, *Cestrum, Erythrina, Fuchsia, Gardenia, Heliotropium, Hibiscus, Lantana, Laurus, Pelargonium, Pittosporum, Plumbago,* and *Punica.*

Climbing tub plants and annuals in pots can be trained along wire or wire mesh. In rectangular flower boxes you can construct a support with stakes and, if necessary, wire.

TIP

Never put plants that are sensitive to frost in wet places, and plant them in a place that is shielded from the east wind. Mix some sharp sand with the soil for better drainage. Be careful when you cover them that plants do not rot. Fir branches are ideal for protecting sensitive plants, as they allow sufficient air circulation. Evergreens that are sensitive to frost cannot endure morning sunlight.

Biblical Plants

At least some of the plants mentioned in the Bible can be in our gardens no matter where we live. With only one exception (purple looosestrife), all the plants need soil that is not too damp, and a sunny location. Except for the tub and greenhouse plants, all these plants can survive a mild winter without long periods of freezing temperatures.

Plants are mentioned in many of the books of the Bible. *Allium* can be found in Deuteronomy, for instance, although we do not know exactly what kind of allium is meant. Some biblical scholars say that manna looked like coriander seed, and coriander can be found in Numbers (11:5). Myrtle is also explicitly mentioned, in Isaiah (55:13), among other places. *Prunus* is named in the Song of Songs, as is narcissus, which is also mentioned in Isaiah (35:1). Read the Bible with an eye out for the plants, and you'll see that you could fill a large garden with them!

Perennials:
Onosis repens
Galium verum (yellow bedstraw)
Papaver somniferum (opium poppy)

Annuals:
Linum (flax)
Triticum (wheat)
Hordeum (barley)
Panicum (millet)
Vicia sativa (vetch)
Ricinus communis (castor-oil plant)
Delphinium ajacis (larkspur)

Bulbs and tubers:
Crocus sativus (saffron crocus)
Colchicum autumnale (autumn crocus)
Anemone coronaria (anemone)
Narcissus jonquila (jonquil)

Vegetables:
Cucumis melo (melon)
Allium (shallot, onion, garlic, chives)
Lens culinaris (lentil)

Herbs:
Anethum graveolens (dill)
Mentha × *piperita* (peppermint)
Brassica nigra (black mustard)
Cuminum cyminum (cumin)
Coriandrum sativum (coriander)

Perennials for drying

Apart from the annual strawflowers (immortelles), numerous perennials make excellent dried flowers. Hang them in a dry, well-ventilated place. The faster the plant dries, the better it retains its color.

Suitable perennials are:

Achillea

Anaphalis

Dipsacus

Eryngium

Echinops

Alchemilla

Gypsophila

Astrantia

Solidago

Morus nigra (black mulberry)
Cedrus libani (Lebanon cedar)

Roses:
Rosa canina (brier rose)
Rosa phoenicea
Rosa foetida
Rosa damascena (damask rose)

Tub plants:
Myrtus communis (myrtle)
Punica granatum (pomegranate)
Laurus nobilis (laurel)
Cistus (rock rose)

For the greenhouse:
Cinnamomum
Phoenix dactilifera (date palm)
Olea europaea (olive)
Cyclamen indicum (cyclamen)

Lavandula (lavender)
Ruta graveolens (rue)
Origanum (marjoram)

Shrubs:
Vitis (grape)
Ficus carica (fig)
Tamarix (tamarisk)
Buxus (box)

Trees:
Juglans regia (English walnut)
Prunus (wild almond)

Seedpod of Papaver sommiferum.

"The desert shall bloom like a rose." However, in the Bible it is Narcissus tazetta *that is meant.*

Anemone of the Caen type. This anemone looks perfect in *the old-fashioned kitchen garden.*

As no consistent names were yet in use in biblical times, it is not always clear what exact variety is meant. For instance, for *Buxus* we are not sure whether *B. lingifolius* or *B. sempervirens* is indicated. Naturally, all the plants mentioned must be the wild varieties. Some, such as cyclamen, can usually be bought today only as a cultivated variety. As there are few flowering perennials mentioned in the Bible, it is difficult to lay out a "biblical" garden that looks nice all summer. It would be wiser to plant only a section of the garden with these plants, or plant them among the other plants

Plants for the Rock Garden

Rock-garden plants are often also called "alpine" plants, as they often are native to alpine regions. Many come from the Alps themselves, others from the Pyrenees and the Carpathians, and from mountainous areas in other parts of the world. What these plants have in common is that they like soil that is not rich and that drains well. Always plant them in a dry spot; this is especially important in the winter. Most damage sustained by rock-garden plants is caused by freezing weather combined with wetness. A solution to the wet-cold combination can be found in placing old glass panes over the plants in autumn.

Many rock-garden plants are hardly suitable for the climates of gardeners who want to grow them. Special greenhouses are often built for this group of plants, built low, with half-height nursery tables. The center aisle is sunken, so that one can stand upright in the greenhouse. The greenhouse is always built on an east–west axis, to obtain maximum sunlight exposure.

Rock Garden Plants for Shade

Almost all rock plants are sun-worshipers. After all, in nature they grow (most of them) above the tree line, where there is always sun in abundance. Under those conditions, they enjoy relatively more ultraviolet light. This light causes compact plants to grow, in contrast to light from which the ultraviolet portion of the spectrum has been filtered out; here, the plants will grow spindly, stretching, as only the infrared rays remain.

You can see this phenomenon with your houseplants, which receive only filtered light without ultraviolet rays. Some plants suitable for the rock garden can grow well in half shade:

Adonis vernalis
Aquilegia caerulea

Apple blossom.

Aster alpinus
Campanula cochlearii folia
Ceratostigma plumbaginoides
Cyclamen hederifolium
Dryas octopetala
Limmaea borealis
Mertensia virginica
Ourisia varieties
Polygala varieties
Saxifraga varieties
Viola odorata
Viola pedata

Cichorium intibus.

TIP

Carnivorous plants

Do not take plants from nature, even though it would be fun to have a carnivorous plant in the garden. These plants grow only in damp, poor soils. That is why they are not suitable for planting in the garden. Sometimes botanical gardens make room for these plants; they must create a humid environment for them—not always a simple business. Carnivorous plants require a great deal more water than most other "thirsty" plants, too, and therefore are that much more susceptible to the damaging effects of any water-borne contaminants, which accumulate in the plant tissue. Many of the 450 varieties of carnivorous plants grow in Australia and southern Africa. In climates that are temperate and colder, these plants can be cultivated in a cold frame. They like a humid environment and fresh air, but do not let direct sunlight reach them. Soft peat and peat moss (*Sphagnum*) can be used in the growing medium. There are carnivorous plants that occur naturally in such different climates as alpine regions and desert, too. If you are interested in obtaining a specimen plant, inquire of specialty nurseries and catalogs.

Shrubs in the Rock Garden

Whether the rock garden is large or small, room must be made for a few shrubs. Look to create diversity of flower, leaf shapes, the color and size of berries, whether bright or not.

Many shrubs have a creeping growth habit that is wonderful for growing over walls and rocks. You do not need any special soil for the following list of plants. Give them soil that drains easily. Plants identified with * need acid soil. The indicated height is that of the full-grown plant; take slow growth into account.

A single pillar-shaped conifer brings the necessary depth to the garden.

Abelia chinensis	5 feet (1.5m)
Acer palmatum 'Dissectum'	4 feet (1.2m)
*Andromeda**	4 feet (1.2m)
*Arctostaphylos uva-ursi**	1 foot (0.3m)
Berberis, several kinds	
Caryopteris × *clandonensis*	3 feet (0.9m)
*Cornus canadensis**	1 foot (0.3m)
Corokia cotoneaster	5 feet (1.5m)
Daphne cneorum	1 foot (0.3m)
Daphne rupestris	4 inches (0.1m)
*Gaultheria procumbens**	8 inches (0.2m)
Genista tinctoria	2 feet (0.6m)
Hedera helix	8 inches (0.2m)
Helianthemum	1 foot (0.3m)
Olearia × *haasti*	4 feet (1.2m)

Abies procera *'Glauca'* and other conifers can grow over walls. Garden peat should be added, though. Most rock garden plants like soil that is rich in lime, or neutral soil; conifers, on the other hand, prefer acid soil.

*These rock-garden plants
have been combined with
low-growing conifers and
small shrubs.*

*A smooth transition from the
rock garden to a pond with
natural stone.*

Rubus arcticus
Sambucus nigra 'Pygmea'   1 foot (0.3m)
Viburnum opulus 'Nanum'   16 inches (0.4m)

Succulents for a Sunny Spot

In plant dishes or next to a terrace in a small rock garden,
you want small rock-garden plants that look attractive
in summer and winter. Many saxifraga and sedum
varieties and the sempervivums are eligible. They are all
succulents that wouldn't be able to hold their own in a
large garden. They take root near the soil surface, so they
would easily be pulled out together with any weeds. (If
you want to remove a weed growing right next to a plant,
it is best to hold on to the plant with one hand while
you pull up the weed with your other; this will keep the
garden plant from loosening in the ground so that it dries
out.) Never put artificial fertilizer directly on the plants,
as it is too caustic for them; dilute it first before applying
it.

The following list proposes succulents suitable for the
garden:

	Color	Size	Flowering time
Sedum acre	yellow	4 inches (10cm)	June to July
Sedum album	white	6 inches (15cm)	June to July
Sedum cauticola	pink	4 inches (10cm)	August to September
Sedum cyaneum	pink	8 inches (20cm)	July to September
Sedum ewersii	dark pink	8 inches (20cm)	July to September
Sedum kamtschaticum	yellow	6 inches (15cm)	July to August
Sedum lydium	white-pink	6 inches (15cm)	June to July
Sedum reflexum	yellow	6 inches (15cm)	June to July
Sedum spathulifolium	yellow	6 inches (15cm)	June to July
Sedum spectabile	light pink	12 inches (30cm)	August to October
Sedum spurium		4 inches (10cm)	July to September
Sempervivum arachnoideum	pink	6 inches (15cm)	July to August
Sempervivum × fauconnettii		6 inches (15cm)	June to July

*Within a few years, several
mosses will grow on porous
lava rock or sandstone and
other soft kinds of stone
spontaneously, especially on
exposures that receive no
direct sunlight.*

| Sempervivum × funckii | pink | 6 inches (15cm) | July to August |
| Sempervivum tectorum | pink | 6 inches (15cm) | June to July |

The genus *Sempervivum* includes several species with leaf rosettes in various colors: reddish and gray-blue; the flower is always pink. With both sedum and sempervivum, the leaf has great ornamental value. Sometimes the sempervivums do not flower, but many gardeners feel the foliage makes up for this. Include a selection of sempervivums in your garden, and you will be rewarded with an always-interesting display.

Sedum and sempervivum varieties grow well on roof tiles. In this way, you can literally grow a garden on the roof of an old shed.

You can grow hosta, primula, trollius, and caltha in a low-lying and wetter part of the rock garden.

Bamboo

In the last decade of the previous century, bamboo came into fashion. The mild climate of England made the plants a popular choice there. There are also bamboo varieties that thrive in a cooler climate. Bamboos have an eastern appearance, and for that reason they do not always harmonize with our other garden plants. You must consider well what will look pleasing with bamboo in your garden, or plant the bamboo as a solitary clump. There is another reason why you should not plant it in the border or among shrubs: In the winter the leaves wither or become brown at the edges. It takes at least until June before this ugly leaf is grown over with fresh green again. When the shrub border is at its best, the bamboo is at its ugliest.

Bamboo is difficult to divide and to transplant. Transplant only in May (in temperate climates), and water during dry periods and during the entire summer. The roots cannot be cut with a spade (even a sharp one). To divide, partly unearth the roots and saw them through with a small tree saw. All large portions will take root; small root divisions must be potted first and set in a very

A garden with considerable differences in grade lends itself to a naturalistic rock garden.

The Unified Garden Picture

Some people greatly admire just a few sorts of plants, and devote their gardens exclusively to them. You have surely seen gardens consisting of greensward bordered and accented by shrubs and hedges of various types, a sort of symphony in green; gardens planted through and through with bright impatiens; and gardens where the owner's passion was clearly for perennials. Other people tend to be plant collectors, and feel they must have one of everything, making their purchases without a thought as to where they will be planted in the garden, or how they will look with their neighbors' gardens.

Most gardeners can't get away with planting willy-nilly. Even rock-garden enthusiasts, whose gardens may have a naturalistic, almost random appearance, acknowledge that the most successful efforts start with some planning. It is very important to consider the design of your garden before you do any planting. You may be excited about combining a biblical garden, a rock garden, and a flowering shrub collection, but before you make your purchases, draw some sketches on paper of the garden you want to have, as described in chapter 1.

humid place, preferably a greenhouse, to take root. Of two genera, several varieties are widely available, producing plants that can grow up to a height of more than 16 feet (5m): *Arundinaria* and *Phyllostachys*.

In climates and under growing conditions where bamboo is very happy, it can spread vigorously and become a terrible nuisance, as it is not easy to eradicate. If you live where bamboo thrives, consider "planting" it out in your garden by sinking a large tub of it into the soil. The tub will be invisible and will keep the bamboo where you want it.

Pernettya mucronata is a small, acid-loving shrub that is suitable for the rock garden. In order to produce berries, this female specimen must be planted near a male. Pernettya may produce red, pink, or white berries.

Rhododendron obtusum flowers in April. This lush plant is tumbling over the stones.

5 Roses

The rose is undoubtedly the flower represented most in all art forms, both in literature and in the visual arts. What captivates people so about roses? Is it the striking combination of prickly stems with petals that are as soft as velvet? Or is it all those different shades of color and glorious fragrance?

A lush wall of Rosa 'Seagull', a rambler rose. A garden shed may be completely overgrown with it. The blooming period is short, but the foliage looks attractive.

Anyway, it is a fact that the rose grows in so many shapes that it will always be an intriguing plant for that reason alone. You have an extraordinary selection to choose from when it comes to roses. You can alternate modest plants with large shrubs, and there are scarcely any limitations concerning the choice of colors. There aren't very many gardens in which roses don't make an appearance in some way or another, and in view of their many applications, this is not surprising at all.

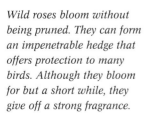

Wild roses bloom without being pruned. They can form an impenetrable hedge that offers protection to many birds. Although they bloom for but a short while, they give off a strong fragrance.

Already by about 1800, hundreds of different roses were cultivated at the Château Malmaison of Joséphine Bonaparte in France. Today, there are many thousands of varieties, and every year dozens of varieties are added. Until 1970, the size of the flowers was a priority; now for many it is the fragrance that is the most important feature.

A rose needs a sunny location with good air circulation if it is to grow and prosper. If wind can blow through the foliage of the plant, you will have less trouble with disease and insect pests. For this reason, small city gardens are frequently unsuitable for roses, which doesn't mean that you *cannot* plant a rose there. But before planting roses, you must consider the probability of having a bit of trouble, and it may be better to limit yourself to cultivating only a few roses in the small city garden.

dig them into the soil in autumn. There are some lovely, small-flowered African marigolds that fit in well with other garden plants, even with roses.

Roses can grow in any kind of soil, but a clay soil is preferable. If the clay is heavy, which you will notice immediately, you can work in some sharp sand and compost to loosen it.

Rosa 'Sally Holmes'. The single-flowered roses are suitable for planting between perennials in the border. Other single-flowered roses that serve

the same purpose are 'White Wings' (white), 'Dainty Bess' (pink), and 'Golden Wings' (yellow).

This garden is dominated by the round habit of the mounded plant (center foreground). The rose border, which could have been

extended a bit farther, clearly shows that a single kind of plant can create a beautiful effect.

A rose growing on a south-facing wall can be afflicted with mildew; the moldy-looking, whitish leaves certainly are no asset to the garden. Plant rambler roses against a southeast or southwest wall, so that the sun does not burn them quite as much. There are also roses that will grow on north-facing walls. A rose growing in soil that is too damp will be damaged by winter frost more easily. The choice is yours: either do not plant roses in damp places, or see to it that the drainage is improved before you do. Many beginners do not know that roses make heavy demands on the soil in which they are growing. Verify whether roses have already grown in the location where you wish to plant them within the past five years. Rose "exhaustion" may occur if roses are grown year after year in the same, unimproved soil. If you wish to plant immediately, it is best to replace the soil. The soil that is dug up can be used somewhere else in the garden—just don't plant roses in it. If, on the other hand, you are willing to wait a year before planting your roses, first grow African marigolds on the spot for a year, and

Planting Roses

Never hurry the planting of the rose. Doing it quickly before going shopping on Saturday morning does nothing to give the rose a good start. Planting it correctly gives it the best chances for flowering well later. It is the digging of the planting hole that is most time-consuming. A hole 16 × 16

Contrary to what many people think, you must never pour water into the planting hole before you have finished planting.

The planting distances of hybrid teas and polyantha roses.

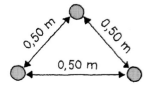

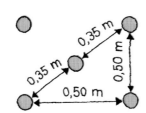

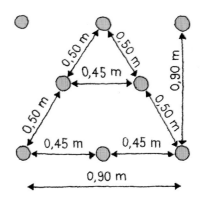

When planting roses, allow the roots to fit into the planting hole easily. Do not bend them apart or force them together. The bud union is most sensitive to frost and must be buried under an inch (3cm) of soil for protection.

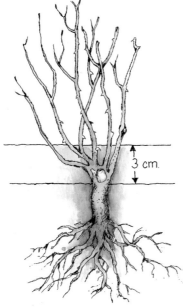

hole. Planting is easier if you do it with someone to help you. When the planting hole is half filled, press down on the soil firmly with your fist, and finish filling up the hole. Firm the soil again, and water only after planting. You must never pour water in the planting hole; the soil will become mushy, and then harden, so the young roots have difficulty growing through it. In professional terms this is called "structural deterioration."

When to Plant

If you wish to have healthy roses in your garden, you need patience. Don't plant if it is not the right time. The best time for planting is in November. By then any roses you have ordered will almost certainly have arrived. In spring, many varieties will already be sold out, and then, although you might indeed be able to buy a red, yellow, or pink rose, it probably won't be the one pink rose that you really wanted. You can still plant roses up to about the middle of April in most temperate areas. However, it is important to prune back the plant a bit more then.

Roses aren't easily damaged by night frost, but the roots must never freeze. Overnight, your unplanted rose must be

Rosa 'Pink Meidiland'.

× 16 inches (40 × 40 × 40cm) may seem very large, but if you hold the plant in the hole, the roots should hang free. They must not be forced apart, nor should they be bound together. The bud union, the spot where the hybrid rose has been grafted onto the rootstock, must be an inch (3cm) underground. If the rose sits too high, it will become loose, and there is also a good chance of frost damage. If the bud union is too low, you will have problems with pruning later on.

For standard, or "tree" roses, place a supporting stake in the planting hole before the rose, so as not to damage the roots. Mix some of the soil from the planting hole in a wheelbarrow with well-rotted stable manure, or dehydrated cow manure and compost. If the roots of the plant are dry, immerse and soak them in a bucket of water first, so that they go into the soil moist and the root hairs that grow first will find soil immediately. It is not necessary to let them "drink." Spread the crumbled soil over and around the roots while holding the plant at the bud union, or place, an inch (3cm) below the edge of the

stored in a plastic bag inside the house or garage, or temporarily heeled in out in a corner of the garden (see page 79). Snow in the planting hole is bad news. It takes a long time for snow to thaw underground, and the soil would stay cold and delay growth of the newly planted rose. You can still plant when there is snow on the ground, as long as the soil is not frozen. After planting, you must shovel the snow back over the closed planting hole, as it will provide insulation, maintaining more even temperatures and reducing the chance of damage from frost heaves.

Rosa *'Bingo Meidiland' var.* © *Meipotal.*

Nutrition

Good soil preparation may seem to be a big investment in time and money. The effort of planting well, though, is amply rewarded later by better growth and flowering. This applies to all plants, not only roses. Good nutrition is essential to roses. If you do not have the discipline to take care of your roses regularly, you should not plant them. With the exception of modern climbing roses and shrub roses (on their own rootstock), all roses need considerable care. In autumn you give the roses well-rotted manure. Be careful! Fresh stable manure contains ammonia, which easily burns foliage; you must use only old stable manure, or commercially prepared dried manure. Hobby farmers use too much straw. Straw "fixes" nitrogen–that is, makes it unavailable–for a year so that your roses suffer a shortage. After about a year, when the nitrogen is released, the roses are in danger of getting too much (especially if you have tried to balance the previous

Rosa *'Alba Meidiland'.*

shortage by adding nitrogen yourself). Remember, stable manure contains weed seeds, which can mean a lot of weeding later. It is best to use dried cow manure, preferably in autumn.

Contrary to popular wisdom, stable manure contains few nutrients. Therefore, it is desirable to add fertilizer. Organic fertilizers work slowly, but do not drain away; you need to use them less often. At the end of June, you fertilize for the last time before winter, because fertilizer encourages new growth, and new growth late in the year enters the winter season too soft, not "hardened," and is susceptible to frost damage. The degree of acidity of the soil is important when it comes to roses. The ideal pH value is 6.5. This is true for the lawn, too, so that you can adjust the pH all at once with lime or peat moss as indicated, and fertilizer when you lay out the garden.

TIP

Roses for shade

Most roses prefer a sunny spot. Some roses that bloom for a short period of time do not mind shade, and brighten up a dark corner nicely.

Some examples:

Rosa alba 'Celestial'	light pink	6½ feet (2m)
Rosa alba 'Maiden's Blush'	pink	5 feet (1.5m)
Rosa alba 'Maxima'	white	8 feet (2.5m)
Rosa filipes 'Kiftsgate'	white	65½ feet (20m)
Rosa 'Albéric Barbier'	soft yellow	16½ feet (5m)
Rosa 'Félicité et Pérpétue'	small-flowered, white	16½ feet (5 m)

With the exception of *R. filipes* 'Kiftsgate', these are all old-fashioned roses created before the mid-1800s. Although the flowering period is short, the fragrance is magnificent.

Pruning

You can prune in spring when the last period of frost has passed, usually around the beginning of April. You do not have to take night frost into account.

Pruning doesn't refer to keeping the roses in check during flowering, nor does it refer to deadheading or trimming away overhanging canes for cosmetic reasons. That work is normal garden maintenance, whereas pruning is taking care of the plant. In autumn, you cut back roses a bit (but not too much), to avoid a chance of frost damage; rose twigs always freeze a little. When the growth buds become thicker in spring and can be seen clearly, you can start pruning. The plants have come alive again and the pruning wounds will heal quickly, making for less chance of infection. Use clean, very sharp pruning shears; you must not economize foolishly when it comes to pruning shears. Good shears are good for your plants and easier for you to use, and if you maintain them well, they will last a lifetime.

Different types of roses have different pruning needs. The more precise you are, the better the roses will reward you.

Pruning Different Roses

Among the several groups of roses, there are differences in flower color, duration of flowering, tolerance of rain,

Rosa 'Duftwolke' (syn. R. 'Fragrant Cloud') is a hybrid tea that reaches a height of 30 inches (75cm). The red flowers look lovely among the dark leaves. They smell nice, too.

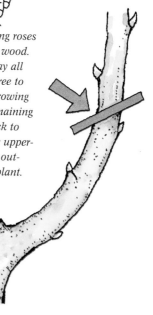

The first step in pruning roses is to remove the dead wood. Subsequently, cut away all thin canes, leaving three to five heavy, outward-growing canes. Each of the remaining canes must be cut back to three to five buds. The uppermost bud should face outward, away from the plant.

Rosa 'Allotria' is a polyantha   *Here it grows in combination*
rose that blooms until autumn.   *with* Lysimachia clethroides.

sensitivity to diseases and pests, the formation of rose hips, fragrance, and size. But there are all sorts of other aspects to rose care that are important to consider in order to make a well-considered choice of rose. Ask yourself, for example, whether you are prepared to prune precisely, or whether you mind cleaning up the petals.

It is better to be realistic in recognizing how much responsibility you are willing to take on. There is a rose for everybody, whether they have green thumbs or not (there is a rose even for people who do not prune at all). Below, you will find some guidelines for pruning different kinds of roses.

Hybrid Tea, Polyantha, and Floribunda Roses

Begin by cutting away the dead wood. Next, cut the smallest branches down to the ground. Three to five large canes should remain. Locate the buds of each cane. It is difficult to spot dormant buds; they can be identified by a small ring on the branch. Count three to five buds up the branch; the uppermost bud must be facing outward, away from the plant. Cut off the cane about a quarter of an inch (0.5cm) above the outward-facing bud. The

uppermost bud will sprout fastest, giving you a nice, open shrub with room for more flowers in the summer. Following this method, the canes will all be of a different height after pruning. This is one way you can recognize a professional rose-pruning job.

Suckers

Hybrid tea roses, polyantha roses, miniature roses, and standard roses are grafted, joining a hybrid rose variety to the roots of a wild rose. This combines qualities of endurance with the desired flowering characteristics. Grafted roses grow better. It sometimes happens that the plant sends up shoots, or suckers, just below the graft. These wild shoots growing from the rootstock portion of the plant, are easily recognizable because they don't look like the growth of the other canes. Do not let suckers grow too long, because they grow at the expense of the grafted rose.

Remove enough soil from around the base of the rose to see where the rootstock is suckering. Cut off the sucker at the base. The closer to its base the sucker is cut, the less likely it will sprout again.

Botanical Shrub Roses

Cut to the ground only third-year branches. If you do this each year, you will have a completely rejuvenated shrub at the end of three years. This technique is recommended for rugosa roses, too. Public parks often have these roses mowed nearly completely to the ground once a year. This can save time and effort pruning, but it looks less attractive because the rose has to start all over again. Species roses and old-fashioned roses that do not repeat

Rosa 'Ferdy Keitoli'.

bloom flower best on the last year's wood. You can prune the roses directly after flowering. Cut away the canes that have flowered, near the ground, leaving the young canes. The happy result is a shrub that remains perpetually young, looks good, and flowers well. Don't prune roses that form ornamental hips until winter or spring, or you will forgo the gorgeous display. If roses are long neglected, they will have to be cut down altogether. Then, you will have to accept a year without any flowering at all.

Trained Roses

Often, trained roses are called "ramblers," but they do not climb by themselves; you must train them. Trained roses that flower perpetually flower best on last year's wood. You must train the young canes that grow near the ground in the summer. At that time, the older canes will be flowering. The next spring, it is these old canes that must be cut away, and the young ones must be trained again. (These pruning instructions apply equally

Ramblers can be trained up over pergolas and garden fences. This white-painted fence needs a rambler such as Rosa *'New Dawn', a pink, large-flowered rose with a long bloom period.*

Rosa *'Zépherine Drouhin' can be grown as a shrub rose. As a rambler, the rose attains a maximum height of 11½ feet* *(3.5m). This rose, which was already being cultivated in 1868, has no prickles.*

to blackberry bushes and *Rubus phoenicolasius*.) If you prune the rose back all the way to the ground, it will hardly flower, if at all, for a full year.

Ground-Cover Roses

For this group, the same instructions apply as for the species roses. Start by cutting off those branches that stick up too much in the summer. The roses can be thinned out in early spring.

Park Roses

"Park" roses are perpetual flowering shrub roses. Prune them in spring, leaving about five good canes. All the other branches must be pruned down near the ground. You can shorten the remaining canes somewhat, too, if you like.

Rugosa Roses

Public gardens tend to mow rugosa roses to the ground. This saves maintenance costs, but for the appearance of the garden it is preferable to cut away the three-year-old wood. This is better for the plant, too, and fortunately you can take that into consideration over efficiency. Again, by pruning out three-year-old wood every year, you will have a shrub completely rejuvenated. The finer *Rosa nitida* can withstand more neglect and can look attractive without pruning.

Modern Varieties on Their Own Rootstock

Several modern varieties of French origin (Meilland) are not grafted or budded. Suckering isn't a problem when growing these roses. They don't require deadheading and you do not need to prune each year, either. You can just cut these roses back or even prune them mechanically.

These modern roses are much used in public parks. They are very suitable for private gardens where maintenance is not always done consistently.

Old Roses

Many roses, from such groups as damask roses, centifolia, Bourbon, alba, and Gallica, are described as "old-fashioned" roses. They often have large flowers with many petals. The petals may be arranged in four quarters, and these roses are in fact called "quartered" roses. They grow into large, rather wild-looking shrubs, with overhanging canes and strong fragrance. The flowering period is usually brief, perhaps only three weeks. Even so, you will undoubtedly remember their fragrance throughout the other forty-nine weeks of the year. Few of these roses are sensitive to frost. Some offer repeat bloom, that is, they have a second flowering period in one season.

Rosa rugosa *is the best producer of hips.*

Rosa 'Blairii No. 2' is an old
rambler developed in 1845.
The rose climbs to a
maximum of 16 feet (5m). It
does not bloom perpetually.

In recent years, there has been a revival of interest in old roses. Many different varieties have been lost forever, as they are not commercially available and have died out from the gardens and, typically in the United States, the cemeteries where they were planted. Old (hence, non-grafted) roses can survive even after long periods of neglect, though, fifty years and longer. It is possible that some of the varieties thought to be lost can be tracked down near old farms, churchyards, and abandoned homesteads.

Nowadays, old roses can be found budded (grafted onto a rootstock) and on their own rootstocks. With a budded plant, remember that suckering calls for maintenance. Prune away the suckers for a more vigorous, and more floriferous, plant. An old rose variety growing on its own rootstock may send up many shoots, and soon cover large areas; such roses are therefore less suitable for small gardens. If you want an old rose that forms a compact shrub, you must buy one that has been grafted. These are more suitable for the smaller garden, too. Roses growing on their own rootstock are fine for a less manicured garden, where the luxury of space allows for wilder, lankier, or more sprawling growth. Some rose suppliers offer both options for the same rose variety, so you can take advantage of the growth habit that best suits you.

A Closer Look at Some Roses

David Austin Roses

Over the past few decades, the English rose grower David Austin has been crossing old rose varieties with modern ones, aiming to combine the old-fashioned voluptuous flower shape and fragrance with the advantages of disease- and pest-resistance, and a longer flowering period. The loose, natural-looking shape is preserved in Austin roses. The first old-fashioned roses developed by Austin have a rather short flowering period (for example, the last week of June and the first two weeks of July). Austin recognized this problem and has worked to remedy it. His roses are very popular today.

Some examples:

Rosa 'Chaucer'	1970	pink	3 feet (1m)
Rosa 'Shropshire Lass'	1968	creamy white-pink	8 feet (2.5m)
Rosa 'Graham Stuart Thomas'	1983	butter yellow	3 feet (1m)
Rosa 'Pretty Jessica'	1983	warm pink	2 feet (0.6m)
Rosa 'Constance Spry' (not a perpetual bloomer)	1961	deep pink	6½ feet (2m)

New Austin roses that combine well with perennials:

Rosa 'Moon Beam'	1983	cream to pink	4 feet (1.3m)
Rosa 'Wild Flower'	1986	creamy white yellow center	1½ feet (0.5m)
Rosa 'Dapple Dawn'	1983	pink with creamy white	5 feet (1.6m)
Rosa 'Windrush'	1984	like 'Wild Flower' but fuller	4 feet (1.3m)
Rosa 'Scintillation'	1968	light pink	4 feet (1.3m)

With almost all Austin roses, the colors shade from yellow into pink or pink into cream. The soft hues harmonize beautifully in a border in the sun; a selection of these roses does not create a restless feel. You do not need large numbers of roses; a single rose is beautiful by itself. These roses can be ordered by mail from a number of rose suppliers.

Hybrid Tea Roses

These were crossbred from original tea roses (themselves of Chinese origin), and other roses popular at the

A yellow hybrid tea. This group of shrub roses boasts the most varieties.

beginning of the nineteenth century. The oldest hybrid tea still commercially available is 'La France' from 1867. This is a perpetually flowering rose, an unusual characteristic for a rose of its time, as only repeat-bloom roses were grown then.

Many thousands of varieties of hybrid teas have been bred. In breeding these roses, people concentrate on making them resistant to mildew. The buds of 'La France' themselves rot during rainy periods. For many years, rose hybridizers worked to enhance the shape and the size of the flowers, and neglected fragrance. In the past few years, fragrance and maintenance of roses have grown in importance. Every year new varieties are added; it would be impractical to try to name them all, as the selection will have changed completely again in a number of years.

Roses are susceptible to fashion. The use of color in the garden changes with time, and there are changes in the public taste for use, size of flowers, and how "natural" a rose looks. At the moment, people seem very much interested in single-flowered roses in pastel hues reminiscent of some species roses, and in the thickly petaled old-fashioned type of rose.

Repeat-Blooming Roses

This group of roses is descended from the Chinese roses too. It is not clear why these roses have not been classified among other groups of roses, such as the Bourbons. Repeat-blooming roses have large, showy, fragrant flowers. These roses offer a second flowering during a season. The English call this group the "hybrid perpetuals." This name is misleading, as it suggests that the roses flower perpetually. They clearly have a first and a second flowering. Of this group, only several dozen varieties remain today of the 661 varieties that were mentioned by William Paul in his book *The Rose Garden* (London, 1848).

Musk Roses

The ancestor of this group of roses is *Rosa moschata*. At the beginning of this century, two rose growers applied themselves especially to crossbreeding within this group: Lambert, in Germany, and the Reverend Pemberton, in England, who became so enthralled with roses that he left the church in 1914 to devote himself entirely to their hybridization. Nowadays, a good deal of hybridization of musk roses is done by the Louis Lens nursery in Belgium; you can recognize their hybrids immediately,

Rosa 'Baronne Prévost' is a repeat bloomer that reaches a maximum height of 5 feet (1.5m) when it flowers for the second time.

Page 149:
Rosa 'Mozart'. This popular musk rose grows to 4 feet (1.2m).

as they all bear names of composers.

Musk roses flower profusely at the end of June and the beginning of July, with good continued flowering in September, with medium-size clusters of half full to completely full flowers. The manner of growing is identical to that of the shrub roses.

Some examples:

Rosa 'Cornelia'	pink and apricot yellow	5 feet (1.5m)
Rosa 'Felicia'	apricot pink	6 feet (1.8m)
Rosa 'Katleen'	creamy white with light pink	6½ feet (2m)
Rosa 'Penelope'	light apricot pink	6 feet (1.8m)
Rosa 'Prosperity'	creamy white with pink	6 feet (1.8m)
Rosa 'Vanity'	rose red	6½ feet (2m)

Moss Roses

Many moss roses descend from *Rosa centifolia* var. *muscosa*, a variety of the ordinary *R. centifolia*. These hybrids were grown most widely in the middle of the nineteenth century. At that time, there were more than eighty varieties, of which half have vanished. This group of roses has branches that are thickly set with thorns. The "mossy" bud is characteristic, with greenish glands that look like moss, soft and hairy. Sometimes it feels as if the bud were covered with aphids, it feels so sticky.

Some examples:

Rosa 'Général Kleber'	striking	5 feet (1.5m)
Rosa 'Mousseline'	creamy pink	4 feet (1.2m)
Rosa 'Nuits de Young'	velvety purple	4 feet (1.2m)

Rosa *'La reine Victoria'*.

Rosa *'Souvenir de la Malmaison'*.

Rosa 'René d'Anjou'	pink to lilac pink	5 feet (1.5m)
Rosa centifolia var. *muscosa* (1824)	old rose	6 feet (1.8m)
Rosa 'William Lobb' (1855)	violet to red	6½ feet (2m)

Bourbon Roses

From a serendipitous cross between Chinese and damask roses, a group of roses was created that had the long-flowering characteristics of the Chinese rose and the vigor and the size of flowers of the damask rose. Of the more than four hundred varieties created, only a few dozen are still grown today. As with most of the other old varieties, they are stocked by specialized growers.

Some examples:

Rosa 'Boule de Neige'	bud red, flower white	5 feet (1.5m)
Rosa 'Gruss an Aachen' (1909)	warm pink	2 feet (60cm)
Rosa 'La Reine Victoria' (1872)	dark pink	6 feet (1.8m)
Rosa 'Louise Odier' (1851)	old rose with lilac	6 feet (1.8m)
Rosa 'Souvenir de la Malmaison' (1843) (sensitive to frost)	soft pink	2⅓ feet (70cm)

Miniature Roses

These are low-growing polyantha roses, most of which have been grafted, varying in height from 6 inches to 1½ feet (10 to 50cm). These small roses are very suitable for growing around other roses and in rose beds by themselves. For the latter application, you need about fifteen miniature roses per square yard (meter). As you can see, this rose can be quite expensive to use. Because of this, miniature roses are most often used to edge borders, and in flower boxes. They are often sold as houseplants. Be warned: They are absolutely unsuitable for growing indoors.

Some varieties:

Rosa 'Baby Gold Star'	yellow and apricot	12 inches (30cm)
Rosa 'Baby Carnaval' (syn. 'Baby Masquerade')	lemon yellow with red and pink	12 to16 inches (30 to 40cm)
Rosa 'Colibri'	apricot with orange	7 to 12 inches (20 to 30cm)
Rosa 'Cinderella'	white and pink	12 inches (30cm)
Rosa 'Frosty'	pink, later white	7 to 12 inches (20 to 30cm)
Rosa 'Little Buckaroo'	bright red	16 inches (40cm)
Rosa 'Peon' (syn. 'Tom Thumb')	crimson with white	3½ inches (10cm)
Rosa 'Phoenix'	carmine with orange	12 inches (30cm)
Rosa 'Pink Heather'	lilac pink	7 to12 inches (20 to 30cm)
Rosa 'Rouletii'	deep pink	10 inches (25cm)
Rosa 'Royal Salute'	rose red	12 inches (30cm)
Rosa 'Scarlet Gem'	orange-red	7 to12 inches (20 to 30cm)
Rosa 'Yellow Doll'	creamy yellow	12 inches (30cm)

TIP

Roses with decorative foliage

The following are recommended for flower arrangements:

Rosa moyesii

Rosa multibracteata

Rosa nitida

Rosa rubrifolia

Rosa willmottiae

Rosa farreri var. *persetosa*

Rosa omeiensis var. *pteracantha*

The hips of the Rosa *willmottiae.*

When it comes to roses you think of flowers. Don't underestimate the splendid hips! Roses that bear beautiful hips in autumn are:

Rosa rugosa

Rosa pomifera

Rosa pendulina

Rosa moschata

Rosa setipoda

Rosa fargesii

Rosa virginiana

Rosa multibracteata

Rosa rubrifolia

All of these roses tend to look rather "wild" and require considerable space.

A York-and-Lancaster rose, Rosa damascena *'versicolor', painted by Redouté. This rose is often mistaken for the* Rosa gallica *'versicolor' (*Rosa mundi*). They both produce striped flowers and were grown during the sixteenth century.*

Patio Roses

We try to categorize roses into groups from which the manner of growth can be deduced immediately. The patio rose group is an exception to this method. The name "patio" has more to do with the application. This modern group of roses has a leaf density similar to that of miniature roses, and a height similar to that of polyantha roses, but the flowers are smaller.

The plants do not spread as much as climbing roses. Patio roses are exclusively of modern varieties, with fragrance. All the following varieties were bred after 1980:

Rosa 'Anna Ford'	orange-red	18 inches(45cm)
Rosa 'Apricot Sunblaze'	orange-red	16 inches(40cm)
Rosa 'Arctic Sunrise'	pink to white	18 inches(45cm)
Rosa 'Cider Cup'	apricot	18 inches (45cm)
Rosa 'Clarissa'	orange-yellow	24 inches(60cm)
Rosa 'Dainty Dinah'	salmon	18 inches (45cm)
Rosa 'Hotline'	bright red	12 inches (30cm)
Rosa 'Little Prince'	orange-red, yellow center	18 inches (45cm)
Rosa 'Meillandina'	red	16 inches (40cm)
Rosa 'Perestroika'	bright yellow	12 inches (30cm)
Rosa 'Striped Meillandina'	red-white stripes	12 inches (30cm)
Rosa 'Yellow Sunblaze'	yellow, pink edges	16 inches (40cm)

Standard Roses

All different heights are available in this group of elegant accent roses. For growing in pots, the shorter roses of about 20 inches (50cm) are most suitable. For gardens, roses of 4 feet (1.20m) are appropriate, while the small-flowered trained roses that are grafted onto a tall rootstock are often 5 feet (1.50m) tall. Most grafted roses are sensitive to frost. Only a few are so winter-hardy that they do not have to be protected in the winter. Naturally, the latter are preferred by many garden owners, as they save time and effort. You must consider whether you do not mind looking at straw or plastic bags all winter long over your roses, or whether you would rather buy a rose that is not quite the color you wanted, but still looks good all through the year. Many think small-flowered roses are the most beautiful. Large flowers can seem out of proportion compared to the thin canes.

Striped Roses

Old-fashioned roses with intense fragrance, but with a brief bloom period, but with beautifully striped flowers, are few. It is worthwhile looking for a specialized rose grower who can supply them.

Some examples:

Rosa 'Variegata di Bologna'	white, purple stripes
Rosa 'Tricolore de Flandre'	light red, purple stripes
Rosa 'Pompon Panache'	cream, pink stripes
Rosa 'Gros Provins Panache'	pink, white stripes
Rosa 'Chateau de Namur'	soft pink, white stripes
Rosa 'Mécène'	white, lilac-pink stripes

This "trompe l'oeil" support is a frame for ramblers, and the depth it seems to have is an illusion. The open habit of trained roses allows some of the framework to show even in summer, which heightens the dramatic effect.

Rosa 'Frankfurt'	red, scarlet stripes
Rosa 'Sophie de Marsilly'	pink, white stripes
Rosa 'Commandant Beaurepaire'	deep pink, purple and white stripes
Rosa 'Ferdinand Pichard'	pink, crimson stripes

The best-known striped rose is *Rosa Mundi*, or *Rosa gallica* 'versicolor', grown as far back as the sixteenth century. This rose still can be found growing around old farms and country houses in Europe. The color is rose red, with irregular, soft pink and pale stripes.

Ramblers
Always plant ramblers at least 4 inches (10cm) away from a wall. The foundations of a building jut out

Some roses grow to a length of no less than 33 feet (10m). The usual, ready-made arch or rose trellis is much too small for many rambler roses.

underground. If you plant the rose on the foundations rather than over good garden soil, there is a danger the rose will dry out. Check whether your newly planted roses need extra water. Depending on the sun exposure, they may require a little extra attention for the first two years after planting. It is preferable to plant the roses facing southeast or southwest. A trained rose on the south side of a building is more likely to be affected by mildew, which grows on roses especially during dry summers.

Roses can be trained to grow along chains. The poles to which the chains are fastened can also serve as supports for standard roses.

The following list sorts rambler roses by color.

red: *Rosa* 'Dortmund'
  Rosa 'Flammentanz'
  Rosa 'Parkdirektor Riggers'
  Rosa 'Paul's Scarlet Climber'
pink: *Rosa* 'Albertine'
  Rosa 'American Pillar'
  Rosa 'New Dawn'
yellow: *Rosa* 'Elegance'
  Rosa 'Golden Showers'
  Rosa 'Leverkusen'
white: *Rosa* 'Snowflake'
  Rosa 'Direktor Benshop'

Rugosa Roses

Rosa rugosa, famous for its abilities to thrive at the seashore and to produce hips in brilliant tones of orange and red, makes a fine hedge about 4 feet (1.2m) high. Unfortunately, this rose is often supplied only in a mix of colors, combining white, pink, and red. Order rugosa roses by variety name; that way you can mix them or choose just one color. The following list may help.

Rosa 'Blanc Double de Coubert'	pure white	double
Rosa 'Cibles'	red with a yellow heart	
Rosa 'F.J. Grootendorst'	red small-flowered	double
Rosa 'Hansa'	dark purple-red	double
Rosa 'Mrs. A. Waterer'	red	double
Rosa rugosa var. *rubra*	red	single

(this rose has the largest hips)

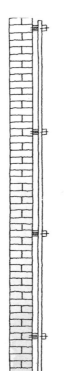

Position the slats at least an inch (3cm) from the wall. This makes it easier to fasten the wire along the slats. In addition, the slats will not rot so quickly if they are not held flush against the wall.

Rosa 'Sarah van Fleet'	pastel pink	semi-double
Rosa 'Roseraie de l'Hay'	crimson	double
Rosa 'Pink Robusta'	fresh pink	semi-double
Rosa 'Scabrosa'	violet pink	single
Rosa 'Schneezwerg'	pure white	semi-double

More than two thousand different rose varieties can be bought. You will not find all of them for sale anywhere; if you want something special, you will have to order it and wait. A rose should not be an impulsive buy. You may enjoy browsing through rose books and catalogs. Some people choose their roses with a great deal of forethought, so they

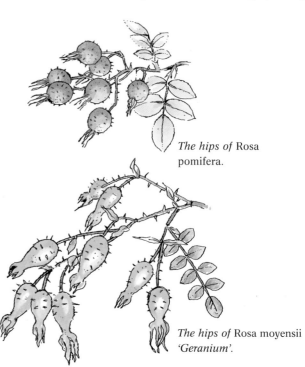

The hips of Rosa pomifera.

The hips of Rosa moyensii *'Geranium'.*

don't often object when they must wait for their order to be filled. And whatever the wait, it is sure to be much shorter than the time you'll have to enjoy your rose.

Weeping Roses

Some kinds of roses are grafted to a rootstock that has a height of some 5 feet (1.5m), and from the top of this the rose canes hang down. These are called weeping roses. The canes need to be thinned out when pruning, but they must not be cut back entirely.
Here are some popular varieties:

Rosa 'Albéric Barbier'	creamy white
Rosa 'Albertine'	salmon
Rosa 'Aloha'	cyclamen pink
Rosa 'Dorothy Perkins'	light pink
Rosa 'Excelsa'	crimson

Rosa *'Mme. Pierre Oger'*.

Rosa 'Green Snake'	white
Rosa 'New Dawn'	soft pink
Rosa 'Swany'	white
Rosa 'Zépherine Drouhin'	dark pink

(The last four varieties are perpetuals.)

Roses in Trees

Roses that can climb trees are a spectacular sight, especially when in bloom. The following varieties are suitable for this:

Rosa 'Bobby James'
Rosa 'Kiftsgate'
Rosa 'Kew Rambler'
Rosa 'Albéric Barbier'
Rosa 'Frances E. Lester'
Rosa 'René André'
Rosa 'Seagull'
Rosa longicuspis

Rosa gentiliana
Rosa helenae
Rosa multiflora

Old fruit trees that are no longer productive, or that do not have a pleasing shape, can be made more attractive by growing ramblers in them. The roses from the previous list are all suitable for this. These are the so-called ramblers, which are climbing roses with longer canes. There is hardly any difference between climbers and ramblers. Ramblers look less cultivated and can overgrow a tree. The bloom period is short, generally limited to the last week of June and the first two weeks of July. But when they bloom, they show a breathtaking number of roses and they give off a strong fragrance.

Winter Hardiness

Roses today are imported from China, Japan, North America, and Europe. The winter hardiness is very different depending on the variety. There are well-known rose growers in Germany (Kordes, Tantau), France (Meilland), England (Austin, Harkness), Belgium (Lens), the Netherlands (Buisman, De Wilde, Moerheim), and Denmark (Poulsen), and these are only a few of them. In England, winter hardiness is less important than in other countries.

Some old-fashioned varieties are very sensitive to frost. As a rule, grafted roses are not hardy. This is not an unsolvable problem with shrub roses, as we can "earth them up" in autumn by mounding the soil that lies between the shrubs up against them. At the same time,

Spent blooms do not simply drop off old-fashioned roses such as this gallica. The dead flowers must be cut off. This group of roses has only one short flowering period, about the last week of June and the first two weeks of July. The unsurpassed fragrance, however, will be remembered all year long.

we can add well-rotted stable manure, too. Usually roses will not freeze once they have been earthed up, so that more than enough buds remain to form shoots in spring.

With standard roses it is a different story. The head or crown must be wrapped for protection, and this can be done with straw for insulation. You may see a plastic bag wrapped around the head of a standard rose, and wonder whether the beauty of the rose compensates for the ugliness of the winter protection. One way to avoid wrapping up plants is to grow standard roses in pots (do not forget to use large pots, so that they will be stable), and wintering these roses in a cool but frost-free shed. Standard roses can sometimes be bent to the ground carefully and then the head can be covered with sod or soil. The stem must be gently held down so that it will not bounce up again.

Some standard roses have proved to be reasonably resilient in severe winters, among them *Rosa* 'Excelsa', *Rosa* 'De Meaux', and *Rosa* 'White Dorothy Perkins'.

Color Schemes and Combinations

There are thousands of rose varieties in commerce today. At most garden centers you will find only a few; the specialized grower may advertise hundreds. If you are fond of roses, you will surely want to grow more than one variety. Avoid planting bright colors together. Visit rose gardens where the roses are identified during the summer, and take note of what you like. Many private gardens are sometimes open to the public, and of course, there are many parks, botanical gardens, and rose growers' nurseries where you can see roses.

Roses that are sensitive to frost shouldn't be considered for planting in combination with perennials; after all, they would have to be earthed or even dug up for the

A rose bed with bright red 'Allotria' roses. The bright color is softened by a haze of fennel (Foeniculum vulgare *'Giant Bronze'). Plant fennel in combination with only those hybrid tea roses that grow quite large; otherwise, the fennel will dominate.*

winter. Bulbs are not wisely grown with roses that aren't hardy, for the same reason. Roses with open, single flowers are extremely suitable for planting between perennials; among them *Rosa* 'Dainty Bess', *Rosa* 'White Wings' and *Rosa* 'Sally Holmes' are especially notable.

Species roses can be "set free" in your wild hedge and in the bird lover's garden. Park roses are suitable for a shrub border.

It is possible to design a perennial border dominated by roses. Beautiful combinations to try: *Rosa* 'Schneewitchen' with columbine, *Stachys*, *Allium caeruleum*, and woolly thyme. Weeping standard roses lend themselves to marking a corner of a bed, preferably with a low-growing perennial beneath. They may also be planted in a long row, such as along an edge of the lawn or by the side of a path. Just one standard rose in a border seems not to have the desired effect. If a single standard rose is what you have, it would be better placed in a large pot or tub. Under the rose, an evergreen ground cover such as *Campanula portenschlagiana*, *Vinca minor* or *V. major*, or a creeping rose that cascades down the sides of the container would be a pretty addition.

Taller perennials that can be combined well with roses are:

Alchemilla mollis	green-yellow
Aster dumosus	several colors
Campanula carpatica 'Alba'	white
Campanula lactiflora 'Loddon Anne'	pink
Chrysanthemum maximum	
'Little Silver Princess'	white

Roses and perennials often make good combinations. On the left, the rose 'Maiden's Blush'; to the right, 'Aloha'.

Geranium endressii 'Walgrave Pink'	pink
Lavandula, several varieties	blue-purple
Nepeta × faassenii	light blue
Potentilla nepalensis 'Miss Wilmott'	pink
Salvia nemorosa	blue
Veronica spicata	blue

Typical for a farmhouse garden is a low, trimmed hedge. Passersby can enjoy the cheerful flowers. The trained rose 'Dorothy Perkins' flourishes against the dark wall together with a single standard rose and hollyhock (Alcea rosea).

A rose garden: full sunlight in an open space. Diseases and pests will be kept to a minimum in this sort of arrangement. For this garden, it was decided to plant only old roses that were already in cultivation by 1868, when this house was built. (Rosarium Oosterhouw, Leens, the Netherlands).

Once there are perennials between the roses, the technique of earthing is no longer possible. That is why the roses must be planted an inch or two deeper, and some peat should be used as a mulch in order to raise the soil around the roses in autumn. In winters with more than 5 degrees of frost, almost all roses need some covering. Consult professional roses growers if you have any doubts about this.

Roses with Clematis

When you combine roses with clematis, you will be delighted by the lovely result. Large-flowered clematis varieties flower at the same time as many roses, but mostly start into bloom a bit earlier on. All clematis flower on the previous year's wood, and because of that, they must not be pruned back too far. That is why these varieties are suitable for growing through rambler roses; select large-flowered trained roses for this, so that the two different flowers are of compatible proportions.

Suitable clematis for combining with roses include:

Clematis 'Henryi'	white
Clematis 'Kathleen Dunford'	pink-purple
Clematis 'Mme. le Coultre'	white
Clematis 'Mrs. Cholmondeley'	lavender-blue
Clematis 'Nelly Moser'	pink stripes
Clematis 'Rouge Cardinal'	wine red
Clematis 'The President'	purple-blue
Clematis 'Vina'	rose red

You can choose a great contrast in the shades of color of the two flowers or, on the other hand, a light color scheme. In a garden, personal style is expressed not only in the overall design, but especially in the details.

Diseases

Just like other plants, roses are susceptible to diseases and pests. Here are the most important of these, together with measures you can take to deal with them.

Prevention is better than cure; that is why you must plant roses only where the wind can blow through them freely. That way, once wetted by dew and rain, the roses will dry faster, and the likelihood of damage from mildew will decrease. Plant roses in full sunlight; only a very few can take shade. Consequently, small city gardens that lie between high walls are unsuitable.

If you want an optimally flowering rose garden, you cannot avoid using chemicals from time to time. In the trade, chemical use is called "crop protection" instead of "disease combat." Unfortunately, this term encourages carelessness in the use of chemicals. You can damage roses by "treating" them with a chemical concentration that is too high; one result of this is leaf burn. Environmental contamination is the outcome of reliance on "crop protection."

Check your roses for mildew and black spot (sooty mold), and spray as soon as you detect these problems. If only a few roses are affected, it is best to collect and remove any fallen leaves, too, to limit damage the next season.

Where to Buy Roses

Rose enthusiasts usually buy roses directly from the grower. Almost all rose growers send roses by mail or by parcel post. You can choose from an enormous selection compared to that offered by garden centers, whose small selections change each year. If a rose in your garden dies, it can be difficult to buy another of the same variety to replace it the next year. Roses in containers are best

Rosa *'Souvenir du Dr. Jamain'*.

Rosa gallica *'Officinalis'*.

Rosa *'Tour de Malakoff'*.

Damage caused by the rose gall wasp.

bought at a garden center, as the mailing costs will be high.

It is very important to know the variety name of every one of your roses. Just "tall double red" or "yellow rambler" does not guarantee you another specimen of the rose variety you once had.

You can often buy packaged roses in supermarkets and warehouses, especially in spring. Before buying, it is best to open the package and see whether the quality is good. Are the roots sufficiently damp? Have the plants sprouted too much? Be warned that shops are too warm to store roses properly. Another important consideration: Are there three heavy canes? A first-quality rose is difficult to package; it is most often plants with one or two canes that are sold this way. All reputable growers and garden centers guarantee the "authenticity of the variety," so you know what you are buying. Nobody can guarantee regrowth. There are many possible causes to consider when a plant does not strike root. Remember that not growing is almost always caused by the care during and after planting, and not by the plant itself.

Rose Associations

There are rose associations that help distribute and exchange information to rose lovers around the world. Many of these associations publish their own magazines.

Buxus hedges and such perennials as lavender and santolina can form a border for rose beds. Hybrid tea and polyantha roses especially need the definition of a border.

For more information, you may wish to contact:
The American Rose Society
P.O. Box 30,000
Shreveport, LA 71130

TIP

Roses in the perennial border

Some roses produce single flowers and keep a neat shape. Many of them are hybrid teas and polyanthas, and do not grow taller than 3 feet (1m). The large, single flower looks very pretty combined with perennials. Flowering continues throughout the summer.

The following varieties are suitable:

Rosa 'Mrs. Oakely Fisher'	yellow
Rosa 'White Wings'	white, dark stamen
Rosa 'Sally Holmes'	pink
Rosa 'Dainty Bess'	bright pink

6 The Vegetable Garden

Anyone who has a garden is very much in tune with the changing of the seasons, because the garden so clearly reflects the special characteristics of each season. This may be true for no one more than the owner of a vegetable garden.

One of the most pleasant aspects of a vegetable garden is watching the growth of the vegetables and determining when they are ready for harvest. Whoever has a vegetable garden always seems to have something to offer unexpected guests, if not fresh from the garden itself, then from the freezer or preserving jars. The harvest itself is a delight.

The colors of this Renaissance garden are contributed by the various vegetable crops (Villandry, France).

Design

A vegetable garden requires a sunny location. It's a good idea to plan a vegetable garden so it is sheltered from the prevailing winds. A warm spot for the vegetable garden yields quicker results after sowing, and greater yield in produce. Vegetables look beautiful, especially when planted with some thought to design, so it isn't necessary to hide the vegetable patch at the back of the garden. Give your vegetable garden a place near the kitchen door and–this is very important–make a good all-weather path through it so as to allow you to walk into your garden with pleasure for that one handful of parsley for the soup even if the weather is bad. If the vegetable garden is in view from the house or terrace–or in the front garden–it should be kept orderly, of course. With the terrace nearby, allowing you to look out at the garden often, maintenance will probably become a matter of course. Garden cloches of glass and terra-cotta pots are decorative in the vegetable garden. Against a south-facing fence around the vegetable garden you can grow grapes and other climbers, both for ornament and produce. More skills are required for training peaches and apricots,

Like cucumbers and pumpkins, gourds need space to grow well.

which are rather delicate, but protected plants in particular are very decorative and can be more than worth the extra care. Do not make your vegetable garden too large. If you regularly plant again on the spots from which you just finished harvesting, a plot 16 x 26 feet (5 x 8m) is enough to provide fresh vegetables daily for two people from April to November. It is better to start small so that maintenance doesn't get out of hand.

In a garden plot of the size mentioned above, it won't be possible to have every sort of vegetable; some beans, for example, take too much space, and potatoes and leeks are not very nice to look at. Red cabbage is smaller than white, and adds a lovely accent of color. Lettuce can be found in a large number of varieties. It may be nice to let one or two lettuce varieties bolt—that is, go to seed unharvested—for a pretty look.

The planting of a small vegetable garden is a true pleasure, in part because you can enjoy refining combinations in form and foliage colors. Many vegetable varieties can be planted among other plants in the rest of the garden. However small your garden may be, there is always room for a small vegetable garden. In the very small garden, you may want to plant decorative vegetables only. Strawberry plants are a good example, as they can be used outside the vegetable garden, too, to define the edge of a garden path, or in a flower bed.

A vegetable garden requires some maintenance, so before planting, you must realize that it will be an investment in time. Not only does caring for your garden make demands on your time, but freezing vegetables and cleaning and putting up fruit do, too.

Planning

Sketch a plan for your vegetable garden, just as you did for your overall garden layout. The layout of the vegetable garden is of the utmost importance for crop rotation. Make a drawing on which you clearly indicate what should be sown where, dividing the garden into three areas: one for peas and beans, one for the varieties of cabbage, and one for the other crops. You will rotate these

Every spring it is a joy to watch the magnificent large leaves of rhubarb develop.

A combination of herbs and vegetables marinated in oil or vinegar not only looks appealing in the kitchen, but is delicious.

areas annually. Crop rotation is necessary to prevent illness in crops, and it is also necessary for a good manuring plan. For professional market gardening, crop rotation is more complicated, but the amateur will manage with this simplified version.

Preparing the Soil

Turn over the soil in the vegetable garden in autumn. Depending on where you live, it may freeze during the winter, and besides, the soil will crumble more easily in spring. You may have to turn the soil over again lightly in spring.

When the soil dries in spring and becomes lighter in color, you can start raking. Make straight beds and rake them even. If the weather has been good the soil will crumble easily. Don't try to work soil that is very wet, as you will only compact it, turning its light texture hard.

Sowing

Seeds should be stored in a cool, dry place. If you have not stored seeds in the correct manner, their ability to germinate will be decreased, and you had better obtain new seeds from a reputable source. Nothing is more bothersome than to have gone to the effort of prparing and planting a vegetable garden only to discover that the seeds do not germinate.

There are two methods for sowing: broadcast, and in drills. In broadcasting,

Mespilus germanica.

the seeds are cast evenly over the desired section of the bed. This method is preferable for crops such as purslane and turnips. Once broadcast seed begins to come up from the soil, it is difficult to distinguish between the seedlings of weeds and those of the culture crops because the crop seeds were sown randomly. You may prefer to sow in drills if you are not yet very experienced at identifying seedlings. To sow in drills, dig straight trenches at the recommended depth and drop the seeds into the trench. Sowing in drills has a number of obvious advantages: The crop will come up more evenly, pulling out weeds will be easier (you can clean out the area between the drills), and thinning can be done more regularly during growth. For vegetables that must be cut for harvest (leafy vegetables), drills are more practical. Chances are that the first time you sow, you will sow too thickly. Of course, spinach should be sown more thickly than carrots, for example, but keep in mind how big the plants will grow, and follow spacing directions on the seed packet. Thinning out young plants will be necessary anyway. After sowing, rake carefully to cover the seeds

Seedlings of weeds are difficult to distinguish from those of culture crops. Clues to the plant's identity can be found in the true leaves that follow the first leaves the seedling unfolds.

to the recommended depth, but not so vigorously as to rake the seeds away. A good method for covering seeds is to scatter some crumbled soil over the drills by hand, then press down lightly with a rake. Pressing the soil down is necessary to prevent dehydration. To germinate, the seed needs moisture, but there is a risk to the fragile seedling of dehydration just after germination, too. Water daily–gently–during this time. This is how a good vegetable garden gets its start: It doesn't require much care, but it does require some attention often: Tend to your young garden regularly, preferably daily. A vegetable garden that is tucked away behind hedges at the back of the garden will probably never get the attention it needs. Plan your vegetable garden in a spot you visit often, so that you can keep a close eye on its progress.

Presowing

Vegetables that require more warmth can be presown in a greenhouse or cold frame. This is also necessary for cabbage plants in a small seedbed; later, they can be planted farther apart. Planting out seedlings should be done in overcast or even rainy weather, so the sun's rays can't dehydrate–or even scorch–the vulnerable young plants. If the weather is sunny, planting out should be done in the evening, to avoid stressing the seedlings too much. Cut off part of the long tap roots;

These herbs and flowers, hung to dry outside a garden shed, add to the charm of the herb garden.

this is better than planting them bent or crooked. Plants set too close in the seedbed won't have enough air circulation for healthy growth; check often to see whether thinning is necessary. Plants that have sufficient room will grow less spindly, and more sturdy.

Weeding

In places in the garden where the atmospheric humidity stays high, many varieties of moss may be encouraged to grow. You need not remove moss from your fruit trees; it will not damage the tree.

Row covers promote more rapid crop growth, but are suitable only for large vegetable gardens.

Most of your time in the vegetable garden should be spent on weeding–do not neglect your vegetable garden in this respect. The annual weeds that occur most often in gardens set seeds quickly. Letting weeds set seed once means years of extra weeding. Weeding should preferably be done in dry, sunny weather; any small weeds remaining will soon shrivel in the sun. If weeds have grown rather big, pull them out in humid weather, as the chance of pulling out your culture crops inadvertently with the weeds is smaller.

Perennial root weeds do not occur in a well-kept garden. If they are in evidence in the beginning, make sure that these weeds do not grow above soil level; weekly weeding is enough, contrary to what some people think. But you have to keep this up for a whole summer!

After every rain shower, hoe the soil lightly. This prevents weed growth because the soil dries faster, and allows more air for the roots of the culture crops. The drier soil will take up more of the sun's warmth. Between narrow drills, you can use a hand cultivator for this. With regular attention, weeding will no longer be necessary, and hoeing the dry, upper layer of soil means weed seeds cannot germinate. Hoeing may seem superfluous if there seem to be no weeds, but remember that weeding would be a lot more work. You've heard it before: An hour now will save you many hours later.

Watering

Rainwater is better for your plants than tap water. Try to get water from a well or ditch. Always fill up the watering can immediately after you finish watering the plants. The water in the watering can then has one day to warm up. Water the plants in the evening, as evaporation during the day is much quicker. Some say that watering plants during the day is bad, but this isn't true; crops do not get burned. Although the water drops on the plants act like tiny magnifying glasses, the plants stay cool because of evaporation.

The Plants

It is striking that most of the plants we eat belong to the same few families of plants. A number of examples are:

Saxifragaceae (saxifrage family): gooseberry and kiwi fruit
Rosaseae (rose family): apple, pear, plum, peach, blackberry, raspberry, and strawberry
Urticaceae (nettle family): hop and fig

Fruits

Fruits can be divided into the large fruits and the small fruits. Large fruits include apple, pear, cherry, apricot, plum, and so forth. Small fruits are red and black currants, gooseberry, blackberry, strawberry, and raspberry.

Sowing and Taking Cuttings

Fruit trees such as apple and pear are always bought as grafted trees. This means that an improved apple–for

The fruit of the pear tree is popular, of course, but the tree itself is very decorative in a large garden.

example, 'James Grieve'–has been grafted by the gardener onto a wild apple. Both quick-growing and slow-growing stocks can be used for grafting. Trees that are grafted on slow-growing stock do not grow tall, and are therefore suitable for small gardens. Other advantages are that they bear fruit quickly and yield large fruit. A ladder isn't needed to pick them. Trees grafted on a slow-growing stock should always be provided with a stake for support when young, and grass around them should be kept short. Tall grass attracts vermin, and mice in particular. Voles love the roots of fruit trees.

You can sow your own fruit tree, but you won't harvest the same type of apple as that from which you sowed the pip, and that may be a disappointment. Nor is it possible to propagate from cuttings of these fruit trees, as can be done with the red currant, black currant, and gooseberry, among others. Make sure that the tree you buy has a label, and that you obtain it from a reputable supplier. That is your best guarantee that you have a healthy, purebred tree, free of illnesses at the time of purchase. And, unless you are an expert at identifying apple trees, this is the only way to be certain of the variety.

Because paper labels rot within the year, after a short while it won't be possible to read which variety was planted where. For that reason, make a sketch to show where you have planted the various fruit trees and smaller

Blackberries that have been pruned and trained well produce more flowers to enjoy, and picking the fruit is much easier.

fruits in the garden. This is also nice for any future inhabitants of the house, so they will know what sorts of fruit trees are in the garden.

Manuring

Because there are different types of soil–sandy, clayey, peaty, and so on–different sorts of manuring are called for. Consult your local agricultural extension agent for

The banana is a fruit for the greenhouse in all but tropical climates. It can be grown in the garden as a potted plant, but it will produce little or no fruit.

Fruit can serve as a medium for the most fanciful imaginations. You can fashion a "bouquet" of fruit as easily as a bouquet of flowers.

advice on improving soils in your area. Manure is a superb organic soil amendment.

Keep in mind that it is useless to spread manure directly around the rootstock base. The roothairs that take in the nutrients aren't near the base of the main stem of the plant, but spread out many feet away. Usually a tree's roots extend into the soil as far away from the trunk of the tree as the tree is tall. Quick-acting fertilizers should be applied in March or April. The last manuring is best done in August. Remember, if plants continue growing late in the year because of a late manuring, they won't have a chance to harden off for the winter, and the new growth is susceptible to frost damage because it is still tender.

With slow-release fertilizers, this risk is smaller. These fertilizers can be used from February on. (Note: Bulbs that flower in spring should be manured in late autumn, because they have an inverted growth cycle.)

Fruit Trees

At some point during fruit season, take a look at an existing orchard in your area. Compare the trees to your own, even if you have only a few. Make a record of when your trees produce fruit. Most trees yield fruit at about the middle of the season. If you know fairly accurately when your trees yield fruit, you may decide to add a few varieties that yield their fruit earlier or later. This way you will be able to enjoy fruit for a longer period of time.

Orchards must be maintained, and this may call for cutting down a tree and replacing it with a young one—

a relatively simple matter, though of course not when the trees are arranged in allées, or for solitary ornamental trees, in which cases the loss of a tree is quite noticeable. Even at an aesthetic cost, it is best to remove a poor tree.

Location

To produce well-ripened fruits of such heat-lovers as peach and apricot, the insulation that is provided by a wall may be necessary, depending on where you live. The orientation of the wall may vary from southeast to southwest, right in the sun. Not only are the cold north winds broken in this way, but the wall absorbs a lot of warmth in the daytime, and it gives that warmth off again at night. The trees then no longer suffer as much from spring night frost, and later in the season the fruits have a better chance of ripening. Peaches, apricots, nectarines, figs, and mulberries all will do better when grown against a wall. To take use of the wall a step further, you can grow your fruit trees as espaliers—the branches trained in one plane—or as cordons—a single trained stem. The espaliered or cordon branches (which you should check and fasten weekly during growth of the young plant) will all receive an even share of sun and won't have to put up with shade that may be cast by other branches.

Layout

The layout of the garden can be as formal or informal as you like. Here again, symmetrical planting creates a more

Blossoms of the 'Bramley Seedling' apple.

formal atmosphere. The training of fruit trees into espaliers will give the garden a formal look. The technique of espalier has virtually disappeared since the Second World War, as it requires a great deal more time and effort than ordinary pruning, and such highly skilled labor has all but disappeared with the demise of private gardeners as professionals. Still, training is a very suitable technique for small gardens; alongside any path, or as fencing between two parts of a garden, espaliered apple and pear trees can grow without taking up too much space.

Because of the stylized form of espaliered trees, the blossoms, and the fruits, the trees are nice to look at all year round, instead of only when they are blooming and bearing fruit.

It is best to choose fruit trees that are grafted on a slow-growing stock. The roots will not spread out too much, and manuring around the stock will directly influence the setting of fruit. Because of the small root system, these trees need supports. The elegant silhouettes, so obviously trained with care, are uniquely graceful.

The trees should be planted, not too deep, in well-drained soil. Because of vermin, but also to make maintenance easier, the trees should not be planted in a lawn, but rather alongside a border or in a bed. Tall grass around the stock is always bad news; keep a circle around

A coat of paint on the lattice on which fruits or tomatoes are trained can affect the growth of the crop. White paint reflects sunlight, and can raise the surface temperature 5.5°F (3°C).

A stone wall should be dark; the warmth it absorbs during the day will be given off again as radiant heat during the night. Even a few degrees of radiant heat can ward off damage by night frost.

the stock of some 30 inches (80cm) free of grass and weeds. This circle can be planted with low-growing perennials such as lady's mantle, or with such bulbs as daffodils.

Form: Apples and Pears

When buying fruit trees, our first thought is of all the fruits that will grow on them—the anticipated harvest. Of course, this is important, but the form of the tree is equally important. In one garden one could sit under the trees; in another, there is no room for large trees. In the ornamental garden the form of a tree or bush is as important as the fruit it will bear, and this is true all year long. You can choose from a number of tree forms:

Cordon trees trained here in the style of Belgian fencing, can serve as a garden fence very nicely. The pear is best suited to this application.

Stake each tree with bamboo and reinforce the "fence" with horizontal wires. The result is an extravagant effect.

Standard Tree

This is a tree with a stock of about 6½ feet (2m), above which point the branches start. For a medium-size garden, you may decide this standard tree is the best choice. You will have to pick the fruits with the help of a ladder. Under the tree there would be enough room for people to pass so the tree could be planted next to a terrace.

Half Standard

The branches start to grow at a height of 2½ feet (75cm). This form of tree is very popular. It is still possible to mow the grass underneath a tree this size, and of course, harvesting is a relatively simple matter. Do use a stake for support during the first years.

Shrub Tree

The branches form a wedge at soil level. You can cultivate these shrubs between other plants, or even plant strawberries beneath them. It is better not to sow grass underneath, because mowing may be a problem in the future. It is not necessary to sink a supporting stake; a bamboo cane will suffice.

Cordon Tree

Trees trained as cordons bear fruit (usually apples or pears) only along the main branch. They take up little space, and can even be grown in a large pot. Cordons grow slowly because of the type of stock onto which they have been grafted. Due to the small number of roots, a thin supporting stake should be used for the lifetime of the tree. To keep the trees in shape, you can prune them once a year. This will put a halt to any quick growth, but it has no effect on the size of the fruits. Cordons add a rich and formal note to the garden.

Crab Apple (*Malus*)

All apple trees are elegant, especially in spring when they are covered with pink and white flowers. Crab apples have particularly elegant fruits. They are edible, not when picked straight from the tree, but they are excellent for making jam. (The fruit of *M.* 'John Downie' is best for making jam).

The 'Bramley Seedling' apple. In the case of cordon trees, fruit is borne on the single stem.

Page 169: A cordon tree bearing fruit.

Variety	Height	Habit	Color of fruit
Malus 'John Downie'	26 feet (8m)	erect	orange
Malus 'Golden Hornet'	19½ feet (6m)	erect	yellow
Malus 'Butterball'	13 feet (4m)	round	golden yellow
Malus 'Lizet'	small	compact	red
Malus 'Red Jane'	13 feet (4m)	weeping	red
Malus 'Red Sentinel'			deep red
Malus 'Wintergold'		round	yellow
Malus 'Royalty'			dark red
Malus 'Georgeous'	16 feet (5m)	weeping	red

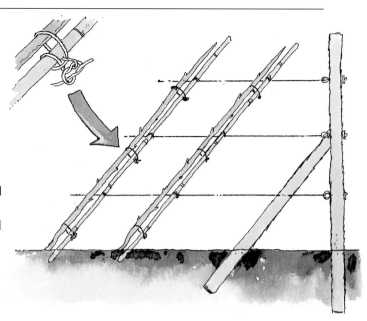

Cordon trees are often planted and trained at an angle of 45°. Do not plant them very deep, but make sure they are sufficiently supported.

Cordon trees.

Vegetables

Potato (*Solanum tuberosum*)

The potato is usually grown as commercial crop. The earliest varieties are recommended for the vegetable garden, because you can enjoy new potatoes earlier. Choose from the various different kinds of potatoes— Idaho, russet, Maine, long white, round new—and the varieties that mature when you want them. Potatoes are suitable only for clayey soil. Follow guidelines for crop rotation accurately, and buy new seed potatoes (that have been tested for disease) every year. Depending on the size of the seed potatoes, plant them about 18 inches (45cm) apart. The rows should also be 18 inches (45cm) apart. Let the tubers sprout in a box in a frost-free area and plant them in the garden about the middle of April. Earth them up in case of night frost, to make sure that the parts above the soil will not freeze.

Some varieties:

Very early:	'Eersteling'
	'Gloria'
Early:	'White Cobbler'
	'Lekkerlander'
Medium early:	'Red Pontiac'
Medium late:	'Kennebec'
	'Surprise'
Late:	'Bintje'
	'Irene'

Endive (*Cichorium endivia*)

Do not sow endive outdoors before mid-May, or when

Curly endive or chicory.

the night temperatures reach 50°F (10°C). Autumn endive should be sown the last week of June or the first week of July. Deprive the plants of light (this is called "blanching") as soon as they are fully grown, so the inner leaves will be pale yellow and tender. Use tape to bind around the top of each head; do this when the plants are dry, to prevent them from rotting. Do not tie them too tightly. Another way to blanch endive is by putting a large cabbage leaf over the top of the plant. To be able to enjoy endive progressively through the season, buy a few plants every week at the nursery; do not buy too many at once, because they will all be ready for consumption at the same time. Bolted endive yields beautiful blue flowers. Chicory and endive belong to the same genus and produce flowers that are identical.

Artichoke (*Cynara scolymus*)

The artichoke is a perennial for the vegetable garden, but only in warm regions and under dry circumstances. Even in fairly temperate areas, the plant can freeze or rot in winter if covered up. To avoid this, dig up the plants in autumn and

Early in spring is the time to earth up potatoes; in summer, earth up your celery plants to blanch them.

Asparagus.

you have a warm spring, you will be able to harvest one week earlier, and during a cold spring, one week later. After the end of May, you should no longer cut asparagus. Be careful when harvesting; don't damage the crown and other shoots. You can get young plants by sowing them yourself; they can be bedded out one year later.

Eggplant (*Solanum melongena*)

This tender crop is for the warmest spot in the vegetable garden, though it is even better to grow eggplant in the greenhouse. Eggplants are sold as plants in spring. They are annuals, and there are varieties with white, yellow, violet, and purple-black fruit. Do not plant them outdoors too early: it is preferable to wait until June. The eggplant needs good garden soil; sand and clay are not very suitable.

store them in a cool place indoors. Put lots of well-rotted manure in the planting hole if you plant them out again. If you think growing your own artichokes is worth the effort, you will enjoy elegant plants for many years. You can rejuvenate plants by dividing them. Keep the lower leaves in place to prevent rotting.

Asparagus (*Asparagus officinalis*)

Asparagus is a crop best grown in sandy soil. It is not a very suitable crop for someone starting a vegetable garden for the first time. The soil must be turned over deeply, to at least 25 inches (60cm), and well-rotted manure should be mixed throughout the whole layer. Good drainage is necessary, and it is recommended that you make a separate, raised bed for asparagus. Plant in April. The crowns should be planted very deep, about 15 inches (40cm). After two years you will be able to harvest for the first time, about the middle of April; if

Asparagus in autumn. The fresh green of the ferns in summer and the unsurpassed autumnal colors give enormous ornamental value to

this plant. Asparagus officinalis, the common garden asparagus, used to be grown as an ornamental plant; the foliage is beautiful. in

Cucumber (*Cucumis sativus*)

Outdoors you should grow cucumbers so their vines trail across the soil; in a greenhouse they should be grown vertically, held by supports. Cucumbers ripen a few at a time. If you have only one plant, wait until all fruits are ripe. Cucumber varieties have been specially developed for pickling and for enjoying as a fresh vegetable. If you pick them when they are large and yellow, they will last for months as a decoration in a fruit bowl.

Take into account that garden plants each need at least 20 square feet (2 sq m). Give cucumber plants lots of water. A moist soil, combined with high humidity, will

The asparagus blossom.

yield many good fruits. To prevent rotting, it is good to put a sheet of glass or some straw underneath the fruit. Cucumbers need a lot of warmth: do not plant them before June. The type of soil is not important, but lots of well-rotted manure is.

Beans (*Phaseolus vulgaris*)

Sow beans when the soil has warmed (about the middle of May in temperate areas) until the middle of June at the latest. Beans are sown three to a hole, in holes about 12 inches (30cm) apart, with 20 inches (50cm) between rows. Add well-rotted manure, but little nitrogen. Beans actually increase the amount of available nitrogen in the soil in which they are grown. Too much nitrogen will make the beans grow, but at the expense of the fruits.

Climbing beans

Bean vines should be trained along poles or up into tripods. Bean poles should be at least 8 feet (2.5m) long. Set the poles straight into the soil in rows 20 inches (50cm) apart, or tie them together in groups of three or four, strengthened by horizontal poles. Sow six seeds

Scarlet runner bean.

4 inches (10cm) away from each pole and 1¼ inches (3cm) deep. Reserve a few beans or plant them in a flowerpot so that you can to replace any seedlings that fail to thrive.

Scarlet runner (*Phaseolus coccineus*)

The scarlet runner blooms more elegantly than other beans, with black, red, or variegated flowers. Scarlet

The pergola brings to mind blooming roses and other climbers. Its usefulness doesn't stop here; in the vegetable garden, it offers a handsome support for the climbing vines of beans.

Bamboo canes erected as bean poles should be fastened well to be able to support the weight of the growing plants.

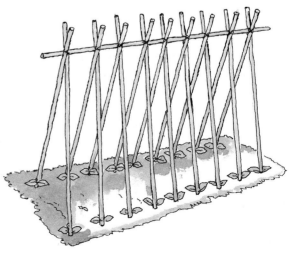

Broad bean.

runners require the same treatment as above, but are a somewhat hardier crop. The vines can be used as a windscreen in summer. The crop is good even during a cool, rainy summer.

Broad bean (*Vicia faba*)

Broad beans can be started in a cold frame in January or February. As soon as the soil has warmed after the last period of frost, the young plants can be planted into the garden. Broad beans can also be sown directly outdoors from about the beginning of March to the middle of May in most temperate areas. Plant them 6 inches (15cm) apart, 2 inches (5cm) deep. The space in between the rows can be used for other, low-growing crops. At the first setting of fruit, the tops can be removed. Removing the tops is a good method for fighting the mites and flea beetles that often appear in large numbers.

Stinging nettle (*Urtica dioica*)

Though the stinging nettle is a plant we would rather not see in the vegetable garden, this plant may be a pleasant supplement to the menu if grown at the back of the garden. Instructions for growing are not necessary: They start to grow spontaneously on nitrogen-rich soil. Pick

the tops of the large nettle if the plants are approximately 6 inches (15cm) high. The quantity to be used and the method of preparation are identical to that of spinach. (See page 181.)

Zucchini (*Cucurbita pepo* var. *melopepo*)

This is a crop for a warm, sunny spot. Do not plant zucchini in a greenhouse, as the fruits will rot. This is not a trailing plant like the cucumber. Give it ample space, at least 3½ square feet (1 sq m). They can be planted outdoors when the soil has warmed, at least a week after the last frost. You need only one or two plants; zucchini are abundant producers, and with more plants you might be overwhelmed. Buy zucchini as plants, because sowing them yourself is hardly worth the trouble.

Peas (*Pisum sativum*)

The pea can be sown outdoors when the ground has thawed, often by the middle of February. Peas can withstand some frost. Sow the peas in rows 4 inches (10cm) apart, three together, 1¼ inches (3cm) apart. You can grow vining types of peas, which do best when provided with support on which to grow, and bush types, which reach 1½ to 2 feet (45 to 60cm) in height. If birds come to feed on your freshly sown peas, crisscross heavy black thread a couple of inches above your crop; this will stop in their tracks any birds it doesn't thoroughly confuse.

Not only the fruit of the zucchini, but also the flower, can be eaten.

Pea.

Garlic (*Allium sativum*)

Take apart a head of garlic and carefully separate the cloves so they come away with part of the roots. These cloves can be planted individually, 6 inches (15cm) apart, when the weather is reliably milder, in autumn and in April. When the flower and foliage have yellowed, the bulbs can be dug up and dried. Save a few in a cool, dry place for planting again next year. Of the several types,

This wide-mesh setup offers good support for peas and pods.

"elephant" garlic, which produces very large heads, is a notably mild garlic.

Brassicas: Cabbages and Their Relatives (*Brassica oleracea*)

All brassicas can be sown on a large seedbed, then the seedings can be bedded out. Even so, beginners (and many experienced gardeners) are better off buying young plants at a nursery.

Nowadays plants are often supplied in peat pots, which drastically reduces the chance of failure when bedding out; when the seedling in its peat pot is set out in the garden, the peat pot softens and disintegrates, leaving the young roots undisturbed as they grow and reach out into the surrounding soil. Drench the peat pots in water before bedding out.

When growing brassicas, you may have to deal with clubroot, an illness of the roots that is caused by a fungus. You can prevent this illness by practicing crop rotation. Completely remove the affected plants. Never put the stalks, healthy or infected, into compost that will be used again on the vegetable garden! Then, do not plant any members of the brassica family in the same location the following year, as the fungus can remain there and infect new plants.

Cauliflower

Like roses, cauliflower needs good light and good air circulation. Early varieties can be sown outdoors in early spring, as early as the middle of March, and the late varieties until the middle of April. Sow sparingly, planting 20 inches (50cm) apart. Between the rows, early crops such as lettuce and radishes can be grown. As soon as the cabbage flowers start to set, the upper leaves should be bent inward; snap the midrib while doing this. This shields the head from sunlight and rain; the cabbage will remain white and will not rot.

Oxheart cabbage.

Brussels sprouts and red cabbage have all the advantages of ornamental brassicas when touched with frost or snow. The vegetable garden can be attractive in winter if you plant crops that will show something green throughout fall and winter. Spinach beets, kale, and leeks remain attractive to look at for a long time.

Kale

Like brussels sprouts, kale can stand very cold weather. The plant grows in every type of soil, and needs less manure than other members of the mustard family. There are short, medium, and tall varieties. Sow them in early spring; you can bed them out until September, but the plants bedded out late in the year will grow less big.

Broccoli

Don't allow broccoli to bolt. A loose flower will result if you cut off the leaves around it as soon as it starts to set. After some time the resulting side shoots can be harvested when they reach 5 or 6 inches (15cm) long. These stems do not keep for a long time.

Sow outdoors in April to May, and bed out eight weeks later, setting the plants about 20 inches (50cm) apart. Harvest will be in July and August.

White cabbage.

Chinese cabbage (*Brassica napus* var. *chinensis*)

Though not an easy crop, this is the most beautiful cabbage variety. The Chinese cabbage resembles bolted chicory rather than cabbage, and the flavor is like that of savoy cabbage. Do not sow before the end of July or the beginning of August, to prevent bolting. Plant 16 inches (40cm) apart. Chinese cabbage is the only one that can be sown directly where it is to grow and be thinned out later. Do not forget to manure.

Red cabbage, white cabbage

The so-called headed cabbages are best grown in a clay soil with good humus, well turned over and manured. Try to buy young plants. Early cabbages should be sown before winter in a cold frame. Plant cabbages at least 24 inches (60cm) apart and check regularly for caterpillars. The young plants can be destroyed by cabbageworm in a short period of time. Do not leave the cabbages "headed" for too long, as they may split; you can prevent this by cutting off a portion of the roots, thus curbing growth. Red cabbages especially keep for a long time if stored in a cool, airy, and dark place; hang them from the stalks, or put them up on shelves.

Savoy cabbage

Do not despair if you are not very successful with red and white cabbage, because the savoy cabbage is less demanding. This variety of cabbage can endure more frost and does not absolutely require a clay soil. Early varieties can be sown in April, the late ones in May or June. They should be planted at least 20 inches (50cm) apart.

Brussels sprouts

Sprouts should be sown in April or May in a nursery row or directly in the garden where they are to grow. Bedding

Red cabbage.

out can be done until the end of July. Select a low- or medium-low-growing variety for a small vegetable garden. A low-growing variety is also recommended for growing in a windy location because taller plants can be blown over. Brussels sprouts are said to improve in flavor with very cold weather, and the plants will give the vegetable garden a touch of elegance in winter if left standing.

Rutabaga (*Brassica napus* var. *napobrassica*)

Sow rutabaga in the beginning of June. Sowing can be done in a nursery row or directly where the plants are to grow. Plant seedlings (or thin them) to 16 inches (40cm) apart. Give lots of water after sowing and when bedding out. Lift them before the start of frost and keep them in a cool place.

Kohlrabi

Kohlrabi grows an enlarged, turniplike bulb aboveground. Both early- and late-season cultures are possible.

Sow a small quantity at a time; the vegetable should be eaten fresh and does not keep long on the field. Early varieties can be sown from the middle of June to the middle of July. The last harvest of the late crop can be stored in a cool place. Kohlrabi is not a very popular crop, and this is a pity. Raw kohlrabi, peeled and sliced, with

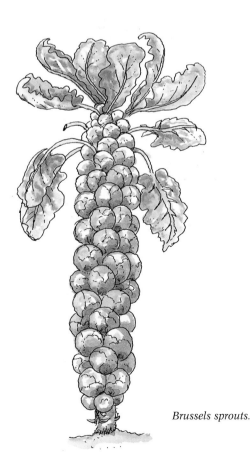

Brussels sprouts.

Do not allow grass to grow tall around the vegetable garden, as it provides a cool and moist hiding place for slugs. From there, the slugs will seek out the young plants in the vegetable garden in the evening.

a bit of salt or horseradish sauce, is a delicious, crisp snack (especially welcome for those who want to watch their diets).

Lentils (*Lens culinaris*)

This crop needs dry, sandy soil and is sown from mid-April to mid-May. Before the lentils fall from the pods, the plants can be hung upside down to dry.

Turnip (*Brassica rapa*)

Turnips can be sown in March. They must be thinned in time so growth is not slowed. You can harvest at the end of May and beginning of June. This crop is not suited for a vegetable garden with dry, sandy soil. Adequate water is essential.

Purslane (*Portulaca oleracea* var. *sativa*)

This heat-loving crop should not be sown in an open bed before mid-May; do not sow deep. After a fortnight you will be able to harvest. Because purslane matures quickly, sow often to be able to harvest a number of times during the season. The seed may fail because of less than ideal culture or weather.

Miner's lettuce or winter purslane (*Montia perfoliata*)

This plant is not related to the *Portulaca oleracea* (above). Heat is not required for this crop. Some people look upon this crop as a nice evergreen creeper, others consider it one of the worst weeds in the garden. Sow in July and harvest in the autumn and in spring. Remove

the plants in April, before the seeds mature and spread over the rest of the garden.

Leeks (*Allium porrum*)

Leeks should be sown before the middle of April, in a separate seedbed. It is easier to buy plants in June. Plant leeks 10 inches (25cm) apart. Replenish soil only at the roots; leave some room at the base of the stem so the plant can thicken. You can transplant the leek when it has the diameter of a pencil. Leeks can withstand frost very well.

Turnip Greens (*Brassica rapa*)

This is the first edible leafy green in the vegetable garden, and one that lends itself to a long harvest. Sow from the beginning of February at intervals until mid-April, in well-manured soil. Sow again in September for a late harvest. Cut the leaves and stems at soil level and prepare the vegetable as you would spinach.

Rhubarb (*Rheum rhaponticum*)

This perennial does not need many instructions for culture. It grows in every type of soil in full sun or partial shade, preferring partial shade; the leaves may go limp in the blazing sun. Do not pick rhubarb much after the first day of summer, so the plant can start preparing for the next year's crop. In early spring, rhubarb can be dug up to force the stems in a dark room; that way you can eat rhubarb very early in spring.

Radish (*Raphanus sativus* var. *radicala*)

Radishes grow in various shapes and colors: red, red and white, and white, and from round to tapered like a carrot. Radishes are a fast-growing crop. You can sow them in between the rows of such crops as carrots, lettuce, or peas. Sow thinly, from the end of March. You may broadcast the seed or sow it in drills. Thin out to 12 to 18 seedlings per foot (30cm). The flat heart-shaped leaves can be easily distinguished from those of weeds. To enjoy radishes for many

Leek.

weeks, sow a small quantity every two weeks starting in early spring. Radishes are a crop for cooler weather; it is useless to sow them in summer.

Harvest rhubarb stems up until the longest day of the year. Stopping then gives the plant a chance to recover for next year's crop.

Winter radish (*Raphanus sativus* **var.** *major*)

Winter radishes are sown from the end of June to the middle of July, directly in the garden where they are to grow. Thin to 6 to 8 inches (15 to 20cm) apart. Harvest before the flower stalk appears, about six weeks after sowing.

Garden Lettuces (*Lactuca sativa*)

It is not surprising that lettuce is a popular vegetable, in winter as well as in summer. What vegetable grows in such variety? You have your choice of loose-leaf or tight heads, crisp and brittle leaves or buttery soft ones, and varieties that produce for a nice long season.

Loosehead lettuce (*Lactuca sativa* var. *romana*)

This lettuce with broad leaves forms elongated, loose heads. The modern varieties no longer must be tied as they once were, to keep them from splitting. Distance between the plants should be 16 inches (40cm). Sowing is as easy as with the usual varieties of lettuce; start seed in nursery rows or directly where it is to grow in the garden.

Head lettuce, cabbage lettuce (*Lactuca sativa* var. *capitata*)

In February, sowing can be done indoors in pots, and at the end of March the young plants can be transplanted outdoors. Sow a small quantity a number of times, never too much all at once. With one packet of seed, you can sow throughout the spring. Plant at least 8 inches (20cm) apart. Lettuce bolts easily in hot weather. The flowers of some varieties, such as 'Lollo Rosso', are very elegant, and you might plant them in the ornamental garden with the purpose of letting them bolt.

Leaf lettuce (*Lactuca sativa* var. *acephala*)

This is the tallest-growing variety of lettuce. Plant 16 inches (40cm) apart. The leaves are picked separately, one by one. Start doing this early to force the plant to grow new, tender leaves. Sowing can be done in April and May, earlier in a cold frame. (This goes for other varieties of lettuce, too.)

Romaine, cos lettuce (*Lactuca sativa*)

Romaine should be sown at the beginning of April in

The striking flowers of the rhubarb justify a place for this plant in the ornamental ·garden.

Celery, celeriac (*Apium graveolens* var. *dulce, Apium graveolens* var. *rapaceum*)

This crop is usually cultivated as for parsley. Like parsley, it can be purchased as a plant. You only need a few. Celeriac can be sown from March onward. At the end of October, the vegetables can be lifted and, if stored in a cool and frostproof place, they will keep for the whole winter.

Blanched celery

Buy plants and plant them in rows mid-May, 12 inches (30cm) apart. By mid-August, the stems should blanch; using the soil in between the rows (which is one reason for a good distance between rows), the plants must be earthed up (see page 155). This is a job for two people, one holding the plant together and the other mounding the soil up around it. Another method is to use blanching pots, like those used for blanching sea kale. (The forcing pot used for rhubarb is also suitable.) Blanching time varies between two and three weeks. The later you start, the longer the blanching process takes.

Shallot (*Allium ascalonicum*)

The shallot is suitable for every type of soil. It is an elegant crop, one that would form a nice border around a vegetable bed. Plant the sets 6 inches (15cm) apart. The

You can store beets as you would winter carrots, in a box filled with dry sand.

a warm location. Always sow in drills to facilitate cutting. You can start harvesting when the leaves are only a few inches tall. Do not cut them off too far down, so the heart of the plant can grow again for a second cutting.

Lamb's lettuce, corn salad (*Valerianella locusta*)

To harvest in early spring, sow at the end of September or the beginning of October. In winter, when nature seems to stand still, lamb's lettuce will grow even under the snow. Sow by broadcasting seed or in drills. This crop soon produces seed, and at that point is no longer suitable for harvesting.

Beet (*Beta vulgaris* var. *hortensis*)

This is an easy crop for the beginner. It can be sown, but nowadays beets are also sold as plants. Early beets can be sown from the middle of April. For consumption during winter, beets can be sown from the first half of May. Thin the small plants, sown in drills, so the roots will have enough room to grow large. Try 'Pacemaker III Hybrid' for an early harvest, or the heirloom variety 'Lutz Green Leaf' for an autumn crop.

bulbs may be pushed up out of the soil by vigorous root growth, so press down on the soil well after planting them. When the foliage becomes yellow, the shallots can be dug up and allowed to dry. Then, separate the clusters of bulbs and store them in a cool, dark, well-ventilated place. Many cooks enjoy the mildly oniony flavor of these pale lavender bulbs both raw and cooked.

Blanched celery.

Swiss chard, spinach beet (*Beta vulgaris* var. *cicla*)

This is an easy crop with which beginners can try their luck. The leaves can be cut at 2 inches (5cm), but bolted leaves are edible, too, if the midrib is removed. Sow in early spring, or in August for a late crop. Even after a night of frost, harvest is possible. Cultivate as for spinach. Swiss chard can be blanched, like celery.

Brassica napus var. *crispa*

Sow in March in a sunny spot in drills that are 8 inches (20cm) apart. You can begin harvesting as soon as four leaves have developed on the plant. Cut them off at soil level, but be careful to leave the inner leaves intact for harvest later.

Spinach (*Spinacia oleracea*)

Sow between mid-February and mid-April, in drills. Spinach is an early crop, and for that reason it can be sown between such vegetables as peas and broad beans. Do not sow after mid-May: the spinach will soon bolt. Spinach for harvest in August should be sown in a shady spot, in moist soil. Spinach needs rich, moisture-retentive soil. Overfertilizing results in a lush crop. Lots of things can go wrong with spinach, and it is the earliest spring crop that offers best results.

New Zealand spinach (*Tetragonia tetragonioides*)

This rather unknown vegetable is very easy to grow and bears little resemblance to ordinary spinach. Unlike spinach, it is an excellent hot-weather vegetable. The plants are large and broad. Pick the thick leaves one at a time. Harvesting can be done whenever the plant has enough leaves. It is best to sow in pots and transplant to the garden later, 16 inches (40cm) apart.

Corn (*Zea mays* var. *saccharata*)

Sweet corn can be sown mid-May, three grains together, 20 inches (50cm) apart in rows spaced 20 inches (50cm) apart. You can sow corn earlier in a cold frame and transplant the young plants out in the garden in mid-May. Harvest the corn by the end of August. The timing of harvesting is important. Too early means too little flavor, and a late harvest means tough kernels so examine each ear before harvesting your corn. Without pulling the husk back from an ear, you can tell when it is ripe: The silk turns brown while the husks are still green. If the husks are starting to go yellow, harvesting time is over.

Tomato (*Lycopersicon*)

Tomatoes can be sown in the cold frame in spring, but it is better to buy plants. Tomatoes can be planted out at the end of May. Immediately position stakes, to support the plants later on. There are special tomato-cages, wide-

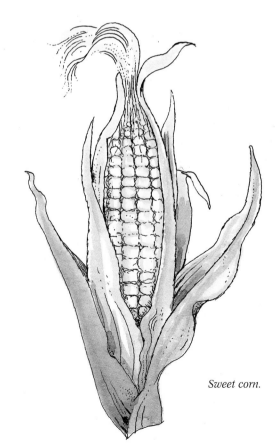

Sweet corn.

*When tomatoes are properly
trained, they don't look
untidy as they do here.*

mesh cylinders 3 to 6 feet (1 to 2m) tall, designed to encircle the plant, supporting it and holding the fruit off the ground. Plant tomatoes at least 24 inches (60cm) apart in a warm, sheltered location that receives 6 to 8 hours of full sun per day. It is best to encourage only one stem on the tomato plant. All side shoots should be removed regularly; if this is not done, the crop will grow wild at the cost of fruit production. Late in the year, and sometimes during cold summers, tomatoes do not ripen well. Unripe, green tomatoes can be enjoyed in a number of dishes, but remember not to eat many all at once.

Garden cress (*Lepidium sativum*)

Garden cress, or peppergrass, can be sown in the first half of March. The crop grows very quickly and can be harvested every week. Sow only a small quantity at a time. Garden cress likes lots of moisture. Failure is almost impossible, and this is an ideal crop for children to raise. (See also page 201.)

Onion (*Allium cepa*)

This crop for both clay and sandy soils is sown in March. Consider how thick onion bulbs can grow, and do not sow them too close. Thinning out will be necessary later on. The mature onions can be lifted from the soil and dried in the field (or in a cool, well-ventilated area) in September. Take care not to damage the onions during lifting; they will not keep very long then. You can store onions for a long time in a cool, dark room.

Fennel (*Foeniculum vulgare*)

The fernlike foliage of fennel strongly resembles that of dill. Fennel grows in any moisture-retentive soil. Florence fennel has a thickened stem and forms a large white bulb just above soil level. Because this bulb is formed in the second year, for an annual crop you must plant every year. It is best to buy fennel as started plants, because the seeds need a lot of time to germinate and grow. Harvest when the flowerbuds become visible.

Carrot (*Daucus carota* var. *sativus*)

You can sow from mid-March on, but seed takes a long time to produce results. Sow a small quantity once every three weeks, and you will be able to eat carrots all summer. Crop rotation is important with carrots, to prevent the occurrence of carrot rust fly and carrot beetle.

Tomatoes that do not ripen before the onset of cold weather can be used in the kitchen even though they are still green. Do not eat too many green tomatoes all at once, because they contain solanine, which is slightly poisonous.

Late-season carrot varieties should be sown very thin in May. Late carrots that are stored in a dry, cool box filled with sand can be eaten until spring. If you have harvested more carrots than anticipated, you can preserve them (shredded and pickled).

Foeniculum vulgare *(fennel)*.

Sea kale (*Crambe maritima*)

Do not confuse this crop with *Crambe* for the ornamental garden, which may grow as tall as 8 feet (2m). The sea kale is a perennial that grows on a rootstock. It can be propagated by sowing or division. Buy young plants if you can; sowing doesn't often result in great success. Give the plants well-aerated, sandy soil. Use blanching pots on the crop in spring. (Overturned flowerpots are acceptable substitutes if they don't allow the plant to get any light, thus inhibiting the production of chlorophyll and ensuring plants pale in color). Harvesting can first be done three years after planting. The pale, thin stalks can be harvested when they are approximately 10 inches (25cm) tall. From one bed planted with sea kale, you can harvest for as long as seven years, a remarkable return on your investment.

Garden sorrel (*Rumex acetosa*)

This perennial makes a beautiful edging for the vegetable garden. Buy it as a plant, because seedlings will soon produce seeds of their own. Garden sorrel needs little maintenance; the flower stalks should be cut off as soon as they appear, though. Garden sorrel can be eaten as a vegetable, or used as an herb, often in combination with spinach. To harvest as a vegetable, plant at least twenty plants. (See also page 201.)

Fruits

Strawberry

Strawberries are best planted 10 inches (25cm) apart in rows placed 24 inches (60cm) apart. Do not simply stuff the roots in a planting hole, but gently arrange them—as you would with roses—spread out in loose soil, to give them an encouraging start. Press the soil down after planting so that the plant cannot be pulled up from the soil by tugging on just one leaf.

You can plant strawberries in March and April if the soil has warmed and there is no danger of frost, but the last week of July or the first of August is better; the following year, these plants will immediately yield a good crop. Do not forget to water those planted in summer regularly. Do not plant them too deep; the "heart" or crown of the plant should remain visible, where the sun can get at it and keep it dry. In a wet season the fruit may be splashed with mud, and rotting may occur easily. For this reason, cover the soil between the plants with straw. Commercial growers use black plastic, but this spoils the effect of a beautiful vegetable garden. Straw mulch can be applied once the plants bear fruit. Because the fruit will no longer be in contact with the warm soil, the

The strawberry pot can be planted with ordinary or remontant–second-cropping or "everblooming"– strawberries. The latter develop long runners. Plant a tall pot with the remontant Fragaria 'Ostara'.

harvest will be later if you use a straw mulch. The risk of damage due to night frost will be higher, too, but on the "plus side," the straw mulch will help keep the strawberries clean. Mulching helps the soil retain moisture.

Varieties that bear two crops or are "ever bearing":
  'Tristar'
  'Picnic'
  'September Sweet'

Varieties that bear one crop, in order of harvesting:
  'Karola'
  'Primella'
  'Earliglow'
  'Allstar'
  'Bogota'

Ever-bearing varieties develop long runners and for that reason are often sold as "climbing strawberries." Beware that you don't pay a good deal more for a variety presented impressively as a climbing strawberry! It is nice to see your strawberry plants spread (less weeding, and effective water conservation), but they will never climb.

Apricot (*Prunus armeniaca*)

Like the peach, the apricot tree is suitable for training in city gardens, placed against a warm, south-facing wall. The tree itself is rather hardy, but because it frequently blossoms as early as March, crops may fail rather often, because of uncertain spring weather. Protection from night frost is frequently necessary for fruit set. The flowers of the apricot are beautiful, and if only for that reason, it is worth planting. The leaf shape is different from that of the peach; the apricot has roundish leaves, while those of the peach are more lanceolate (spearhead-shaped). Do not pick the fruit too early, as it will not continue to ripen. They taste best in jams, compotes, or dried; the flavor when fresh can be exquisite, but is not reliable.

Almond (*Prunus dulcis*)

The almond, with its foliage reminiscent of that of the peach tree, is worth planting as an ornamental tree. Early in spring, the branches of the tree are showered with blossoms. Give the tree a sheltered, warm spot in the garden to prevent damage from night frost. Limey, dry soil is preferable. The warmest climates will succeed in producing fruits.

Pineapple (*Ananas comosus*)

In summer this tropical plant does very well in a greenhouse; in winter it should be moved to a warm room. This plant needs the same care as a bromeliad: high humidity. Buy a pineapple with a fresh green top at a greengrocer's. Cut off this green top, leaving as little flesh of the fruit as possible, and pot this "cutting." Keep humidity high by placing a plastic bag over the plant. Transplant the cutting to a larger pot with humus as soon as it has enough roots. The plant may grow quite big, and after three or four years you may even be rewarded with new fruit if the plant has been well cared for. *Ananas comosus* 'Variegata' is an elegant plant, a variety with yellow-rimmed leaves.

Page 185:
The blueberry in acid soil displays unprecedented autumn color.

Apple (*Malus pumila*)

Every garden should have an apple tree. Because of the various forms of growth, apple trees can be planted in very large as well in very small gardens; there is a pleasing variety for every gardener. Apples, like pears and plums, may be wonderful one year and disappointing the next. Depending on where you live, you may experience difficulties with one pist or another; ask apple growers around you how their apples fare, and note their advice. For the home orchard, it is much preferable to avoid pesticides on your crop. We cannot mention all apple varieties here. Consider planting one or more of the older varieties, types not readily found at the supermarket. The following varieties are most often grown by professional gardeners nowadays.

TIP

A bed with bright red apples

Some apple trees bear fruit of a gloriously bright red color. Not only do the flowers have ornamental value, but the fruits do, too. Some varieties:

    'Sterappel'

    'Summerred'

    'Elise'

    'Red Elstar'

    'Elshof'

    'Regal Prince'

Plant these apple trees in the sunniest spot in the garden, and the fruit will color even more beautifully. Train a late-blooming clematis to grow up through the tree, and you will enjoy an extraordinary garden ornament.

Summer varieties:

    'Benoni'

    'Discovery'

    'James Grieve'

    'Summerred'

    'Vista Bella'

Autumn varieties:

    'Alkmene'

    'Delcorf'

    'Elan'

Varieties suitable for storing:

    'Cox's Orange Pippin'

    'Elstar'

    'Gala'

    'Gloster'

    'Golden Delicious'

    'Jonagold'

    'Karmijn de Sonnaville'

    'Lambarts Calville'

    'Schone van Boskoop'

Many old varieties are on the market today, and can be ordered from specialty nurseries. It is especially nice to plant these apples in your garden, beloved types of years gone by. Old varieties are very often regional; to find out which apples are suitable for your region, ask a gardener who lives nearby. Also, many of the sweet varieties such as 'Rode Dijkmanszoet', 'Sweet Caroline', and 'Sweet Orange' are not to be found for sale very often, perhaps a reason to plant a sweet apple in your garden.

Avocado (*Persea americana*)

This plant is not suitable for a cold greenhouse or any garden not located in a hot climate. We mention the avocado because it is fun for children to grow a plant from the pit. The resulting seedling can be grown on as a houseplant. Though the plant will grow very tall, it has little ornamental value and will probably never produce

Lavender, Lavandula, *a woody plant, is suitable for making hedges in the mild-climate herb garden. Choose from various species that grow to various heights.*

Tea from your garden

When we think of tea, usually the leaves that come to us from Ceylon come to mind. We never think of our own gardens as the likely place for a tea bush. *Camellia sinensis*, from which true tea leaves are picked, grows only in certain regions of the world—most of which seem exotic to us. There are, however, other plants from which we can make a cup of "tea" with delightful aroma.

Apple tea

Both apples and crab apples can be used. Pour hot water over apple peels or grated apple and let steep for fifteen minutes.

Lavender tea

Pour a pint (half a liter) of boiling water over a few grams of lavender flowers and steep for five minutes. Although distinctly floral in flavor, lavender has a long culinary tradition.

Lime-blossom tea

Only a few dried flowers are needed for a cup of lime-blossom tea. Pour boiling water over the petals and steep for ten minutes.

Peppermint tea

All varieties of mint are suitable. Put one fresh leaf in one cup of freshly brewed tea. For a tea party, prepare a little dish of fresh leaves to offer separately. Dried leaves can also be used.

Rose-hip tea

This requires some preparation. The dried hips should be soaked for some time and boiled for twenty minutes. This tea can also be served cold.

Elderflower tea

Dry the flowers of an ordinary elder tree. One teaspoon of dried flowers is sufficient for one cup of tea. It steeps quickly. You can also make tea from ripe berries; put them in cold water and bring to a boil. Caution: The green berries are poisonous.

Currants and blackberries taste best. grown in your own garden

fruit. (In nature, avocado trees grow taller than 50 feet [15m]!) Take a fresh avocado pit and push three matchsticks equidistant around the middle, so the matchsticks (or toothpicks) will support the pit on the rim of a glass. Fill the glass with water to reach just the bottom of the pit; the water must touch. Roots will appear soon, reaching down into the water. Don't let the roots get dry. When the pit has sufficient roots, you can pot it, and it will soon start to grow into a tall plant with handsome foliage.

Currants

Currant bushes should be planted more often. What fruit makes a tarter, more brilliant jelly than the red currant? Not all currants taste good, but they attract many birds—a beautiful sight, even though this means that you will have to protect the currants better if you wish to eat them yourself. There are many types of currants; those most significant for the home garden are listed below.

Highbush blueberry (*Vaccinium corymbosum*)
Often mentioned together with the red currant and the black currant, this plant belongs to a different family and requires a different soil. Plant in acid soil with a pH of approximately 4.5. The soil should be moist and rich in humus. Make sure sufficient water is received to obtain good fruit production.

Not every garden can be adapted to the needs of the

highbush blueberry, so consider the growing condition you can offer before planting. Give the bushes adequate space in the garden and do not let them grow too dense. Prune them from the inside to maintain good air circulation and admit adequate sunlight, advice that goes for currants and gooseberries, too.

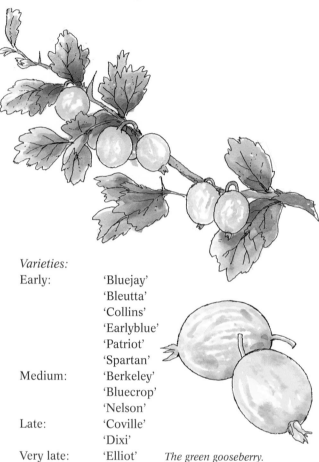

Varieties:

Early:	'Bluejay'
	'Bleutta'
	'Collins'
	'Earlyblue'
	'Patriot'
	'Spartan'
Medium:	'Berkeley'
	'Bluecrop'
	'Nelson'
Late:	'Coville'
	'Dixi'
Very late:	'Elliot'

The green gooseberry.

Chinese gooseberry, kiwi (*Actinidia chinensis*)

This is a dioecious plant, which means that a male and a female plant are required for the production of fruit. This climber needs support, with which it grows up to 20 feet (6m) tall, and quite wide. The large white flowers give off a strong fragrance and give this vine good ornamental value. The Chinese gooseberry requires a warm spot in full sun. Give plenty of water during summer. The plant is hardy, but you should still give young plants some protection. Do not forget which plant is the male and which is the female, so that you can replace one if it dies with the appropriate sex; you don't want to have to replace both plants if you can help it. The male plants usually are the weaker.

Gooseberry (*Ribes uva-crispa*)

Commercially grown gooseberries are planted along wires in a straight hedgerow. In the past, the yellow fruits

The blueberry, Vaccinium myrtillus, *is an attractive bush; you will enjoy a high* *yield only if it is grown in acid soil.*

were grown most often; nowadays the red ones are more in favor. The attractive berries are ornamental and lend themselves nicely to preserves and desserts.

Gooseberries are more vulnerable to night frost in spring than the red and white currants. The most important disease to note is caused by *Spae rotheca morsuevae*, which affects the leaves as well as the fruit.

Gooseberries can be propagated from cuttings, but many of the gooseberries grown today are grafted onto a stock. The stocks used most frequently are *Ribes odoratum, R. aureum,* and *R. divariatum.*

Variety	Harvest	Color
'Achilles'	late	red
'Golda'	medium early	yellow
'Invicta'	medium early	green
'May Duke'	early	bright red
'Winham's Industry' (syn. 'Rote Triumphbeere')	medium early	purple-red
'Whitesmith' (syn. 'Weisse Triumphbeere')	medium early	pale green

Loganberry (*Rubus ursinus* var. *loganobaccus*)

The loganberry grows like a blackberry, but is not of interest to professional growers because of small crop yields. The fruit resembles that of the blackberry, but are red and more elongated in form. The sour fruit is ripe in August and is especially suited for making preserves. There are thornless varieties. Growth and pruning are identical to that of the blackberry. The loganberry is not very hardy, so plant it in a sheltered spot.

Japanese wineberry (*Rubus phoeniculasius*)

The Japanese wineberry produces bunches of red fruit that look like blackberries, but are much smaller. The fruit does not all ripen at the same time. The plant looks attractive, even when the leaves have dropped; the stems with their numerous small spines have a beautiful reddish brown color. The bush can be planted in the vegetable garden as well as in the ornamental garden. Growth and pruning are identical to that of the blackberry.

Red currant (*Ribes rubrum*)

Currants can be planted as solitary bushes, or to form a kind of hedge. Bushes should be planted 5 feet (1.5m) apart. We do not see them very often as a hedge, but particularly for the small garden, this method of planting is ideal: a high crop yield from a small area. To

The Japanese wineberry has rather sticky fruit that do not all ripen at the same time.

create a short partition up to 6½ feet (2m), the currant is useful. Put two sturdy poles about 6 feet (1.75m) tall to mark the ends of the future hedge, and tie a good piece of sturdy wire to the poles at about 20 inches (50cm) off the ground. Below the wire, plant the currant bushes 16 inches (40cm) apart. You want only one main stem; the other branches can be removed at planting. Allow that one branch to grow as it will. Prune the others every year to two eyes (buds). This method of growing requires a lot of attention, but is rewarded with a high crop yield.

Plant a number of varieties, to spread out your harvest over a period of time. You may find that some protection is necessary to protect your harvest from birds; commerical netting may be a solution.

Varieties

Early:	'Jonkheer van Tets'
	'Jennifer'
Medium early:	'Fay's Prolific'
	'Rolan'
	'Stanza'
Late:	'Augustus'
	'Rode Rebel'

The fruit of the dewberry.

'Rondom'
'Rosetta'
'Rotet'
'Rovada'

White currant (*Ribes sativum*)

The white currant is not grown much by professional gardeners. Red currants just look more attractive. The flavor of the white currant is identical to that of the red currant. For birds, the white currants are also less eye-catching. Perhaps gardeners pestered by birds would do well to plant the white currant, so they can eat the currants themselves.

Varieties

Early:	'Zitavia'
	'Werdavia'
Medium early:	'Albatros'
	'White Pearl'
Late:	'Primus'
	'Blanca'

Black currant (*Ribes nigrum*)

The black currant is suitable for use in the kitchen, but not as a fresh fruit. The bushes require the same culture as the red and white currants. They grow bigger, however. Plant the bushes 5 feet (1.5m) apart, placing them behind any other currant bushes.

The black currant can be distinguished easily from other currants because of the strong smell of the branches and leaves. Even bare branches have this characteristic odor in the middle of winter.

Varieties

Early:	'Ben Lomond'
	'Ben Nevid'
	'Black Down'
	'Wellington'
Medium early:	'Tenah'
	'Tsema'
Medium late:	'Phoenix'
Late:	'Baldwin'
	'Black Reward'

Blackberry, thornless (*Rubus laciniatus*)

Especially for the ornamental garden, the thornless blackberry is preferable to the blackberry with thorns. Maintenance around it and pruning of the plant itself will be more pleasant if it does not have thorns. These blackberries, however, are incorrectly called "thornless"–these are prickly. Blackberries are not very demanding as far as soil is concerned; they prefer it not too dry, but well-aerated. Provide support with stakes about 6½ feet (2m) in height, and wire running horizontally between them. Plant 5 feet (1.5m) apart. Pruning should be done in autumn every year by cutting away the branches that have borne fruit.

Cold weather will turn the green color of the leaves of some blackberries to red.

Some blackberries, however, are evergreen.

The evergreen blackberry.

Secure young shoots during the growing season; these shoots will set fruit in the second year. The same treatment applies for the Japanese wineberry and the loganberry.

Varieties

Early:	'Bedford Giant'
	'Himalaya'
	'Hull Thornless'
Medium early:	'Thornless Evergreen'
Late:	'Chester Thornless'
	'Thornfree'

Raspberry (*Rubus idaeus*)

The raspberry can be easily distinguished from the blackberry by its leaves; they are a fresher green, and white on the back. Another difference is that the blackberry grows rank aboveground, while the raspberry does this underground. We usually think of raspberries as bearing red fruit, but there are also black and golden raspberries. Plant raspberries in straight rows 20 inches (50cm) apart. The plants are usually sold in bunches of ten. A row of raspberries is suitable as a hedge around a vegetable garden; around a flower garden they would not be unbecoming, either. Set up support stakes and tie on a number of wires horizontally, the highest 5 feet (1.5m)

above the ground, to which young shoots can be fastened in summer. The old canes can be cut off after harvesting. The raspberry sends out underground runners. Cut off the runners that grow too far away from the wire; allow only the runners that are more or less underneath the wire grow. A good pruning ensures a good fruit crop, and keeps fruit production where you can reach it. Raspberries are not very demanding as far as soil is

A bee pollinates the raspberry.

*The European hazelnut,
Corylus avellana, is often
planted in European public*

*parks. The cultivated variety is
grafted, and produces larger
and more numerous hazelnuts.*

concerned, but they should not be planted in too wet a spot. You can divide and propagate the raspberry by cutting off the underground stolons and planting them elsewhere.

Varieties

'Malling Promise'
'Rode Radbout'
'Spica'
'Schönemann'

In addition to the usual summer-bearing raspberry, there are autumn-bearing raspberries. The autumn raspberry bears fruit on one-year-old wood and therefore requires a different method of pruning. Prune it in autumn, and in spring, new shoots will come up again. Do not confuse this raspberry with the summer raspberry!

Varieties

'Baron de Wavre'
'Scepter'
'Lloyd George'
'Heritage'
'Zefa Herbsternte'

There is little difference between ripening times of the raspberries. Like most berries, raspberries will invite birds into your garden; keep an eye on your ripening crop so that some remains for you to harvest.

Hazelnut, filbert (*Corylus avellana*)

You can expect the first nuts the third year after planting *Corylus avellana* or *C. maxima*, which is sometimes grown as an ornamental shrub. One year may see an excellent harvest, the next year a disappointing one. *Corylus* grows in the wild as a shrub. Grafted, it can also be grown in a tree form. Commercial growers only use the tree form to facilitate the nut harvesting with machines. The first nuts that fall are usually empty, and should be cleaned up.

Varieties

Early:	'Gustav's Zeller'
	'Impératrice Eugénie'
	'Lange Spaanse'
	'Lang Tidlig Zeller'
	'Pearson's Prolific'
Late:	'Gunslebert'

Quince (*Cydonia oblonga*)

Some quince fruits look more like apples, others look more like pears, but they are always golden yellow. The quince is a tree for a sheltered spot. The lush growth makes pruning difficult; prune the tree considerably right from the beginning, which will determine the form of the tree. Quince trees grow about 16 feet (5m) tall. The young

*Corylus avellana, the
hazelnut, can grow well in
part shade. As a shrub it is*

*suitable for growing
underneath trees.*

leaves are downy. The large flowers are of great ornamental value, and large fruits adorn the tree three times each season. Beautiful autumnal color is provided by the foliage.

Quinces cannot be eaten out of hand, but can be enjoyed in numerous preparations, including jelly. The tree was already in culture by the time of the Greeks and

Mespilus germanica (medlar).

Romans, who attributed healing powers to the fruit. *Cydonia oblonga* 'Bereczki' bears large, pear-shaped fruit, and 'Reuzenkwee von Lesovac' bears very large, apple-shaped fruit.

Cultivation of the tree is identical to that of the almond. The blooming period is identical too, and damage by night frost is a concern. Harvest time is early: July and August. The quince is worth growing as an ornamental tree.

Medlar (*Mespilus germanica*)

The medlar, similar to the crab apple, will grow some 16 feet (5m) tall. Its pure white flowers, large downy leaves, and brownish fruit give it great ornamental value. The fruit is not popular for eating, but can be used in the kitchen, freshly picked as well as overripe.

Mulberry (*Morus alba* and *M. nigra*)

The white mulberry is grown as food for the silkworm, which feeds on the leaves. The black mulberry is usually planted for its fruit. Mulberry trees can grow to be very old. They are very hardy, and can be planted as solitary trees or in orchards. Because most of the fruit falls to the ground when it is ripe, don't plant a mulberry tree over a terrace or driveway, or in a lawn that sees a lot of recreational use. The mulberry grows in every type of soil.

The blackberrylike fruit with its sweet flavor is a purplish-red and ripe in July. The fruits of the white mulberry are smaller and sweeter. The flowers of neither one are of ornamental value.

Pear (*Pyrus communis*)

Pears tend to grow vertically, and for that reason are more suitable for the small ornamental garden than apple or plum trees. Even though some pears are self-pollinating, it is better to have other varieties in the neighborhood.

Both the apple and the pear are suitable for training as cordons. The pears shown here grow only on the main stem.

If your neighbors don't grow any pear trees, plant various types yourself. Because pears may experience a short pollination period some years, even a variety of plants still does not guarantee a successful harvest every year. Aside from pollination problems, pears may produce more fruit in some years than in others. Pears are grafted onto rootstocks of the wild pear and of quince.

Varieties

Eating pear,	summer variety:	'Clapp's Favourite'
		'Supertrevoux'
	autumn variety:	'Beurre Hardy'
		'Bonne Louise d'Avranche'
		'Triumphe de Vienne'
Storage pear:		'Beurre Alexandre Lucas'
		'Charneux'
		'Concorde'
		'Conferance'
		'Doyenne du Comice'
Cooking pear:		'Gieser Wildeman'
		'Saint Rémy'
		'Winterrietpeer'
		'Zoete Brederode'

Peach (*Prunus persica*)

The peach is really not very suitable for growing outdoors

The plum 'Reine Victoria'.

If there are too many plums growing on a branch, it is better to thin the fruit. This lowers the risk of breaking the branches, and the remaining plums will grow bigger.

in any but warm climates if fruit is wanted, but for the flowers alone it is worth growing elsewhere, too. Plant it against a trellis at the south side of the house, so that the branches can be trained horizontally. Do not fasten them too tightly, or the branches will be damaged when they grow in thickness. (This isn't readily visible when it occurs because the branches are then covered in leaves.) Peach trees can survive a fairly cold winter, though the branches may freeze a little. Night frost when the tree is covered with blossoms may mean that the tree will not bear fruit in the summer; covering the tree with a garden blanket or sheet may help. Spraying the flowers with water may just save the setting fruit.

If you are the happy owner of a greenhouse, you can tie horizontal wires the length of the greenhouse for training the branches of a peach tree. Spray regularly with water to prevent red spider mite infestations. Regular pruning during the summer is necessary; otherwise, your greenhouse will soon be overgrown.

Plum (*Prunus domestica*)

European, large-fruit varieties belong to *Prunus domestica*, and examples of these varieties are listed below. *P. cerasifera*, which is primarily used as an ornamental shrub, bears the so-called cherry plums. Mirabelles and damson plums belong to *P. insititia*. Some varieties alternate years of heavy crops with years of few plums.

Pick plums when they are ripe on the tree, as soon as

Varieties	Color of fruit	Ripe	Description
'Belle de Louvain'	red/blue	late August	big
'Bleue de Belgique'	dark blue	August to September	oval
'Czar'	purple-blue	early August	small, oval
'Monsieur Hâtif'	purple	mid-August	oval
'Opal'	purple-red	July to August	small
'Reine Claude d'Athan'	red-purple	August to September	large, round
'Victoria'	red	late August	large

the fruit starts to feel a little soft. Plums do not keep well, so eat or make use of them as they are harvested. They can be infected by the fungus *Chondrostereum purpureum*; if many of the leaves turn gray or silvery in color, the tree may die.

Rose hips (*Rosa* species)

Roses are usually planted in the ornamental garden, where rose hips are considerably less important than rose flowers. Even so, the hips can be fetching. A number of rose varieties yield hips good for making jam and compotes. *Rosa villosa* and the *Rosa eglanteria* are attractive roses suitable for small gardens. It is *Rosa rugosa*, which is often used in hedges, that yields the biggest hips.

Varieties

Rose	Height	Flower color	Hip color
Rosa rugosa	3 to 5 feet (1 to 1.5m)	various	red
Rosa villosa	5 to 6½ feet (1.5 to 2m)	pink	red
Rosa canina	10 feet (3m)	red-pink	orange
Rosa eglanteria	3 to 5 feet (1 to 1.5m)	red	orange

Rosa eglanteria varieties may bloom in white, pink, red, or violet. Flowering takes place from May to August. You could plant a few in a flower border, for a change. To keep the bushes pretty, cut them off near soil level every year.

Chestnut (*Castanea sativa*)

This is a large tree for drier soil that is not very limy. In cool, wet summers the fruit set does not amount to much, but even so, in a (large) private garden the gorgeously showy yellow-green male catkins that cover the tree in June are worth the trouble of planting. The tree is not self-pollinating, so you must provide a "mate" or be sure one grows nearby. The Chinese chestnut, *C. mollissima*, is suitable for smaller gardens. The shrub will grow 10 feet (3m) high and is self-pollinating.

Fig (*Ficus carica*)

The fig is related to the rubber tree, which was very popular as a houseplant in the sixties. It hardly seems possible that this plant belongs to the nettle family—they appear to be so little alike. In warm climates the fig can be grown as a shrub, but can also be trained along wires against a south-facing wall. Do not give the young plants too much manure; they will grow too fast and form weak branches at the expense of sturdy growth. If the plant grows too fast, you can cut off portions of the roots to hinder growth. More warmth is required for the setting of fruit than is offered in most temperate climates. Lucky gardeners in

The fruit will not ripen in cooler climates, but that is no reason not to plant the fig (Ficus carica). The tree itself is pretty enough.

warm climates can look forward to exquisite, though homely, fruit. Even without fruit, the fig is nice to look at.

Walnut (*Juglans regia*)

Walnut trees should be planted only in autumn. They do not like being transplanted; therefore, plant carefully so as not to have to transplant later. To increase the likelihood of striking root, do not buy too big a tree; an immature walnut tree offers better chances for success. Walnuts grow tall (82 feet/25m) and for that reason are not suitable for small gardens. In small gardens it is better to plant hazelnuts. The walnut used to be planted for timber as well as for its fruit.

Male and female flowers, which both grow on the same tree, do not blossom at the same time, so self-pollination rarely takes place. If you want to harvest walnuts, you need more than one tree. Look around your neighborhood to see whether there are trees that could pollinate your tree (the distance may be quite substantial). Flowers sometimes are damaged by night frost, and pollination can't take place when this happens—and thus, no walnuts.

Varieties

'Broadview'
'Buccaneer'

Both varieties are hardy. The latter has a more upright growth habit.

TIP

Green manure

Humus-poor soil can be enriched by sowing "green manure" in empty fields. A number of crops that replenish the soil, and thus are called "green manure," are suitable for this. Rye can be sown in autumn and dug under in spring. The plants that are turned over enrich the soil, with nitrogen particularly, and the following culture crops will profit. Most good green manuring crops can be sown in August or September, when the vegetable garden is just about empty again.

Plants for green manuring:

Lupine
Phacelia
Red clover
Vetch

With your own herb garden and old bottles and jars you have saved, you can make wonderful gifts. Label your gifts carefully and include the date on the label.

The Herb Garden

Kitchen herbs make food more attractive and better-tasting. Herbs add to the aroma of the food. Cookbooks will tell you how to use your herbs, and how they should be dried and stored. In this book, the use of herbs in the garden will be discussed. If herbs grow well and look attractive, your curiosity about their use in the kitchen will undoubtedly be aroused.

Herbs do not usually look their best in the vegetable garden. A separate herb garden is nice when low-growing hedges or structural enclosures give it form. Herbs may produce flowers that are uninteresting to look at, or flop over or don't stand up straight. Supports may make them more attractive. Many herbs are so ugly that they should be planted together with other plants. Some can be used in the perennial border. Plant herbs where you can easily pick them, even during inclement weather. You need only small amounts of an herb at any one time; a small herb garden is therefore sufficient. To have to pull on rubber boots for such small quantities shouldn't be necessary: try to find a spot near the kitchen or along a paved path. If you do plant a separate herb garden, lay out a sufficient number of paths. Because these are not "through" paths, you can make them less wide than you would in the rest of the garden.

Most herb varieties like a sunny location; only a few can't endure full sun. Do not use any herbicides in the herb garden: You will often eat herbs raw, and it really is not possible to wash them off well enough. Fortunately, most herbs suffer little from insects, and a weeding session once a week should keep your garden in excellent condition.

Anise (*Pimpinella anisum*)

This annual grows to a height of 20 inches (50cm) and should be sown in spring. The plants will come up one month later. Unlike many herbs, this umbelliferous plant is attractive. Harvest the seeds in August or September.

Borage (*Borago officinalis*)

This annual plant will sow itself every year–you may have to sow it only once. The bright blue, starry flowers look marvelous in a border of perennials. The plant will grow 3 feet (90cm) tall and needs some support. Harvest the petals of the flowers when they are at their best.

Borago pygmaea is hardly ever used. This plant for the rock garden looks much finer with its slender, prostrate stems. It is a perennial plant that can be used in the kitchen in the same way as the more common *Borago*.

Chives (*Allium schoenoprasum*)

Chives can be sown, or they can be propagated by division in early spring and autumn. Chives like rich soil; dig up the plant each year and work compost through the soil. The leaves will then remain green and edible longer. The edible purple flowers are an extra treat, and make chives an attractive addition to the herb and ornamental gardens.

Savory, summer (*Satureja hortensis*)

Bench with Roman chamomile, Anthemis nobilis *'Trenegue', a chamomile variety that can stand up to a limited amount of walking or sitting on.*

Sow only a small quantity, as only a few plants will be necessary. The flavor is more refined than that of winter savory. It is worth the trouble of sowing it every year. The established plant can withstand drought, but moisture is

The form of the herb garden makes the garden attractive. The herbs themselves are useful, but most are not very pretty. The hedges are of Buxus, *which can be pruned to any shape*

Allium schoenophrasum.

needed for the seeds to germinate. Vigilant weeding ensures more water for the emerging plants.

Savory, winter (*Satureja montana*)

This shrublike perennial will grow 16 inches (40cm) tall. Although woody, the stems are weak and may fall over easily; the plant isn't very attractive then. This is a plant for poor soil and attractive to bees.

Stinging nettle (*Urtica dioica* and *Cnidoscolus urens*)

The large stinging nettle is a perennial that spreads by means of rootstocks; the small stinging nettle is annual and often occurs as a weed in vegetable gardens. In a large garden, the large nettle can be assigned a spot to grow. Make sure the plants are mowed twice a year so as not to let them set seed. They like nitrogen-rich soil. Cut off the apical meristem in spring, but make sure you are wearing gloves. After having been boiled for a while, they will not sting anymore. They are delicious in combination with sorrel, which should also be boiled for a short time.

The annual, small nettle takes up so much time in cutting small quantities that growing this plant is not worth the trouble.

Mugwort (*Artemisia vulgaris*)

A weed that thrives in the dry soil by roadsides, and one that has a place in the herb garden. It is not a very attractive plant, with its gray-green, fine leaves and insignificant flowers. Depending on the type of soil, the plant may grow to 6½ feet (2m) high, if pleased with its surroundings. See also "Tarragon."

Lemon balm (*Melissa officinalis*)

Lemon balm is an easy plant to grow. Propagate by cuttings, sowing seed, or by division. In soil that is too dry, the leaves will turn yellow; in too moist or shady a spot, the flavor will not develop. Lemon balm does not produce large flowers, but the leaves look nice and fresh. Damage from early spring frost may occur, but usually does not harm the plant.

Dill (*Anethum graveolens*)

Dill is an annual plant, but it sometimes survives a mild winter. It spreads easily, even between paving stones. The seeds remain capable of germination for a long time. The plants grow too tall for a small herb garden: to 4 feet (1.2m). However, the yellow umbelliferous flowers are of great ornamental value. Like the bronze-colored fennel, dill looks beautiful planted among roses. Dill and fennel look very much alike; you can distinguish between them by their fragrance. Dill is used in the kitchen primarily for fish and vegetable dishes.

A tree trunk hung with herbs in pots. Many herbs grow well in containers, which will allow you to change your arrangements as you please.

Tarragon (*Artemisia dracunculus*)

Tarragon is darker in color than the other *Artemisia* species. It is a tall-growing, ugly perennial, one that develops an enormous root system. A single plant will be sufficient. It is suitable for poor, dry soil; if the soil is too rich, the plant will continue growing for too long in autumn, resulting in damage by frost.

Angelica (*Angelica archangelica*)

This biennial plant will grow 6½ feet (2m) tall, and spreads easily. After a year, the plant "dies" and you will not be able to harvest this herb for a summer. Therefore, buy one plant two years in a row, to be able to enjoy this beautiful umbelliferous plant every year.

Hyssop (*Hyssopus officinalis*)

Hyssop is grown today mostly as an ornamental. This shrublike perennial, with its woody stems, grows 2 to 2½ feet (60 to 80cm) tall. The purple-blue flowers are attractive. Hyssop is very hardy, and can be sown, and propagated by taking cuttings.

Caraway (*Carum carvi*)

This biennial plant must be sown. The foliage looks like that of carrot and coriander. The plant grows to 2½ feet (80cm) tall. It may not be necessary to buy seeds; a few seeds from your spice rack can be used for sowing, if fresh enough. Seeds containing oil are often able to germinate after a long time.

Chervil (*Anthriscus cerefolium*)

Young plants can hardly be distinguished from parsley. The umbelliferous leaves appear at the top of the 2-foot-tall (60cm) plant. Chervil goes to seed quickly, having a short growing season. Sow it again in late summer or even early autumn to ensure a fresh green supply.

Garlic (*Allium sativum*)

This perennial onion variety will grow approximately 20 inches (50cm) tall and should not be allowed to get too dry. The cloves can be planted in autumn and in April. Once the green foliage has yellowed and withered, you can harvest the bulbs. Let them dry in a dry, well-ventilated place for two or three weeks.

Garlic keeps well for a long time when stored in the refrigerator. (See also page 175.)

Cumin (*Cuminum cyminum*)

Cumin is annual with reddish, umbelliferous flowers. The

Angelica.

plant likes a rich soil and lots of sun. The strongly flavored seeds should be harvested at the end of August.
A little cumin goes a long way.

Coriander, cilantro (*Coriandum sativum*)

This herb, too, is umbelliferous and annual, and grows 16 inches (40cm) tall. The foliage resembles that of flat-leaf parsley, but the distinctive flavor is reminiscent of citrus.

Bay leaf (*Laurus nobilis*)

Do not confuse this plant with the much-planted cherry laurel (*Prunus laurocerasus*). This potted plant must overwinter in a cool, frost-free place. The leaves are a beautiful dark green, but the flowers do not amount to much. Check this plant regularly for pests. Always remove bay leaves when serving, as people have been known to choke on the bay leaves.

Lovage (*Levisticum officinale*)

This perennial grows to 8 feet (2.5m) tall. In the right spot—not too close to a path, but in the background—it is a beautiful addition. Give this plant some space to grow.

Sweet woodruff (*Galium odoratum*)

Sweet woodruff is a beautiful border plant for the herb garden. It prefers some shade, but if the soil is rather moist, full sun is also acceptable. The leaves are a beautiful light green in spring, and in April or May the fine white flowers appear.

Marjoram (*Origanum majorana*)

Marjoram is half hardy; in a sheltered spot it may survive the winter. It grows 16 inches (40cm) tall, and pink flowers bloom from July to September. The plant is highly aromatic.

Horseradish (*Armoracia rusticana*)

This is a rampant grower, so plant it in a large pot tub, which you can sink into the garden if you like. The plant has attractive leaves, and will send up a flower 4 feet (1.25m) tall.

Mint

Spearmint (*Mentha spicata*) and peppermint *(Mentha × piperita)* also grow rampantly, and will spread to fill any container in which they are planted. The pretty flowers attract bees. Plant them in a tub near a terrace; one leaf in your cup of tea will taste delicious. (If the plant is too far away, you will not pick from it very often.) Both spearmint and peppermint are perennials.

Laurus nobilis is a magnificent addition to the herb garden, but should be overwintered in a cool, but frost-free place.

Thymus vulgaris *(common thyme).*

Burnet (*Sanguisorba officinalis*)

This is a beautiful perennial, 16 inches (40cm) tall, which flowers from June to August. The leaves become reddish in color in autumn. Burnet is an easygoing plant.

Rosemary (*Rosmarinus officinalis*)

This tender perennial shrub is grown for its richly aromatic, narrow leaves. It blooms with flowers in shades of blue to white. Plant it in dry soil because of its sensitivity to frost. You can train a rosemary plant into an impressive standard.

Sage (*Salvia officinalis*)

Sage has beautiful purple flowers on an otherwise unimpressive plant. You should cut it back in spring to keep the plant in shape. Like peppermint, the leaves can be used for tea (one leaf will do); they are a traditional ingredient in many poultry and meat dishes adding a distinctively pungent flavor that enhances richer foods. *Salvia* is a plant that attracts bees.

Garden cress (*Lepidium sativum*)

Garden cress is the perfect crop for children: Two weeks after sowing it will come up, and very little can go wrong. Be sure to give the plant enough water. (See also page 182.)

Thyme (*Thymus vulgaris*)

Do not confuse this plant with creeping thyme. It forms a rather woody shrub 12 inches (30cm) tall. Give the plant a spot sheltered from wind. It is slightly sensitive to frost. A dry spot in full sun and limy soil is best. This plant is a nice addition to the rock garden. You need only one or two plants.

Sorrel (*Rumex acetosa*)

Cultivated sorrel from a garden is better than the wild variety. The plant can be used to line paths, or in between various kinds of herbs. Unfortunately, the flower stems grow tall and then collapse. Pick them before they fall. Sorrel can be grown as a vegetable (see page 183) or as an herb.

Parsley (*Petroselium crispum*)

Parsley is sown in drills and should be thinned. Sow from May to August. This biennial plant can withstand light night frost. An easy crop for every type of soil. Keep the soil moist.

7 The Small City Garden

A large garden surrounding the house can be a magnificent thing, but it isn't for everyone. The necessary effort and time laying it out and maintaining it doesn't appeal to everyone, and many people who want a garden live in the city, where houses with gardens are scarce.

The garden in March 1990 (above and below).

The owners of city gardens can create pleasing, original, even exciting gardens, small though they may be. In this chapter we will examine the laying out of one city garden. You will see it grow, over a period of a little under three years, from a bare lot to a real garden, a delightful retreat that doesn't demand too much time of the owner. Notice how the owner of this garden decides what features and plants to include, and what sorts of questions facilitate that decision-making process. It's all about what you want!

After some consideration, a design was created for this city garden based on the taste of the owner and the many limitations of the given site. Though every garden is different, the method of planning and laying out is similar for all small gardens. This city garden measures 53 feet (16m) long and 16½ feet (5m) wide, resulting in an area 875 square feet (80 sq m) in all.

The Garden Owner

The owner of the garden has decided in advance how the garden will be used. First he starts to sketch plans himself, but soon comes to the conclusion that he would like professional help. He knows what he wants but is not sure he will handle the practical interpretation of his wishes and requirements correctly.

The Landscape Architect

The landscape architect listens carefully to the wishes and requirements of the owners, taking into account how the garden is to be used, and what the site of the garden is. The budget and costs are not discussed at first, but it is clear in the case of this garden who will do the laying out and the maintenance: the owner himself. Naturally the time and effort available for maintenance have some bearing on the designs, as every good landscape architect knows.

External Factors

The owner of the garden and the landscape architect (for those who design their own garden, this is one and the same person) must take into account external factors. Adapting a desired garden design to accommodate these factors is not always necessary, but they nevertheless influence the architect at the design stage. Should old materials be incorporated into the garden of a new house, or new materials be used with an old house? Are there any municipal or neighborhood restrictions? The period during which a house, or indeed a neighborhood, was built can play an important role in the design. The type of soil and sun exposure will strongly affect the design and plantings.

The Owner's Vision

Bearing in mind the size of garden area, the owner lists everything he and his family would like in their garden:

- a children's play area with a swing, with room enough for grandma's present, a jungle gym
  - a pond
  - a garden bench
  - a rabbit hutch
  - privacy from neighbors
  - a floral arch
  - many kinds of perennials

The garden six months later, August 1990.

- some roses
- many flowering plants
- fruiting plants
- climbing plants
- a round terrace by the house
- incorporate existing paving stones $15\frac{1}{2} \times 24$ inches (40 × 60cm)
- existing trees are to remain
- evergreen shrubs at the back to camouflage a public path.

The landscape architect who is confronted with this list has as an advantage in that he is not familiar with the house and garden, and so can look objectively at the project. Because of his objectivity, he can immediately evaluate the existing elements: what is valuable and should stay where it is, and what can or must be moved. The existing lawn can be turned over quite easily, and isn't a consideration. It is easier for a garden owner to lay out a new garden in an empty lot rather than change an existing garden; this is because his vision is unaffected by existing elements.

Approach a design by looking at the big picture first. In this case, it is known that a round terrace will be located near the house. It is logical, then, to repeat this

The garden in February 1991.

The garden in April 1991.

round shape throughout the garden, and some possibilities for consideration are: a round pond, a floral arch, shrubs cut in a rounded shape, perhaps additional round or semicircular terraces, or even a semicircular garden bench. Small round cobblestones can be used for paving. Of course the orientation of the garden and its environment play important roles. One neighbor has an ugly garden and sits outdoors very often, whereas another neighbor has only a small lawn and never sits outdoors. In addition to nearby human neighbors, there are many cats in the neighborhood. What should be taken into account at the outset is the quality of the soil and site, which in this case is unfortunate: heavy clay, which is difficult to work, a high groundwater level and a lot of shade from the house. There is a difference in grade of 15½ inches (40cm); the existing garden slopes gradually to the back.

The garden owner has not added a pergola to his wish list, but the garden architect proposes this to screen the terrace from the view of neighbors above. The problem of traffic noise might be solved by means of a fountain. At this stage of the project, the question of just which plants are going to be used is not yet very important.

"Homework" for the Owner

The owner of the garden must consult with the neighbors, because if new hedges are to be planted in a garden only 16½ feet (5m) wide, the garden will become considerably narrower if the hedges must be planted so far in on his own property that they don't grow over his neighbors' property. In a small garden one has to make the most of the available space, and so consulting with the neighbors about planting the hedge on the boundary is a priority. Sometimes it is possible to share the costs with the neighbor. Together the garden owner and the neighbor can

Two drawings by the land-scape architect for the planting and layout of the garden. The drawing on the right shows only the trees in position; the drawing on the left shows all sorts of perennials and bulbs. The fixed elements such as the terrace and garden pool are shown in both drawings. The light green areas in the left drawing indicate where perennials were yet to be filled in at the time of the making of the drawing. No grass was planned for this garden, a decision made by the owner at an early stage.

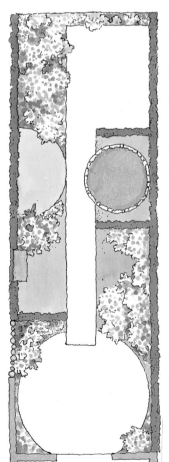

decide on a type of hedge, with advice from the landscape architect. In this case, an agreement has been made with the neighbor on one side to plant a deciduous hedge, and the other neighbor has agreed to an evergreen hedge. One neighbor did not want to share in the costs of the hedge but still wanted a say about its height; the other neighbor agreed to share in the costs, and the height was a mutual decision. Fortunately there are many types of hedges, so that the wishes of both neighbors could be met.

The Design Phase

A garden of this size can be looked upon in two ways: One can try to make it appear wider, and necessarily shorter, or make it appear longer. In this case the owner wants the garden to look longer. It is pleasant to be able to wander about in a garden, but the size of this one offers little possibility for that. Here, a single path must be made interesting by means of design and the selection of plants; interest is increased by the use of a variety of plants, and also by leading the path under something or seemingly to a certain destination. A path that leads to a rather concealed endpoint is intriguing; a layout like this always arouses the curiosity of the visitor, who invariably wonders what portions of the garden are out of sight. A garden path must always be wide enough so that two or even three people can walk on it together instead of in single file. This requires a width of at least a yard (1m), so that a mother can walk on it with a child. A sunken path will look narrower than it is in reality, and when the plants grow taller along the sides, the path will seem narrower still. These "tricks" can enhance the perceived depth of the garden, which is exactly what the landscape architect intended for this city garden. With some thoughtful planning, a small garden can be made to seem more spacious.

Drawing the Plan

After having made an inventory of what is desired in the garden, the owner and the landscape architect are ready to put the outlines of the plan on paper. The lines in the plan must form a good composition; the drawing has to look well-balanced. There ought to be a consistency in the shapes found throughout the garden; these shapes should recall the ones that can be found in the house, as in rectangular windows, an arched doorway, the shape of the roof. After all, the garden is rarely isolated, and usually should link the house with its surroundings. In the case of our city garden, the starting point for the design is a circular terrace by the house. The back of this house doesn't offer much for such a terrace to hold on to, but the view from the living room can be used as a starting point. The main path in the garden is designed to run straight to this living-room window. Thus, a link between house and garden is established.

Three-Dimensional Thinking

Many people find it difficult to visualize three-dimensional space from the flat surface of a drawing. Hedges grow to a certain height. The height, and also the width, of the crown of a tree after a few years adds dimension, rather than making the garden smaller. By comparing the photographs in this chapter you will be able to see how the depth of the garden increases with

*The garden in June 1991
(above left and above).*

the growth of the plants. Vistas do much to give a garden depth. Pergolas do this, too, and the ability to walk alongside elements in a garden makes the garden seem longer. The perceived depth can be further increased by

This overview photograph of the garden was taken in May 1991.

the use of optical illusion. One example of using optical illusion to create false perspective in a garden: a path that is slightly narrower at the far end than at the beginning; the narrowing is so slight that it is not noticeable. This illusion is most effective when gravel or small stones pave the path, because the narrowing will be made obvious from the straight edges of larger paving stones. In the case of our city garden, paving stones were to be used, so it was not possible to use false perspective in this way.

Symmetry and Harmony

By repeating certain elements in a garden, one can achieve a more harmonious effect. A garden with many different kinds of plants, like this one, may be made to seem more "quiet" by the square flowerpots arranged symmetrically on the terrace. Even the usually ugly rope of the swing adds to the quiet mood of this garden. The bench is positioned in the middle of the garden, with the pond directly opposite, and the distances to the left and the right of the bench are more or less equal. The garden has to be level, not only because it looks better in this

case, but also because the pond would otherwise be on a slope. Harmony can be achieved, especially in a small garden, by a sense of unity. Here, the path continues in the large, round terrace.

In the initial drawing, you can see that there are few lines. In a later step, plants will be drawn in. The choice of the plants determines how "quiet" the finished garden will be; the form and colors of the plants can create soothing or exciting effects. The quiet mood of this city garden was not affected by the fact that a few hundred different plants had been used.

Hardscape Materials

A landscape architect can plan to incorporate existing materials or structures into the new garden and should also take the talents and preferences of the client into account. For example, for someone who is a good welder, it is natural to plan a metal pergola; for someone who is handy with a hammer, a wooden one is the more logical choice, provided he builds it himself.

The greatest savings for the garden owner are made when it is the garden owner who does as much of the work as possible. In this way the garden not only bears the signature of the landscape architect, but of the garden owner, too, making it different from the many gardens assembled only from materials purchased from garden centers. For this garden, it was decided to use a pre-fabricated plastic pond, because on one side it touches the path; it is easy to lay bricks on a fixed edge, and the bricks can be attached with concrete glue.

The Budget

The question of how much money someone is willing to spend on a garden has as much to do with the energy of

Growing on the pergola, the evergreen Japanese honeysuckle, Lonicera japonica 'Halliana' flowers. In the background is the Swiss willow.

The floral arch frames a pretty pot, temporarily placed here until the owner finds the proper planting to suit the garden.

the client as with the cost of the materials. If it is to be an inexpensive garden, it is possible to use somewhat cheaper materials. Gravel was chosen for the path in this garden instead of more expensive paving stones, without affecting the design of the garden. The cost of plants is a small part of the total cost; do not try to save on them.

The owner of this garden rolled up his sleeves over the spring holidays and thus saved half of the cost of the garden. His family has enjoyed this garden for three years already, and they do not spend a lot of money on plants each year.

Planting Design

A good landscape architect will first ask a question that does not seem to have much to do with plants: "How much time do you plan to spend maintaining the garden, and how often?" There is quite a difference between a quarter of an hour of maintenance every day and one morning every two weeks. Someone who takes a stroll through the garden every morning before going to work can spot immediately which plants must be tied up, which plants are overgrowing others, where weeds come up,

and which plants need watering. When it comes to maintenance, not only is available time important, but the regularity with which maintenance takes place is critical. A real lover of gardening will walk around the garden with pruning scissors every week. And so for a garden lover, plants that need regular trimming can be included in the garden plan. The owner of this city garden did not know much about garden maintenance, but was prepared to learn on his own. The results of his efforts are clearly visible.

The enthusiasm of the owner of this city garden turned out to be so great that some more delicate and more demanding plants were included in the design: *Epimedium*, which requires acid soil; roses, which require winter protection; *Saxifraga fortunei*, which must be covered; *Lewisia*, which is very sensitive to frost; and *Cotula squalida*, so rampant that it must be controlled continuously. As a matter of good planning, no fast-growing plants were drawn next to slow-growing ones in the plan.

Planting

The garden owner may take pleasure in planting the garden, but the question is, how great is that pleasure?

The remaining corner of the terrace is decorated with laurels and pelargonium.

Solanum jasminoides *grows against the wall.*

A devotee of this work will be prepared to travel greater distances to find that one special plant than the gardener who wants to make things a bit easier for himself. This makes quite a difference to the planting plan. After all, it is useless to include in the plan plants that cannot be found nearby. It is only at this stage, by asking questions

*The garden in July 1992
(above and below).*

of the gardener, that it can be determined whether a given plant should be included in the garden. The owner of this garden wanted many perennials in pink, blue, and white, and the other plants were preferably to fall in with this color scheme. The owners wanted to avoid poisonous plants, and did not demand plants that are quick growers. Compare the photographs: Thanks to good spadework and correct manuring, the slow growers among the climbing plants have grown about 10 feet (3m) in just a few months. The owners were prepared to travel an enormous distance (45 miles, or 75km) to obtain a specific plant they felt would enhance the harmony and color patterns. This made some fine combinations possible. It is not so much the planting as the buying of the plants that takes a lot of time. Don't be discouraged if you do not have the time; with plants from your own neighborhood, you can certainly make a good garden plan, and it is only the gardening specialist who notices the small, subtle differences.

Plant Selections

Fortunately, the existing trees in this garden were of modest size. The largest tree is *Gleditsia triacanthos* 'Sunburst', and in addition to this there were a number of small apple trees.

The hedges that are to be planted must not grow too wide, given the narrow width of the garden. *Thuja* can grow out, but considering the good state of maintenance that is kept up in this garden, the hedge will remain narrow because of trimming twice a year. The deciduous *Carpinus betulus* 'Fastigiata' is the narrowest possible hedge. The short diagonal hedge behind the pond is of the same variety; it does not have to stay green in winter.

The owner found the idea of having many varieties of flowering plants in his garden appealing. To keep a restful feel in the garden, two low hedges were planned alongside the path; in the front, *Rosa* 'The Fairy', and left at the back, *Salix helvetica*, the Swiss willow, with gray leaves, as counterpart. The desire to grow fruit has been fulfilled by training a kiwi to grow on a pergola, and to the existing apple trees a gooseberry was added, placed in the middle of flowers. Underneath the gooseberry, a number of ferns have been planted in shade. The garden owner had summer flowers in mind, but it is the task of the landscape architect to make sure that the garden looks pleasant all year round; this was even more important in the case of this garden because one looks out on the garden directly from the living room. There had to be a good balance between the plants that die back and those that remain evergreen. Some evergreen plants of interest are *Helleborus, Hepatica, Asarum, Tiarella, Symphytum, Lamium maculatum, Iberis, Epimedium, Prunella,* and *Bergenia.*

In this narrow garden there are several trees that it was decided would remain. This caused some problems because the sloping garden was to be graded level; even for a small garden, this means having to replace at least

a truckload of soil. So, as is usual with a new design, all the trees had to be replanted after all. Otherwise, those in the front part of the garden would be left planted too shallowly, and those in the back, too deeply.

The garden owner did the planting himself. Professional workmanship was required only for welding a pergola and for paving, and so these projects were contracted out. Digging a pond is not very difficult, and most prefabricated pools come with a good manual. A lot more work was called for to improve the heavy clay

The garden in July 1992.

soil, because sand and compost, and leaf mold for acid-loving plants, had to be worked in. The soil had to be thoroughly turned over, and piping was installed to improve drainage. Accurate work is essential during the groundwork stage; a tilted pond and pavement that is not level will not only be a visible eyesore, even after the plants have grown, but will have problems in wet weather. The landscaping and pool installation were finished before the plants were planted. The pergola, swing, and garden bench were painted the same shade of dark green, as eye-catching tones would make the garden look smaller.

Installation

In comparison with the tasks of planning, landscaping, and soil preparation, planting does not amount to much. This garden was planted in just one day.

First of all the existing plants, which had been dug out, were planted again. Then the hedges: the evergreen *Thuja plicata* 'Dura' along one side and the *Carpinus betulus* 'Fastigiata', a very narrow deciduous hedge, along the other side. By mid-April the garden was ready for planting the perennials. A separate planting plan had been made for the bulbs, which were planted the following autumn. Especially in a small garden, bulbs are important.

Aftercare by the Landscape Architect

Making a drawing is not the only task of a landscape architect. He or she checks whether the plants that were intended for a certain spot are actually growing there. Checking is done in the summer: If one of the plants that was meant to be part of a beautiful combination blooms a week apart from the rest of the combination, this combination has failed. Professional growers tend to sell "near" varieties, with slightly different colors or bloom times than was intended in the plan.

In spite of what seemed to be good preparation, the plants in this garden did not appear to be growing according to plan. Plants tend to grow differently than expected from one spot to another. Even very knowledgeable gardeners have surprises, and most garden plants require some refinement once the plants come into growth.

Maintenance

As mentioned before, the city garden does not require much maintenance, but it is required often. This garden needs two hours of maintenance every week, although not during the winter. But for those who enjoy their gardens, this can hardly be considered work.

The garden, fully grown after about two and a half years, *is a garden of which the owner is justly proud.*

During the first year the climbing plants need regular training; they should be fastened every week until they reach their full—or desired—height; thereafter, only those branches that stray need to be cut off. The garden pool requires maintenance, naturally, and the fish must be tended to every day, like the rabbits in the hutch on the terrace.

The Result

A garden of this size can easily welcome ten visitors. It offers permanent seats, a play area for children to swing and climb on a jungle gym, a kitchen garden from which herbs can be picked daily and jam can be put up every year, lots of apples for eating out of hand and for storage, roses to cut for vases and to enjoy outdoors. This is not just a garden, but a special outdoor living room that even people who live in the country would envy!

8 Trees A to Z

Every garden should have a tree, and preferably more than one, but trees take up rather a lot of space and to a large extent determine the design of the rest of your garden. Soil type, geographic region, and garden size ought to be taken into consideration in the choice of a tree.

The hawthorn, Crataegus, *can be trimmed into a rounded* *shape, a special look in* *winter.*

I n this chapter we examine characteristics with which you should be familiar before choosing a tree for your garden. Additional important characteristics are noted to help you select the trees most suitable for your garden.

Quick-Growing Trees
Acer negundo
Alnus glutinosa
Betula pendula
Fraxinus excelsior
Prunus padus
Robinia pseudoacacia
Salix

Trees That Only Filter Light
This characteristic is important if underplanting is considered.
Ailanthus
Alnus glutinosa 'Laciniata'
Betula
Gleditsia
Gymnocladus

Juglans
Robinia
Sorbus aucuparia

Trees with Attractive Fruit
Crataegus
Malus
Sorbus
Prunus (some)

Trees with Attractive Bark
Acer campestre
Corylus colurna
Liquidambar styraciflua
Phellodendron amurense

The red weeping European beech Fagus sylvatica *'Purpurea Pendula', after a hundred years, grows taller as a solitary tree than is indicated in most books. This majestic tree should be planted only in very large gardens.*

Trees with a Colored Bark

Betula costata	white
Betula ermanii	yellow-white
Betula nigra	salmon red
Prunus serrulata	dark red
Prunus maackii	golden brown

Salix alba 'tristis'.

Trees with Striking Flowers

Aesculus hippocastanum
Catalpa
Corylus colurna
Crataegus
Fraxinus ornus
Magnolia kobus
Malus
Paulownia tomentosa
Prunus
Robinia pseudoacacia

Trees for Small City Gardens

When considering planting a tree, it is necessary to think ahead at least twenty years. Plant a tree that is suitable for the particular location you have in mind, and where it can grow old enough to be enjoyed by generations to come. If a large tree is planted in a garden that is too small, it will have to be cut down prematurely.

Remember that some trees take a few years to develop the characteristics that make them really beautiful. The following trees are suitable for small gardens.

Crataegus laevigata	20 feet (6m)
	rounded head
Fraxinus excelsior 'Obelisk'	32 feet (10m)
	rising
Fraxinus ornus	23 feet (7m)
	rounded head
Koelreuteria paniculata	13 to 20 feet (4 to 6m)
	rounded head
Laburnum	16½ feet (5m)
	lower part narrow, upper part vase-shaped
Magnolia kobus	23 feet (7m)
	rounded to broad head
Malus	10 to 16½ feet (3 to 5m)
	roundish head
Prunus cerasifera	16½ to 20 feet (5 to 6m)
	rounded head
Prunus subhirtella 'Autumnalis'	
Pyrus salicifolia 'Pendula'	20 to 26½ feet (6 to 8m)
	rounded weeping form
Robinia pseudoacacia 'Umbraculifera'	13 feet (4m)
	wide weeping form
Sophora japonica 'Pendula'	13 feet (4m)
	wide weeping form
Sorbus aucuparia 'Fastigiata'	20 feet (6m)
	rising (dry soil)

The silhouettes of trees add to the beauty and charm of the landscape.

The Value of Trees

We do not usually think of money when we think of trees, except when purchasing one. Nevertheless, a tree has a certain value, greatest when it is full-grown. In 1970, Mr. A. Raad, M.Sc., developed a method to determine the financial value of trees. The "Raad Method" can be used to determine value for an insurance claim, both of damages to a tree that can be repaired, and damages that cannot be repaired.

How can one determine this? Factors that are important for determining the value of a tree are:
• *The diameter of the trunk at the height of 4 feet (1.3m)*: a unit price per inch is determined;
• *The location*: it is obvious that the value of a single tree in a large forest is different from that of a solitary tree in a city center, or a specimen tree in a private garden;
• *The condition of the tree*: a diseased or dying tree is less valuable than a healthy one; an expert should determine this;
• *The use*: a solitary tree is more valuable than a tree planted as one of many in a row along a street, or than a tree that is one of a small or large group of trees.

To calculate the damage, we take into account the relative damage to the trunk diameter at 4 feet (1.3m) high. We look at both the superficial and the deeper tissue damage, and any damage to crown and roots is considered. A calculation of the damage can then be made; the devaluation percentage is compared to the value of the tree.

Quick-Growing Windbreaks

First, manure well and make sure the soil is free of weeds. Suitable trees that will soon enclose a garden are:
Alnus glutinosa (black alder)
Alnus cordata (Italian alder)
Alnus incana (white or gray alder)
These trees can withstand strong winds and high groundwater level.

Salix alba and *S.* 'Belders' can withstand brackish groundwater and are suitable for coastal areas; however, there is a risk that the trees may be affected by *Erwinia salicis*.

Populus nigra 'Italica' grows very fast, though the branches will break easily when it grows older; this can be prevented by regular maintenance.
Cupressocyparus leylandii 'Haggerston Gray' and *C. l.* 'Leighton Green' are sensitive to salt winds and severe frost. They root only superficially—they can easily be blown over—and are green in winter. A windbreak that is very tall

and dense can cause wind shears, too, just as tall buildings can. Do not choose *Cupressocyparus* if this danger seems likely, but one that will let through more wind.

Plants for an Asian Atmosphere

Picture a Chinese or Japanese garden, and large areas of gravel, bamboo fences, artfully placed rocks, natural stone, moss paths, and of course naturalistic ponds come to mind. However, the choice of plants is equally important, and this goes for trees. With plants from the following list you will be able to create a pleasantly Eastern atmosphere.

Azalea and dwarf rhododendron
Buxus microphylla
Acer palmatum, a number of varieties
Ilex crenata
Astilbe
Hemerocallis
Hosta
Mahonia (*M. bealei* is most suitable)
Juniperus horizontalis
Arctostaphylos uva-ursi
Thymus serpyllum
Cornus florida
Amelanchier lamarckii
Cryptomeria japonica
Tsuga heterophylla
Enkianthus campanulatus
Syringa vulgaris
Spiraea japonica
Weigela purpurea
Polygonatum
Liriope muscari
Ligularia and other foliage plants such as *Astilboides*
    and *Darmera*
Pieris japonica
Cercidiphyllum japonicum
Equisetum hyemale
Iris

Unfortunately, it is only the variegated *Aucuba japonica* that is usually offered, but do try to get one with green leaves. Plants that go well with this are the mosslike ones, such as *Sagina*, ferns, among which there are evergreen varieties, and of course bamboo and ornamental grass varieties. For trees, the various *Prunus* (ornamental cherry) and *Malus* (crab apple) are particularly recommended. In a small garden, in which there is no space for fruit trees, a cherry, morello, plum, or cherry apple could replace the ornamental cherry or crab apple.

Acer (Maple)

The maple includes trees and shrubs of all sizes. The most important thing they have in common is that they grow in nearly every type of soil; the Japanese maple (p. 235) does not grow very well in limy soil, however.

A. campestre (hedge maple, field maple)
height: 26½ to 33 feet (8 to 10m)
type of soil: all types, not very wet

One of the red maple trees.

A. negundo (box elder, ash-leaved maple)
height: 33 to 50 feet (10 to 15m)
    The crown admits light, and therefore underplanting is possible. This tree sometimes suffers from breaking branches.

A. platanoides (Norway maple)
height: 66 to 83 feet (20 to 25m)
    This tree is not very demanding, though it should not be planted in too wet a spot. The varieties 'Crimson King',

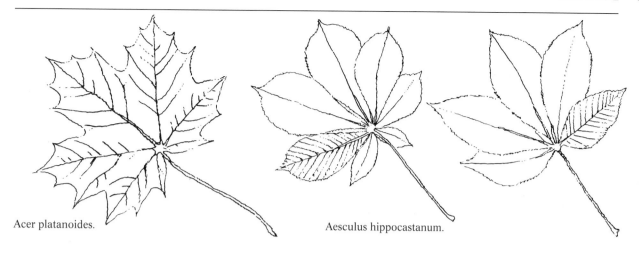

Acer platanoides.

Aesculus hippocastanum.

'Goldworth Purple', and 'Royal Red' have brown-red leaves and grow less tall.

   A. pseudoplatanus (sycamore, sycamore maple, mock plane)

   All have some characteristics as *Acer platanoides*.

Aesculus hippocastanum (Horse chestnut)
height: 66 feet (20m)
   This tree is suitable only for large gardens, but is not very demanding. Do not locate a terrace underneath a chestnut; if you do, you will have to sweep all summer—first the scales of the leaf buds will fall, then the flower petals, then small chestnuts all

Chestnuts on the tree. The heavy fruits fall in September.   *Avoid planting a chestnut next to a terrace.*

summer, after which large chestnuts will follow in autumn, and finally the leaves. The tree allows little undergrowth.
   The rare *Aesculus pavia* will grow 20 to 26½ feet (6 to 8m) tall and can be used in smaller gardens.

Alnus cordata (Alder)
height: 46 feet (14m)
   This tree likes a

Alnus gutinosa.

very moist garden. The growth habit is irregular. *Alnus incana* needs a slightly drier soil than *A. cordata*, and *A. incana* 'Laciniata' has a prettier form.

Betula pendula (syn. B. verrucosa) (White birch)
height: 50 feet (15m)
   This tree is suitable for smaller gardens. This birch lets through so much light that underplanting is possible. It is suitable for poor, dry soil. *Betula pendula* 'Youngii' does not grow as tall (20 to 26½ feet/6 to 8m), with drooping branches. *Betula costata* has a tighter form and a pure white bark. *Betula jaquemontii*, (50 feet/15m), which has a pure white bark, grows wider at the top as it ages. This tree is often sold as *B. utilis*.

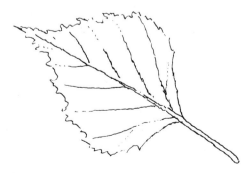

Betula pendula.

Carpinus betulus (Hornbeam)

height: 50 feet (15m)

The hornbeam will do best in dry, loamy soil. It grows very wide and is therefore suitable only for large gardens. Application as a hedge is possible in any garden, and the hornbeam can be trimmed into any shape. The leaves remain on the trees in winter, when they turn gray-brown, in contrast to the beech hedge, the leaves of which are chestnut. The *Carpinus betulus* 'Fastigiata' is narrow only when young, but will grow into a very wide tree later. This tree can be shaped into tall columns. The leaves of this variety will not stay on the trees.

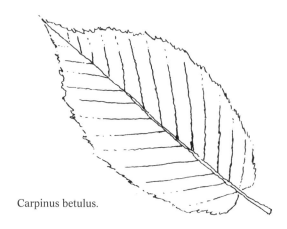

Carpinus betulus.

Castanea sativa.

Castanea sativa (European chestnut, Spanish chestnut)

height: 66 feet (20m)

This tree is not very demanding and can endure a lot of drought. It is suitable for large gardens, but sensitive to coastal winds. The fungus *Endothia* can occur and will spread.

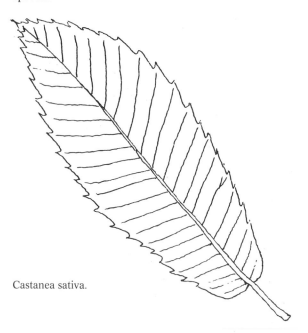

Castanea sativa.

Catalpa bignonioides (Indian bean)

height: up to 50 feet (15m)

The large, light green leaves are striking. The tree blossoms in June or July with large whitish flowers. It is sensitive to frost when young. The crown grows very wide. Because of the large leaves it is suitable only for public gardens and other gardens of appropriately large scale.

Catalpa *with pods*.

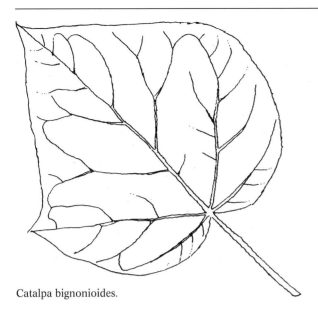

Catalpa bignonioides.

Cercidiphyllum japonicum (Katsura tree)

height: 32 feet (10m)

This small to medium-large tree is usually sold as a shrub, but will grow into a tree with more than one trunk. The small round leaves may freeze off during a late night frost. The leaves develop a beautiful color in autumn.

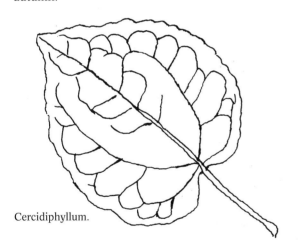

Cercidiphyllum.

Corylus colurna (Tree hazelnut)

height: 50 feet (15m)

This tree is suitable for drier soils. It has an evenly shaped crown, and the bark feels remarkably soft. The tree produces edible hazelnuts (filberts).

Crataegus (Hawthorn)

height: 13 to 30 feet (4 to 9m)

Hawthorns are excellent as street trees, in city gardens, and in the landscape. They can be grown as hedges as well as trees. The caterpillars that may eat all the leaves off the tree can be a nuisance.

C. laevigata (English hawthorn)

height: 10 to 20 feet (3 to 6m)

The best-known varieties are the double pink-red 'Paul's Scarlet' and the double white 'Plena'. They are very suitable for country homes. Caterpillars may be a nuisance, but will not kill the tree.

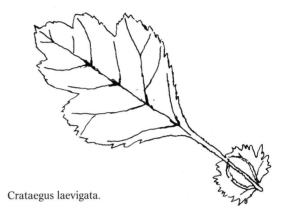

Crataegus laevigata.

C. monogyna (English hawthorn, single-seed hawthorn)

This is the most common European variety. The variety 'Stricta' grows up to 26½ feet (8m) tall. This narrow, rising tree is sensitive to wind.

The English hawthorn, Crataegus monogyna, *is suitable for street plantings and also as a hedge. The berries are popular with birds.*

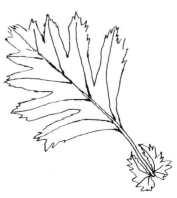

Crataegus monogyna.

C. × prunifolia
height: 20 feet (6m) maximum

This tree has dark green, glossy leaves. The dark red fruit, which remains on the trees after the leaves have dropped, is remarkable. The tree forms a wide, flat top.

Davidia involucrata (Handkerchief tree)
height: 26½ to 33 feet (8 to 10m)

This medium-large tree has large leaves. The common name is derived from the large white leaf bracts. The "handkerchiefs" hang on the trees in May and June.

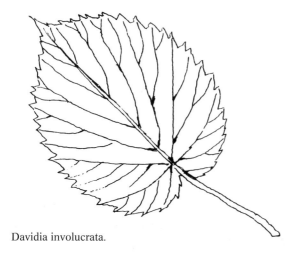

Davidia involucrata.

Fagus sylvatica (European beech)
height: 100 feet (30m)

This large denizen of the forest is suitable for large gardens. Avenues of country estates are often bordered by beeches. The tree does not let through much light, and for that reason underplanting is discouraged. The beechnut is edible. The beech grows slowly. Some notable

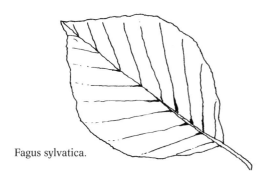

Fagus sylvatica.

varieties are:

F. s. 'Asplenifolia' (fern-leafed beech)
height: up to 50 feet (15m)

This is a smaller beech with deeply cut leaves.

F. s. 'Dawyckii' (syn. 'Fastigiata')

This is a large beech with a fastigiate (columnar) shape.

Beechnut seedling.

F. s. 'Pendula' (weeping beech)
height: up to 83 feet (25m)

This tree grows very broad and has hanging branches. Give it enough space!

F. s. 'Purpurea'

This tree has purple-brown leaves. Because they are grown from seed, the color of the leaves is not the same for every plant. For that reason, select a tree from the nursery in summer—when you can examine the color of the leaves—and transplant it in autumn.

Fagus sylvatica 'Pendula'.

F. s. 'Purpurea Pendula'

This is a smaller, weeping tree with red leaves. It also is suitable for the smaller garden.

Fraxinus (Ash)

height: 66 to 83 feet (20 to 25m)

Fraxinus excelsior, the European ash, is a strong tree that is not demanding as far as soil, sun, and wind are concerned. A number of remarkable varieties are available:

Fraxinus excelsior.

F. e. 'Diversifolia'

This ash does not have the pinnate leaves of the other varieties of ash.

Save the leaves of beech trees. They will decompose slowly, and are excellent mulch for placing under acid-loving plants. Moreover, the leaves on the soil surface will discourage the growth of weeds.

F. e. 'Jaspidea'

This tree has yellow leaves, like 'Aurea', but the latter grows more slowly.

F. ornus (flowering ash).

The Fraxinus excelsior *'Aurea' grows much more slowly than F. e. 'Jaspidea'. The tree starts to color yellow in September. The silver fir on its left is 125 years old.*

height: up to 26½ feet (8m)
F. o. 'Obelisk'

This variety, with its rising shape, is suitable for smaller gardens.

Ginkgo biloba (Maidenhair tree)
height: 50 to 66 feet (15 to 20m)

The maidenhair tree has a tendency to grow more than one trunk. Regularly remove the double tops from the tree to get a nice single trunk later. There is a difference in appearance between the male and female trees: the female will grow broader. *Ginkgo biloba* 'Fastigiata' forms a column; 'Pendula' has hanging branches.

Ginkgo biloba, *a class apart.*

Gleditsia (Honey locust)
height: 66 feet (20m)

This tree has an open structure and fine pinnate leaves. It can live to be very old. The variety 'Inermis' is thornless. 'Rubilace' will remain smaller, as will 'Sunburst', which is often planted for its yellow to yellow-green foliage.

Gleditsia triacanthos.

Gymnocladus
height: 33 to 50 feet (10 to 15m)

Gymnocladus dioicas will remind you of an ash because of its leaves. Do not plant it in dry soil. It is sensitive to wind and therefore not suitable for coastal areas.

Juglans (Walnut)
height: 66 feet (20m)

As you may have read in the section on fruit crops, there are two varieties, of which *Juglans nigra* is less sensitive to frost. It is suitable only for larger gardens. Juglans used to be planted near kitchens to repel flies.

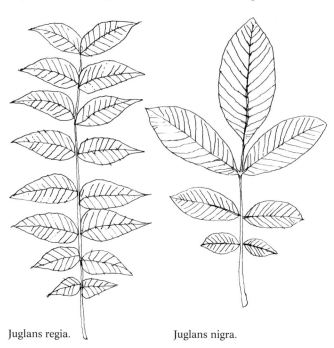

Juglans regia.   Juglans nigra.

Koelreuteria (Golden-Rain tree)
height: 16½ feet (5m)

Koelreuteria paniculata (varnish tree), an ideal city tree, is not very demanding. It is sensitive to frost when young.

Koelreuteria paniculata.

Laburnum (**Laburnum**)

height: 16½ feet (5m)

The laburnum is sold as a bush as well as a standard tree. It is one of the best trees for small gardens. See page 249 for more information.

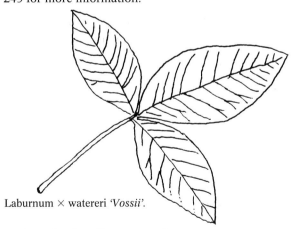

Laburnum × watereri *'Vossii'*.

Liquidambar (**Sweet gum**)

height: 50 feet (15m)

Varieties of this tree are suitable for virtually any location. The leaves look like the foliage of ivy; their color in autumn is unsurpassed.

Liriodendron (**Tulip tree**)

height: 66 to 83 feet (20 to 25m)

Koelreuteria paniculata.

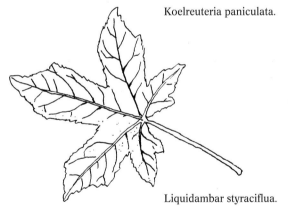

Liquidambar styraciflua.

The tulip tree is a large, wide tree that shows to advantage only in large parks or large gardens. The leaves have the form of tulips, hence the name *Liriodendron tulipifera*. The variety 'Fastigiatum' grows into a narrower tree suitable for medium-large gardens. *Liriodendron tulipfera* 'Aureomarginatum' has foliage with yellow-green margins.

Liriodendron tulipiferum.

The leaves and flower bud of the true tulip tree (Liriodendron tulipifera). *The magnolia is often called "tulip tree," but the difference is obvious: the leaves of* L. tulipifera *resemble the flower form of the tulip.*

Magnolia (Magnolia)

height: 20 to 26½ feet (6 to 8m)

Except for limy soil, the tree magnolia, *Magnolia kobus*, grows in every type of soil. It is fully hardy. The flowers suffer greatly from wind and late night frost in spring. The pure white flowers appear in April and May before there are any leaves. This tree is suitable for smaller gardens. See also page 251.

Magnolia *'Kewensis'*.

Malus (Crab apple)

height: 10 to 16½ feet (3 to 5m)

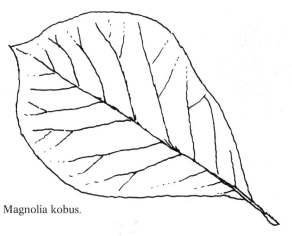

Magnolia kobus.

The crab apple flowers abundantly in spring and has beautiful fruit in late summer and autumn. Most crab apples have a wide, full crown. Buy the standard tree; height of the trunk is 7 feet (2m). Crab apples—you can make jam of the fruits—are suitable for smaller gardens.

Malus baccata *'Mandshurica'*.

Morus (Mulberry)

The white mulberry, *Morus alba*, is a small tree with white, red, or dark purple fruit. The black mulberry, *M. nigra*, is a large bush, which you can buy as a standard or small tree. As a bush it is often trained. The fruit is red to black. Do not plant mulberries in soil that is too moist, and give them a spot sheltered from frost. Mulberry trees can live to be as old as five hundred years.

Nothofagus

height: 16½ to 26½ feet (5 to 8m)

Nothofagus has fanciful branches with white lenticels. The small leaves color yellow in autumn. It is a suitable tree for large tubs, roof terraces, and small city gardens, and also fits in very well in the heather garden.

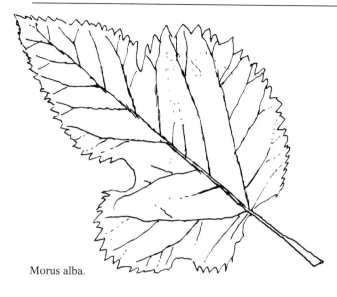

Morus alba.

Parrotia persica
height: 20 feet (6m)

This tree is always sold as a bush. You will have to make a tree out of the bush yourself, by pruning and leaving only one trunk, and gradually pruning to fashion a crown. *Parrotia* is suitable for partial shade and has unsurpassed autumnal colors.

Paulownia
height: more than 33 feet (10m)

This tree is popular for its light purple, trumpetlike flowers. Though it is not a tall tree, it is unsuitable for small gardens. The large leaves (up to 15½ inches/40cm) are out of proportion to the surrounding plants, and are all the more noticeable for their striking light green color. Especially young trees suffer from frost, and the flower buds of older trees are particularly susceptible to frost damage. A sheltered location is desirable.

Platanus (Sycamore, plane tree)
height: 66 to 100 feet (20 to 30m)

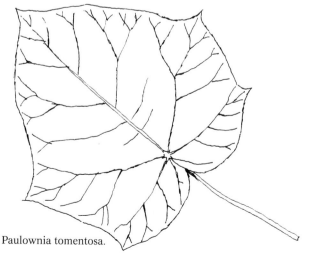

Paulownia tomentosa.

Sycamores are suitable for large parks and for lining avenues. When the tree is older, portions of the bark fall off. The trunk looks like a jigsaw puzzle with pieces missing, as those places that have shed bark are lighter in color.

Populus (Poplar, aspen, cottonwood)
height: 83 feet (25m)

The poplar grows very quickly, and this may induce you to select it for a new garden, but remember that you will have to cut down the tree later—and that may ruin your garden. Though the tree can live more than one hundred years, large branches start to break off in strong winds after only fifteen years. This can cause considerable damage around the tree. In addition to this, the roots can push up pavement. The poplar is not suitable for gardens, but we could make an exception for the *Populus simonii* 'Fastigiata', which grows 50 feet (15m) tall at most; though the cultivar name suggests otherwise, this tree becomes very broad.

Prunus

The ornamental cherries with the large pink flowers are well known. Most people are so taken with the

Poplar.

striking flowers that they overlook the decidedly ugly form of the tree. There are other ornamental cherries, some of European origin, which are better suited for use in the garden because their form is more beautiful.

P. cerasifera (cherry plum)
height: 13 to 23 feet (4 to 7m)

This tree is not often grown. There are four varieties with red leaves: *Prunus cerasifera* 'Atropurpurea' (syn.

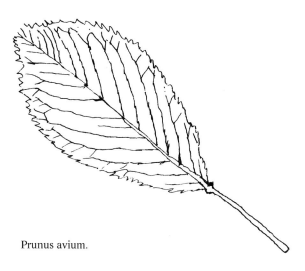

Prunus avium.

P. pissardii) with white flowers; *P.c.* 'Hollywood' (syn. 'Trailblazer') has pink flowers and also yields large edible red plums; *P.c.* 'Nigra' has rather large leaves; the smallest is *P.c.* 'Woodii'.

P. avium (sweet cherry)
height: 33 to 50 feet (10 to 15m)

The sweet cherry is suitable for many purposes: It can be used in a street, it looks pretty in a landscape, and it is suitable for larger city gardens. It has white flowers, like the variety 'Plena', which has fully double flowers.

P. padus (European bird cherry)
height: 26½ to 40 feet (8 to 12m)

This tree can grow in some shade and is nice in combination with all kinds of plants, in the landscape, and in small city gardens.

P. serotina (black cherry)
height: 80 feet (24m)

This large tree or shrub has glossy leaves in profusion. Because it has spread in European forests, it is discouraged there. It produces abundant small white flowers.

P. serrulata (Japanese flowering cherry)
height: 20 to 26½ feet (6 to 8m)

Who is not acquainted with this tree? The large pink bunches of flowers in spring create a brief, but memorable blossoming. *Prunus serrulata* 'Amanogawa' grows into an erect tree up to 20 feet (6m) tall, and is suitable for smaller gardens. *Prunus serrulata* 'Kiku-shidare-sakura' also has pink flowers and is a weeping variety. As a street tree we often come across the *P.s.* 'Kwanzan', a broad tree with semidouble pink flowers and brown-red buds. The *P.s.* 'Shimidsu-sakura', with fully double flowers, is a large spreading tree.

P. subhirtella (higan cherry)
height: 16½ feet (5m)

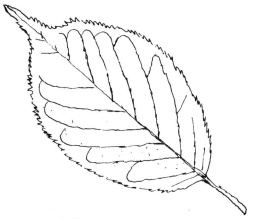

Prunus serrulata *'Kwanzan'.*

Various varieties of this species are grown as shrubs and trees. *Prunus subhirtella* 'Autumnalis' produces small white flowers from November to April, depending on the weather. *Prunus subhirtella* 'Rosea' flowers during

Prunus *'Kursar F₂'*.

the same period, but has light pink flowers, and its branches are sturdier. *Prunus subhirtella* 'Fukubana' has semidouble, dark red flowers; this small tree blossoms throughout the month of April.

P. triloba (flowering almond)
height: up to 5 feet (1.5m)

This is actually more of a shrub, but grafted onto a small tree it is suitable for large pots and in very small gardens. Important: Immediately after flowering, prune all branches just above the grafting scar. If this is not done, the tree will lose its form and will yield fewer flowers. In the case of all ornamental cherries, suckers and shoots from rootstocks should be removed.

Pterocarya (Wingnut)
height: 50 feet (15m)

These large, broad trees are suitable for planting in parks. *Pterocarya fraxinifolia* is most often planted; the name indicates that the leaves look very much like those of the ash.

Pyrus (Pear)
height: 20 to 26½ feet (6 to 8m)

Pyrus salicifolia, the willow-leaved pear, with narrow gray-green leaves is an ideal tree for smaller gardens. The

Prunus serrulata.

Pterocarya fraxinifolia.

form of the tree is pretty; the flowers do not amount to much. *Pyrus salicifolia* 'Pendula' is a weeping form of *P. salicifolia,* very decorative, with an extremely delicate appearance.

Pyrus salicifolia *'Pendula'.*

Quercus (Oak)

height: 83 feet (25m)

Oaks are large trees for parks and avenues. They grow slowly. There are few gardens in which oaks can be used. You can make an exception for *Quercus robur* 'Fastigiata', an erect, columnar oak.

Acorns on an oak.

Robinia (Locust)

height: 66 feet (20m)

Though these are large trees, they can be planted in smaller gardens. The crown is airy and open, so underplanting is possible. The trees grow so quickly in rich soil that the branches will remain soft and break easily. For that reason, plant it by preference in relatively poor soil, and do not give the tree any manure. If the tree grows in rich soil, you must be watchful. 'Umbraculifera' has a nice round form, but brittle branches are a problem; regularly prune the top to prevent this from happening.

Robinia pseudoacacia.

Salix (Willow)

height: 66 feet (20m)

These quick-growing trees, like poplars, are not suitable for the average garden. In a pollarded form the ordinary willow can be planted in medium-size gardens; it should be pollarded once every three years. *Salix matsudana* 'Tortuosa' is often planted; the "corkscrew" branches are unusual. Give this tree much space: it will soon grow 40 feet (12m) tall! *Salix alba* 'Tristis', the weeping willow, also takes a lot of room. A small weeping willow is *S. caprea* 'Pendula', for small and even very small gardens. From the height at which it was grafted, this tree grows only downward. Many willows have the form of shrubs and are suitable for use in gardens.

Willow catkins early in spring.

Page 227: The oak is planted for its handsome foliage.

Salix alba *'Tristis'*.

Sophora

height: 33 to 50 feet (10 to 15m)

This tree requires dry soil. It looks somewhat like an acacia, and yet is suitable for smaller gardens. *Sophora japonica* is sensitive to frost, especially when it is still young. The beautiful weeping form *S. j.* 'Pendula' is especially nice in smaller gardens.

Sophora japonica.

Sorbus (Mountain ash)

height: 13 to 40 feet (4 to 12m)

Sorbus likes dry soil; heavy clay is not suitable. The trees all bear bunches of white flowers and orange or red berries. Do not plant them too close to the front door, as berries that travel indoors on the soles of your shoes will stain the carpet. The common variety is *Sorbus aucuparia*. A particularly nice variety is *S. intermedia*, the Swedish whitebeam, the foliage of which is gray and soft underneath.

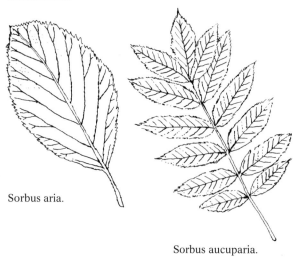

Sorbus aria.

Sorbus aucuparia.

Tilia (Linden, lime tree, basswood)

height: 66 feet (20m)

These strong trees can live to be very old, perhaps more than a thousand years. They are suitable for avenues and as city trees. Do not plant them next to a terrace or a parking place because of the sticky honeydew excretion of the aphids that can plague these trees. This sweetish discharge causes sooty mold, turning the leaves black. *Tilia* are not demanding as far as soil is concerned. Cultivated varieties are:

Tilia americana	(Basswood)
T. cordata	(Small-leaved European linden)
T. × euchlora	(Crimean linden)
T. × europaea	(Common lime)
T. petiolaris	(Pendant silver linden)
T. platyphyllos	(Large-leaved linden)
T. tomentosa	(Silver linden)

Ulmus (Elm)

height: 66 feet (20m)

Dutch elm disease is still the reason that planting on a large scale is advised against. Even in gardens in which one tree can determine what the garden looks like, it is recommended to choose a different tree. Instead of *Ulmus glabra* 'Camperdownii', *Betula pendula* 'Youngii'

Sorbus aucuparia.

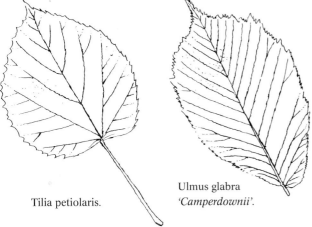

Tilia petiolaris.

Ulmus glabra
'Camperdownii'.

and suitable for all types of soil, but it cannot endure wind. It is related to the elm and, like the elm, susceptible to Dutch elm disease. The seed of the zelkova can be sown immediately after harvesting. Layering is another good method of propagation. The zelkova can be grafted onto the elm, too. The tree requires a fertile, well-aerated soil.

is now recommended. Varieties of the past twenty years are 'Dodoens', 'Plantijn', 'Lobel', and 'Clusius'. They are less sensitive to Dutch elm disease, but not entirely immune. Dutch elm disease is caused by a fungus that is passed on by the *Scolytus scolytus*. The best way to fight it is to remove the bark of the cut-down tree immediately. Never keep firewood cut from elm trees with bark; elm trees still growing nearby will surely be affected after one year.

Zelkova

height: 33 to 40 feet (10 to 12m)

This medium-tall tree with a flat, round crown is strong

Zelkova serrata.

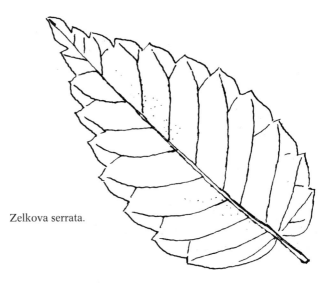

9 Shrubs A to Z

Shrubs have a place in every garden, and for every type of soil and environment, an appropriate shrub can be found. You can select a shrub for its flowers, size, pleasing color, form, or its ornamental berries. Many shrubs are suitable as underplanting for trees. Others create a nice background against which to view a border of perennials.

Shrubs with Aromatic Leaves

Shrubs with pleasant-smelling foliage are lovely in a garden, especially for the visually handicapped. Sometimes the fragrance is noticeable simply when you pass the shrub; in other cases, you must touch or crush the leaves between your fingers to be able to enjoy the fragrance.

Artemisia arborescens
Caryopteris
Escallonia
Gaultheria
Lavandula
Myrica
Perovskia
Ribes sanguineum
Rosmarinus
Santolina
Skimmia

Viburnum opulus, *the guelder rose, bears fertile and sterile flowers. The V.o. 'Roseum', the snowball bush, has sterile flowers only.*

Shrubs for Beautiful Autumn Color

Acer (most species)
Aesculus parviflora
Amelanchier
Aronia
Berberis (most species)
Callicarpa
Cornus (most species)
Corylopsis
Cotinus
Enkianthus
Euonymus
Fothergilla
Hamamelis
Rhus
Rosa (species roses)
Stephanandra
Viburnum (most species)

Prunus spinosa.

If a garden is close to the seashore or otherwise receives a considerable amount of wind, autumn foliage really isn't a particular concern for you; the effect would be wasted. If your garden is sheltered from the wind, however, you will be able to enjoy the exciting change of colors every year.

Shrubs for Deep Shade
Arctostaphylos
Aucuba japonica
Buxus
Cornus canadensis
Elaeagnus × *ebbingei*
Euonymus fortunei
Hedera helix 'Arborea'
Hyperiacum calycinum
Ilex aquifolium
Ligustrum
Lonicera nitida
Lonicera pileata
Mahonia aquifolium
Osmanthus
Prunus lusitanica
Ribes alpinum
Rubus odoratus
Skimmia
Symphoricarpos
Viburnum davidii
Vinca species

Most of these shrubs will also do well in full sun. In general, shade-loving plants can withstand the sun (though not the brightest of afternoon sun in some cases), while true sun-worshipers do not thrive in shade. (This goes for perennials, too.)

Shrubs with Red Leaves
Give the garden variety by planting one or two shrubs with reddish foliage. It is easy to use too many of them, as it is with variegated plants. A shrub with red or variegated leaves makes a nice endpoint to mark the termination of a path. Use it as an accent. Here are a number of shrubs with red foliage:
Acer palmatum 'Atropurpureum'
Acer palmatum 'Dissectum Atropurpureum'
Berberis thunbergii 'Atropurpurea'
Corylus maxima 'Purpurea'
Cotinus coggygria 'Royal Purple'
Euonymus europaeas 'Atropurpureum'
Phormium tenax 'Purpureum'
Prunus spinosa 'Purpurea'
Sambucus nigra 'Purpurea'
Weigela purpura

The alder buckthorn can withstand a lot of wind, and in nature it can be found growing near the seashore; it stands up to salty coastal winds well. Use this shrub as a quick-growing windbreak around the new garden.

Shrubs That Stand Up to Wind

Suitable for a windy spot inland, and also for the seaside balcony:

Colutea
Cotoneaster
Cytisus
Eleagnus
Escallonia
Euonymus
Fuchsia magellanica
Garrya
Hippophae
Hydrangea
Lavatera olbia
Lonicera pileata
Myrica
Prunus spinosa
Rhamnus
Rosa (species roses)
Sambucus
Spiraea
Tamarix
Viburnum
Yucca

   The art of good garden design for a certain spot (in this particular case, a windy spot), is to find the right plants. A plant that grows under conditions it likes is better equipped to fight off disease and pests. The plants from the above list will do even better when they are in a more sheltered location. They will, however, grow well in the wind's path, in places where other plants will give up.

Flowering Shrubs for Every Month of the Year

January

Garrya	6½ feet (2m)	yellow-green
Hamamelis	10 feet (3m)	yellow
Jasminum (as shrub)	5 feet (1.5m)	yellow
Lonicera standishii	6½ feet (2m)	
Viburnum × bodnantense	8 feet (2.5m)	pink
Viburnum farreri	10 feet (3m)	pink
Viburnum tinus	10 feet (3m)	pink

February

Cornus mas	13 feet (4m)	yellow
Daphne mezereum	6½ feet (2m)	purple
Mahonia japonica	6½ feet (2m)	yellow
Ulex europaeus	6½ feet (2m)	yellow

March

Corylopsis	5 feet (1.5m)	yellow
Forsythia	8 feet (2.5m)	yellow
Magnolia stellata	10 feet (3m)	white
Mahonia	5 feet (1.5m)	yellow
Osmanthus	6½ feet (2m)	white

April

Amelanchier	11½ feet (3.5m)	white
Berberis species	10 feet (3m)	various colors
Chaenomeles	6½ feet (2m)	orange/yellow
Cytisus	6½ feet (2m)	yellow
Kerria	8 feet (2.5m)	yellow
Magnolia × soulangiana	13 feet (4m)	pink/white

The flowers of the Prunus × serrulata *'Kwanzan', the Japanese flowering cherry, will not stay perfect for long, but when they bloom, they do so abundantly.*

Pieris	6½ feet (2m)	pink
Prunus species		
Ribes	8 feet (2.5m)	white, red, pink
Spiraea × arguta	8 feet (2.5m)	white
May		
Cornus florida	13 feet (4m)	white
Cotoneaster	10 feet (3m)	white
Enkianthus	11½ feet (3.5m)	pink
Halesia	20 feet (6m)	white
Kolkwitzia	6½ feet (2m)	pink
Ledum		
Lonicera		
Paeonia	5 feet (1.5m)	various colors
Potentilla	3 feet (1m)	various colors
Pyracantha	6½ feet (2m)	white
June		
Abelia	3 feet (1m)	pink
Buddleia globosa	6½ feet (2m)	yellow
Colutea	6½ feet (2m)	yellow
Cornus kousa	13 feet (4m)	white
Deutzia	8 feet (2.5m)	white
Genista	3 feet (1m)	yellow
Kalmia	3 feet (1m)	pink
Neillia	5 feet (1.5m)	various colors

The alder buckthorn, Rhamnus frangula, *belongs in the garden of every bird lover. It tolerates shade.*

Philadelphus	3 to 10 feet (1 to 3m)	white
Rhododendron	(0.5 to 4m)	various colors
Rubus	3 to 10 feet (1 to 3m)	various colors
Spiraea	1½ to 8 feet	various colors
	(0.5 to 2.5m)	
Syringa	3 to 10 feet (1 to 3m)	various colors
Viburnum	3 to 10 feet (1 to 3m)	various colors
Weigela	3 to 6½ feet (1 to 2m)	various colors

Prunus padus.

July

Buddleia	6½ feet (2m)	various colors
Fuchsia	3 feet (1m)	red-pink
Hydrangea	3 to 6½ feet (1 to 2m)	various colors
Hypericum	3 feet (1m)	yellow
Indigofera	6½ feet (2m)	pink-purple
Yucca	3 feet (1m)	white

August

Buddleia	6½ feet (2m)	various colors
Caryopteris	5 feet (1.5m)	blue
Ceanothus	6½ feet (2m)	pink and blue
Hibiscus	8 feet (2.5m)	various colors
Hydrangea	6½ feet (2m)	various colors
Lavandula	3 feet (1m)	blue
Perovskia	3 feet (1m)	blue

September

Aralia	13 feet (4m)	white
Campsis radicans		red
Hebe species		various colors

Plants listed under August will still be in flower.

October

Fuchsia *magellanica*	5 feet (1.5m)	red

November

Prunus subhirtella 'Autumnalis'	10 feet (3m)	pink
Viburnum	10 feet (3m)	pink

December

Prunus subhirtella 'Autumnalis'	10 feet (3m)	pink

Acer japonicum *'Aureum'*.

Acer palmatum.

The following have beautiful buds:
Hedera helix 'Arborea'
Skimmia
See plants listed under January.

Shrubs with Brown Leaves

Sometimes it is necessary to give a border a special accent. Especially in places where a path meets up with a border, it is nice to have some sort of punctuation. This accent mark might take the form of a garden bench, a planted container, a chair, a statue, or a shrub that stands out from the surrounding foliage. A shrub with bronze or brown foliage makes a nice contrast in a perennial or shrub border.
Some examples:

Acer palmatum 'Atropurpurea'
Berberis thunbergii 'Atropurpurea'
Corylus maxima 'Purpurea'

All shrubs with the variety name 'Purpurea' or 'Atropurpurea' have bronze-brown leaves that may shade to purple or red. (In the case of perennials, this varietal name sometimes denotes the color of the flowers.)

Remember that plants with brownish leaves prefer sun; the color of the leaves will look better if the plant is in a sunny location. These plants need more light because they have less chlorophyll, the compound plants use to convert sunlight into food. The same goes for variegated plants that have a lot of white in their leaves–give them sun.

Acanthopanax

height: 10 feet (3m)
bloom: June, July

Acanthopanax sieboldanius has hand-shaped leaves that remind one of the chestnut. The name has as many syllables as there are leaves on the compound leaf. This shrub flowers with small, green-yellow flowers. The whole shrub bears sharp thorns and is suitable for a rather thick, impenetrable hedge.

Acer (Maple)

This is a diverse genus of trees and shrubs. *Acer palmatum* may be the best known and is especially suitable for the Japanese garden. The shrub is somewhat sensitive to frost.

	leaves	height
A. palmatum	green	10 to 16½ feet (3 to 5m)
A. palmatum 'Atropurpureum'	red	10 to 13 feet (3 to 4m)
A. p. 'Dissectum'	green, pinnate	6½ feet (2m)
A. p. 'Dissectum Atropurpureum'	red	3 to 5 feet (1 to 1.5m)
A. p. 'Dissectum Nigrum'	dark purplish red	3 to 5 feet (1 to 1.5m)
A. p. 'Dissectum Ornatum'	purplish red	3 to 5 feet (1 to 1.5m)

Amelanchier lamarckii.

The low-growing varieties are especially suitable for small sunny gardens. They grow very slowly.

Aesculus (Chestnut)

height: 13 feet (4m)

The common *Aesculus*, the white horse chestnut, is generally known. *Aesculus parviflora* is more suitable for smaller gardens. It grows in the form of a shrub. The maximum height is 13 feet (4m), but the shrub usually remains smaller. The flowers are similar to those of the common chestnut, but they appear later in summer and with wispy flowers.

Amelanchier (Serviceberry, juneberry)

height: 13 feet (4m)
bloom: April, May

This shrub has an open structure. *Amelanchier lamarckii* is often planted. In early spring the leaves are bronze-colored. The shrub offers white flowers

Amelanchier lamarckii. *The flowers appear almost at the same time as the budding leaves.*

and has beautiful autumnal color. It is propagated by seed.

Andromeda (Bog rosemary)
height: 4 inches (10cm)

This genus used to be listed under *Pieris. Andromeda polifolia* (syn. *A. rosmarinifolia*) looks like heather, with very narrow leaves and pink flowers. This creeper shrub needs acid soil.

Aralia

The most common shrub of this genus is *Aralia elata*, which grows 16½ feet (5m) tall and has large leaves. The entire plant has thorns. Large cream-white umbels are borne at the top of the plant. The genus *Aralia* includes some perennials and some plants suitable for indoor culture.

Arbutus (Manzanita, strawberry tree)

The shrub is suitable only for very sheltered spots. In warmer climates *Arbutus unedo* grows quite tall; in temperate climates it grows into a large shrub. It is most suitable as a potted plant. The white flowers and red leaf stalks are most striking. The fruit reminds one of strawberries.

Arctostaphylos (Bearberry)

This creeping shrub with heatherlike white flowers blooms in May. The round, red berries are attractive. This shrub is an evergreen and requires acid soil.

Aronia (Chokeberry)
height: up to 5 feet (1.5m)

These nice, low-growing shrubs flower in pink or white; black fruit follows. They are easy shrubs for every type of soil in the sun or partial shade.

Aronia.

Aucuba japonica *'Rozannie' has green leaves without the* yellow spots. This shows the *berries to advantage.*

Aucuba

The aucuba, which will grow up to 10 feet (3m) tall, is hardy only if planted on a sheltered spot. Do not plant them in a location that bakes in morning sun. Plants with yellow-spotted leaves are usually offered, but do try to find one with green leaves. Aucuba looks best combined with the other plants in the garden. The flowers are insignificant; it is the leaves and berries that make it beautiful. The berries remain on the shrub for a long time. Aucubas are the best evergreens for city gardens, especially when given acid, humus soil.

Varieties with green leaves (without spots) are:
Aucuba japonica 'Borealis'
A. j. 'Longifolia'
A. j. 'Dentata'
A. j. 'Rozannie'
A. j. 'Hillieri'

Azalea
See *Rhododendron*, page 414.

Page 237: Arbutus unedo.

Berberis *species.*

Berberis (Barberry)

The genus *Berberis* has more than two hundred species. Some of these are evergreens. *Berberis thunbergii*, the green *Berberis* used for hedges, is most common. *Berberis thunbergii* 'Atropurpurea' has red leaves.

Evergreen *Berberis*
B. *darwinii*
B. *frikartii*
B. *candidula*
B. *gagnepainii*
B. *julianae*
B. *linearifolia*
B. × *stenophylla*
B. *verruculosa*

Deciduous *Berberis*
B. *aggregata*
B. *koreana*
B. × *ottawensis*
B. *thunbergii*
B. *wilsoniae*

All *Berberis* varieties have thorns. This makes pruning the shrubs very unpleasant, even more so because these thorns immediately cause inflammation. Wear good gloves during pruning.

Buddleia

This shrub is cherished because it attracts butterflies. What is less well known is that it is sensitive to frost; earth up the shrub in winter to help prevent damage. This shrub is different from all other shrubs as far as pruning is concerned. Cut off all branches to 20 inches (50cm) after the last frost in spring. If you do not cut the branches back, the shrub will grow very tall and produce fewer flowers. Buddleias can be propagated easily from cuttings. The flowers appear in August and may remain until late in autumn.

Some species and varieties of note:
Buddleia globosa	yellow
B. × *weyeriana* 'Sungold'	orange
B. *davidii* 'Ile de France'	dark violet
B. *d.* 'White Profusion'	white
B. *d.* 'Royal Red'	purple-red
B. *d.* 'Empire Blue'	bright blue
B. *d.* 'Pink Delight'	pink

Buxus (Box)

Box is an evergreen that is often used for hedges and for topiary. The shrub can grow as tall as 16½ feet (5m) if planted as a solitary shrub. There are varieties that differ in size, shape and color of foliage, and growth habit.

When planting *Buxus* for hedges, you should take into account that shrubs bought a year later may grow differently and not fit in very well with the existing hedge. Buy the *Buxus* from a professional who propagates them using the same "mother" plants. Taking cuttings yourself is not very difficult; it does, however, take a year before roots develop on the cuttings. Plant the cuttings close together on a shady spot, and do not let them dry during the summer.

Callicarpa (Beautyberry)

height: 10 feet (3m)

This plain-looking shrub has a fastigiate growth habit. The clusters of purple berries are elegant, and they remain on the shrub for a long time. The branches and berries

A cut branch with berries of Callicarpa bodinieri *remains beautiful when dried. Plant it close to a window to be able to enjoy the beautiful berries all winter.*

can be dried and will keep virtually forever. An especially desirable shrub is *Callicarpa bodinieri* 'Profusion', because it is self-pollinating.

Calycanthus (Sweet shrub)
height: up to 8 feet (2.5m)

This slow-growing shrub bears dark red flowers. *Calycanthus floridus* is the best known, but the variety 'Purpureus' has nicer foliage and flowers more abundantly.

Camellia
Though hardy varieties are sold nowadays, it is not recommended to plant camellias outdoors in an unsheltered location except in warmer climates. They cannot endure any morning sun after frost. Plant them preferably in acid soil in an unheated greenhouse. These evergreen shrubs have beautiful leathery leaves.

Caragana (Pea tree, pea shrub)
height: 10 feet (3m)

A rising shrub with fine, light green leaves is *Caragana arborescens*. The yellow flowers blossom in small bunches between the leaves. The shrub can be planted in sun or partial shade. The weeping variety is grafted onto a rootstock. The shrub, especially attractive during blossoming, is worth looking at all summer long.

Buxus is suitable for growing in a container.

Caryopteris (Bluebeard)
This shrub flowers on one-year-old wood. After freezing in winter it can be cut down to the ground. The light blue flowers appear in August and September. The most common species is *Caryopteris × clandonensis*, of which the varieties 'Heavenly Blue' and 'Kew Blue' flower more abundantly. The species *C. incana* has gray tomentose leaves and fits very nicely in the butterfly garden.

Ceanothus
The *Ceanothus* slightly resembles *Caryopteris*, and blossoms around the same time too. The plant is evergreen and can withstand only light frost. It is recommended only as a potted plant, but it may thrive against a sheltered warm wall with a western exposure. The *Ceanothus* hybrid 'Gloire de Versailles' is often available. Less hardy varieties can be found that bloom in bright blue and pink.

Chaenomeles (Flowering quince)
Chaenomeles has flowers resembling those of apple trees, in the colors pink, orange, and red, and fruit that looks like apples, varying in color from yellow, and yellow-

Chaenomelis japonica.

green to green. Some varieties :

shorter than 2½ feet (75cm)

C. japonica 'Sargentii'	orange
C. speciosa 'Simonii'	blood red
C. × superba 'Crimson and Gold'	dark red
C. × s. 'Stanford Red'	pink-red

2½ to 3 feet (75 to 100cm)

C. × superba 'Nicoline'	scarlet

4 feet (1.25m)

C. × superba 'Fire Dance'	dark red

5 feet (1.5m)

C. speciosa 'Rosa Plena'	pink
C. × superba 'Clementine'	orange-red
C. × s. 'Coral Sea'	

6½ feet (2m)

	salmon pink
C. speciosa 'Spitfire'	crimson
C. s. 'Umbilicata'	bright pink
C. × superba 'Bright Hedge'	orange
C. × s. 'Ernst Finken'	red

Clethra (Summer sweet)

This special shrub for the heather garden requires acid soil and flowers in August and September with white flowers. *Clethra alnifolia* will grow 6½ feet (2m) tall and has handsome yellow autumnal color.

Colutea (Bladder senna)

Best known is *Colutea arborescens*, a fastigiate shrub with very fine, light green foliage. The flowers of this 13-foot-tall (4m) shrub are yellow. It flowers in May and June.

Cornus (Dogwood)

There are many varieties of this garden shrub to use for the lovely flowers, the color of the leaves or branches, the shape of the shrub, or the eye-catching autumn color. Among the creepers is *Cornus canadensis*, with white flowers and red berries. *Cornus alba* has beautiful reddish branches; more beautiful still is *Cornus alba* 'Sibirica', with bright red branches. (This shrub also has tidier growth and reaches 10 feet [3m] high.) *Cornus alba* 'Elegantissima' has white variegated leaves; *C. a.* 'Gouchaultii' has yellow leaves. Remarkably yellow twigs are borne by *C. sericea* 'Flaviramea', which, like *C. sanguinea*, is not among the tidy garden shrubs. Branches touching the soil will immediately grow roots, and the result is a mess after a number of years. Tall shrubs with large white flowers include *C. florida* and *C. kousa*. The flowers very much resemble those of clematis. Best known is the *C. mas*, with yellow flowers in early spring. The shrub grows tall and can't be considered a jewel in your garden until it ages some.

Corylopsis (Winter hazel)

At the sight of yellow flowers early in the year, people usually think of the forsythia. A more refined shrub with

Cornus alba.

Cornus mas.

Cotinus coggygria.

slow growth is *Corylopsis pauciflora*, which grows 5 feet (1.5m) tall at most. The slow-growing *C. spicata* grows slightly taller. These more expensive shrubs deserve to be used more often, especially in the smaller garden. They will grow in sun and partial shade.

Corylus (Hazelnut, filbert)

The European hazelnut, *Corylus avellana*, is a nice addition to the ornamental garden; for yellow leaves, try *C. a.* 'Aurea', and for red leaves, *C. a.* 'Fusco-rubra'. In winter, *C. a.* 'Contorta' is notable for its corkscrew branches, but the sick-looking leaves on this tree are less than attractive—try to give it a spot that makes it eye-catching in winter but not in summer. The best hazelnut for red foliage is *C. maxima* 'Purpurea', a shrub that grows 13 feet (4m) tall. The Turkish hazelnut, *C. colurna*, has the form of a tree and produces nuts. Hazelnuts grow in sun and in shade, in every type of soil.

Cotinus (Smokebush)

height: up to 13 feet (4m)

Cotynus coggygria is an evergreen and much more beautiful than *C. c.* 'Red Beauty', 'Royal Purple', or 'Rubrifolius', which are usually offered. Enormous

panicles of fine flowers make *Cotinus* a popular shrub. It is a pity that the branches can freeze off in winter. Cut off damaged branches, even though it may be at the expense of the form of the shrub.

Cotoneaster

Cotoneaster is susceptible to fire blight, which calls for vigilant pruning. *Cotoneaster dammeri* and *C. d.* 'Skogholm' and 'Coral Beauty' have a handsome creeping habit. Against walls, and especially under windows, *C. horizontalis* can be planted to pleasing effect. All cotoneasters bear white flowers and red berries, which birds love.

Deciduous

C. bullatus	8 feet (2.5m)
C. horizontalis	3 feet (1m)
C. moupinensis	8 feet (2.5m)
C. dielsianus	6½ feet (2m)
C. divaricatus	6½ feet (2m)
C. wardii	4 feet (1.25m)
C. franchetii	6 feet (1.75m)
C. zabelii	8 feet (2.5m)

Evergreen

C. dammeri	6 inches (15cm)
C. microphyllus	20 inches (50cm)

Cotoneaster dammeri 'Coral Beauty'.

C. salicifolius	3 feet (1m)

The tallest cotoneasters are *C. racemiflorus* var. *soongoricus*, *C. salicifolius* var. *floccosus*, and *C.* × *watereri* 'Cornubia'. Evergreen cotoneasters may suffer from frost in unsheltered locations.

Cytisus scoparius *(Scotch broom)*.

Crataegus (Hawthorn)

Hawthorn grows as a large shrub or a small tree. As a shrub it is suitable only for large gardens. In rural areas the hawthorn can be grown into a nice hedge. Fire blight may affect the whole shrub, and caterpillars are often pests. See also page 217.

Cydonia

See *Chaenomeles*, page 239.

Cytisus (Broom)

Everyone knows the yellow broom that grows naturally along the roadside. Its sensitivity to frost is less well known. Every now and then, broom freezes to the ground even in fairly temperate climates; usually, it will start to grow again. Keep broom young by pruning; the result will be more abundant bloom. Plant broom in a dry, sunny spot that is to be its permanent home, because the shrub does not like being transplanted. For that reason, nurseries sell only container-grown plants.

It is useless to try to take a plant from nature and transplant it in your garden. The long tap root will be damaged too much, and the plant will not survive. People used to make brooms out of wild broom, hence the common name. The cultivated broom *Cytisus* x *praecox* can be found in a number of colors: yellow and white, white, dark yellow, golden yellow, light yellow, and pink to pink-red.

Daphne

Very early, sometimes as early as March, the daphne blooms. The light and dark purple flowers are followed by poisonous red berries; the white-flowered variety 'Alba' has yellow berries. The shrub grows rather vertically to about 3 feet (1m). The garland flower, *Daphne cneorum*, is a procumbent shrub ideal for the rock garden; it bears pink flowers in April. Propagation can be done by layering: Bend a branch to touch the soil, and anchor it there on the soil surface by putting a stone on it to weight it down and keep it from springing back up. Cut the branch free of the mother plant as soon as it has grown roots.

Daphne mezereum.

Davidia

Davidia, often cultivated as a shrub, can grow to be a medium-size tree. The white flower bracts that hang on the branches (they look like handkerchiefs) are eye-catching.

Decaisnea

height: 10 feet (3m)
There is only one variety in culture: *Decaisnea fargesii*. The steel blue pods hang from the shrub, looking like pickles. Propagation takes place by sowing.

Page 243:
Pods of Cytisus scoparius.

Davidia involucrata *var.*
vilmoriana.

Deutzia

This old-fashioned shrub, of which the lower-growing varieties are now preferred, deserves to be planted more often. *Deutzia gracilis* will grow 30 inches (75cm) tall and bears pure white flowers in May and June. A pink version to be recommended is *D. × rosea*. *Deutzia × kalmiiflora* grows to medium height, and produces white flowers in May that are carmine pink on the outside. A particularly old-fashioned shrub is *D. scabra*; it grows to 10 feet (3m) tall and can be found with white, light pink, and even double flowers. *Deutzia* grows in every type of soil and prefers full sun.

Diervilla (Bush honeysuckle)

This low shrub has flowers that resemble those of *Weigela*. It flowers in July and August on one-year-old wood. You can cut these shrubs right down to the ground, and give them dry soil. They prefer full sun or partial shade. This is a good shrub for small gardens.

Elaeagnus

The evergreen varieties are especially valuable for the garden. *Elaeagnus* is suitable as a solitary shrub, and also for hedges. *Elaeagnus* species can withstand a lot of wind. *Elaeagnus × ebbingei* is the best evergreen shrub for coastal areas. Further inland the shrub should be planted in a sheltered spot because it is somewhat sensitive to frost. If winter sun shines much on a frozen plant, it may cause considerable damage. *Elaeagnus pungens*, of which the variety 'Maculata' is most often sold, has variegated leaves. This thorny shrub has a more beautiful structure. *Elaeagnus angustifolia* is deciduous, and the undersides of the leaves, like those of *E. × ebbingei*, are silver-gray. *Elaeagnus commutata* has leaves which are entirely silver-gray.

Enkianthus

height: 10 feet (3m feet)

This shrub belongs to the heather family and therefore requires acid soil. *Enkianthus campanulatus* is well known, with bunches of hanging pink flowers.

Euonymus (Spindle tree)

This genus includes a variety of shrubs. The most beautiful is *Euonymous alata*, which boasts attractive characteristics throughout the year. In winter the corky wings on the branches are shown to advantage. The shrub grows 6½ feet (2m) tall and has a round, full shape. The variety 'Compactus' remains shorter. *Euonymus europaea* grows in nature, a tall shrub, and a suitable addition to the bird-lover's garden. More beautiful than the European spindle tree is *E. sachalinensis*, with striking, large red flowers. This shrub grows 13 feet (4m) tall.

Like the other members of this genus, the autumn color of this shrub is magnificent. *Euonymus fortunei* is a low-growing evergreen creeper that can be trained as a climber, too. A number of varieties have foliage variegated with gold or silver, some leaves have three colors, and there are *Euonymous* with golden yellow leaves.

Eunonymus europaeus.

Exochorda (Pearlbush)

Exochorda giraldii grows up to 13 feet (4m) tall and has eye-catching white flowers. For small gardens the variety 'The Bride' is recommended. This compact shrub grows 3 feet (1m) tall. It is suitable for all types of soil in full sun.

Forsythia

Whether this shrub is justifiably one of the most often planted shrubs is questionable. Of course, the flowers are beautiful. But is the homely form of the shrub during the fifty weeks a year it is not in flower less important? Always plant this shrub in the second line of a shrub border, not out in front. The flowers make their impact at a time when other shrubs do not yet have any leaves. Forsythia branches are good for cutting. Flower buds do not develop until after the first period of frost, and it may occur once in a while that the plant does not flower after a winter without freezing weather. *Forsythia × intermedia* 'Lynwood' flowers most abundantly. *Forsythia suspensa* has arching, flexible branches that allow the plant to be trained as a vine.

Fothergilla

It is a pity that fothergilla is one of the least planted garden shrubs. Like the forsythia, this shrub flowers very early. Because of its slow growth it is an expensive shrub.

Eunonymus europaeus, *flower with fruit set.*

Fothergilla gardenii remains short, growing up to 3 feet (1m). *Fothergilla major* and *F. monticola* grow 6½ feet (2m) high. Fothergilla is related to the well-known *Hamamelis*, or witch hazel; the foliage resembles that of *Hamamelis*. Grow *Fothergilla* for beautiful autumn color. The brushlike, cream-yellow flowers appear early in spring.

Exochorda racemosa 'The Bride'.

Fothergilla major.

Fuchsia

The shrub fuchsia, with small red, pendant flowers, is an ideal shrub for a city garden. In a sheltered spot, the branches may not freeze to the ground; if this does happen, the plant will just come up again in spring. *Fuchsia magellanica*, native to southern Chile, is commonly known as the hardy *Fuschia*.

Gaultheria

There are two species in culture: *Gaultheria procumbens*, a creeper, and *G. shallon*, a low-growing shrub. Both require partial shade and acid soil, and are evergreen. The berries are pretty.

Genista (Broom)

This broom is much smaller than *Cytisus* (see page 242). The shortest of these are suitable for the rock garden, and can be grown to drape over low walls. The flowers are yellow. This shrub is suitable for poor soil in full sun. The following species are cultivated:

G. sagittalis	6 inches (15cm)
G. tinctoria 'Plena'	12 inches (30cm)
G. germanica	20 inches (50cm)

G. lydia	20 inches (50cm)
G. hispanica	20 inches (50cm)
G. pilosa	20 inches (50cm)
G. tinctoria 'Royal Gold'	28 inches (70cm)
G. tinctoria	31 inches (80cm)
G. anglica	31 inches (80cm)

Gleditsia (Honey locust)

This is actually a tree, but it is often cultivated as a shrub. It bears yellow flowers, sharp thorns, and beautiful, fine pinnate leaves. Only one species is cultivated: *Gleditsia triacanthos*, of which the cultivar 'Sunburst' has yellow leaves.

Hamamelis (Witch hazel)

Hamamelis, which flowers in red or yellow in January and February, is often used in gardens that are much too small for it. The shrub grows up to 13 feet (4m) tall and equally wide. Pruning is not necessary, and it will spoil the beautiful shape. Give the shrubs ample space and, preferably, a sunny location. Partial shade is acceptable, but witch hazel doesn't flower very abundantly under those conditions. There are a number of species, and of these a number of interesting varieties are cultivated. Their requirements are more or less the same. Visit a botanical garden in February to pick the variety you find most beautiful.

Hamamelis 'Westerstede'.

Hebe

Hebes are low-growing and sensitive to frost; they come originally from New Zealand. They will successfully overwinter only in locations close to the seashore and sheltered. It may be best to think of them as potted plants.

The shrubs are popular for their lovely blossoms in August and September.

Hibiscus.

Hibiscus

height: 8 feet (2.5m)

Most hibiscus are indoor plants. *Hibiscus syriacus* is a 6½ foot (2m) tall sturdy shrub originating in Asia Minor, with flowers that resemble those of *H. rosa-sinensis*.

Hibiscus bloom in many colors:

H. 'Blue Bird'	blue
H. 'Caeruleus'	blue
H. 'Rubis'	dark pink
H. 'Hamabo'	red
H. 'Meehanii'	white
H. 'Totus Albus'	white

Hippophae (Sea buckthorn)

height: 10 feet (3m)

The sea buckthorn is the ideal shrub for coastal areas: It can withstand the strongest winds. The shrub grows in every type of soil and can endure drought well. Its charm lies in the combination of narrow gray leaves and bright orange berries. The shrub itself looks rather untidy and is therefore not recommended for every garden. Plant it where other shrubs will not grow. *Hippophae rhamnoides* is cultivated.

Hydrangea

Three obviously different species are cultivated: *Hydrangea paniculata* (pointed flowers), *H. macro-*

phylla (flowering round or flat), and *H. petiolaris* (climbing). The shrub with the round shape is what we envision for gardens. The hydrangea does not mind shade and for that reason can be a practical choice for the city garden. *Hydrangea paniculata* always flowers in white. Do not plant these shrubs along a path: the branches break rather easily. The globe-shaped flowers of *H. macrophylla* are often admired in floral arrangements.

Hippophae rhamnoides.

Hydrangea macrophylla.

The flowers may be dark pink, light pink, white, or various shades of blue. For a very deep blue, grow hydrangea in a light acid soil, to which aluminum sulfate has been added. The largest flowers are produced by *H. arborescens*; the white-flowering variety 'Annabelle' is often seen. Give this shrub, as you would *H. paniculata*, a lot of space. The shrub is handsome as a solitary plant in the lawn. *Hydrangea macrophylla* is suitable for symmetrical use because of its even shape. Try planting one at either side of an entryway or flanking the sidewalk.

Do not give hydrangeas too dry a location. They will go limp in strong sunshine. If the large terminal buds are removed in spring, the plant will flower more evenly over the whole shrub.

Hypericum (Saint-John's-wort)
height: 2½ to 3 feet (75cm to 1m)

These shrubs flower yellow on one-year-old wood, and can be pruned back to the soil in winter or early spring. *Hypericum calycinum* is evergreen and a good creeper to grow under other, taller shrubs. Plant *Hypericum* in full sun; they do not require anything else.

Ilex (Holly)
Only a small number of the four hundred species of holly are in cultivation. Some are evergreen; others are deciduous. There are enormous differences in manner of growing hollies. The best-known shrub from this family is *Ilex aquifolium*. Male and female plants are required for the production of berries on this holly. *Ilex aquifolium* 'Pyramidalis' is self-pollinating. In addition, this variety has less prickly foliage than the common wild

The hydrangea does not become blue unless the soil is acid, low in phosphorus, and is given aluminum sulfate.

holly, and this makes maintenance under and around the shrub a lot more pleasant—you can pull out weeds without gloves. A number of species have gold or silver variegated leaves.

Less well known is the Japanese holly, a shrub that grows 6½ feet (2m) tall and looks like *Buxus* with round leaves. *Ilex crenata* 'Convexa' has round, dark green leaves, and *I. c.* 'Golden Gem' has golden leaves. *Ilex verticillata*, which grows 10 feet (3m) tall and is unsurpassed as a shrub for ornamental berries, is deciduous. (However, birds can eat all of the berries in one day.) Here again, you need a male and a female shrub for berries. Plant the male at some distance, out of sight if you like, as berries will not appear on it. Prune the holly (except for *I. verticillata*) when it is young; clip off the ends of the branches to get fuller growth.

Kerria (Japanese rose)
Kerria has light green leaves and green twigs, and flowers in May and June with buttercuplike yellow flowers. A fresh-looking shrub, it can look rather shabby after the winter because of frozen branches. It is best to prune out all two-year-old branches after blooming, but if it still does not look good after the winter, cutting the shrub off to the ground is the solution. Flowering will not be affected by this. *Kerria japonica* 'Pleniflora', which has dark yellow fully double flowers, is the cultivar most often sold. Still, *K. japonica*, with single flowers, blooms in a more beautiful bright yellow. *Kerria japonica* 'Aureovariegata' boasts variegated leaves and single flowers.

Kolkwitzia
height: 6½ feet (2m)
This shrub, relatively unknown to private gardens, flowers like *Weigela*, with pink blossoms on arching branches. It usually flowers just after most of the commonly grown spring flowering shrubs. One species is cultivated: *K. amabilis*.

Laburnocytisus
This is a *Cytisus* grafted onto *Laburnum* stock. The plant looks like something in between broom and laburnum, as the compound name suggests. This botanical curiosity is of little value for the garden. The scientific name is *Laburnocytisus adamii*.

Laburnum
The laburnum, more a tree than a shrub, is suitable for larger gardens. In a small garden, let it serve as a tree. The wild laburnum, *Laburnum anagyroides*, has short bunches of flowers. *L. × wateri* 'Vossii' is grafted, and

Lespedeza.

flowers with long yellow bunches of up to 20 inches (50cm) long. This shrub is much more expensive, but a great deal more beautiful. Do not plant Laburnum in soil that is very wet, and never prune it to keep it small—only thin it.

Laurus (Laurel)
Do not confuse this plant with the cherry laurel (*Prunus laurocerasus*). See also page 396.

Lespedeza
This late-blooming shrub is one of a group of shrubs that do not get enough attention. After most flowering shrubs have bloomed in spring, the garden usually looks green in the shrub border. *Lespedeza thunbergii* offers purple-pink flowers in September and October, and as it grows only 3 feet (1m) tall, it is suitable for small gardens. *Lespedeza bicolor* grows 5 feet (1.5m) tall. This plant can be cut down to the ground every year in spring. *Lespedeza* flowers on one-year-old wood.

Leycesteria
height: 5 feet (1.5m)
This shrub somewhat resembles the shrub honey-suckle. It has large pseudo-spikes with red bracts,

Leycesteria formosa.

between which the flowers hang. Give it a warm, sheltered location to protect it as much as possible from freezing. The only species suitable for temperate climates is *Leycesteria formosa*.

Ligustrum (Privet)

Privet is more than neatly trimmed hedges. You can enjoy their beautiful blossoming of white flowers on the solitary shrub. *Ligustrum* includes a large number of species and varieties. Some have golden or silver variegated leaves, others have yellow leaves. They are evergreen.

L. amurense
This privet has green leaves and black berries.

L. delavayanum
A privet with flowers in almost hairy bunches.

L. japonicum
A compact plant sensitive to frost.

L. lucidum
This very tall shrub has brownish green flowers.

L. obtusifolium var. regelianum
This shrub has large black berries and is the best solitary privet.

L. ovalifolium
This is the best hedge plant of the family, a good evergreen.

L. quihoui
This has light gray branches, which can be a nice complement to greens in the garden.

L. vulgare
This is the wild privet, which is not a very reliable evergreen. It is a nice addition to the bird-lover's garden.

As a hedge it is less sensitive to frost than *Ligustrum ovalifolium*.

L. × vicaryi
This privet has beautiful yellow leaves.

Lonicera (Honeysuckle)

Climbing honeysuckles are discussed with the other climbing plants (page 322); here, the shrub honeysuckle is discussed. There are evergreen and deciduous honeysuckles.

Evergreen honeysuckles

L. nitida	4 feet (1.25m)	small leaves, good for hedges
L. pileata	2 feet (60cm)	suitable for short hedges and beds

Deciduous honeysuckles

L. fragrantissima		blooms in winter
L. korolkowii	8 feet (2.5m)	gray-green leaves, white, red berries

Lonicera.

Magnolia soulangeana.

L. ledebourii		grows very wide, withstands strong wind, purple berries
L. maackii	10 feet (3m)	white flower, red berries
L. tatarica	10 feet (3m)	pink flower, red berries
L. xylosteum	10 feet (3m)	yellowish flower, red berries

All these honeysuckles bud early in spring, and are therefore very eye-catching when other shrubs do not even have any leaves yet. These shrubs are attractive to birds.

Magnolia

The magnolia is often, and erroneously, called the "tulip tree." This name is correctly applied to *Liriodendron tulipifera*. Magnolia includes many species, taking the forms of small shrubs, large shrubs, climbing shrubs, and trees. The purpose you have in mind determines the species you choose.

M. stellata (Star magnolia)
height: up to 6½ feet (2m)

This rounded shrub has white star-shaped flowers. It is one of the most beautiful shrubs for the smaller garden.

The flowers appear before the leaves.

M. kobus
height: 20 feet (6m)

This small tree has white flowers that appear before the leaves.

M. × soulangiana (Chinese magnolia, smaller magnolia)
This magnolia with large pink-white flowers can grow very wide, and for that reason is less suitable for a small garden. It is nice grown as a solitary shrub in a lawn. Leaves and flowers appear at the same time.

M. quinquepeta 'Nigra'
This magnolia has dark pink flowers and grows into a large shrub. The leaves appear first, followed by the flowers. It is slightly remontant.

M. grandiflora (Southern magnolia)
This magnolia has very large white flowers and is not fully hardy. For that reason, plant it only against a warm wall sheltered from wind. The large leathery leaves remain on the shrub in winter.

M. sieboldii

This large shrub is the magnolia that flowers latest in the season, in June and July.

Mahoberberis

This is a cross between the genus *Mahonia* and the genus *Berberis*. This evergreen shrub is a botanical curiosity of interest to the specialist, but it is not a really beautiful shrub, and flowers sparsely.

Mahonia

This sturdy evergreen can be used in a number of ways in the garden. The plants are undemanding, fairly quick growers that bear yellow flowers early in spring. Mahonias can be used the fill large spaces, and they are effective hedging plants. Plant them where they will be visible from the house in winter.

M. aquifolium

height: 5 feet (1.5m)

This may be the most popular *Mahonia*, but it is not the best one. The leaves do not remain entirely green at the end of the winter; the edges turn brown.

M. wagneri 'Pinnacle'

This shrub is more or less the same as the previous one, but stays green better. The plant has a slightly finer appearance.

M. bealii

height: up to 6½ feet (2m)

This branched shrub flowers very early and has large, leathery green leaves.

M. japonica

This resembles *Mahonia beali*, but the main stem is 8 feet (2.5m) long. The leaves reach 11 to 12 inches (30cm) long.

M. repens

This is a creeper with blue-green glaucous leaves; the plant forms runners.

Malus (Crab apple)

The crab apple can be purchased as a shrub, half standard, and standard tree, as can many fruit trees. It is suitable for large gardens. The birds will benefit as much as you. For a naturalistic look, try planting a crab apple next to a ditch; it may look like a chance seedling that took root there. The crab apple offers virtually endless possibilities. You can create color combinations with red, white, or pink flowers, red or green leaves, red, yellow, or orange fruit in a variety of shapes, from perfectly round to elongated. There are various tree shapes from which to choose, from the almost fastigiate to the more spreading. A crab apple can be found to suit any purpose.

Myrica (Bog myrtle)

The European bog myrtle grows in acid wet soil. This shrub, which grows 5 feet (1.5m) high, can even be in water. It is an aromatic plant; there are male and female plants. It blooms in April and May with brownish flowers—slightly mysterious when the sun shines on them in early spring. The American myrtle grows to 6½ feet (2m) tall and needs drier conditions. Both shrubs look somewhat like willows.

Neillia

Neillia affinis resembles *Spiraea*. The lime green leaves are most beautiful when the shrubs are not in bloom. The medium-tall shrubs can be planted in partial shade. There are species that bear pink, red, and white flowers.

The budding leaves of Pieris *'Forest Flame' are decorative, but—watch out!—very sensitive to frost. The shrub is an evergreen and flowers abundantly.*

Nothofagus
See page 222.

Paeonia (Tree peony)
height: 5 feet (1.5m)

No shrub has flowers as big as those of the tree peony. They are so big, they even look out of proportion to the size of the shrub. The shrub looks like the common peony. The plants will grow tallest in a sheltered location. They are sensitive to late night frost. The tree peony flowers in April/May in the brightest of colors: purple, yellow, pink, red, and white.

Parrotia
Every member of the witch hazel family is a sure thing for beautiful autumn color. *Parrotia persica* can be grown as a tall shrub or a small tree. The small reddish flowers appear between January and March. Young plants do not flower and are slightly sensitive to frost.

Pernettya
This plant, a member of the heather family, requires acid soil. These low-growing shrubs produce large red, pink, and white berries. A male plant (which does not grow berries) is always required. Plant them in humid soil in half shade.

Pieris japonica *'Forest Flame'*: young red shoots and white *bunches of flowers on the same shrub.*

Philadelphus (Mock orange)
This well-known, fragrant shrub deserves a place in every garden. It grows in every type of soil. The following species and varieties are cultivated:

P. coronarius	common mock orange, up to 16½ feet (5m)
P. c. 'Aureus'	yellow-green leaves
P. 'Belle Etoile'	up to 6½ feet (2m)
P. 'Lemoinei'	up to 6 feet (1.8m), elegant, spreading, pendulous branches
P. 'Manteau d'Hermine'	3 feet (1m), fully double flowers
P. 'Virginal'	6½ feet (2m), pure white, semidouble

Pieris
height: up to 5 feet (1.5m)

These evergreen shrubs produce bunches of pink or white flowers. The best-known is the *Pieris japonica*, which has glossy, leathery leaves. A variety with bright red runners is *P. japonica* 'Forest Flame'. Protect *Pieris* from late night frost. Give them acid soil in partial shade, but absolutely no morning sun in winter, a situation that can kill them.

Prunus laurocerasus.

Poncirus

The foliage of this shrub, which resembles the citrus tree, colors a beautiful golden yellow in autumn. In winter the green branches with large thorns are striking. *Poncirus trifoliata*, the trifoliate orange, yields small, inedible lemons. In spite of its tropical appearance, the shrub can withstand frost well. It is also suitable for cultivation in a pot.

Potentilla (Cinquefoil)

This genus includes perennials and shrubs. The shrub cinquefoil, *Potentilla fruticosa* will grow up to 3 feet (1m) tall. The flowers usually are yellow, but there are also pink and white ones. The shrub is suitable for planting in beds and for hedges. Prune the old branches every year to keep a nice shape.

P. 'Abbotswood'	white	spreading	28 inches (70cm)
P. 'Arbuscula'	yellow	creeper	12 inches (30cm)
P. 'Fruticosa'	yellow	fastigiate	3 feet (1m)
P. 'Klondike'	golden yellow	fastigiate	3 feet (1m)
P. 'Moonlight'	lemon yellow		4 feet (1.2m)

P. 'Primrose' Beauty'	creamy yellow	pendulous	2 feet (60cm)
P. 'Tangerine'	orange		16 inches (40cm)

Prunus (Cherry laurel)

The cherry laurel, *Prunus laurocerasus*, is an evergreen with leathery leaves and can be used for hedges and for planting in beds. The shrubs, which bear bunches of white flowers, are quick growers for every type of soil, and can manage in sun and shade. This is the easiest evergreen for the garden. There are fastigiate, spreading, broad-leaved (suitable as a noise barrier), and narrow-leaved, tall and short varieties. Before you select a cherry laurel, decide to what height you want the shrub to grow.

P. 'Caucasica'	10 feet (3m), narrow fastigiate, very hardy
P. 'Rotundifolia'	13 feet (4m), wide fastigiate, do not plant it in a spot in full wind, slightly sensitive to frost
P. 'Van Nes'	6 feet (1.75m), wide, very dark green
P. 'Mischeana'	3 feet (1m), very wide-growing
P. 'Otto Luyken'	3 feet (1m), compact, eye-catching flowers
P. 'Reynvaanii'	6 feet (1.75m), sinuate leaves, fastigiate

Another evergreen variety is *P. lusitanica*, a rather stiff-looking shrub 6½ feet (2m) tall. The dark green leathery leaves with red stems are striking. Deciduous indigenous shrubs include *P. padus* and *P. spinosa*, the bird cherry and the blackthorn. Both will grow 13 feet (4m) tall and bear

Prunus padus.

white flowers. With the blackthorn, the flowers appear before the thorny shrub develops any leaves. Both shrubs are must-haves for the bird-lover's collections.

See also page 224.

Pyracantha (Fire thorn)

The fire thorn is generally grown as a shrub against a wall. In a sheltered spot, this is a beautiful solitary shrub. Protection is required to prevent freezing. The berries are left alone by the birds until all other food is gone. Then, the birds throw themselves on the shrubs and eat all the berries in just one day.

Rhamnus (Buckthorn)

Rhamus frangula, alder buckthorn, and *R. cathartica*, common buckthorn, are shrubs suitable for use as underplanting. As they produce berries, birds find them attractive.

Rhus (Sumac)

Rhus typhina, staghorn sumac, is a large open shrub with hairy branches and beautiful autumn color. *Rhus typhina* 'Laciniata' grows slower and has very laciniate, fine leaves. When the leaves have fallen, the red fruit spikes at the end of every branch can be better admired. Because they are rather open, these shrubs can be underplanted with evergreens. Cut off the runners regularly to encourage growth.

Ribes

There are numerous species of this common garden

Prunus × serrulata 'Amanogawa' has a fastigiate habit, and so this shrub is suitable for small gardens after all.

shrub. The yellow-flowering *Ribes alpinum* can grow in deep shade; *Ribes viburnifolium* is an evergreen. The common *R. sanguineum* offers a number of varieties; the species grows 10 feet (3m) tall and the pink flowers appear at the same time the forsythia blooms.

Rhamnus cathartica, *the buckthorn.*

Rhamnus frangula.

S. cinerea	6½ to 10 feet (2 to 3m)
S. exigua	13 feet (4m)
S. hastata	3 feet (1m)
S. irrorata	6½ to 10 feet (2 to 3m)
S. repens	up to 6½ feet (2m)

See also page 226.

Sambucus (Elder)

Elders grow into large shrubs, and can be pruned into small trees. They grow in every type of soil, and in sun and shade; they also sow easily.

S. canadensis 'Aurea'	13 feet (4m), golden yellow leaves, black berries
S. nigra	16½ to 23 feet (5 to 7m), black berries
S. nigra 'Pygmy'	18 inches (50cm), suitable for the rock garden
S. nigra 'Laciniata'	16 feet (5m), fine pinnate leaves
S. racemosa	16 feet (5m), red berries

There are many varieties of *S. nigra,* with many different leaf shapes and colors. *Sambucus nigra* 'Hamburg' is cultivated for its larger berries, which make fine jam.

Skimmia

height: up to 3 feet (1m)

These evergreen shrubs have firm, leathery, oval

R. s. 'King Edward VII'	red
R. s. 'Splendens'	red
R. s. 'Tydemans White'	white

Rubus

Rubus odoratus is a shrub of 8 feet (2.5m) with pink-red flowers in clusters. The shrub forms many underground runners and can be divided easily. Cut off the old branches in winter to keep a tidy bush. *Rubus biflorus* is very striking in winter because of its gray-white branches. It grows 10 to 13 feet (3 to 4m) tall and is suitable for planting under tall trees.

Salix (Willow)

The genus has several hundred species, many of which remain low-growing. They are suitable for damp areas of the garden. The stamens of the male catkins give the willow an elegant look. It is strange that low-growing varieties are not often found at nurseries. We always see *Salix matsudana* 'Tortuosa', which is sold as a shrub, and grows into a tree. Its twisted branches are ornamental.

Some worthy examples from the large selection:

| *S. aurita* | 6½ feet (2m) |
| *S. bockii* | 3 to 6½ feet (1 to 2m) |

Sambucus nigra.

leaves. They require acid soil in partial shade. The flower buds are already formed in autumn and are attractive all winter. The leaves of the white-flowering shrubs are lighter in color than the leaves of red-flowering shrubs. Skimmia can make a beautiful underplanting for magnolias.

Spiraea douglasii.

Sorbaria (False spirea)

height: up to 10 feet (3m)

The flower panicles of this shrub remind one of goatsbeard and false goatsbeard. Five species are in cultivation, and they all look alike. *Sorbaria* form underground runners; the plants can be divided easily. Plant them at the back of the shrub border; the panicles at the top of the shrubs can be enjoyed from a distance. These shrubs grow in every type of soil, in sun or partial shade.

Spiraea (Spirea)

This genus has many species. *Spiraea* grow in every type of soil, in sun or partial shade. They will grow, but flower less, in deep shade. Late-flowering species can be cut down to the ground in winter; they flower on one-year-old wood. Those that flower early should only be thinned in winter. Some varieties of note are:

	Color	Height	Flowering period
S. arcuata	creamy white	6 feet (1.75)m	April to May
S. × arguta	white	6½ feet (2m)	April to May
S. × cinerea	white	5 feet (1.5m)	May
S. prunifolia	white	6 feet (1.75m)	May
S. × vanhouttei	white	6 feet (1.75m)	May
S. albiflora	white	20 inches (50cm)	June
S. bullata	dark pink	16 inches (40cm)	June
S. × bumalda	pink	20 to 40 inches (50 to 100 cm)	June
S. billiardii	pink	6½ feet (2m)	July
S. douglasii	pink	6 feet (1.75m)	August
S. japonica	dark pink	5 feet (1.5m)	August

Stephanandra

These low-growing shrubs, which are often used as creepers, have lime green foliage that resembles that of *Neillia*. *Stephanandra incisa* remains low-growing. Unfortunately, *S. i.* 'Crispa', with sinuate and sick-looking leaves, is usually what is offered by nurseries. Do try to find the species. *Stephanandra tanakae* is slightly taller. Both bloom with small white flowers that cover the shrub.

Stranvaesia

On this more-or-less-evergreen shrub, the leaves color slightly red in winter. The shrub is somewhat sensitive to frost, but very sensitive to fire blight—a reason to consider whether to plant this susceptible shrub at all.

Symphoricarpos albus.

Symphoricarpos (Snowberry)

This shrub is ideal as an underplanting for trees. In full sun, more white or pink berries are produced, and they will stay on the shrub for some time. Regular pruning of the two- and three-year-old branches is required to keep the snowberry nice-looking. If pruning is done regularly, the branches will be so thin that they can be cut off easily with pruning shears.

Syringa (Lilac)

height: up to 13 feet (4m)
flowering: May

Give lilacs room to grow; they can be kept small only with difficulty. They grow in every type of soil, in full sun. Many botanical species are cultivated by specialized growers. The following varieties of the *Syringa vulgaris* have large flowers.

Varieties of *Syringa vulgaris* with single flowers

S. 'Andenken an Ludwig Spaeth'	purple
S. 'G.J. Baardse'	lilac blue
S. 'Cavour'	blue
S. 'Decaisne'	dark blue
S. 'Ester Staley'	light blue

S. 'Flora'	white
S. 'Leon Gambetta'	lilac
S. 'Lucie Baltet'	pink
S. 'Primrose'	creamy white

Varieties of *Syringa vulgaris* with fully double flowers

S. 'Charles Joly'	purple
S. 'Mme. Lemoine'	white
S. 'Belle de Nancy'	blue
S. 'Paul Thirion'	pink-red
S. 'President Loubet'	wine red

Tamarix (Tamarisk)

The tamarisk is always portrayed in catalogs in flower, when the ugly shape of the shrub is disguised. Even pruning the shrubs cannot make them tidier. It is only during flowering, when the shrub is colored purple-pink, that the beauty of the shrub can be enjoyed. It requires dry soil and full sun.

Ulex (Gorse)

This shrub resembles broom in appearance and flowering. All branches of the shrub have large thorns. *Ulex* is even more sensitive to frost than broom, and it requires a sunny place in the garden.

Syringa vulgaris. The flower buds appear at the same time as the leaves.

Viburnum

This genus includes evergreen and deciduous shrubs, both early and late flowering. Perhaps best known is *Viburnum plicatum* with white umbels and bright red berries. The shrub very much resembles *V. opulus*

'Roseum' (syn. *V. o.* 'Sterile'), the snowball-bush. The viburnum is an old-fashioned shrub with round flowers.

Ulex europaeus, *the gorse, very much resembles broom. Pruning is more difficult though, because the plant is covered with thorns.*

Evergreen viburnums

V. × burkwoodii	6 feet (1.75m)	March to April
V. davidii	20 inches (50cm)	May to June
V. rhitidophyllum	11½ feet (3.5m)	May to June

Viburnum opulus. *When ripe, the berries are soft and bright red, and though birds love them, they will eat the berries from other shrubs first.*

Deciduous viburnums

V. x bodnantense		
'Dawn'	10 feet (3m)	February to March
V. × carlcephalum	6½ feet (2m)	April to May
V. carlesii	6½ feet (2m)	April to May
V. farreri	11½ feet (3.5m)	February to March
V. lantana	13 feet (4m)	May to June
V. plicatum	10 feet (3m)	May to June

Weigela

height: 8 feet (2.5m)

Weigela is a pleasant shrub, though it is a pity that the flowers do not appear until the shrub has all its leaves; they are not very noticeable. *Weigela florida* flowers profusely. The variety 'Purpurea' is especially handsome, with dark red leaves and light pink flowers; it grows about 3 feet (1m) tall. Taller cultivars (about 8 feet/2.5m) are:

W. 'Ballet'	pink-red
W. 'Bristol Ruby'	carmine
W. 'Candida'	white
W. 'Eva Supreme'	bright red
W. 'Rosabella'	pink with lighter edges

10 Conifers A to Z

If there is one garden design element with which care should be taken, it is with conifers. As has been mentioned in previous chapters, with conifers, especially, it can be hard to imagine how a small plant could grow into a giant that dominates your garden.

But for whoever goes to the trouble of noting the most important characteristics of the many sorts of conifers, these varied trees will offer a beautiful complement in the garden. There is a wide range of growth habits, and foliage types and color from which to choose. In many cases, conifers are just the right accent against which flowering plants can be shown to best advantage.

A typical branchlet of Pinus.

Nomenclature

Scientific, or botanical, names are a lot easier to remember if you know their meaning, and this is particularly true for evergreens. *Taxus baccata* 'Fastigiata Aureomarginata' means, in plain English, a yew with a fastigiate shape, berries, and needles with golden margins. And the name *Juniperus pisifera* 'Filifera Aurea' means a juniper with berries and threadlike golden foliage.

Familiarity with the following terms will help you recognize quickly the conifer in question:

alba	white
argentea	silver
atrovirens	dark green
aurea	golden
baccatus	with berries
communis	common
compacta	compact
fastigiata	fastigiate, columnar (Lat. *fastigium* = top)
filifera	threadlike
glauca	blue, or covered with a whitish bloom
globosa	spherical
grandis	giant, large
heterophylla	bearing more than one form of leaf
hibernica	from or of Ireland
koreana	from or of Korea
lutea	yellow
marginata	rimmed
nanus	dwarf
obtusa	rounded, blunt
pendula	hanging, weeping
pisifer	bearing pealike seeds
plicatus	folded
plumosus	feathery
procumbens	prostrate
repandens	with wavy edges
sabina	broomlike
squamata	scaly
variegata	having various colors, variegated
verticillatus	verticillate, whorled

Choose the Right Plant

Conifers that can withstand a lot of wind
Larix kaempferi
Picea pungens 'Glauca'
P. sitchensis
Pinus mugo
P. nigra

Evergreens that thrive in, or can endure, some shade
Abies alba
Chamaecyparis obtusa 'Nana Gracilis'
Juniperus sinensis 'Pfitzeriana'
J. communis
Sciadopitys verticillata
Taxus baccata
T. × media 'Hicksii'
Thuja occidentalis
Thujopsis dolabrata
Tsuga canadensis
T. heterophylla

Deciduous conifers
Larix decidua
L. kaempferi

A good proportion of ever-green conifers, flowering plants, and gray-foliaged plants. Even when only a few plants are in flower, this garden is very attractive.

Metasequoia glyptostroboides
Pseudolarix kaempferi
Taxodium distichum

Fast-growing conifers
Abies nordmanniana
Cedrus atlantica
× Cupressocyparis leylandii
Juniperus virginiana
Picea
Pseudotsuga menziesii
Thuja plicata
Tsuga heterophylla

New pine branches adorn the trees in spring with "candles."

Evergreens for very dry soil

Abies concolor
A. homolepis
Juniperus communis
Picea omorika
Pinus mugo
P. nigra
Pseudotsuga menziesii

Evergreens for hedges

× *Cupressocyparis leylandii*
Juniperus communis
Taxus baccata
Thuja occidentalis
T. plicata
Tsuga canadensis
    Plant twenty-five to thirty plants per 33 feet (10m).

Conifers for birds

    These conifers provide berries and attractive nesting possibilities.
Juniperus
Larix
Picea
Taxus

Pinus sylvestris. *This is a young tree, which has sown spontaneously.*

Evergreens for growing on a slope

	Height	Width
Juniperus communis 'Hornibrookii'	20 inches (50cm)	6½ feet (2m)
J. c. 'Repanda'	12 inches (30cm)	5 feet (1.5m)
J. horizontalis	16 inches (40cm)	6⅔ feet (2m)
Picea abies 'Repens'	20 inches (50cm)	5 feet (1.5m)
Taxus baccata 'Repandens'	24 inches (60cm)	8 feet (2.5m)

Conifers for the rock garden

	Height	Habit	Color
Abies balsamea 'Nana'	32 inches (80cm)	round	green
Cedrus libani 'Sargentii'	4 feet (1.25m)	shrub	blue-green
Chamaecyparis lawsoniana 'Ellwoodii'	8 feet (2.5m)	columnar	blue-green
C. l. 'Minima Glauca'	3⅔ feet (1.1m)	round	blue-green
C. obtusa 'Nana Gracilis'	6½ feet (2m)	irregular	light green
C. o. 'Pygmaea'	5 feet (1.5m)	round	blue-green
C. pisifera 'Filifera Aurea'	3 feet (1m)	round	golden yellow
Cryptomeria japonica 'Vilmoriniana'	32 inches (80cm)	round	light green
Juniperus communis 'Repanda'	12 inches (30cm)	creeping	green
J. virginiana 'Grey Owl'	5 feet (1.5m)	shrub	gray-blue
Picea glauca 'Conica'	5 feet (1.5m)	cone	light green
Pinus mugo 'Mughus'	6½ feet (2m)	shrub	green
Thuja occidentalis 'Rheingold'	5 feet (1.5m)	cone	yellow
T .o. 'Globosa'	6 feet (1.75m)	round	green

A Separate Class

Two plants are difficult to fit into the botanical system. For the sake of convenience, they may be grouped with the conifers. These are *Ginkgo biloba*, the maidenhair tree, and *Ephedra*, a low-growing plant that looks like *Equisetum*, but is more woody. In books on flora, you will find these plants in a separate group between ferns and evergreens.

Conifers A to Z

Abies (Fir)

The firs, some of which grow quite large, are not very demanding as far as soil is concerned. Most are quite cold-hardy. They do object to drying east winds. Some species of *Picea* and *Abies* are confused. *Abies* has blunt needles with an incision at the tip; *Picea* has sharp needles. Another difference: If you pull a needle from the twig of some *Abies* species, a piece of bark from the base of the needle will remain; this does not happen with *Picea*. Furthermore, *Picea* has pointed buds, and the *Abies* buds are blunt.

A. alba

This is the common silver fir, up to 66 feet (20m) tall with a straight trunk. *Abies alba* 'Pendula' grows up to 50 feet (15m), also with a straight trunk. The branches hang down along the trunk. The branches of *A. a.* 'Pyramidalis' are angled upward; this tree does not grow taller than 33 feet (10m).

A. balsamea

The dark green needles have two clear white stripes. *Abies balsamea* 'Nana' has a round dwarf shape.

A. grandis

This tree grows in the shape of a pyramid to a maximum of 66 feet (20m) tall.

A. homolepis

This columnar tree grows to 83 feet (25m). The branches are regularly spaced and grow out at right angles to the trunk.

A. koreana

This conifer is popular for the violet-purple cones that grow vertically on the branches. This tree will grow 50 feet (15m) tall.

Cedrus atlantica *'Glauca'*.

A. nordmanniana

The undersides of the glossy dark green needles have two white stripes. The height of this conifer will be 66 feet (20m) at maturity.

A. procera

Of this fine silver fir, the variety 'Glauca' is most often used. The maximum height is 83 feet (25m).

Araucaria (Monkey puzzle tree)

Araucaria araucana is suitable only for a sheltered spot. The young tree is very sensitive to frost. Give this tree enough space; it will grow 50 feet (15m) tall. This dark green tree has a mysterious, gloomy appearance. The twisted branches form regular rings (whorls) on the tree.

Cedrus (Cedar)

Cedrus atlantica, the Atlas cedar, is a large tree of 100 feet (30m). During severe winters the needles may freeze; though the tree may look dead the following spring, it will start to bud again. *Cedrus atlantica* 'Glauca' has blue-gray needles and grows as tall as the species, while *C. a.* 'Glauca Pendula' and 'Aurea' remain considerably shorter.

Cedrus deodara is a wide pyramidal tree, growing to 66 feet (20m) tall. The needles are softer than those of the Atlas cedar, and the branches are more pendulous. Its sensitivity to frost is comparable to that of C. atlantica. There are many varieties: golden, dwarf forms, fastigiate growers, creeping, and weeping varieties.

Chamaecyparis (False cypress)

Chamaecyparis lawsoniana is a tree that will grow up to 83 feet (25m) tall. It has green to blue-green scaly foliage.

C. l. 'Alumnii'

This conifer is often wrongly sold as a hedge plant. It has a blue-green color, less blue than the variety *C. l.* 'Columnaris'.

C. l. 'Columnaris'

This conifer has a columnar habit, as its name implies. It has a blue-gray color, and is less wide than *C. l.* 'Alumnii'. This is not a good hedging plant; as its shape is narrow, many plants would be required to create an uninterrupted hedge suitably dense. These evergreens are difficult to prune, and it is preferable to use *Thuja* for hedges.

Pinus mugo.

C. l. 'Erecta Viridis'

This conifer offers a fresh green color and grows 33 feet (10m) tall at most. It has a pyramidal, fastigiate shape.

C. l. 'Lane'

This conifer has a narrow fastigiate habit and is golden yellow.

C. l. 'Minima Glauca'

This blue-green, rounded dwarf conifer grows to 5 feet (1.5m) tall at most.

C. l. 'Silver Queen'

'Silver Queen' grows slowly and will reach 33 feet (10m).

C. l. 'Stewartii'

Golden yellow to yellow-green, this tree has a pyramidal shape and grows to 26½ feet (8m) tall.

C. l. 'Triomph van Boskoop'

This silvery blue pruinose conifer grows to 50 feet (15m).

C. l. 'Wisselii'

This narrow, tall conifer has small blue-green needles.

C. l. 'Spek'

This conifer is gray-blue and grows 33 feet (10m) tall at most. A grouping of these trees gives a nice effect.

C. nootkatensis

This pyramidal tree grows 100 feet (30m) tall, with fresh green needles and pendulous branches.

C. n. 'Pendula'

'Pendula' grows up to 33 feet (10m) tall. The horizontal branches have drooping branchlets.

C. obtusa

This species includes some shorter trees of note. They are slow-growing and very ornamental.

C. o. 'Filicoides'

This slow grower reaches 5 feet (1.5m) at the most and is a glossy dark green.

C. o. 'Nana Gracilis'

This is one of the best known dwarf conifers. It grows—slowly—to a height of 6½ feet (2m). The ends of the branchlets have the shape of a shell. The young conifers are often offered as bonsai trees. Buy these as garden plants, rather than as trees, and you will pay a lot less.

C. o. 'Pygmaea'

This spreading dwarf conifer grows 6½ feet (2m) tall at most.

C. pisifera

These medium-tall conifers have foliage that may be scalelike as well as threadlike or needled.

C. p. 'Filiformis'

This conifer has threadlike, dark green foliage.

C. p. 'Filifera Aurea'

This conifer can be pruned into a round shape up to 3 feet (1m) across. Let alone, it can grow up to 13 feet (4m) tall.

C. p. 'Plumosa'

'Plumosa' grows in the shape of a pyramid up to 33 feet (10m) tall, with horizontal branches. The branchlets end in panicles and give a feathery effect. The green foliage becomes somewhat bronze-colored in winter. The variety 'Plumosa Aurea' is golden yellow.

C. p. 'Squarrosa'

'Squarrosa' grows up to 33 feet (10m) tall, is dense and wide, and blue-green in color.

Three examples of Picea glauca *'Conica', a fresh green when* *budding in spring.*

Cryptomeria

C. japonica is a large tree that grows to 83 feet (25m) tall. The color of the bark is reddish brown, like that of *Sequoiadendron*. The dark green needles radiate from all sides of the branchlets. *Cryptomeria* is beautiful when pruned into shapes. The variety 'Compacta' will remain about 33 feet (10m) shorter than the species. 'Cristata' is cultivated for its fasciated (flattened) branches.

C. j. 'Globosa Nana'

This conifer grows in a cone shape up to 5 feet (1.5m) tall with blue-green needles.

C. j. 'Jindai-Sugi'

'Jindai-Sugi' is a dense tree and grows 8 feet (2.5m) high at the maximum. 'Bandai-Sugi', shorter, resembles it .

C. j. 'Vilmoriniana'

This is the shortest variety. The rounded conical plant will grow up to 32 inches (80cm) tall.

× Cupressocyparis

× *Cupressocyparis leylandii* is the result of a cross between two plant genera, *Cupressus* and *Chamaecyparis*. It is, like *Metasequoia*, one of the quickest-growing conifers. It is sensitive to frost, but can be used very well as a hedge. This conifer endures coastal winds well.

Juniperus (Juniper)

This genus includes narrow, fastigiate species and spreading species. They are all undemanding, and can withstand dry soil well.

J. chinensis (Chinese juniper)

The many varieties of Chinese juniper include:

J. c. 'Blaauw', 3 feet (1m), gray-blue, shrub

J. c. 'Hetzii', 6½ feet (2m), blue-gray, spreading

J. c. 'Keteleeri', up to 33 feet (10m), blue-gray, columnar

J. c. 'Pfitzerana', wide and tall, bright green

J. c. 'Pfitzerana Aurea', golden yellow when budding, smaller in every way than 'Pfitzerana'

J. c. 'Plumosa Aurea', up to 6½ feet (2m), irregular shape

J. communis (Common juniper)

The common juniper grows to 16½ feet (5m) tall in the shape of a column. The foliage feels prickly. This tree is suitable for coastal locations.

J. c. 'Hibernica' is denser than the species. This columnar tree has blue-green needles and reaches a maximum height of 13 feet (4m).

J. c. 'Hornibrookii' grows 20 inches (50cm) tall and as wide as 6½ feet (2m). The green needles have white stripes.

J. c. 'Repanda' is similar to 'Hornibrookii', although smaller and less prickly.

J. horizontalis 'Glauca'

This conifer grows slowly to about 10 feet (3m) broad and 12 inches (30cm) tall. It is a good prostrate evergreen, suitable for the rock garden.

This weeping spruce creates a pretty scene amid the rocks.

J. sabina

J. sabina has an irregular shape and forms a number of fastigiate branches. It grows up to 10 feet (3m) tall. The variety 'Tamariscifolia' with blue-green needles remains shorter, but grows wider.

J. squamata 'Meyeri'

This conifer is attractive as a young plant. Your mistake in acquiring it will become apparent later: The plant will look dry and brownish. Though it is one of the conifers sold most often, a responsible supplier or nurseryman should not sell it without informing the customer about the future appearance of the plant.

J. virginiana

This is the North American red cedar, and it is an exception: This conifer likes to grow in limy soil. It is one of the best tall conifers. It can withstand coastal wind, and is not sold often enough. It will grow up to 66 feet (20m) tall. The variety 'Grey Owl' grows only 10 feet (3m) tall and is gray-blue in color. 'Glauca', more columnar, grows up to 16½ feet (5m). The narrowest variety is *J. v.* 'Skyrocket'. Unfortunately, the branches will have to be bound together every now and then to keep the narrow column shape; the color of the plant is blue-gray.

Larix (Larch)

Most conifers are best transplanted in September or October. The larch, however, is an exception to this rule, as its planting time is March and April. The larch is deciduous.

L. decidua (European larch)

This larch appears in gardens less than it used to. It displays nice autumn colors.

L. kaempferi (Japanese larch)

The Japanese larch has rather bluish needles. It can reach 100 feet (30m) high at most, and grows wider than the European larch.

Libocedrus (Incense cedar)

Libocedrus decurrens has a columnar shape. In spite of the height it can reach (up to 66 feet/20m), the narrow form makes its use in medium to large gardens possible. The foliage is dark green.

Metasequoia

The metasequoia is deciduous. *Metasequoia glyptostroboides* grows very quickly to 100 feet (30m). This is the most recently discovered large tree, found in central

China in 1945. Though this tree was imported to Europe less than fifty years ago, gigantic specimens can be admired already in several botanical gardens. It grows in every type of soil.

Picea (Spruce)

Spruces prefer dry soil. Spruces and pines are often confused, but differences are easily seen: Pines have long, to very long, needles in bunches of two, three, or five. Spruces have short single needles.

P. abies (Common spruce, Norway spruce)

This spruce is often used for Christmas trees. It grows up to 66 feet (20m) tall and has horizontal branches.

P. a. 'Clanbrasiliana'

This spruce grows 3 feet (1m) tall at most. It is compact and rounded, and wider than it is tall.

P.a. 'Inversa' (Weeping spruce)

It reaches 50 feet (15m) at most. The branches hang along the trunk and spread over the ground.

P. a. 'Nidiformis'

'Nidiformis' grows 3 feet (1m) tall and has a pleasing dwarf form.

In the right foreground is Picea glauca 'Conica'. The large tree in the background is Cedrus atlantica 'Glauca'.

P. a. 'Procumbens'

'Procumbens' grows like the species, but as though in miniature. This prostrate plant reaches 3 feet (1m) in height.

P. a. 'Repens'

'Repens' grows low and wide, and has creeping branches.

P. brewerana

This is a sad tree: All the branchlets droop limply.

P. glauca 'Conica' (White spruce)

This is one of the most beautiful cone-shaped conifers, which buds a beautiful light green in spring. Dwarf, it can be grown as a potted plant, as a specimen, and in the rock garden. In a large garden it would probably be overlooked.

P. omorika (Siberian spruce)

Picea omorika is more narrow than the common *P. abies*. It is a quick grower that can reach 100 feet (30m) tall.

A number of Pinus *species are not grown in gardens very often. Especially in England,* *Wales, and Scotland,* Pinus radiata *is often planted as a forest tree.*

P. pungens (Colorado spruce)

This species, with very sharp needles, is sown. From sown seed, green, blue-green, and blue-gray offspring may arrive. The bluer the color, the more expensive the plant. The most beautiful blue spruce is *P. p.* 'Koster', which ordinarily grows up to 66 feet (20m) tall. A dwarf form is *P. p.* 'Glauca Procumbens', and a weeping form is 'Glauca Pendula'.

P. sitchensis (Sitka spruce)

Picea sitchensis requires a moister location and can withstand coastal winds. This tall tree—it grows 165 feet (50m) tall at maximum—has very short needles, green on top and blue-white underneath.

Pinus (Pine)

Pines make few demands as far as soil is concerned. They will grow in the poorest of sandy soils. Pines are more suitable than spruces for many applications in gardens. There are many species, of which we will discuss the ones most often encountered.

P. mugo (Mountain pine)

Pinus mugo grows up to 33 feet (10m) tall and has dark green needles. For use as hedges that do not need to be clipped, the *P. mugo* var. *mughus* (up to 6½ feet/2m) and *P. mugo* var. *pumilio* (up to 10 feet/3m) are suitable. They can withstand coastal winds.

P. nigra var. austriaca (Austrian pine)

This tall, wide dark green tree is strong and can withstand coastal winds. It is the best tall pine for gardens. The needles are rather soft and long.

P. parviflora 'Glauca' (Japanese white pine)

This medium-large pine has irregular branches. It is suitable for use as a specimen tree.

P. sylvestris (Scotch pine)

P. sylvestris is much cultivated for timber. It is less suitable for gardens; *P. s.* 'Globosa' has a more or less rounded shape and grows 3 feet (1m) tall at most. 'Pumila' has the same shape and grows up to 6½ feet (2m) tall.

P. wallichiana (Himalayan white pine)

This tall tree has a pyramidal shape. It has long blue-green needles with white stripes, and which hang down limply.

Pseudolarix (Golden larch)

A singular deciduous tree is *P. kaempferi,* a tall tree with a wide pyramidal shape. The needles are light green in color.

Pseudotsuga (Douglas fir)

In its natural habit—northern North America—the tree will grow up to 200 feet (60m) tall. It is a quick grower, wide, and in the shape of a pyramid.

A vista with Taxus baccata *as an accent at the end of the view.*

Sciadopitys (Umbrella pine)

The umbrella pine is named for the position of the needles around the branchlets; the whorls look like umbrellas. This pyramidal tree looks a rather gloomy dark green from a distance. Only one species is being cultivated: *S. verticillata*.

Sequoiadendron (Giant sequoia)

This tree grows to more than 330 feet (100m) tall in California. It is suitable only for enormous gardens or parks. It is sensitive to frost when young. The larger trees are often struck by lightning. The bark feels softer than that of any other tree.

Taxodium (Cypress)

These large deciduous trees grow well in very moist, even wet, soil. Around the tree, large knots push up through the soil from the roots, and are known as "knees." The swamp cypress shows beautiful autumn color.

Taxus (Yew)

The yew is one of the few conifers indigenous to Europe. It can grow in limy soil, provided that it is well supplied with humus. *Taxus baccata* is one of the best evergreens for hedges. It grows slowly and for that reason makes an expensive purchase. *Taxus baccata* 'Fastigiata' has a columnar shape. For a wide shrub with yellow needles, choose *T. b.* 'Semperaurea'.

Taxus baccata 'Repandens' grows only 2 feet (60cm) tall, with more or less horizontal branches. As a hedge, *T. × media* 'Hicksii' is often employed. The upright-growing branches will bow away from the trunk from the weight of snow, resulting in disfigurement or damage, and for that reason *T. baccata* should be chosen for planting a hedge where the genus *Taxus* is desired.

Pseudolarix kaempferi.

Thuja occidentalis *'Ericoides'*.

Thuja (Arborvitae)

Chamaecyparis is often wrongly used for hedges. *Thuja* is easier to shape, and as a hedge it does not tend to go bald near the base, either. Arborvitae can withstand wind and water-retentive soil.

T. occidentalis

This *Thuja* can grow up to 66 feet (20m) tall. It is often used for hedges; this is a pity, because *T. plicata* will stay green in winter more beautifully. Many varieties are being cultivated, of which *T. occidentalis* 'Globosa' is particularly striking for its rounded form. For wide and conical growth, choose *T. o.* 'Rheingold'. The yellow color sometimes shows to advantage in a rock garden. *Thuja occidentalis* 'Spiralis' grows tall, with remarkably twisted branchlets and foliage of nice green color.

T. plicata (Giant arborvitae)

This is the best and quickest-growing hedging conifer, which will remain a shining dark green both summer and winter. The varieties 'Atrovirens' and 'Dura' have proved to be sturdy.

Thujopsis

This conifer can withstand partial shade. It is too large even for medium-large gardens. The glossy scales feel leathery and are white underneath.

Tsuga (Hemlock)

It is virtually never used for a hedge, yet *T. canadensis* is suitable for it. It can grow rather tall and can withstand, like *T. heterophylla,* shade. The latter will endure coastal winds, but is sensitive to frost when young. For a weeping dwarf form, choose *T. canadensis* 'Pendula'.

11 Perennials A to Z

Only a few perennials keep their good looks throughout the year. Most have a short period of flowering, but by combining various perennials, you can create a border or bed that is a virtual sea of flowers for a much longer period of time—months, if you plant with some care.

It takes some thought to figure out which plant should be planted in which spot. Never purchase plants just because you think they look nice. Remember, you must first take a close look to see whether the sun exposure, type of soil, and so forth in a particular location are

Iris 'Edith Wolford'.

agreeable with the plant you have in mind for that location. Variety is important in a garden, and you will want to combine your perennials with other plants such as bulbs, shrubs, roses, annuals, even vines.

Variety in the Garden

In this chapter you will find information on the demands many different perennials make as far as soil, water, and sun are concerned, rather than elaborate descriptions of the plants themselves. Very often, just perennials are used in borders. But bulbs are necessary to extend of the flowering period in spring; so few plants flower in the early spring months. Perennials die back in autumn and come up again in spring. Before they return, the area will look bare throughout the winter months if you insist on cutting off the stems and foliage they leave. For winter interest, don't cut your perennials down to the soil, and do plant some evergreen perennials.

In a small garden, a few crops such as strawberries and sorrel can be planted among the flowering plants. If you find it difficult to achieve the ideal spacing of plants for lush flowering, plant annuals between your perennials to make sure that the border will flower all summer. Note

Ranunculus ficaria. The wild lesser celandine is considered a weed by some, while others think it a beautiful plant.

There are varieties with yellow foliage, and with white flowers.

Teasel head with brimstone butterfly.

over the course of the summer those times when there are not enough plants in bloom, and plan to remedy this the year after.

Planting Time

The best time for planting perennials is spring. A number of perennials shouldn't be planted in late autumn. Because they will not have enough time to become established before the winter, they may rot or freeze. A general rule is that trees and shrubs are planted in autumn, perennials in early spring.

When looking over plants at the nursery, it is rather difficult to assess how large they will grow. Therefore, it is important to make a well-considered list beforehand of the plants you wish to have. A great many bad bargains can be prevented by taking the trouble of doing some preparatory research. Perennials do not look attractive in early spring and you may be tempted to buy plants that seem to offer spectacular flowering at the nursery. Stick to your garden plan, and remember that you are trying to create a long period of bloom and garden interest in the years to come. You are unlikely to achieve utter perfection your first year, and ought to use that first season to observe carefully how the effect can be improved.

Rampantly Growing Perennials

Some perennials grow rapidly into large plants, pushing aside slower-growing or more delicate plants. With some plants, say, creepers, this is an advantage, but in the perennial border it may be bothersome. The following plants often need regular attention so they don't overwhelm their neighbors in the border:

Alstroemeria
Convallaria majalis
Doronicum pardalianches
Helianthus
Macleaya
Matteuccia struthiopteris (fern)
Petasites
Pulmonaria
Viola odorata and *Viola sororia*

Fragrant Perennials

It would be a pity not to include sweet-smelling plants in your garden. If the garden is regularly visited by people who are blind or partially sighted, fragrant plants are an important inclusion. There are gardens specially designed for blind people to enjoy, and you can add such pleasing

Eryngium giganteum is a perennial suitable for the heather garden.

plants as those with very soft leaves, such as *Stachys byzantina*, or fragrant flowers from the following list:
Arabis caucasica
Galium odoratum
Convallaria majalis
Dictamnus albus
Doronicum
Lavandula
Monarda
Paeonia
Primula
Salvia × superba
Smilacina
Viola odorata

Perennials That Repel Rabbits
Anchusa
Echium vulgare
Eryngium maritimum
Helleborus foetidus
Iris × germanica
Nepeta

Polygonatum
Salvia nemorosa
Saponaria
Thymus

Plants for Coastal Locations
Armeria maritima
Convolvulus soldanella
Crambe maritima
Eryngium maritimum
Glaucium flavum
Lavatera olbia
Santolina

Plants That Spread Easily
Aquilegia
Campanula lactiflora
Heracleum
Lupinus
Lychnis chalcedonica
Myosotis
Papaver nudicaule
Thalictrum aquilegifolium
Verbena bonariensis

Lysimachia vulgaris, loosestrife, is not often grown in gardens. It can be admired in botanical gardens and "wild" gardens.

Perennials That Need Protection from Frost
Acanthus
Alstroemeria
Eremurus
Fuchsia
Incarvillea

Astilbe *species.*

Kniphofia
Lavatera
Thalictrum dipterocarpum
Yucca

Flowers for Cutting

The flowers you usually love to cut are perennials. You can plant flowers for cutting in your perennial border; you don't need a separate cutting garden to enjoy flowers indoors. What could be better than strolling through your garden, stopping to cut flowers for an arrangement? The following includes the best cut flowers for the perennial garden.

Yellow flowers:	*Achillea*
	Buphthalmum
	Coreopsis
	Doronicum
	Helenium
	Helianthus
	Heliopsis
	Solidago
	Telekia
	Trollius
Orange flowers:	*Alstroemeria*
	Kniphofia
	Papaver
	Physalis

Red flowers:	*Astilbe* (also pink and white)
	Geum (also orange and yellow)
	Heuchera
	Paeonia (also pink and white)
	Penstemon
Blue-purple flowers:	*Aconitum*
	Campanula
	Centaurea
	Delphinium (also pink and white)
	Erigeron (also pink)
	Thalictrum (also white)
White flowers:	*Achillea* (also yellow)
	Anemone sylvestris
	Anaphalis
	Aruncus
	Astilbe (also red and pink)
	Chrysanthemum maximum
	Gypsophila (also pink)
	Dictamnus (also pink)
	Phlox (all colors)
	Smilacina
Pink flowers:	*Anemone* × *hybrida* (also red and white)
	Aster (also blue, violet and white)

Lathyrus cyaneus *flowering in spring.*

Chrysanthemum × *rubellum*
Dianthus
Paeonia (also red and white)
Lavatera (also white)
Sidalcea
Lathyrus latifolius (also white)

Lythrum salicaria *flowers for a long time and attracts butterflies: It is a must for any* *naturalistic pond. The plant will grow in a damp or dry location.*

These are only a few of the many possibilities for flowers that are excellent for cutting. You may admire some other flowers in a neighbor's garden, and if you can offer similar growing conditions, chances are those flowers will thrive for you, too. Short flowers–those with short stems–were not included in the list above. Of many of the listed genera, varieties in other colors exist, but within the varieties there often are various shades of a color, say, dark red and light pink. *Delphinium*, for example, offers red, white, blue, and violet, all of which can be further distinguished in darker and lighter shades.

Perennials to Attract Butterflies

Plants that attract butterflies, in short, "butterfly plants," should be planted on warm sheltered locations, where they will attract the most butterflies. There is a difference between the host plants for caterpillars, and the plants with nectar-filled flowers often visited by butterflies. Host plants include cabbages and other cruciferae, nettles large and small, and even various grasses. Caterpillars rarely appear on garden plants and will not cause damage in the ornamental garden. In most gardens, there is no room for typical host plants. Concentrate on the nectar plants for butterflies. You will find butterflies are attracted particularly to the aster, globe thistle, dame's violet, and sedum.

Latin name	Common name	Height	Color	Flower
Achillea millefolium	common yarrow	12–24 in./30–60cm	pink/white	June/July
Ajuga reptans	carpet bugleweed	10 in./25cm	blue	May/June
Alyssum saxatile	gold dust	4–12 in./10–30cm	yellow	April/May
Aster amellus	Italian aster	12–24 in./30–60cm	pink/violet	July/Sept.
Aster novi-belgii	aster	39–47 in./100–200cm	various	Sept./Nov.
Aubrieta deltoidea	purple rock cress	2–4 in./5–10cm	blue	April/May
Buphthalmum salicifolium	oxeye	20 in./50cm	yellow	June/Sept.
Centaurea species	knapweed	various	various	July/Sept.
Centranthus ruber	red valerian	71in./180cm	red	May/July
Dianthus deltoides	maiden pink	10–12 in./25–30cm	purple-red	June/Sept.
Echinacea purpurea	purple coneflower	24–39 in./60–100cm	purple	Aug./Oct.
Echinops species	globe thistle	31–39 in./80–100cm	blue	July/Sept.
Erigeron species	fleabane	20–31 in./50–80cm	violet	June/July
Euphorbia	spurge	4–16 in./10–40cm	yellow/green	May/June
Galium odoratum	sweet woodruff	4–12 in./10–30cm	white	May/June
Hesperis matronalis	dame's violet	24–36 in./60–90cm	lilac/white	June/Sept.
Humulus lupulus	common hop	157 in./400cm	white/green	July/Sept.
Liatris spicata	gayfeather	20–39 in./50–100cm	purple-red	Aug./Sept.
Ligularia dentata	*ligularia*	39–59 in./100–150cm	various	July/Sept.
Lychnis flos-cuculi	ragged robin	24–31 in./60–80cm	pink	May/July
Lythrum salicaria	purple loosestrife	39–59 in./100–150cm	purple	July/Sept.
Nepeta	catmint	12–24 in./30–60cm	blue-purple	June/Aug.
Phlox	phlox	24 in./60cm	pink	various
Polemonium caeruleum	Jacob's ladder	31–39 in./80–100cm	blue	various
Primula	primrose	4–39 in./10–100cm	various	various
Prunella	self-heal	6–10 in./15–25cm	various	various
Ranunculus	buttercup	12–35 in./30–90cm	yellow	May/July
Saponaria ocymoides	soapwort	10–20 in./25–50cm	pink-red	June/Sept.
Scabiosa caucasia	pincushion flower	20–31 in./50–80cm	blue/violet	June/Sept.
Sedum spectabile	stonecrop	20 in./50cm	pink	Sept.
Sedum telephium	orpine	12–20 in./30–50cm	pink	Aug./Sept.
Senecio jacobaea	ragwort	12–35 in./30–90cm	yellow	July/Oct.
Taraxacum officinale	dandelion	2–12 in./5–30cm	yellow	April/May
Thymus	thyme	2–12 in./5–30cm	lilac	May/Sept.
Valeriana officinalis	garden heliotrope	24–35 in./60–90cm	red	June/Sept.
Verbena bonariensis	verbena	59 in./150cm	blue-purple	July/Oct.
Viola	violet	4–10 in./10–25cm	yellow/blue/white	March/May

Caterpillars are usually considered to be harmful. Unfortunately, there are no butterflies without caterpillars.

The hosta is an excellent solitary plant for shade. Remember that the plant will not put up foliage until late in spring: The spot will be bare all winter.

Perennials with Notable Foliage

These plants show to advantage in the border, and they can make excellent plantings through vines and ground covers. In addtion to their beautiful leaves, they all flower, too.

Astilboides
Bergenia
Hosta
Macleaya
Petasites
Rheum
Rodgersia

A red flower border in the garden of Beth Chatto.

Perennials Suitable for the Heather Garden

To make the heather garden look natural, plant a number of those perennials that are reminiscent of the wild plants that grow on the heath. Obviously, large-flowered plants would not be appropriate–the likes of tulips and peonies. Plants that are more suitable are listed below, and many plants are options for you if your garden is in partial shade. The plants in the following list, however, will be happy only if your heather garden is in full sun:

Aster alpinus
Eryngium alpinum
Geranium, species with small flowers
Helianthemum
Hypericum calycinum
Iberis sempervirens
Lavandula
Limonium latifolium
Nepeta
Potentilla nepalensis
Prunella webbiana
Santolina
Saxifraga cotyledon
Sedum, various species
Thymus, various species
Veronica incana and *V. spicata*

Most ferns and ornamental grasses will happily add variety to the heather garden. Because few of the above plants flower early, it is recommended to add a number of species bulbs as well.

Thematic plantings

Variety in the garden is a conscious effort. Some people yearn to grow indigenous plants, or plants typical of a Japanese garden; others want medicinal herbs or old-fashioned plants only. You may choose heather species only, or, for a shady garden, a collection of ferns. You could plant an entire garden completely full of roses from the past century. It is a little trickier to make a kitchen herb garden attractive; often the plants themselves are beauties, often with small flowers that put in only a late appearance. The same goes for plants that are used for dyeing fabrics (even wool you've carded yourself). A garden designed uniquely with plants that can be used for dyeing doesn't make a very attractive garden. But, a selection of dyeing plants from the following list can be used in every garden, if the plants are spread throughout the garden.

Page 277:
Anjuga reptans. *Bungleweed occurs in nature, too.*

Common name	*Botanical name*	*Part used*	*Height*	*Color*	*Plant type*
African marigold	*Tagetes*	flower	8–31 in./20–80cm	yellow/brown	annual
Apple	*Malus pumila*	leaves/bark	6½–16½ ft./ 200–500cm	white	tree
Aster	*Aster*	flower	20–47 in./50–120cm	yellow	perennial
Barberry	*Berberis vulgaris*	roots	3–10 ft./100–300cm	white	shrub
Bearberry	*Arctostaphylos uva-ursi*	leaves	8–35 in./20–90cm	pink	shrub
Birch	*Betula*	leaves	10–25 ft./300–700cm	x	tree
Beech	*Fagus*	leaves	6½–33 ft./300–700cm	x	tree
Tansy	*Tanacetum vulgare*	whole plant	16–47 in./40–120cm	yellow	perennial
Clematis	*Clematis vitalba*	leaves	39–59 in./100–150cm	white	perennial
Blackberry	*Rubus* species	young branches	6½–16½ ft./ 200–500cm	white	perennial
Stinging nettle	*Urtica dioica*	tops	5–6½ ft./150–200cm	green	perennial
Broom	*Cytisus scoparius*	flower	3–4 ft./100–120cm	yellow	perennial
Yarrow	*Achillea millefolium*	whole plant	14–18 in./35–45cm	white/pink	perennial
Oak	*Quercus robur*	leaves/acorns	6½–100 ft./200–3000cm	green	tree
Alder	*Alnus glutinosa*	bark	6½–16½ ft./200–500cm	green	tree
Maple	*Acer*	leaves	6½–131 ft./200–4000cm	yellow/green	tree
Sumac	*Rhus*	leaves/panicles	3–6½ft./100–200cm	red	perennial
Goldenrod	*Solidago canadensis*	whole plant	2⅔–5 ft./80–150cm	yellow	perennial
Ground ivy	*Glechoma hederacea*	whole plant	2–10 in./5–25cm	purple	perennial
Hop	*Humulus lupulus*	hops	13–16½ ft./400–500cm	green	climber
Horse chestnut	*Aesculus hippocastanum*	leaves	100 ft./3000cm	white	tree
Sweet chestnut	*Castanea sativa*	nutshells	100 ft./3000cm	white	tree
Cherry, sweet	*Prunus avium*	leaves/bark	10–65½ft./300–2000cm	white	tree
Ivy	*Hedera helix*	berries	3–13 ft./100–400cm	white	climber
Dogwood	*Cornus sanguinea*	roots	6½–9 ft./200–260cm	white	shrub
Larch	*Larix*	needles	6½–65½ ft./200–2000cm	purple	tree
Privet	*Ligustrum vulgare*	berries/ branches/leaves	6½–10 ft./200–300cm	white	perennial shrub
Mahonia	*Mahonia aquifolium*	roots/berries	3–6½ ft./100–200cm	yellow	shrub
Queen-of-the-meadow	*Filipendula ulmaria*	flower	1⅔–4 ft./50–120cm	cream-white	perennial
Horsetail	*Equisetum palustre*	whole plant	12–20 in./30–50cm	x	perennial
Pear	*Pyrus communis*	leaves	6½–33 ft./200–1000cm	white	tree
European aspen	*Populus tremula*	buds	6½–33 ft./200–1000cm	x	tree
Red flowering currant	*Ribes sanguineum*	flower	3–5 ft./100–150cm	pink	shrub
Larkspur	*Delphinium*	flower	3–5 ft./100–150cm	blue	perennial
Rudbeckia	*Rudbeckia purpurea*	flower	2–2⅔ ft./60–80cm	yellow	perennial
Thyme, wild	*Thymus serpyllum*	whole plant	x	purple	perennial
Onion, common	*Allium cepa*	skin	2–4 ft./60–120cm	purple	annual
Royal fern	*Osmunda regalis*	whole plant	2–6½ ft./60–200cm	x	perennial
Dyer's greenweed	*Genista tinctoria*	flower	1⅓–2 ft./40–60cm	yellow	shrub
Foxglove	*Digitalis purpurea*	whole plant	2⅔–5 ft./80–150cm	purple	biennial
European elder	*Sambucus nigra*	leaves/berries	3–19½ ft./100–600cm	white	shrub
Bird cherry	*Prunus padus*	bark	3–5 ft./100–150cm	white	shrub
Lady's mantle	*Alchemilla mollis*	whole plant	8–20 in./20–50cm	green/yellow	perennial

Alder buckthorn	*Rhamnus*	leaves/bark	3–10 ft./100–300cm	white	shrub
English walnut	*Juglans regia*	leaves/shells	6½–33 ft./200–1000cm	green	tree
Plantain	*Plantago lanceolata*	whole plant	1⅓–1½ft./40–45cm	yellow	perennial
Buckthorn	*Rhamnus cathartica*	bark	6½–10 ft./200–300cm	yellow	shrub
Willow	*Salix*	leaves	10–33 ft./300–1000cm	green	tree

Perennials A to Z

Acaena microphylla
'Kupferteppich'.

Acaeana

This is a good creeper from New Zealand. The flowers are not very striking, but the fruits give a nice reddish-brown glow to the plants. They are quick growers, and sometimes need to be pruned back; do not plant slow-growing short perennials next to them.

The species *A. buchananii* has glaucus leaves, and the variety 'Kupferteppich', with reddish-brown leaves, is the one sold most often. The plant can be propagated easily by cuttings. It does not look attractive in winter.

Acanthus (Bear's breech)

This good cut flower for sun and part shade originated around the Mediterranean; give it a warm location. *Acanthus mollis* grows 3 feet (1m) tall and bears sturdy flowers. The plant flowers in August. The leaves are decorative, too.

Achillea (Yarrow)

Most yarrows need full sun and a dry site. The common yarrow (*Achillea millefolium*) and sneezewort (*A. ptarmica*) have white flower umbels. Good hybrids flowering in yellow are 'Altgold', 'Coronation Gold', 'Moonshine', 'Neugold', and 'Schwefelblüte'. These all grow about 2 feet (60cm) tall and are sturdy enough to be able to stand without having to be fastened. They are good cut flowers, and the umbels are nice in bouquets of dried flowers.

Aconitum (Monkshood)

The blue-purple flower is formed in such a manner that only bumblebees can reach the nectar: a good example of the unique relationship that can arise between a certain plant and a certain animal species. Unlike the larkspur, this plant likes shade. Of the more than sixty species,

Adonis.

quick-growing type with green leaves. *Ajuga reptans* produces blue flowers and grows 6 inches (15cm) tall. Of this plant, a number of varieties are cultivated with purple, white, or pink flowers. *Ajuga genevensis* has nice green leaves and large blue flowers. Bugleweed flowers in May and forms runners aboveground, which can be cut off and easily planted elsewhere.

Alchemilla (Lady's mantle)

Alchemilla mollis definitely qualifies as a garden plant. This plant flowers a greenish yellow and grows 12 inches (30cm) tall. Because of its shape and manner of flowering, this plant is ideally suited, like *Nepeta* (catmint), for bordering flower beds or paths. It requires soil that is not very dry, in sun or partial shade. You can propagate the plant by division; sowing is simple.

Allium

See page 328.

Alstroemeria (Peruvian lily)

The not entirely hardy Peruvian lily is one of the cut flowers that can be kept longest, and grows between 2 and 3 feet (60 to 100cm) tall. *Alstroemeria aurantiaca*

Alchemilla mollis, *lady's mantle.*

Aconitum henryi and *A. napellus* are the most significant. They both have nice dark green, laciniate leaves, and flower in July and August.

Adonis (Pheasant's eye)

The old-fashioned *Adonis amurensis* and *A. vernalis* flower in March and April. The yellow flowers resemble those of the peony. They grow 8 to 16 inches (20 to 40cm) tall. The foliage is finely pinnate. They require a dry, sunny spot.

Aegopodium podograria 'Variegata' (Goutweed)

This shade plant grows rampantly, like a weed, and for that reason is not recommended for the garden. It is difficult to exterminate. The best method to get rid of this plant is by continously grubbing or picking all leaves, thus forcing the plant to grow to death. This should tell you that this plant is suitable only for use in flower boxes.

Ajuga (Bugleweed)

This dense creeper grows green, red, or variegated leaves. In dry soil the plant is very sensitive to mildew. Therefore, plant it in shade or partial shade in every type of soil, if moist. If the growing conditions are not ideal, choose a

Althaea rosea.

flowers in orange and will be fairly hardy after a few years in the same location. This plant requires well-aerated, humusy soil that is not too wet, and sun. You can propagate it by dividing the rootstock in spring.

Althaea (Hollyhock)

Althaea officinalis' roots are valued for medicinal applications. The plant grows 5 feet (150cm) tall and flowers in August and September. The pale pink-violet flowers are small in proportion to the size of the plant. The well-known hollyhock *A. rosea* is, in fact, biennial, but often behaves as a perennial. The plants grow 6½ to 10 feet (2 to 3m) tall and are available in many colors, with single and fully double flowers. The plants are often supplied in mixed colors. Pick the flowers of the plants with undesirable colors in time to prevent them from sowing, and, after two years, you will have left the colors you like. The plant needs a sunny spot, not too wet.

Anaphalis

Anaphalis triplinervis from the Himalayas withstands drought well and grows 8 to 16 inches (20 to 40cm) tall, depending on the type of soil. In a sunny spot *Anaphalis* will flower in July and August. The small white flowers remain on the plant for a long time in dry weather. The plant has striking gray leaves.

Anchusa (Bugloss)

Anchusa officnalis is a very hairy plant with rough leaves 3 feet (1m) tall and bright blue, boragelike flowers. Depending on the variety, the flowers are sky blue to dark blue-purple. In drier soil, these plants will survive the winter better; they require full sun. You can propagate the plant by division. Flowering is in June and July.

Anemone (Windflower)

Windflowers with bulb and rootstock flower in spring; the perennials discussed here flower in autumn. Though they originate from south and east Asia, they are called Japanese anemones. Hybrids that are very suitable for application in gardens have been developed.

Varieties	Height	Color	Flowering period
'Albadura'	32 inches (80cm)	white/pink	July-Aug.
'Honorine Joubert'	4 feet (1.2m)	white	long
'Königin Charlotte'	3 feet (1m)	purple-pink	Sept.-Oct.

The Aquilegia *(columbine) fits very well into both the wild* garden and the most sophisticated of borders.

'Praecox'	32 inches (80cm)	pink	long
'Robustissima'	3 feet (1m)	bright pink	July-Sept.
'September Charm'	32 inches (80cm)	pink	Aug.-Sept.
'Whirlwind'	3 feet (90cm)	white	Sept.-Oct.

Antennaria

This gray creeper is short (2 to 8 inches/5 to 20cm), and recommended for a sunny spot. *Antennaria dioica* is dioecious; the male flowers are whitish. The bright pink color of the female plants usually combines poorly with other plants in the border. As a ground cover, *Antennaria* will endure a moderate amount of being walked over.

Anthemis (Chamomile)

This sun-lover is indigenous to western Europe and the Mediterranean. This small plant flowers like a daisy, with white rays (outer petals and yellow inner petals). A number of species is cultivated, of which *Anthemis nobilis* is the best known.

Aquilegia (Columbine)

There are 120 species of columbine, and of those, there are many varieties and hybrids. The columbine is often sold as a mixture of colors, which obviously is not suitable for every flower border. Ask your local garden center for the varieties you want in the colors you want. A plant for the rustic garden is *Aquilegia vulgaris*, a tried-and-true European plant in cultivation for a great many years.

Arabis (Rock cress)

This early-flowering plant for the sunny rock garden may be planted in every type of soil. The plants grow 4 to 12 inches (10 to 30cm) tall and are perfect for defining a long ledge.

Aruncus (Goatsbeard)

Goatsbeard suffers from drought easily, so do not plant it in full sun. In June the plants grow up to 5 feet (1.5m) tall with nice large, white panicles. It is a good solitary plant, and deserves a place by itself to show off its beauty. The plant is long-lived.

Asarina

With gray woolly leaves, creamy yellow flowers, and a height of 8 inches (20cm), this is the ideal plant for the dry rock garden. It flowers from May to October.

Asarum (Wild ginger)

With its dark green, kidney-shaped leaves, this is a beautiful plant for the deepest shade. In such a location in particular, the plant will not be overgrown by competitors. Because of its slow growth, this plant usually is a rather expensive purchase. It is a good evergreen and only 6 inches (15cm) tall. It requires a moist soil.

Aruncus sylvester.

Aubrieta.

Asparagus (Asparagus fern)

The asparagus fern is the familiar cut foliage at the florist's. This old-fashioned garden plant, with ornamental foliage, has a beautiful green color, followed by yellow in autumn. It fits nicely into perennial borders and can also be planted in groups among creepers. The red berries are an extra treat.

Asperula

See *Galium*, below.

Asphodeline (Jacob's rod)

This hardy plant for dry soil originated in the Mediterranean region and belongs to the lily family. The yellow flowers grow on long spikes. The yellow flowers of *Asphodeline lutea* appear in May and June. Immediately after ripening, sowing can be started; you will have flowering plants after three years. Division can be done in spring.

Aster

Asters are appreciated for their long and abundant flowering in late summer. The choice of flower color and height is enormous. However, be prudent when you buy them, because many asters need staking. The lover of cut flowers will not mind doing this.

Apart from a few exceptions, asters suffer from mildew on the leaves, which diminishes the beauty of the plants.

Aster alpinus flowers as early as June. Like all asters, this 10-inch-tall (25cm) plant likes full sun. Of those flowering in autumn, *A. amellus* and *A. dumosus* are shortest, between 12 to 24 inches (30 and 60cm); these plants do not need any support. The tall asters are suitable for the background of a border in the casual or farm garden. *Aster cordifolius* 'Silver Spray' is a pleasing aster with small white flowers, suitable for filling any bare spots in a border. In a border of taller perennials, *A. laterifolius* 'Horzontalis' is suitable for the same purpose. Neither of these suffers from mildew on the leaves.

Astilbe (Spiraera)

For a moist shady corner, various astilbes can be recommended. The loose panicles flower in red, white, or shades of pink. If the soil is too dry, the leaves will shrivel and die. The height varies from 20 to 32 inches (50 to 80cm). Flowering is in July and August. The dwarf form *Astilbe crispa* 'Perkeo' has scalloped leaves and grows only 8 inches (20cm) tall. The low-growing *A. simplicifolia* flowers a bit earlier, the purple dwarf *A.*

Astilbe.

chinensis 'Pumila' slightly later. This plant is a stunning ground cover. The other species are suitable for the woodland garden or for along the banks of a pond. What garden wouldn't benefit from the addition of *Astilbe*?

Astilboides

Despite its name, this plant does not look like the plant described above. The large round leaves of *Astilboides tabularis*, the only representative of this genus, have ornamental value. A moist, humusy soil is required. The richly flowering dense panicles grow up to 5 feet (1.5m) tall, provided the plant is in the right spot. It looks beautiful next to a pond in the shade, in combination with *Primula bulleyana*.

Astrantia (Masterwort)

Astrantia major and *A. maxima* are real meadow flowers, suitable for the moist, rough shoulders of roadways, flower meadows, or the border. They are not very demanding, as you might guess from their natural habitat. They flower in July and August and grow 24 inches (60cm) tall. *Astrantia minor* requires acid soil and is more difficult to cultivate.

Aubrieta (Purple rock cress)

This plant resembles *Arabis*, and flowers in early spring. It is suitable as a border plant, or creeper, an excellent candidate for planting between stones and to spill over walls. It flowers in violet and blue, and it requires a sunny location that is not too dry. It's a nice candidate

for the rock garden. Propagation is easiest by division in autumn, but sowing in April is also possible.

Bergenia

This large-leafed evergreen flowers in April and is a good border plant. It produces many flowers bunched together on a long stem. The large leaves are beautiful in combination with ferns, grasses, and other fine-leafed plants. You can also plant it in large groups next to a pond. Because it is an evergreen, *Bergenia* is a good pond border plant.

Variety	Flower color	Height
'Abentglut'	dark red/ semidouble	10 inches (25cm)
'Bressingham White'	nearly white	12 inches (30cm)
'Glockenturm'	pink-red	12 inches (30cm)
'Morgenröte'	dark purple-red	16 inches (40cm)
'Perfect'	lilac-red	24 inches (60cm)
'Rotblum'	pink-red	12 inches (30cm)
'Silberlicht'	white, later light pink	16 inches (40cm)
'Sunningdale'	carmine-lilac	18 inches (45cm)

Campanula.

Bergenia.

Borago (Borage)

This kitchen herb can also be used very well in the perennial border. It dies off, but sows easily. The individual blue flowers look festive in salads. This is a good plant for attracting bees.

Brunnera

Brunnera macrophylla can endure rather deep shade. The plant has large round, decorative leaves. The blue flowers are small and start to bud as early as April.

Caltha (Marsh marigold)

See page 357.

Campanula (Bellflower)

There are tall campanulas for the borden and low-growing ones more suitable for the rock garden. They are all sun-lovers. *Campanula carpatica* forms patches of 12 inches (30cm) tall with large blue bells. Flowering is in July and August. A creeping habit and starry bells are features of *C. clatines*. *Campanula glomerata* flowers a month earlier, and is a good cut flower for the border. It will do best in clayey soils. *Campanula lactiflora* grows more than 3 feet (1m) tall, with small pink flowers in July. This plant can take light shade. *Campanula latifolia* has the same height as *C. lactiflora*. A number of varieties

remain slightly shorter, and for that reason will stand up straight more easily. *Campanula persicifolia*, with soft lilac-blue flowers, can also withstand partial shade. The look-alikes *C. poscharskyana* and *C. portenschlagiana* flower in blue-purple. They are creepers and suitable for use as edging plants. They are somewhat evergreen. *Campanula poscharskyana* should be cut back immediately after flowering in June and July, after which it will flower for a second time. All bellflowers are rewarding plants for every garden.

Cardamine (Lady's-smock)

In nature this plant grows in moist meadows and on the banks of ditches. *Cardamine pratensis* 'Plena', which flowers from March to June, is cultivated. The pink flowers are fully double, and for that reason, eye-catching from a distance. The evergreen *C. trifolia* prefers a moist spot in shade and flowers in May and June. Both plants grow 12 inches (30cm) tall.

Centaurea (Cornflower)

The cornflower is sold both as an annual and as a perennial. The one least resembling the common cornflower is *Centaurea macrocephala*, which grows 3

Consider planting a long edging of one plant species. On the left, Campanula *portenschlageana. Their blue-violet color is lovely with the pink roses.*

forming a carpet in the garden. The plants are indispensable for the gray-white border, and they are ideal as rock-garden and border plants.

Ceratostigma

This low-growing plant has gentian blue flowers. The leaves, which turn red, may give you the feeling early in summer that autumn has arrived. The 12-inch-tall (30cm) plant flowers in August.

Cheiranthus (Wallflower)

This rather spindly biennial produces orange or yellow flowers. Plant it among neighbors that will offer it support if it is floppy, but that won't crowd it out.

Chelone (Turtlehead)

This 30-inch-tall (75cm) plant, which flowers in autumn, does not need any support. It prefers a sunny spot, but will be satisfied with partial shade. It is a good cut flower, and a strong plant that can do well in poorer soils. *Chelone obliqua* still bears its pink flowers in September, a nice plant to brighten up the end of the summer.

Chrysanthemum

With the exception of blue, this plant flowers in all colors. *Chrysanthemum zawadskii* var. *latiobum* is a medium-tall plant for full sun. Geese love them. They flower in September and October with slightly smaller flowers than the florist's chrysanthemum. This old-fashioned plant must be staked, but is suitable for all types of soil. It flowers in autumn. Better known is *C. maximum*, the daisy chrysanthemum. There are varieties in many heights. All flowers are white with a yellow heart and appear in May and June. They are rewarding cut flowers that grow well in every type of soil in full sun, and just a few will enhance any flower arrangement.

Chrysanthemum.

feet (1m) tall with round yellow flowers. It is a good cut flower that can also be dried. The most common is *C. montana,* an old-fashioned plant that has large, bright blue flowers. Cut back the plant after flowering, and it will flower again. The pink *C. dealbata* has smaller flowers than the previously mentioned plant, and also grows 24 inches (60cm) tall. All cornflowers prefer full sun.

Centranthus (Red valerian)

The blue-green leaves and pink-red flowers are difficult to fit into the border. The plant does well on old walls and in stony places in the garden. It really shows to advantage in combination with gray-leaved plants, and that goes for the *C. ruber* 'Albus' in particular, which has white flowers.

Cerastium (Snow-in-summer)

Two species are cultivated, of which *Cerastium bierbersteinii* has the larger flowers. *Cerastium tomentosum* has more compact growth. They have gray feltlike leaves and flower in May, the white flowers

The clematis from the "Viticella" group flowers at the same time as the first autumn asters.

Chrysoplenium

This lush, small, green-yellow plant requires a wet place in shade. It grows over stones quickly in moist conditions and can be combined very well with primulas, ferns, and marsh marigolds. In western Europe, this is a protected plant, sold only by specialized nurseries.

Clematis

When one thinks of clematis, usually a climbing plant is pictured. The perennial plant clematis is not used often enough. *Clematis* × *bonstedtii* 'Crepuscule' flowers in light blue from July until autumn, with upright growth to 3 feet (1m) tall. *Clematis hirsutissima* grows to 20 inches (50cm) tall and bears violet-blue flowers. If its site is not too wet, it will flower in May and June. The most beautiful violet-blue is produced by *C. integrifolia*, which flowers from June to September. Though only 24 inches (60cm) tall, they need support. As a rule, you will have to plant them at least as deep as they were planted previously in their nursery containers. Plant clematis (climbers, too) 4 inches (10cm) deeper, and their disease resistance will be better.

Codonopsis (Bonnet)

Of the thirty cultivated species, the delicate *Codonopsis clematidea* and *C. rotundifolia* are usually grown. The bell-shaped flowers are not very striking, but will give an extra dimension to the richly contrasting shapes in the garden. With their limp stems, they manage to grow 20 inches (50cm) tall. Let them sprawl over dwarf conifers, and plant them near a path or terrace, as these delicate plants will not be very effective seen at a distance.

Convallaria (Lily of the valley)

This plant is related to Solomon's seal and May lily. A low-growing evergreen plant, it can cover large areas in partial shade. Propagation is simple–by division–in summer. The white flowers appear in May.

Coreopsis

Coreopsis verticillata, 28 inches (70cm) tall, flowers from July to September with yellow, daisylike flowers and fine, light green foliage. *Coreopsis* is a plant for full sun. Because of its fine foliage and ability to withstand drought, this is one of the few perennials that is nicely

Convallaria majalis. *Large areas are quickly filled with the lily of the valley, thanks to its rapidly increasing underground "pips."*

Coreopsis verticillata *has fine foliage that offsets the flowers prettily.*

suited for planting in large flower tubs. *Coreopsis grandiflora* grows to the same height, a very good cut flower, of which there are many varieties.

Cornus

Cornus canadensis flowers in June. It requires humusy soil; the rootstocks grow only through a thick layer of leaf mold or peat, which should always be slightly moist. The shrublike plant grows 8 inches (20cm) tall and bears starry white flowers. Flowering is in May, and is followed by bright red fruit. The less-often cultivated *C. suecica* requires a wetter soil.

Corydalis

Corydalis lutea grows 24 inches (60cm) tall and spreads

Corydalis lutea *can spread quickly. It is an easy, long-   flowering perennial.*

a lot in soils that please it. The bright yellow flowers show to advantage in shade. The long period of flowering is from May to September. *Coryldalis ochroleuca* is finer in all its parts, a good addition to any border with its creamy white flowers. For other species refer to "Bulbous and Tuberous Plants A to Z," page 334.

Cotula

This genus from New Zealand looks like something between a fern and a moss. The creeping plants grow quickly. After a year, this ground cover can be walked on carefully. The creamy white flowers are not spectacular. Of the seventy species, *Cotula squalida* is the one most often planted.

Crambe (Sea kale)

Crambe cordifolia resembles gypsophila, but reaches 8 feet (2.5m) tall. The plant fits very well at the back of the border, and is nice as a solitary plant in the lawn. It looks best at the far side of a pond, as the reflection in the water makes the plant even more impressive. It bears small white flowers, and can be recommended for any garden that is not quite small. The plant requires soil that is not too wet in winter.

Cymbalaria (Mother-of-thousands)

Cymbalaria muralis flowers from May to November with small, whitish purple flowers. The small, succulent leaves can help it endure considerable drought. Mother-of-thousands grows in partial shade on walls and stony places. It spreads easily, making it a pest in the more refined rock garden. It forms threadlike stems of several yards (meters), but it does not grow very high.

Daboecia (Saint Dabeoc's heath)

This beautiful green plant is larger than the common bell heather and is sensitive to frost. The flowers are available in red, purple, and white. The plant grows 12 inches (30cm) tall.

Darmera

See *Peltiphyllum*, below.

Delphinium (Larkspur)

This tall plant (5 ft./1.5m) requires full sun. The torchlike flowers have remarkable colors, varying from pink to blue and purple. It looks marvelous with all large-flowered perennials, and also with roses and lilies. Larkspur is a good cut flower. If the plant is cut back

immediately after flowering (June and July), it will start to flower again later in the year, though it will remain shorter. Some of the many garden hybrids:

Variety	Color	Height
'Aristolat'	pink/black eye	5 feet (1.5m)
'Azurriese'	azure blue/ white eye	5½ feet (1.7m)
'Black Knight'	dark violet blue	5 feet (1.5m)
'Blue Bird'	gentian blue/ white eye	5 feet (1.5m)
'Blauwal'	blue/brown eye	6½ feet (2m)
'Berghimmel'	bright blue/ white eye	6 feet (1.8m)
'Capri'	bright blue/ white eye	2⅔ feet (80cm)
'Galahad'	snow white/ large bunches	5 feet (1.5m)
'Guinevere'	mauve	5 feet (1.5m)
'King Arthur'	violet/white eye	5 feet (1.5m)
'Kleine Nachtmusik'	dark purple	2⅔ feet (80cm)
'Piccolo'	azure blue	2⅔ feet (80cm)
'Summer Skies'	light blue/ white heart	5 feet (1.5m)
'Waldenburg'	deep, dark blue/ black eye	5 feet (1.5m)

The bleeding heart, Dicentra spectabilis, *grows about 30 inches (80cm) tall. It is considered to be an old garden plant, but was not introduced from China until 1847.*

'Zauberflöte'	blue with pink/ white eye	6 feet (1.80m)

Dianthus

Of the many species, the maiden pink, *Dianthus deltoides*, is the best for edging. It can also be used very effectively at the front of the border and in the rock garden. It flowers in spring with small flowers on stems 6 inches (15cm) tall. The variety 'Albus' is white, 'Splendens' is carmine, and 'Brilliant' is a bright dark red.

Dicentra (Bleeding heart)

This old-fashioned plant prefers partial shade. The taller *Dicentra spectabilis* flowers in rosy red and white. *Dicentra formosa* is finer in all its parts and is more pinkish. Like *D. formosa, D. eximia* 'Alba' grows approximately 12 inches (30cm) tall. This plant remains beautiful after flowering in June because of the gray-green foliage; it is magnificent for the gray-white border. The delicate flowers indeed look like tiny puffed hearts.

Delphinium *at a nursery.*
Beautiful combinations can be
made with the large range of
colors.

Dictamnus (Gas plant)

You can actually make the flower burn: Hold a lit match to it on a night without wind. Flame will erupt above the bunch of flowers, giving off a spicy smell. The flower does not suffer from this. This perennial blooms for a short time in June and July with large racemes of flowers. It requires full sun and dry soil. The color of the flower is pinkish. *Dictamnus albus* 'Albiflorus' flowers are white.

Dodecatheon (American cowslip)

Humusy, nutritious, and moist soil should be provided for *Dodecatheon meadia*. This plant is closely related to *Primula* and cyclamen, and most resembles the latter. Stems of 24 inches (60cm) stand in a circle of leaves. The color of the flowers, which appear in July and August, is pink.

Doronicum (Leopard's bane)

Of the approximately thirty species only three are important for the garden. *Doronicum orientale* flowers earliest (April and May). *Doronicum pardalianches* and *D. plantagineum* flower later and grow taller (32 in./80cm). They are all daisylike with yellow flowers. They require sun to partial shade in soil that is not too dry.

Draba

Draba sibirica is a fine, rampantly growing plant for the rock garden. This yellow-flowering perennial flowers in early spring. It spreads easily, but propagation is also possible by dividing the rootstock. Give it limy soil and full sun.

Dryas

Dryas octopetala requires full sun and well-aerated, rather dry soil. Give *Dryas* this, and the shrublike plant will reward you with an evergreen carpet. After a short flowering period in June, the plant becomes a sea of silvery fruit fluff. It is obvious from the white flowers why the plant belongs to the rose family.

Duchesnea

This plant most resembles the wild strawberry, but has yellow flowers. The small "strawberries" look delicious, but do not have any flavor whatsoever. The plant is a good creeper in partial shade and grows very quickly.

Echinacea (Purple coneflower)

Echinacea purpurea is often sold as *Rudbeckia*. This sun-loving plant flowers from July to September and grows 32 inches (80cm) tall. The flowers are pink-red with orange-brown hearts. This is a good cut flower.

Echinops (Globe thistle)

Echinops ritro comes from eastern Europe. Depending on the type of soil, it can grow to 3 feet (1m) tall. The blue flowers dry well. This plant is not very demanding. It will show to advantage in full sun. It flowers from July to September. The globe-shaped flowers are perfect for arrangements.

Echinacea purpurea *(purple*
coneflower) used to be called
rudbeckia. This plant is one of
the better cut flowers.

Erica, *bell heather.*

Empetrum (Crowberry)

The soil must be absolutely free of lime for *Empetrum nigrum*, which requires a moist to wet soil in full sun. This is an excellent evergreen creeper if its requirements are met. The flowers are not very striking, but the black berries, which appear after June, are.

Epimedium (Barrenwort)

"Shade," "humus," and "moist" are the buzzwords for *Epimedium.* The leaves of this exotic-looking plant most resemble those of the tree *Cercidiphyllum.* Both are appropriate in Oriental garden design. The various species, which resemble each other closely, flower in April and May. The leaves remain green through winter. This is an effective creeper, but it may not thrive everywhere, even though all its requirements seem to have been met.

Erica (Bell heather)

Unlike common heather, this heather can be sited in a moister spot. Acid soil (add peat moss) is required. Clay is not suitable, and heather would look out of place, anyway, in a landscape with clay-loving plants. This plant can also be grown in containers. The flowering period of the various species of bell heather is broader than that of common heather, and the plants look better when they are not in bloom. (Remember that August and September see the bloom of *Calluna.)* Prune immediately after flowering; this is done at a different time for each species. For Saint Dabeoc's heath, see *Daboecia*, page 288.

Erigeron (Fleabane)

The genus *Erigeron* has as many as 150 species. The ray (outer) petals are finer than those of the aster, but as to the rest, there is hardly any difference. There are many colors among the hybrids, also like the aster. An advantage of the aster is that the leaves do not get mildew. The cultural requirements are the same.

Erodium (Heron's bill)

This plant resembles the geranium, but prefers drier soil. *Erodium manescavii* is the species to be found most often, and it spreads easily; for that reason, it is an excellent plant for the wild garden.

Eryngium (Sea holly)

Eryngium planum is the easiest to cultivate. It is suitable for very dry soil, and grows 32 inches (80cm) tall, and for that reason is very suitable for the perennial border.

Eryngium, sea holly, is marvelous for the rock garden, among ornamental grasses and gray-leafed plants.

It is handsome in combination with ornamental grasses in the heather garden.

Eupatorium

Of the six hundred species, we will mention only *Eupatorium purpureum* (Joe Pye weed) here: a sturdy, 6½-foot-tall (2m) border plant, which can be used as easily in the naturalistic garden as in a tidy border. The

Note the characteristic yellow-green flower of Euphorbia, *spurge.*

purple flower umbels are eye-catching in August and September. Though the plant should not be planted in too wet a spot, it looks good as a backdrop for a pond; their height guarantees the plants can be enjoyed from some distance.

Euphorbia (Spurge)

This plant is the same yellow-green as the flower of lady's mantle. There are tall and short species, all with this characteristic green-yellow color. *Euphorbia epithymoides* is the best known and fits in very well with such other spring-flowering plants as leopard's bane. It can withstand some shade, and grows 16 inches (40cm) tall.

Filipendula

Filipendula rubra 'Venusta Magnifica' makes a beautiful combination with *Eupatorium*, a tall perennial with loose carmine flower panicles. *Filipendula palmata* grows to 3 feet (1m) tall with pink flowers, and *F. ulmaria* with white flowers. *Filipendula ulmarina* 'Plena' has fully double flowers.

Foeniculum (Fennel)

The green-leafed fennel is a kitchen herb, while the brown-leafed *Foeniculum vulgare* 'Purpureum' is more suitable as a border plant, and is particularly beautiful among tall hybrid tea roses. The brightly colored roses are toned down by the airy, ocher-yellow umbels of the fennel. The umbels look great by themselves, set off by the brown foliage.

Fuchsia

Though it does not belong with perennials—the plant is woody—*Fuschia* is usually considered to be a perennial because it dies to the ground in winter and comes up again in spring. A semishrub from the south of South America, *F. magellanica* 'Riccartonii' is most often cultivated. This semishrub is suitable for locations in full sun to part shade. If winters are mild, or if the plant is well protected, it will freeze less or not at all, and may then grow up to 6½ feet (2m) tall. If not protected, the plant will grow approximately 3 feet (1m) tall in one summer.

Galium (Sweet woodruff)

The plant has bright green foliage, with small white flower umbels on top of starry rings of leaves. Sweet woodruff is a good border plant, one usually planted in the herb garden. It requires full sun to part shade. Putting one sprig

Page 293: Galium odoratum.

Gentiana asclepidea.

of this 12-inch-tall (30cm) plant in a bottle of cheap white wine will give it a distinctive taste. The plant used to be called *Asperula;* nowadays the official name is *Galium odoratum*.

Gaultheria

Gaultheria procumbens is usually classified with the perennials, while *G. shallon* is listed with the shrubs. See page 246 for both.

Gentiana

This genus contains more than eight hundred species. Only a few species are being cultivated, because of the special cultural requirements of the plant. It is admired for its deep blue color, which can also be found in speedwell. Species that are cultivated are:

G. acaulis, 2–4 inches (5–10cm), blue

G. asclepiadea, 16–24 inches (40–60cm), hyacinth blue

G. clusii, 2–4 inches (5–10cm), blue

G. farreri, 2–4 inches (5–10cm), inside light blue with white

G. septemfida, 4–12 inches (10–30cm), violet-blue

G. sino-ornata, 4–6 inches (10–15cm), bright blue

G. pneumonanthe, 10 inches (25cm), chionodoxa blue

G. lutea, 39 inches (100cm), yellow

With *G. lutea*, a few years may pass before the first flowers appear.

Geranium (Cranesbill)

This genus offers unlimited possibilities for the perennial border. The blue, purple, and pink flowers of various heights do not make things difficult for the designer, because—excepting in orange-red and in the yellow borders—they can be applied in countless numbers and

species. With the exception of *Geranium phaeum,* all geraniums will grow in full sun, but partial shade is usually best. Keep in mind that the taller species may fall apart; if they do, cut them off, after which they will grow and flower again. For the rock garden, *G. cinereum* 'Ballerina' with lilac-pink flowers is most suitable. As underplanting for trees, the creeper *G. macorrhizum* is appropriate; it greatly resembles the spreading *G. robertianum*, a wild cranesbill.

Geum (Avens)

Genum rivale is an old-fashioned plant. Its beauty does not lie in the orange flowers, but rather in the "fluffs" that follow the flowers. This plant is a rampant grower for shade. The varieties 'Album' (white), and 'Leonard' (copper-red) may harmonize better in your garden.

Glaucium

Glaucium belongs to the poppy family. It has blue-green leaves and very long seedpods. It can withstand salty coastal winds. *Glaucium* is not a particularly nice plant, but in the coastal areas *G. flavum* may offer a solution to some of your gardening puzzles.

Geranium phaeum, *cranesbill,*   *sheltered spot.*
is suitable for naturalizing in a

not very well known. Its leaves give a special contrasting effect in the border, on a plant 6½ feet (2m) tall. The most beautiful species is *H. × superbus*, which has bright yellow flowers 8 inches (20cm) across atop dark-colored stalks. (The Jerusalem artichoke belongs to this genus, too.)

Helleborus (Hellebore)

Helleborus niger, the Christmas rose, bears white flowers; "niger" refers to the black roots. The flowering period is from December to January. Other notable species include *H. viridis*, a green-flowering species that blooms from March onward; *H. foetidus*, a nice evergreen plant that grows at most 24 inches (60cm) tall and bears green-yellow flowers in March and April; *H. orientalis*, the Lenten rose, a finer plant with dark purple flowers.

Hemerocallis (Daylily)

The daylily is available in the colors red-brown, yellow, and orange. This old-fashioned garden plant of the lily family blooms in July with large flowers on stems 3 feet (1m) tall. This easy garden plant offers ornamental value in the early emerging foliage. Daylilies look pretty on the banks of a naturalistic pond, or along a shrub border. A

Give Gunnera *enough space; it grows tall and wide.*

Gunnera

Gunnera is not entirely hardy, and it is suitable only for larger gardens. The rhubarblike leaves of this foliage plant grow 13 feet (4m) tall. The flowers are at the bottom of the plant—green spikes 3 feet (1m) tall—and are not very eye-catching from a distance. This plant can be used very effectively by a pond. The early emerging leaves may freeze easily in a late night frost. These leaves can be covered for night protection, but you can also wait for new leaves.

Gypsophila

This genus includes annual and perennial plants. The perennials have smaller flowers that bloom in July and August. *Gypsophila* is a good cut flower and needs a dry, sunny site. The flowers may be white or pink. Filling any bare spots in a border with *Gypsophila* may create a more peaceful unity out of a rather untidy border.

Helianthus (Sunflower)

The common annual sunflower is a member of this genus. There are perennial sunflowers, too, with much smaller flowers, but which grow tall. *Helianthus salicifolius* is

Hemerocallis *'Delightsome'*.

Hemerocallis *'Will Return'*.

Hemerocallis *'Betty Woods'*.

Hemerocallis *'Indonesia'*.

Hesperis matronalis flowers twice if the plant is cut back after blooming.

banks of a naturalistic pond, or along a shrub border. A few scattered clusters, or even banks, makes for a natural effect. All parts of the plant are edible.

Heracleum (Cow parsnip)

This is a large and sometimes appeciated garden plant. See also under poisonous plants, page 123. In large gardens where a shaggy look is desired, this 13-foot-tall (4m) plant may have a place. Keep in mind, however, that it spreads easily. To prevent this, remove the flowers.

Hesperis (Rocket)

The fragrance of *Hesperis matronalis*, dame's violet, is strongest in the evening. The flowers are pink. If the 3-foot-tall (1m) plant is cut off immediately after flowering, it will flower a second time. The white *H. m.* 'Alba' is the one usually cultivated, but there are shorter varieties with fully double flowers.

Heuchera

The name "Plui de feu" (rain of fire) of this sun-loving perennial for the red border hints at the many small flowers on one long flower stem. The plant height of 24 to 32 inches (60 to 80cm) depends on the richness of the soil. Indicated heights of plants should not be taken too seriously; remember that plants will remain shorter in poor soil, and that they may grow considerably taller in rich soil.

Hosta (Plantain lily)

The plantain lily is also known as funkia. This foliage plant for deep shade makes a wonderful underplanting,

and it will serve you well as a border plant or as a specimen. There are several thousands of species and varieties. Choose from hosta with sea green leaves, white leaves with green edges, golden variegated and silver variegated leaves; there are tall and short hostas, large and small. Often seen is *Hosta sieboldiana* 'Elegans', a variety with blue-green leaves and white flowers. Consider the color hosta can provide; the blue or yellow cast of the foliage can be an enhancement. Whereas most perennials are full-grown after two years, hostas are full-grown after four to five years, and 'Krossa Regal' only after seven years. This, the largest hosta, has a diameter of 5 feet (1.5m). Give hosta the time they need to develop.

Gray-leafed		
Hosta sieboldiana	'Elegans'	28 inches (70cm)
H. tokudama		12 inches (35cm)
	'Big Daddy'	3 feet (1m)
	'Big Mama'	3 feet (1m), leaves slightly narrower
	'Blue Angel'	3 feet (1m)
	'Blue Diamond'	12 inches (30cm)
	'Blue Wedgewood'	12 inches (30cm)
	'Halcyon'	16 inches (40cm)
	'Krossa Regal'	5 feet (1.5m), yellow
Several shades		
H. fortunei	'Gold Standard'	24 inches (60cm)

Iberis.

H. plantaginea		24 inches (60cm)	
H. sieboldiana	'Frances Williams'	24 inches (60cm)	
H. tokudama	'Little Aurora'	6 inches (15cm), green-leaved	
H. sieboldii	'Bianca'	24 inches (60cm)	
H. s.	'Snowflakes'	16 inches (40cm)	

Hypericum (Saint-John's-wort)

This genus of plants includes shrublike plants, perennials, and annuals, and has evergreen as well as deciduous plants. They all flower in yellow. Though *Hypericum calycinum* is woody, it is often classified with the perennials. It reaches 1 foot (30cm) in height, is evergreen, and very suitable for use as a creeper in a sunny location. The stamens of the large yellow flowers are eye-catching.

Iberis (Candytuft)

This low-growing, evergreen border plant bears white flowers in spring. *Iberis sempervirens* requires a sunny site. It is suitable for the rock garden.

Hosta lancifolia *var.* albomarginata *(plantain lily or funkea). Only after five years can hosta be considered full-grown. Only the large-leafed species are suitable as specimen plants.*

Incarvillea

The most well known is *Incarvillea delavayi*. The bulbous fleshy roots are best planted in soil that is not too moist, because of sensitivity to frost. *Incarvillea* is also suitable for container culture. The large pink flowers appear as early as June. The height depends on the growing conditions; the plants grow 12 to 20 inches (30 to 50cm) tall, on average.

Iris

The German iris (*Iris* × *germanica*), the Japanese iris (*I. kaempferi*), and the Siberian iris (*I. sibirica*) are easily distinguished. The rhizomatous plants flowering in spring and summer will be found in the chapter on bulbous plants (page 344). *Iris pseudacorus*, the yellow iris, can be found under water plants (page 360). *Iris germanica* requires a dry site, one preferably with limy soil.

Notable varieties are:

I. germanica	'Constant Wattez'	pink
	'Blue Rhythm'	pure blue
	'Empress of India'	light blue

Iris sibirica *'Creme Chantilly'*.   Iris *'Olympiad'*.

Iris *'Designer Gown'*.   Iris *'Navajo Jewel'*.

'Sable'	dark purple
'Nightfall'	blue/violet
'Red Orchid'	red
'Wabash'	white/blue

Iris sibirica will grow in a dry or a humid place; it looks splendid growing near a naturalistic pond, and it makes a nice combination with *Hemerocallis* and *Tradescantia*.

Notable varieties are:

I. sibirica	'Berlin Bluebird'	bright blue
	'Perry's Blue'	blue
	'Blue King'	dark blue

Kirengeshoma

Kirengeshoma palmata is the plant most often grown. It flowers late with creamy yellow, pendant flowers. Even for those who think they do not want yellow in their gardens, this plant is recommended. Cover it up in winter. The 3-foot-tall (1m) plants will do well in part shade.

Kniphofia (Red-hot poker)

Red-hot pokers flower in red, yellow, or orange. In preparation for the first winter after planting, you must cover them well. After that, they will prove hardy if the soil is not too wet. In a sunny spot, most varieties will grow more than 3 feet (1m) tall.

Lamiastrum

Of this yellow-flowering creeper, the variegated plant sold most often is *Lamiastrum galeobdolon* 'Florentinum'. The plant forms runners quickly and will grow 20 inches (50cm) tall if the conditions are right. It grows rampantly; for that reason, plant it only in deep shade, which will check its growth.

Lathyrus (Wild pea)

The climbing wild pea is generally known. This annual is perfect for children to grow because it is so reliable. Less well known is the perennial wild pea, *Lathyrus latifolius*. This climbing plant (6½ ft./2m) blooms pink or white. For this plant, too, flowering will increase with deadheading. Sow as early as February in a cold frame.

Lamium (Dead nettle)

A gloomy but beautiful plant is *Lamium orvala*, the only border plant of this genus that grows approximately 2 feet

Lamium maculatum, *the spotted dead nettle, does well* *in shade. It is also suitable for the moist wild garden.*

Lathyrus.

(60cm) tall. It has purple flowers and thrives in partial or full shade. *Lamium maculatum* is a good creeper that never flowers abundantly, but for a very long time. It does not grow as quickly as *Lamiastrum* (above), which used to be sold under the name of *Lamium galeobdolon*, and which flowers in yellow.

Lavandula (Lavender)

Lavender is actually a semishrub, but it is discussed with the perennials here for practical reasons. Various varieties of *Lavandula angustifolia* are in cultivation, all of which grow to different heights. The leaves are grayish, the flowers blue-purple. The maximum height is 20 inches (50cm). Prune the plant every year in March for more compact growth, and the plant will flower abundantly in July. Give lavender a warm spot in full sun, and it will perform well as a border plant. It is beautiful in combination with roses, and always looks attractive with gray-leaved plants.

Lavatera (Tree mallow)

Lavatera trimestris (syn. *Malope)* is an annual that is very popular with enthusiasts. Less well known are *L. olbia* 'Rosea' and L. 'Barnsley', both perennials. They grow up to 5 feet (1.5m) tall. The flowering, from the end of June to late in autumn, is so abundant that we are willing to

put up with its sensitivity to frost. Do not site the plant in a location that is very moist and rather sunny. People with a knack for gardening take cuttings every year at the end of summer and store them in a cool, dry place during the winter. In one year the cuttings will mature into full-grown plants.

Lavatera olbia is worth the trouble of protecting over winter. You will be rewarded with abundant flowering that continues from July to first frost.

Ligularia przewalskii.

Liatris (Gayfeather)

This stiff plant is often grown as a cut flower. Depending on the richness of the soil, it may grow 24 to 32 inches (60 to 80cm) tall. It is rather hardy in a dry location. The flowers are usually light purple, but there are white varieties. It is remarkable that the flower spike blooms from the top down.

Ligularia

These moisture-loving plants grow large. They are excellent for planting near a pond, not only because the location offers sufficient water, but also because the decorative leaves will be reflected on the pond surface. The flowers are yellow or orange. *Ligularia dentata* has daisylike flowers and rounded leaves. The flowers of *L. przewalskii* grow on large spikes; the leaves are very laciniate. These plants can be put in full sun, but prefer to stand in partial shade.

Linaria (Toadflax)

The yellow *Linaria vulgaris* is a beautiful plant that grows well in sandy soil. It requires a dry spot in full sun. It is cultivated by few perennial growers. The mother-of-

thousands, *Linaria cymbalaria*, also called *Cymbalaria muralis*, grows nicely on walls and is suitable for the rock garden. The flowers are small, but the flowering period is unsurpassed in duration. The variety 'Globosa' has larger flowers than the species, and 'Alba' is white. The natural color is pinkish purple with a yellow "mouth."

Lupinus (Lupin)

The genus Lupin includes two hundred species. *Lupinus arboreus* is an exception to the other herbaceous plants, with yellow flowers and a woody stalk that may grow 10 feet (3m) tall. The *L. polyphyllus* is commonly known; it is probably the easiest garden plant as far as cultural demands are concerned. There are various colors. Collect fresh seed from the most beautiful plant and propagate only these. Deadhead the plants that do not have to yield seeds immediately after flowering, and they will flower again in August.

Lychnis (Campion)

The color of *Lychnis chalcedonica* is bright red. The plant is 3 feet (1m) tall and needs support. The red-orange *L. × arckwrightii* only grows 1 foot (30cm) tall, and the flower is more refined, showing to advantage

Linaria cymbalaria, *mother-of-thousands, likes limy soil. The plant can be grown on* *walls facing east, west, or north.*

against the dark brown leaves. *Lychnis coronaria* (syn. *Coronaria tomentosa*) occurs more often. This plant flowers for a long period and has a bright pink color that is difficult to fit in with anything else. The white variety is more beautiful, with gray leaves. All *Lychnis* require full sun.

Lysimachia (Loosestrife)

There are many species of loosestrife, and they all look different. *Lysimaschia nummularia* is a yellow-flowering creeper. A quick grower, it can cover an entire bank in a short period of time. *Lysimachia punctata* flowers from June to August and grows 3 feet (1m) tall. *Lysimachia clethroides* has white flower spikes curved at the top, and is known as gooseneck loosestrife. This is the best border plant; it grows 28 inches (70cm) tall and flowers in August and September. It spreads, however, very rapidly, and requires watchful maintenance. New plants spring up from pieces of root left in the soil.

For a wet spot near a pond, robin) is suitable.
Lychnis flos-cuculi *(ragged*

Lythrum (Purple loosestrife)

The wild *Lythrum salicaria* grows 5 feet (1.5m) tall, and for that reason is suitable only for larger gardens. *Lythrum salicaria* 'Robert' and 'Rosy Gem' remain smaller; they are carmine red and carmine pink, respectively. They flower in July and August and like full sun. They are at home near naturalistic ponds, as they like damp soil. Be warned, however, that *Lythrum* is a rampant spreader and can crowd out other plants.

Left:
*Loosestrife (*Lysimachia nummularia*) is a good plant for moist locations. The plant grows very quickly, then dies back in winter.*

Right:
Lysimachia punctata.

Lythrum salicaria.

Macleaya

Although this plant does not resemble *Papaver* at all, it belongs to the same family. It is a large plant—not suitable for small gardens, but it looks appropriate at the back of a large border. It does need support. The maximum height is 8 feet (2.5m). It flowers in late summer, the flowers an insignificant yellow-green growing in loose panicles. The plant forms large underground suckers. It looks best growing with other tall perennials such as sunflowers, *Echinops*, and *Eupatorium*.

Maianthemum (False lily of the valley)

This plant does not appear often in gardens, but is suitable as an underplanting for rhododendrons, or in the woodland garden. From its appearance it is obviously related to Solomon's seal and lily of the valley. It is a low-growing plant with only two leaves, hence its scientific

*For the woodland garden in deep shade, the false lily of the valley (*Maianthemum *bifolium) is a sensible choice. Each stem carries two leaves.*

name *Maianthemum bifolium*. The plant will spread slowly with thin root stocks in humusy soil.

Malva (Mallow)

The *Malva moschata* most often cultivated reminds one of the woody *Lavatera*, and it prefers a similar site. However, it will do well on poorer sandy soil. Mallow flowers are most often pink, but there are white varieties, too.

Meconopsis (Himalayan poppy)

This delicate plant that is sensitive to frost is, like *Salvia patens*, desired for its extraordinary blue color. Flowering is in June. *Meconopsis betonicifolia* requires well-drained soil to overwinter successfully. However, the soil must also be rather moist. If you succeed in keeping the plant alive, it will grow 2 feet (60cm) tall. *Meconopsis cambrica* is easy of culture, though, and grows 1 foot (30cm) tall. The plants spread easily and can become invasive. The flowers are yellow and orange.

Mertensia (Bluebell)

This forget-me-not–like plant is intensely blue, grows well in shade, and is fairly hardy. Various species are being cultivated, of which *Mertensia virginica* is best known. The plant dies back early in the year, to come up again the following spring.

Mentha × piperita (Peppermint)

There are many mint species, all of which tend to grow enthusiastically. Therefore, do not plant them in a small herb garden, but rather in containers. Peppermint is a kitchen herb. A single leaf in a cup of ordinary tea will make it memorable.

Monarda (Bergamot, bee balm)

Monarda is related to the dead nettle—the flowers look much alike. These plants will bring butterflies and hummingbirds to your garden. The most significant species is *Monarda didyma*, of which many varieties are being cultivated:

'Croftway Pink'	pink
'Cambridge Scarlet'	scarlet
'Prairiebrand'	dark red
'Adam'	carmine
'Alba'	white
'Violacea'	dark lilac

Page 303:
Meconopsis betonicifolia.

Malva.

Nepeta (Catmint)

Two species—*Nepeta mussinii* (up to 1 foot/30cm tall) and *N.* × *faassenii* (more than 1 foot/30cm tall) are often, unfortunately, mixed up. The first is suitable for borders in small gardens; the latter is desirable for large gardens. The choice of species also depends on whatever is to be planted behind the *Nepeta*. Both species bear blue flowers from June until autumn. The less well known *N. grandiflora* grows 28 inches (70cm) tall. With bigger flowers, this plant is suitable for the border. The color is violet-blue.

Oenothera (Evening primrose)

This genus includes annual, biennial, and perennial species. The shortest of the perennials is *Oenothera missourensis*, 8 inches (20cm). The large yellow flowers are not in proportion to the small plant. This *Oenothera*, like the following species, requires a sunny, dry location in sandy soil. *Oenothera fruticosa* has reddish stems and grows 2 feet (60cm) tall; *O. tetragona* has green stems and larger flowers than the *O. fruticosa*. Both bear yellow flowers from May to September.

Omphalodes (Navel wort)

The most well known is the blue-flowering *Omphalodes*

verna. The flower very much resembles that of the common forget-me-not. The plant needs moist soil in partial shade or full shade, and will spread quickly in humusy soil. If the soil is too dry, the leaves will soon shrivel. The plant grows 6 inches (15cm) tall and is a good creeper. It flowers early.

Opuntia (Prickly pear)

It is unusual to mention a cactus with the perennials, but this plant is an exception: Some *Opuntia* species are hardy. Planted in a sheltered, dry spot in sandy soil, this cactus will do very well in the garden.

Pachysandra (Spurge)

Pachysandra terminalis, an evergreen creeper, bears white flowers in March and April and is suitable for a shady site. The height is 8 inches (20cm). This thick cover of glossy leaves ensures that weeds do not stand a chance. The plant will not grow well in every soil or situation; try a few plants first before planting a large area.

Paeonia (Peony)

Of the many species, we will mention only *Paeonia officinalis* here, the old-fashioned large-flowered double peony, and *P. lactiflora*, a more delicate flower on more

Oenothera, *evening primrose*.

Paeonia *'Madame Alert Claude'*.

Paeonia *'Kansas'*.

Paeonia *'King of England'*.

Paeonia *'Madame de Vatry'*.

Papaver orientale. The flowers of this, the Oriental poppy, seem almost unnaturally large and will dominate the border. They are available in a number of clear, sometimes harsh colors: red, orange, white, and pink. Cut the plants back immediately after flowering, and they will flower again later that year. Because of the heavy flowerheads, they may need staking. They will grow in all types of soil, in full sun.

Peltiphyllum

Peltiphyllum peltatum, which is sometimes sold under the name *Darmera*, flowers in April with pink flowers on bare stems 32 inches (80cm) tall, which arise from the soil without foliage. The large round leaves come up later and turn reddish in autumn. In spring the plant may be damaged by frost, but it is rather hardy. It is good in combination with narrow-leaved plants such as iris and grasses. Give it a place in sun or partial shade that is not too dry.

Penstemon

This is the first plant that comes to mind when thinking about making a red-flowering border. Though it is not entirely hardy, this plant resembling the foxglove deserves

Papaver somniferum.

elegant, straight stalks. As a cut flower, *P. officinalis* will droop too much from the weight of the flower head, but a few blooms can be floated in a bowl of water. *Paeonia officinalis* tends to flower two weeks earlier. *Paeonia lactiflora* is an ideal cut flower. There are a great many types and varieties of peony: single, semidouble, and fully double flowers; anemonelike flowers; Japanese; and so on. A specialized nursery can best inform you. Peonies require nutritious, humusy soil that is not limy. Plant peonies in a large hole, and mix well-rotted stable manure into the soil. Unlike other perennials, peonies should be left undisturbed in the same place for a long time. Flowering will be enhanced, and it is not unusual for one plant to bloom for twenty years or even much longer. You ought to supply manure every year. If you must transplant a peony, do so in September or October, so the plant can establish itself before winter. Peonies require full sun or partial shade. Questions concerning peonies that do not flower are among the complaints heard most often at nurseries, so give your peonies the care they need. (For tree peonies, see "Shrubs A to Z," page 253.)

Papaver (Poppy)

A number of species occur in nature, all annuals. Of the perennial *Papaver*, the garden species descended from

Penstemon.

a place in the garden. It is a good cut flower, and depending on the species, from 16 to 40 inches (40 to 100cm) tall. It requires full sun in a warm spot and dry, well-aerated soil.

Petasites (Butterbur)

An old English book on gardening describes this plant as an unworthy pest. Many gardeners share this opinion, but for a different reason: The foliage will be eaten by insects early in summer, and die in August. For the same growing conditions, *Peltiphyllum peltata* is more suitable. In addition, this plant offers attractive autumn color. The much smaller *Petasites albus*, the white variety, is suitable for use in gardens. The white flowers

Petasites hybridus (butterbur) is beautiful in spring, but in August large holes will appear in the leaves. By September the plant will have died back, leaving bare soil. For that reason, plant it in combination with Arum italicum *(arum).*

appear early, in March and April. This is an attractive waterside plant, too.

Phlomis

The creamy yellow flowers are attached like little bulbs along the stems of this plant, an ideal addition to the border in a sunny spot. It flowers in July, and even after the flowers have passed, the plant still looks attractive in autumn. Its grows to 32 inches (80cm).

Phormium (Flax lily)

Suitable only for a very sheltered garden, this plant can be uprooted in autumn to overwinter in a frost-free place. Dark gray-green leaves stick straight up from the soil. *Phormium* is nice on its own, and at the front of a border it brings peace in an otherwise colorful riot. It grows to 5 feet (1.5m). Flowers appear only in warmer regions. This is a plant for the connoisseur, and is not appreciated by everyone.

Physalis (Japanese lantern)

It's not the flower of this plant, but the calyx—bright orange in late autumn—that makes it attractive, and a delight for lovers of dried flowers. In the garden, the plant behaves like a weed; the rootstock is difficult to stop. It grows to 32 inches (80cm). *Physalis alkekengi* is the species most often cultivated.

Phytolacca.

Physostegia (False dragon's head)

One of the best and easiest border plants, this makes a good cut flower, too. It blooms in summer and does not need staking, growing to 24 to 32 inches (60 to 80cm). The flowers are pink or white. The plant needs full sun for sturdy growth.

Phytolacca (Pokeweed)

Phytolacca acinosa, indigenous to North America, has gone wild in many parts of Europe. Straight panicles of pink flowers bloom from July to September. In autumn, the clusters are full of black berries. The 5-foot-tall (1.5m) plants will do best in full sun or partial shade. You can propagate it by division and seed.

Plantago (Plantain)

A variety of the broad plantain, *Plantago major* 'Rubrifolium', has beautiful, brownish red leaves. It is well suited for planting casually in gravel.

Polemonium (Jacob's ladder)

Polemonium coeruleum is the best-known species of the genus *Polemonium*. It is a good border plant, and at 32 inches (80cm) tall makes a good cut flower. It grows sturdily and does not need support. It flowers from June to August.

Polygonatum (Solomon's seal)

Except for *Polygonatum verticillatum*, *Polygonatum* varieties resemble one another a great deal. The heights vary, though. Choose the appropriate height for your garden setting.

P. commutatum	4 feet (1.2m)
P. latifolium	28 inches–4 feet (70–120cm)

Plantago major, *the common plantain, is a weed that likes growing between paving stones and in rubble. The cultivated plant* P. major *'Rosularis' does, too.*

The berry of Solomon's seal.

P. multiflorum	24 inches (60cm)
P. odoratum	16 inches (40cm)
P. verticillatum	28 inches (70cm)

Give the plants a humusy, moist soil, and partial to full shade.

Polygonum (Knotweed)

Polygonum is a genus of versatile plants, and includes creepers to perennials 13 feet (4m) tall. There are nice annuals, and also some bothersome weeds. The flowers are spiky and whitish to pink. See "Climbing Plants A to Z," page 324.

P. affine	up to 12 inches (30cm)
P. amplexicaule	24–36 inches (60–90cm)
P. bistorta	12–28 inches (30–70cm)

Polygonum bistorta.

P. compactum	16–24 inches (40–60cm)
P. cuspidatum	6½–10 feet (2–3m)
P. sachalinense	10–13 feet (3–4m)
P. weyrichii	24–32 inches (60–80cm)

Potentilla (Cinquefoil)

Cinquefoils can be found growing as shrubs, perennials, rock-garden plants–and weeds. The border plants resemble somewhat the strawberry, though they do not

Potentilla anserina *(cinquefoil) is usually considered a weed. The plant grows in limy and stony soil, where few other plants will grow.*

bear fruits. *Potentilla atrosanguinea* grows 16 inches (40cm) tall with bright red flowers. *Potentilla nepalensis* bears pink flowers and grows to the same height as *P. atrosanguinea*. Smaller and yellow-flowering are *P. aurea*, *P. ternata*, and *P.* × *tonguei*, all flowering in the middle of summer.

Primula (Primrose)

All primroses require some shade and a rather moist soil, conditions that cannot be found in every garden. Trees take up a lot of moisture from the soil in summer, so any primroses nearby would get too little water. A shady spot on the north side of the house, without trees, would be better. Some examples from the enormous selection of primroses available:

Botanical name	Color	Flowering time	Height
P. beesiana	purple-red	June/July	20 inches (50cm)
P. chionantha	white	May/July	16 inches (40cm)

P. florindae	yellow	July/Sept.	36 inches (90cm)	Primula.
P. pulverulenta	purple-red	May/June	20 inches (50cm)	

and the rock garden.

Prunella (Self-heal)

This low-growing pink perennial flowers in June and July. *Prunella webbiana* should not be confused with the weed that grows in the lawn; the cultivated plant has larger flowers. It requires full sun and rather dry soil.

Pulmonaria (Lungwort)

Flowering in early spring, this is an attractive plant for bees. Except for the varieties with the name 'Alba', they flower in a mixture of blue and pink. They all have spotted leaves, except for *P. angustifolia* 'Blaues Meer', which has deep blue flowers. In a dry location they are often affected by mildew (like *Ajuga reptans*). Spraying to remedy this is useless: The location is wrong for the plant.

Pulsatilla (Pasqueflower)

This plant used to be classified with the anemones. It flowers in April and May, after which beautiful silvery fluffs appear. The rather large flowers are blue. The plant grows 10 inches (25cm) tall and is suitable for the border

Raoulia

This silver-gray, creeping perennial requires a dry, sheltered place in full sun. It is very suitable for covering large areas of the rock garden. In July it bears very small yellow flowers. The only species that is being cultivated is *Raoulia australis*, which originated in New Zealand.

Rheum (Rhubarb)

As a specimen ornament by a ditch or pond, the moisture-

loving, tall rhubarb will look its best. The flowers are dark red, but the ornamental value lies mainly in the deeply laciniate leaves. The

Pulsatilla vulgaris, *pasqueflower.*

Rheum palmatum.

Sambucus ebulus (Danewort, elder)

Although not woody, this plant is considered to be a perennial. It is propagated by division or by sowing. Suitable for every type of soil in full sun or partial shade, it grows rampantly. It is nice in landscape gardens. The plant dies back in autumn after reaching a height of 8 feet (2.5m). It very much resembles the common elder, often planted in gardens and parks, and which occurs in natural landscapes.

Saponaria (Soapwort)

This plant resembles the weed chickweed because of its limp stems. It bears pink flowers in May and June and requires full sun. It is suitable for the rock garden and is a good plant to let grow over walls.

Sedum (Stonecrop)

This genus has as many as five hundred species, most of which are not hardy. The lowest-growing yellow species, only a few centimeters tall, is *Sedum acre*. This mat-forming plant is rather loose, giving weeds an opportunity to grow through it. When the weeds are pulled, the stonecrop is often uprooted, too.

Saponaria officinalis, *bouncing bet, is also called soapwort for its soapy smell. The plant flowers especially well in the* evening, *and is attractive to moths then. There are also white and fully double cultivated varieties.*

plant is suitable for full sun to partial shade. Only a few plants are needed to make an impact.

Rodgersia

The leaves are especially elegant. The hand-shaped leaves of *Rodgersia aesculifolia* very much resemble those of the horse chestnut. Flowering is in June and July. The plant grows 3 feet (1m) tall. Moist soil in part shade will suit it best. *Rodgersia* will also show to advantage on the shady bank of a pond.

Sagina (Pearlwort)

This prostrate plant can be used in the rock garden or the soil between flagstones. It has small starry flowers that appear in June and July. It is an easy garden plant, but one that looks nice only in combination with other garden plants.

Salvia (Sage)

The bright red annual sage is the best known. *Salvia nemorosa* is a beautiful border plant. The violet-blue 'Ost Friesland' and the pink 'Roze Queen' grow 20 inches (50cm) tall and flower from June to August. Use the spiky flower heads to contrast with other shapes in the flower border.

Sedum acre.

Another yellow species is *S. kamtschaticum*, with prostrate stems; this is an easy, slow-growing, long-flowering stonecrop. *Sedum spurium* is another low-growing species, with pink-red flowers; most species require full sun, but this one can also be planted in partial shade. *Sedum spectabile* and *S. telephium* are taller species. Both attract butterflies. Sedum combines well with *Sempervirens* species, which also are succulent, but have fewer flowers. As succulents, the plants can withstand a lot of drought. Except for *S. spectabile*, all species require a sunny spot and well-aerated soil. Wet soil in winter is damaging.

Sidalcea

This is the ideal plant for the flower border: long-flowering, with sturdy stems that do not need support, attractive after having flowered, a good cut flower, requires little care, with flowers in shades of light pink, carmine, and white, and a height of 20 to 32 inches (50 to 80cm). In addition, it grows in every type of soil. It belongs to the family of mallows, as do *Lavatera* and *Hibiscus*. The plant is nice in combination with purple loosestrife, phlox, and lavender.

'Brilliant'	shiny carmine
'Rosy Gem'	camine with lilac
'Rose Beauty'	dark red, flowering early

Smilacina

This plant very much resembles Solomon's seal, but the flowers are borne in panicles at the end of the stems. It is a plant for the deepest shade, though it does not mind more sun. It is beautiful in combination with *Primula*. *Smilacina* is a good cut flower.

Solidago (Goldenrod)

This plant grows rampantly. The lower leaves are often affected by mildew, so for most gardeners this plant will

Sedum reflexum.

Symphytum.

not be a first choice. An old-fashioned plant, it bears yellow panicles that grow 3 feet (1m) tall. There are some shorter varieties suitable for the border. Aside from locations in deep shadow, you can plant *Solidago* anywhere. Flowering is in August and September.

× *Solidaster*

This plant used to be classified as × *Asterago*; the name "Solidaster" combines the words "aster" and "solidago." (When a cross is made between two plant genera, the new name is usually a combination of the two.) In nature this cross could not have occured, because the different genera occur on different continents. *Solidaster lutea* is yellow and requires the same growing conditions as goldenrod and aster. The plant topples over easily, and for that reason it may not be very suitable for your garden. It is a good cut flower.

Stachys (Betony)

Stachys is suitable for borders, and is pretty mixed with roses as well as in the heather garden. The carmine flowers of *S. byzantina* grow 16 inches (40cm) tall. *Stachys lanata* does not flower. Plant large groups of these at the front of a gray-white border. The hairy foliage is deliciously velvety.

Symphytum (Comfrey)

Symphytum officinale is an easy plant for moist locations in full sun or partial shade, with white or blue flowers. It grows 3 feet (1m) tall. The creeper *S. azureum* flowers with sky blue flowers. This plant flowers early in spring and can grow in deep shade. Another creeper, and one that flowers virtually in the middle of winter, is *S. grandiflorum*, with creamy white flowers.

Thalictrum (Meadow rue)

Thalictrum aquilegifolium has leaves that resemble those of the columbine, and flowers that resemble those of *Gypsophila*. The height is 4 feet (1.2m), the color is violet. Meadow rue is a good border plant, and suitable for cutting. It will do well in a sunny place, but can also withstand deep shade. Flowering is in June. Later, in July and August, *T. dipterocarpum* bears rounded flowers in large panicles. The yellow stamens are striking. Of this species there are also a white and a fully double variety. Height, between 5 to 6½ feet (1.5 and 2.m).

Thymus (Thyme)

Do not give thyme soil that is too moist because of its sensitivity to frost. There is a creeping thyme with gray woolly foliage. *Thymus* x *citriodorus* 'Aureus' has golden leaves and grows slightly taller. This species is also available in silver: *T. c.* 'Silver Queen'. The color of the flowers is the same for all species: lilac-pink.

Tiarella

This evergreen creeper has lime green leaves in spring and a beautiful reddish color in autumn. The creamy yellow flowers appear in April. This quick grower forms a thick carpet. It can be planted in full sun, but partial shade is better, and deep shade is also possible. *Tiarella* is an ideal underplanting for shrubs and in the woodland garden. *Tiarella cordifolia*, foamflower, blooms only for a short period, but abundantly. *Tiarella wherryi* flowers for a lot longer, from May to September, but the blooms are less pretty. *Tiarella cordifolia* 'Rosalie' is light pink.

Tricirtus hirta, the toad lily, is not glamorous, but the small waxlike flowers are fascinating.

Page 313:
Sedum cauticola, like S. spectabile, attracts many butterflies.

Veronica, *speedwell.*

Tricyrtis

Tricyrtis hirta belongs to the lily family. Though the color of the flowers is insignificant (brownish with spots), the plant is interesting because of its glossy leaves and late flowering. Plant this special, waxlike flower where it can be seen and appreciated. It requires acid soil, so you will probably need to add peat moss.

Trollius (Globeflower)

Trollius resembles the buttercup, but has round flowers in the colors yellow and orange. It prefers a moist, sunny location. It is a good cut flower for the border and flower meadow, and grows 20 inches (50cm) tall. It flowers from April to June. The harsh colors strike a false note in the border; choose the soft yellow 'Lemon Queen' for a quieter effect.

Verbascum (Mullein)

Verbascum nigrum, the black mullein, is a biennial plant that grows to 6½ feet (2m) tall. The slightly shorter *V. blattaria*, yellow, *V. chaixii*, purple, and *V. phoeniculum*, purple, are perennials. They all flower between June and August. Give them a dry spot in poor soil in full sun.

Veratrum (False hellebore)

This tropical-looking plant originated in the mountains of central Europe. It can be recognized immediately by its leaves, which are folded like fans. After having grown in the same place for years, the plant will start to flower, and will grow 5 feet (1.5m) tall. The flower panicle of *Veratrum album* grows 20 inches (50cm) long, with greenish white flowers. *Veratrum* is a good woodland plant for partial shade, but it also fits beautifully in the border. It is a very good solitary plant, but only for people with patience. It is nice in combination with *Gentiana lutea*, for which you will need just as much patience; they make good partners.

Veronica (Speedwell)

Veronica filiformis, which flowers in the lawn in May with pale blue flowers, is a veronica. Picture these flowers and you will be able to recognize any veronica, even though the flowers might be held in thick panicles or on spikes. *Veronica filiformis* grows rampantly as a creeper with rounded leaves, in moist soil in full sun. It is suitable for meadows. More suitable for the rock garden is *V. repens*, which forms a mat with blue-white flowers in May and June. *Veronica gentianoides* is worthy of its name. It flowers for a short period in May, at the time when most people visit nurseries. A drier location is required for *V. spicata*, native to the south of Europe; it is a good border plant 20 inches (50cm) tall, and it flowers in July and August. One month earlier, *V. incana* bears dark blue flowers, and it thrives in dry soil. There may be a veronica for just about any garden.

Vinca (Periwinkle)

With *Pachysandra*, periwinkle is among the creepers planted most often. The following plants are also evergreens: *Vinca minor* has small, dark green leaves, does well in shade, and bears blue flowers in spring. There are several varieties in purple and white; these varieties flower less abundantly. The white variety 'Gertrude Jekyll' flowers for a longer period than the ordinary variety. The silver variegated 'Argenteovariegata' and the golden variegated 'Aureovariegata' grow less well in deep shade. The large-leafed *V. major* is less often planted. Plant it only in sheltered locations. The evergreen trees are most beautiful, but often difficult to find. More often, it is the yellow-veined 'Reticula' and the yellow-rimmed 'Variegata' that are offered. These plants are suitable for growing over walls, for a cascading effect of tiny, softly colored blossoms.

Viola (Violet)

Viola odorata and *V. labradorica* are creepers. They have small, but fragrant, flowers. *Viola odorata* is called "sweet violet" and flowers in April/May. The beauty of *V. labradorica* lies in its purple-brown leaves, against which the blue-purple flowers show to advantage. *Viola sororia* grows rampantly. It bears a whitish flower with blue spots, and flowers at the same time as other small-flowered *Viola*. Much more like the biennial *Viola* are the Cornuta hybrids. They bloom in the middle of summer with medium-size flowers. They are available in the colors blue, purple, yellow, and white. Unlike the small-flowered *Viola*, they require full sun. Some examples:

Viola cornuta	'Boughton Blue'	blue
	'Gustav Wermig'	pale blue
	'Milkmaid'	creamy white with blue
	'Molly Sanderson'	black-purple
	'Nelly Britton'	lilac-blue

Waldsteinia

Waldsteinia is an evergreen, strawberrylike plant for a shady place. It does not bear any fruit (as is the case with *Duchesnea*). The flowers are yellow. Two species are

Viola odorata (sweet violet) is very fragrant. This creeper is a good underplanting for trees.

The wild Viola arvensis *grows in nature and will spread easily.*

often cultivated: *Waldsteinia ternata* (6 in./15cm tall) and the slightly taller *W. geoides*. The plants flower in April and May. They are good creepers, and are easily propagated.

Yucca (Yucca palm)

Yucca is a good solitary plant for a dry sunny place, with a striking and rather exotic form that serves it well as a specimen planting. The leaves will remain green in winter. The flowers grow up to 5 feet (1.5m) tall. Sometimes it takes a few years before this plant starts to flower. In the center of a raised, round bed for annuals, this plant will really show off.

12 Climbing Plants A to Z

Climbing plants enhance their surroundings wherever they may be— not only in gardens and scrambling up walls, but out in the landscape where their natural elegance runs wild over ditches, hillocks, and shrubs. There are many different types and sizes, they bloom in all colors, and there are numerous manners and seasons of flowering.

Akebia is planted against this lattice to screen a view.

Climbing plants have a unique talent: They can integrate the house and surrounding garden like no other plant. A vine, for example, that is trained from the house via a pergola to the garden creates a scene of "natural" unity.

H. helix is said to eventually weaken the soft cement in old walls.

Climbing plants to train into large trees
Actinidia arguta
Aristolochia durior
Campsis radicans
Celastrus orbiculatus
Clematis montana
Fallopia aubertii
Hydrangea petiolaris
Parthenocissus quinquefolia

Climbing plants to train into medium-size trees
Akebia
Clematis macropetala
C. montana 'Rubens'
C. orientalis
C. tangutica
Lonicera

Clinging vines and climbers
Campsis
Euonymus fortunei
Hedera
Hydrangea petiolaris
H. integrifolia
Parthenocissus

Lonicera periclymenum.

Woody plants to climb a wall or fence, and that require support

Abelia
Ceanothus   evergreen
Chaenomeles
Cotoneaster
Escallonia   evergreen
Euonymus fortunei   evergreen
Jasminum nudiflorum
Magnolia grandiflora   evergreen
Pyracantha   evergreen
Ribes laurifolium

Climbing plants for containers

Clematis, the shorter species and varieties
Hedera
Jasminum (*J. nudiflorum* unsuitable)
Lathyrus latifolius
Lonicera
Passiflora
Solanum jasminoides

Ivy grows abundantly, as a climber and as a ground cover, in the landscape. Many old trees are overgrown with it.

Honeysuckle (Lonicera caprifolium) *grows at the edges of forests. You can plant a climber to grow up into an old tree. Try to approximate in your garden the growing conditions your climber enjoys in nature.*

Actinidia

A. arguta (bower actinidia*)* is self-pollinating and grows up to 26½ feet (8m); the green-yellow fruit is an inch (2.5cm) long. Young plants must be protected in winter. *A. chinensis* grows as high as *A. arguta,* but bears larger creamy white flowers in May/June. It requires a warm site. Damage from frost can happen easily, and then pollination will not occur. The edible kiwi fruits grow 1¼ to 2 inches (3 to 5cm) long. The plant is not self-pollinating, and so both a male and a female plant are required for the production of fruit. The most elegant *Actinidia* is *A. kolomikta,* with leaves of three colors. In June it bears small white flowers.

Akebia

The evergreen *A. quinata* grows up to 26½ feet (8m) and requires sun or partial shade. It is a plant that behaves differently under different growing conditions, and even from one location to the next in the same neighborhood; it cannot be predicted whether or not the plant will do well. Sometimes it does not grow at all during the first year, and it may catch up the second year. Because there are few evergreen climbers for temperate climates, this plant certainly has its uses. Consider it a foliage plant, as the brownish-red flowers are not spectacular.

Ampelopsis

See also *Parthenocissus* (below).

A. brevipeduncalata 'Elegans' is a very good small climber for patios and unheated greenhouses. It is too frost-sensitive to be planted outdoors. The white-spotted and variegated leaves are attractive. This somewhat delicate climber is also suitable for growing in a hanging basket, from which the pretty foliage can trail.

Aristolochia (Dutchman's pipe)

A. macrophylla (syn. *A. durior*) is a large-leafed foliage plant that deserves to be used more often. With support, the plant will climb up to at least 33 feet (10m). The brownish flowers hang behind the leaves, a lush green mass. The flowers indeed resemble pipes after a fashion, hence the common name. Pruning is rarely necessary. The rare *A. tomemtosa* is constructed on a smaller scale.

Campsis (Trumpet creeper)

This clinger needs some support. The first orange-red flowers appear after about five years. *C. radicans* is one of the few climbers appropriate for the south side of the house. It grows up to 33 feet (10m) tall and 20 feet (6m) wide. The variety 'Flava' has yellow flowers, as does 'Yellow Trumpet'. 'Atropurpurea', 'Flamenco', and 'Florida' are red.

Celastrus (Bittersweet)

C. orbiculatus can be trained up into large trees. Do not try this with smallish, young trees; the twining shrub may kill a tender tree by constricting the trunk. For setting of fruit, both a male and a female plant are required. The fruits are highly ornamental in autumn, when the yellow seed capsules open to reveal the orange seeds. Cut branches dry beautifully and are a splendid addition to dried flower arrangements. This climber grows up to 40 feet (12m).

Clematis

Some clematis hybrids should be cut back to about 3 feet (1m) above the ground to encourage abundant flowering. They will grow to 10 to 13 feet (3 to 4m) in spring after such pruning.

Some varieties:

	Color	Flowering period
'Gipsy Queen'	purple	July to October
'Superba'	red-purple	July to August
'Nelly Moser'	lilac-pink	June to July
'Ville de Lyon'	carmine	June to September
'Lasurstern'	blue-purple	June to July
'The President'	dark blue	June to July
'Jackmanii'	dark violet	August to September

Page 319:
Akebia quinata.

Clematis × Jackmanii.

Wild species of clematis are lovely, and not seen in gardens very often, as nurseries tend to sell cultivated varieties. You might try growing one up into a tree. Non-climbing varieties are listed with the perennials in Chapter 11. All species flower in early summer. Pruning is limited to cutting away any straying growth.

	Color
Clematis alpina	light blue
C. alpina 'Frances Rives'	stronger blue
C. macropetala	pink
C. viticella	pale blue
C. v. 'Abundance'	deep pink-red
C. v. 'Alba Luxurians'	white
C. v. 'Etoile Violette'	deep purple
C. v. 'Minuet'	whitish with pink-red
C. v. 'Royal Velours'	dark purple
C. v. 'Venosa Violacea'	purple on a white background

Clematis *(large-flowered hybrid)* 'Nelly Moser'.

C. orientalis	yellow, flowers later
C. paniculata	white
C. tangutica	yellow

Clematis species should be well trained, especially during the first year. They are ideally suited to small gardens because they take up little space. The genus *Clematis* is divided into a number of groups, each group with particular pruning requirements. Take note of the cultural requirements of the clematis that interest you.

Clematis hybrids

Hybrids that do not need pruning, just thinning:

	Height	Color
Clematis montana 'Alba'	up to 33 feet (10m)	white
C. montana 'Elizabeth'	up to 33 feet (10m)	pink
C. montana 'Freda'	up to 33 feet (10m)	dark pink
C. montana 'Rubens'	up to 33 feet (10m)	pale pink
C. montana 'Tetraroze'	up to 20 feet (6m)	pink
C. vitalba	up to 50 feet (15m)	white

Cotoneaster horizontalis

This shrub makes a fine creeper, but can also be trained as a low-climbing shrub against walls. The branches grow in a characteristic fashion, spreading out flat in almost a herringbone pattern. *C. horizontalis* bears small white flowers in autumn. After the leaves have dropped, red berries remain and are enjoyed by birds. The plant is ideal for planting underneath a window, against the wall. Regularly prune any branches sticking out; remove branches entirely, because the stumps will look unattractive in winter.

The plant is very sensitive to the bacterium that causes fire blight, so much so that its importation is restricted in a number of countries to keep the disease from spreading. See also *Pyracantha* (page 324).

Euonymus (Spindle tree)

E. fortunei is an evergreen climbing shrub. The plant has dark green, glossy leaves, and bears white flowers in spring, followed by red berries in autumn–it's an attractive addition to the garden all year long. Pruning can be done with hedge clippers if the plant has been trained well against the house. The leaves of *E. fortunei*

Against an open fence, trained roses can be planted handsomely in combination with clematis. The flexible branches of Forsythia suspensa *can be trained through the fence, too.*

'Silver Queen' are finer. The Japanese spindle tree, *E. japonica,* is sensitive to frost; use this shrub only in sheltered patios and courtyards.

Forsythia

The name "forsythia" recalls a commonly seen garden shrub that blooms yellow early in spring. *F. suspensa* resembles this shrub, but has long, thin, limp branches that can be trained for a more dramatic effect. The plant flowers slightly less abundantly than the garden shrub, with green-yellow flowers.

Hedera (Ivy)

Hedera helix is a small-leafed ivy that does very well as a ground cover in shade and as a climber against the east/west/north side of the house. It clings by itself. This small-leafed ivy is most hardy; the large-leafed plants run the risk of frost damage, especially on eastern exposures. During the first years the plant does not grow quickly, but this changes. It is easy to propagate from cuttings. But if you take a cutting of a flowering branch, it won't grow into a clinger, but remain a shrub. The scientific name for this shrub is *H. helix* 'Arborescens'. The Irish ivy, *H. hibernica,* is often planted. Large-leafed and sturdy, it nevertheless is more sensitive to frost than *H. helix.* It grows very quickly. Less sunny walls such as on the north side of the house can be cheered up with *H. colchica,* available in a number of variegated varieties, including silver variegated and golden variegated plants. It clings less aggressively than *H. helix* and the *H. hibernica.*

Humulus (Hop)

H. lupulus can also be considered a perennial; the plant dies back in autumn and comes up again in spring. The young hop shoots that come up from the soil in spring are edible. The female plants are more beautiful, producing green-yellow hops (inflorescences) in August. It is a pity that you cannot determine the sex of the plants when you buy them. You might buy three plants, wait to see them develop, and then discard the male plants, which are not needed for pollination. Give hops enough room—they grow up to 16½ feet (5m).

It is preferable to train them on separate poles, to make sure that other plants are not overgrown by their enthusiasm. Underground stems, which can grow quite some distance away from the plant, should be cut away regularly.

Hydrangea (Climbing hydrangea)

Climbing hydrangea is one of the few climbing plants that prefers full shade. The large white flower umbels in August and the light-colored leaf buds in winter are attractive. These woody plants cling by themselves. Regularly prune any straying branches and those that have grown out too far; if you do not do this, the plant

Hedera helix.

A solid fence requires climbers that pull themselves up by clinging, such as Hedera helix *and* Hydrangea petiolaris.

may fall over. Some support is required for that reason. This climber is hardly ever seen planted against a tree. Nevertheless, it will grow very well against a rather old tree, because it likes shade, and the tree will not suffer. The *H. anomala petiolaris* is available in only one color: creamy white, the umbels 10 inches (25cm) across. The special *H. integrifolia* is evergreen, but needs some protection.

Jasminum (Jasmine)

Flowering of *J. nudiflorum* occurs between November and April, depending on where you live. You may want to plant it in a place you will visit often in cooler weather. The small yellow flowers are very striking. The plant is easily propagated. It requires support and should be secured at regular intervals. The maximum height to which it will grow is 10 feet (3m). This plant can be trained to grow prettily beneath windows, just like *Cotoneaster horizontalis*. Prune for shape as needed. *J. beesianum* flowers in May/June with fragrant pink blossoms. It grows 20 feet (6m) tall and is evergreen. The plant is considered to be sensitive to frost, but it can endure fairly cold temperatures if planted in a sheltered spot.

Kadsura

K. japonica is a rare twining shrub, and evergreen to boot. In June it bears small cream-colored flowers and grows up to 13 feet (4m) tall. Plant it only in sheltered spots, and even then, against a south-facing wall, as this plant will be grateful for all the warmth you can give it.

There are relatively few evergreen climbers, and this is a plant for the gardening enthusiast. It requires acid soil, so you will probably need to work peat moss into the soil.

Lathyrus (Wild pea)

L. latifolius, the everlasting pea, is a perennial. It dies back every year, but will come up again. It flowers in white or pink, producing delicate blossoms that are pretty against the foliage.

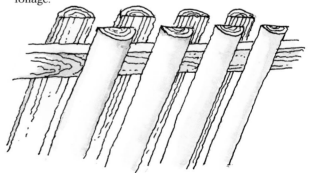

A low gate is a suitable support for Lathyrus latifolius *or* Jasminum nudiflorum.

Lonicera (Honeysuckle)

There are evergreen and deciduous honeysuckles. Woodbine, *L. periclymenum*, grows naturally as a shrub along the edges of the forest, and so it is no surprise that in the garden this plant requires partial shade and good

Lonicera.

air circulation. In enclosed city gardens, honeysuckles may suffer from such pests as aphids, and powdery mildew.

Evergreen honeysuckles

L. henryi	brown-red
Lonicera japonica	creamy yellow

Deciduous honeysuckles

Lonicera × *brownii*	
'Dropmore Scarlet'	orange (pendulous)
L. heckrottii	orange-pink
L. periclymenum 'Belgica'	yellow-pink
L. p. 'Cream Cloud'	white
L. p. 'Serotina'	purple-red
L. × *tellmanniana*	orange-yellow

Always be mindful of the natural growing conditions of a plant. This is the key to a healthier, stress-free plant, one resistant to pests and diseases. A weakened plant is a target. If you can't provide the growing conditions for a plant you admire, then it is preferable to select a different plant. This is a better approach than replacing plants that fail to thrive, or dousing them with toxic chemicals. Replacement plants are—most often—an avoidable expense.

Magnolia

The magnolia is not a true woody climber. However, *M. grandiflora*–a large-leafed, evergreen magnolia–can be planted against a sunny wall, protected from harsh winds. The young branches can be trained easily for an elegant look. This is one of the most expensive, though beautiful, species. And although it takes a number of years before the first (large) flowers appear, this magnolia is worth trying, because its flowering is absolutely spectacular.

Parthenocissus (Woodbine)

Two species are used in gardens. *P. tricuspidata* is suitable for walls. For pergolas, choose *P. quinquefolia*. The latter can also be employed very well as a creeper, as one might guess from the common name, "Virginia creeper." As pleasing as *Parthenocissus* can be as a climbing plant, it is also a hanging plant. Both of the above species are clinging plants that like sun and partial shade. *P. quinquifolia* yields blue berries (that look like small grapes) in autumn. Birds love them. Both plants bear small flowers, of no ornamental value. The autumn color of the foliage is magnificent, and the plants reach a maximum height of 50 feet (15m). Unlike ivy, woodbine

An elegant screen should remain visible. Climbers with an open structure include the small-flowered clematis varieties. Grapes could also be grown against a screen such as this.

does not weaken old walls. Some climbing plants damage those walls that were constructed using soft (limy) cement (fortunately, this building material has fallen from common use) by pushing into and breaking apart the cement "glue."

Passiflora (Passion flower)

This plant is for the real go-getters. The passion flower will easily freeze when young, but once it is five years old, it can endure a lot more frost. *P. caerulea* grows quickly the first year, and bears blue flowers abundantly as early as the first year, too. Freezing can be avoided by planting *Passiflora* in a large container and overwintering it indoors, where it will be comfortable and can be enjoyed. In autumn, cut the plant back, and in spring it will grow out again. The edible passion fruit (*P. edulis*) will not grow in temperate climates.

Polygonum (Silver lace vine)

Fallopia aubertii is better known under the name *Polygonum aubertii*, and it is the quickest-growing climber. You might compare it with *Clematis vitalba* for sheer speed, and the small white flowers, and even the period of flowering, are similar. *Polygonum* is sensitive to frost, especially when planted in moist locations. The biggest difference between *C. vitalba* and *P. aubertii* is apparent in late autumn/winter: Then, clematis has fluffy silver seed heads, and the structure of the plant is beautiful to look at; *Polygonum* looks messy and rather dead.

Pyracantha (Fire thorn)

Like clockwork, *P. coccinea* is planted next to the front door, with scarcely a thought. Certainly it offers a dramatic welcome to visitors. Unfortunately, it often happens that once it has been planted, care is forgotten. Straying growth must be pruned to keep this vigorous climber within bounds. Young branches can be trained successfully along heavy garden twine, to ensure that the fire thorn remains close against the house. This treatment enhances the production of berries. It is usually the red-fruited fire thorn that is planted, but you might try a fire thorn with yellow berries for a change. The color is less harsh, and birds will not touch these berries until later in the season, so you can enjoy them longer. This color seems to go better with the rest of the garden, too. Like *Cotoneaster*, the fire thorn is a "carrier plant" for fireblight. This bacterial illness occurs often in members of the rose family, to which fruit trees also belong. In areas where fruit trees are grown commercially, it is sometimes not allowed to plant the fire thorn, hawthorn, *Cotoneaster* and a number of other ornamental shrubs, to prevent spreading of the disease.

A sturdy pergola can handle tall-growing, vigorous climbers such as Celastris *and* Wisteria.

Solanum (Potato vine)

S. jasminoides is less sensitive to frost than the variety *S. jasminoides* 'Crispum', but neither plant should be located on any but the most sheltered site. Flowering is from July to October, the small and delicate flowers like those of the potato plant. Woody nightshade can often be found with variegated leaves, as *S. dulcamara* 'Variegata'. This plant can survive more frost, but requires a moist soil.

Vitis (Grape)

For the warm, southern side of the house, grapes are attractive and useful. They can grow to as much as 50 feet (15m) in length. Prune the woody parts only in late autumn and winter. After February, no more pruning: The branches will start to bleed then, and will not stop. This is harmful to the plant, but it will not bleed to death. Young plants require special treatment. First encourage the main trunk to reach upward by keeping side branches well spaced. Leave two buds (leaves) on the side branches; this is where bunches of grapes will grow later. Let the trunk of the grapevine grow as long as there is room for it. Wire should be used to train the branches horizontally–remember, not so tight as to cut into the branches and wound them. You want at least a foot

By planting Lonicera periclymenum *'Belgica' with* L. p. *'Serotina', flowering can be enjoyed throughout the summer.*

(30cm) between wires if they are fastened one above the other. You can also grow grapes on a trellis over your terrace. For the weekly training during the growing period, you will need a ladder. There are numerous species and varieties. *V. coignetiae* is not edible. This hardy species has great ornamental value, however, especially because of the beautiful autumn color of the foliage, a gorgeous emblem of the season.

Wisteria

Take two species particularly into account when deciding on a wisteria, and note that they wind in opposite directions. *W. floribunda* flowers only after ten years, producing very long racemes of fragrant flowers; for that reason, it is suitable for a pergola where the flowers hang free in the air. These flowers are worth waiting for. The *W. sinensis* flowers after three years. It has short racemes, and the flowers start to bud before the leaves appear, an exciting announcement of the beauty to come. It is suitable for walls and pergolas, too. There are pink and white varieties of both species.

13 Bulbous and Tuberous Plants A to Z

Flowering bulbs in particular are considered the heralds of spring, a time of year full of promise. The first crocus elicits a sigh of relief: Temperatures are on the rise, and the days grow longer.

The famous Keukenhof gardens in Lisse, The Netherlands.

Flowering bulbs are colorful and cheering. And fortunately, the pleasure bulbs can bring is not restricted to springtime. In summer and autumn, too, there are numerous species that bloom.

Summer-flowering bulbs

Bulbs that should be planted in spring and dug up again in autumn:

Anemone hybr. 'St. Brigid'
Anemone hybr. 'de Caen'

A combination of bulbs and biennials lengthens the flowering period in spring.

Here, violets, wallflowers, and forget-me-nots bloom among tulips and hyacinths.

Begonia multiflora
B. × *tuberhybrida*
Dahlia
Galtonia candicans
Gladiolus, large-flowered
Lilium

Spring-flowering bulbs for a white garden

The early-flowering bulbs are usually yellow or blue; nevertheless, there are plenty of candidates for the "white garden." The correct planting time of these bulbs are the months of October and November for temperate climates. In colder climates, September planting is recommended. In warmer climates, plant from late November into December.

Anemona blanda 'White Splendour'
Convallaria majalis
Crocus, large-flowered, white
Fritillaria meleagris 'Alba'
Galanthus nivalis
Hyacinthoides hispanica 'Alba'
Muscari botryoides 'Alba'

Narcissus triandrus 'Thalia'
N. poeticus 'Actaea'
Ornithogalum species
Tulipa, white

Bulbs for a damp location

Most bulbs will rot in soil that is too wet, but for the following bulbs a great deal of moisture is a requirement.
Camassia
Fritillaria meleagris
Leucojum aestivum

Autumn-flowering bulbs

Buy the following bulbs in July and August, to be able to enjoy their flowering in the next months.
Crocosmia
Lilium speciosum
Colchicum
Cyclamen
Crocus speciosus and others
Sternbergia

Bulbs suitable for naturalizing in the lawn

Flowering bulbous plants growing in clusters seemingly

Plan colors for beautiful combinations.

Muscari botryoides *'Album'*.

Lilium tigrinum.

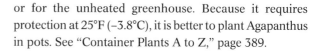

Acidanthera bicolor.

Acidanthera (Abyssinian gladiolus)

Plant the bulbs at the end of April or beginning of May at 4 inches (10cm) deep. Give them a warm, sunny location; they are not very hardy. The gladiolusike white flowers will grow about 2½ feet (80cm) tall.

Agapanthus

This bulbous plant is suitable only for the warmest gardens

naturally here and there about the lawn can be a beautiful sight. The effect is both charming and cheering. Suitable plants for this are:

Crocus
Eranthis
Galanthus
Ornithogalum umbellatum (flowers when the foliage is already gone)
Scilla siberica

or for the unheated greenhouse. Because it requires protection at 25°F (−3.8°C), it is better to plant Agapanthus in pots. See "Container Plants A to Z," page 389.

Allium

The last bulbs to flower in spring are the alliums, the ornamental onions. Plant them in full sun, in limy or neutral soil that isn't too wet. All alliums can be left in the soil over winter.

Scilla tubergeniana.

Allium karataviense.   Allium albopilosum.

Do not plant them too shallowly–8 inches (20cm) deep on average is good. Choose from these species:

Allium sphaerocephalon.

Latin name	Color	Flowering period	Height
A. aflatunense	lilac/pink	May	30 inches (75cm)
A. albopilosum	lilac	May	20 inches (50cm)
A. atropurpureum	purple	May	28 inches (70cm)
A. caeruleum	sky blue	June	20 inches (50cm)
A. cernuum	lilac	July	12 inches (30cm)
A. christophii	silver purple	May	12 inches (30cm)
A. giganteum	violet	July	47 inches (120cm)
A. karataviense	green/white	May	8 inches (20cm)
A. moly	yellow	June/July	8 inches (20cm)
A. oreophyllum	purple	June/July	6 inches (15cm)
A. roseum	white	June	12 inches (30cm)
A. siculum	brown/green	June	2–3⅓ feet (60–100cm)
A. sphaerocephalum	purple-red	July	16 inches (40cm)
A. stipitatum	dark pink	July	5 feet (160cm)
A. unifolium	soft pink	May/June	16 inches (40cm)

Alstroemeria aurantiaca.

Anemone blanda.

| A. ursinum | white | May/June | 12 inches (30cm) |
| A. zebdanense | white | April | 10 inches (25cm) |

The globe-shaped flowers of the ornamental onions show to advantage between perennials; the shorter

Anemone coronaria 'Hollandia', a low-growing jewel.

plants look nice among creepers, and the taller ones between, for example, hosta and lady's mantle. Because the alliums die back rather early in the year, combining them with other plants is necessary for interest all summer long.

Alstroemeria (Peruvian lily)

The Peruvian lily is not really a bulb, but it has a thickened fleshy root stock, or tuber. See *A. aurantiaca* also under "Perennials A to Z," page 280. The Peruvian lily is sometimes sold as a perennial, but it is also often offered during the season for selling bulbs. It makes an excellent cut flower–it keeps for a long time–and there are numerous plants to choose from for this purpose. As a garden plant, *Alstroemeria* offers one species: *A. aurantiaca*. Locate the plant in a warm, sunny spot, and cover it up well with mulch in winter. *Alstroemeria* can remain undisturbed in the same place for years.

Anemone (Wind flower)

Anemone blanda flowers as early as March. It makes a suitable underplanting for a shady spot. Soak the hard tubers before planting them, and plant them 3 inches (8cm) deep. *A. blanda* is usually for sale in lots of mixed colors. Nevertheless, try to buy tubers of a single color, because there is considerable variation in the size of the flowers and culture of the various colors. The most beautiful is *A. blanda* 'White Splendour', a pure white, large-flowered anemone. The 'Charmer' is pink, and 'Blue Shades' offers, unsurprisingly, various shades of blue. *A. coronaria*, a good cut flower, came to Europe from Turkey in the mid-seventeenth century. Varieties were later imported from Caen, France, the so-called "De Caen types":

single flowers:	'The Bride'	white
	'Hollandia'	red
	'Mr. Fokker'	violet/blue
	'Sylphide'	violet
fully double flowers:	'King of the Blues'	dark blue
	'Lord Derby'	violet/blue
	'Surprise'	red
	'Queen of the Violets'	purple

A. nemorosa, the European wood anemone, does not have a tuber, but rather a root stock. It prefers damp, humusy soil in shade. The variety 'Robensoniana' is lavender-blue. Both grow 4 to 6 inches (10 to 15cm) tall and flower in April to May.

Page 331:
Anemone "De Caen" type.

A hanging begonia.

Arum dracunculus (syn. Dracunculus vulgaris)

This good, hardy arum has beautiful arrow-shaped leaves between which large, dark red flowers with black stems unfold. It is suitable as a potted plant and as a specimen plant.

Arum italicum (Italian arum)

Arums have thick fleshy root stocks. They are expensive, and for that reason they are always sold individually. The foliage of Italian arum appears in autumn. The white flower is insignificant, but after the foliage dies in July, dramatic spadixes with orange-colored berries appear. The Italian arum is suitable for naturalizing.

Begonia

Everyone knows the begonia as an indoor plant (often, the rex begonia) and as an annual, for outdoor as well as for indoor enjoyment. Tuberous begonias are best planted outdoors, although a cool room indoors can be adequate. The culture is identical to that for the dahlia. Begonia tubers can be planted outdoors after May 1, after the soil has warmed. If the tubers have sprouted, they should not be planted outdoors if there is any chance of frost; wait until mid-May if you must. Horticultural authorities have divided begonias into 13 groups, among them large-flowered hybrids, medium-large hybrids, small-flowered hybrids, and pendula, or hanging basket, begonias, with large hanging clusters of single flowers.

Though their colors are always bright, the hanging begonias fit in very well with other plants in the garden. In the previous century, bright colors were generally preferred. Tuberous begonias worked beautifully in the highly stylized Victorian flower bed.

Make a well-balanced combination of colors. Avoid planting red, pink, yellow, white, and orange together.

Brodiaea (syn. Triteleia)

Brodiaea requires a dry, warm site. The bunches of blue flowers appear in June and grow to 12 inches (30cm) tall. For that reason, do not plant them among tall perennials. They are pretty at the front of the border.

Calla (Calla lily)

The calla lily is suitable only as an indoor plant in all but the warmest climates. You can "summer" the potted plant outdoors from June to September. Calla lilies are available in pink, yellow, and white. White is the naturally occurring color and the easiest fo find.

Camassia

This bulbous plant is one exception to the rule: It prefers a moist or wet site. *C. cusickii* is the best known, with

Chinodoxa luciliae.

sturdy stems 28 inches (70cm) tall, bearing many pale blue flowers. The bulbs are big. *C. quamash* has dark blue flowers and is much shorter: 14 inches (35cm). The

Page 333: Begonia 'Marmorata'.

Colchicum autumnale
'Waterlily'.

creamy-colored *C. leichtlinii* grows 31 inches (80cm) tall, and flowers—like the other species—in June. *C. l.* 'Alba' produces white flowers.

Canna
See under "Container Plants A to Z," page 392.

Chionodoxa (Glory-of-the-snow)
Some smaller bulbous plants seem to resemble each other very much: *Chionodoxa, Pushkinia,* and *Scilla.* Closer examination reveals that none of the plants is as beautiful a pale blue as *Chionodoxa gigantea.* The plant flowers early, in March, and is very suitable for naturalizing.

Colchicum
This bulbous plant, which flowers in late August and September, can be grown without soil and brought into bloom on the windowsill; the bulb will not suffer if planted in the garden again immediately after flowering. There are *Colchicum* with white, pink, and violet flowers. Only *Colchicum* 'Waterlily' has fully double flowers.

The height is difficult to indicate: The flowers grow 6 to 8 inches (15 to 20cm) tall, but the leaves—which do

not appear until spring, and die back in June—grow to 2 feet (60cm) Do not confuse *Colchicum* with the autumn-flowering crocus (see *Crocus*, page 335).

Convallaria (Lily of the valley)
In spring, these may be found for sale with the bulbs—or "pips"—in flower in bunches of twenty-five. See also "Perennials A to Z," page 287.

Corydalis
Both perennials and annuals can be found in this genus. For the shady spots underneath trees, *Corydalis bulbosa* and *C. cava* offer possibilities. They resemble each other

Crocosmia masonorum.

Crocosmia × crocosmiiflora.

Crocus *'Pickwick'*.

very much. The first is pale pink and smaller in every way than the latter, which in addition to bearing darker flowers, also produces white flowers.

Crocosmia (Montbretia)

This bulbous plant (they are corms, actually) can remain in the garden over winter if temperatures above 10°F (–12°C) are expected, but must be well mulched. Give these summer-flowering plants a warm place in full sun. This old-fashioned garden plant flowers in July–August with small, gladioluslike flowers, usually orange. The scientific name is *C. masoniorum.* The cultivar 'Lucifer' is bright red and grows to 31 inches (80cm).

Crocus

There are crocus that flower in autumn, and crocus that flower in spring. Autumn-flowering crocus particularly prefer a warm and dry location in summer. The most widely known autumn-flowering crocus is *Crocus sativus*, which bears lilac flowers with dark stripes. This crocus is cultivated commercially for the stigmata, from which saffron is produced. A crocus that spreads well is *C. speciosus.* Plant the bulbs among spring-flowering crocus bulbs in spring, and that one spot will flower twice. *C. speciosus* flowers in October-November with silvery lavender blooms. Spring-flowering crocus with

large flowers are the most widely planted. Everyone knows them, with their violet, yellow, and white, sometimes striped, flowers. Buy them in numbers. You can plant keeping the colors separate, or you can mix them. You might want to create gradual shadings in color, for example, from the darkest violet gradually to lighter shades.

This is how magificent crocus can be. This impressive sight was created by the sheer quantity and color combinations used.

Crocus chrysanthus.   Crocus *Spring Pearl*.

You don't want a severe line where one shade ends and another begins, but rather a gradual change in color.

Lots of small-flowered crocus bloom in spring, of which *C. chrysanthus* is the best known. The small bulbs are rather flat. The flowering period is about two weeks earlier than that of the large-flowered plants. Some recommended varieties:

'Blue Peter'	purple-blue with a yellow throat
'Buttercup'	golden yellow, brown interior

Cyclamen persicum.

'E.P. Bowles'	lemon yellow
'Spring Pearl'	
'Zwanenburg Bronze'	bronze, yellow interior

The crocus that will spread quickest is *C. tomasinianus,* a slim, soft lavender-colored flower. Two varieties that will propagate even faster are the darker 'Barr's Purple' and 'Ruby Giant'.

Cyclamen

Although cyclamen are popular houseplants, some varieties are sufficiently hardy for the garden. The most abundantly flowering is *C. hederifolium* (syn. *C. neopolitanum).* In clayey soil, fresh seed can be sown directly. After years, there may be as many as fifty flowers on one bulb. Flowering is in August. The foliage resembles ivy.

Decorative Dahlia *'Garden Wonder'.*

C. persicum has rounded leaves. The leaves appear after flowering, and die back late in spring. The bulbs are "rabbit proof." Make sure, when you buy the bulbs of cyclamen (this goes for snowdrops, too), that the plants were cultivated and not taken from nature in southern countries such as Greece or Turkey. Of course, you wouldn't want to make your garden more beautiful at the cost of nature!

Dahlia

As with the tulip, narcissus, and gladiolus, there seem to be unlimited variations on dahlias. Dahlias are usually sold packed with a color, illustration of the mature plants. The height, color, and classification are printed on the package.

Page 337:
Dahlia *'Duet'.*

Anemone-flowered Dahlia 'Honey'.

Yellow cactus dahlia.

White cactus dahlia.

Pompon dahlias

The pompon dahlia has full flowers and is suitable as a cut flower. These tall dahlias make a handsome addition to the perennial border.

Single-flowered dahlias

These dahlias are suitable for flower beds.

The height can vary from 12 to 60 inches (30 to 150cm).

Every dahlia classification contains plants with many color variations. Do not be tempted to buy a large number of mixed dahlias, but choose a pleasing color combination for yourself.

Plant dahlias at the same time as potatoes, after mid-April. Dig them up (in all but frost-free climates) in November, and store them in a cool, but absolutely frost-free place indoors. The best way to store them is in a box filled with dry sand or peat moss, to prevent deyhdration. Do not add water, as this promotes rotting. Dahlia classifications include:

Anemone-flowered dahlias

These low-growing, richly flowering dahlias are particularly suitable for planting in borders, and pots.

Collarette dahlia

Use like the single-flowered dahlias.

Formal decorative dahlias

These dahlias may be the most satisfying and easiest to grow for tall cut flowers. They reach 4 feet (1.2m) maximum.

Straight cactus and semi-cactus dahlias

These dahlias are exquisite cut flowers. The petals are curled and look pointed.

Water-lily–flowered dahlias

These are small-flowered species of the decorative type, with a maximum height of 3 feet (1m).

Dicentra spectabilis (Bleeding heart)

D. spectabilis is often packaged for sale at the same time as the bulbs. See "Perennials A to Z," page 289.

Eranthis (Winter aconite)

This is one of the earliest plants to flower. A slightly moist location in shade is best for *Eranthis*. As with *Anemone blanda*, you will have to soak the hard tubers before planting, and plant them relatively deep, at 6 inches (15cm). The plant grows in every type of soil, but prefers a clayey soil, where winter aconite will spread easily.

Eremurus (Foxtail lily)

Do not plant *Eremurus* too deep; put the "nose" of the tuber approximately 2 inches (5cm) below the soil surface. Because of sensitivity to frost in the first few years, you should plant the foxtail lily only in dry soil in a sunny spot. Mulch the tubers for the first years in winter well with dead leaves, and mulch every year thereafter if temperatures below 0°F (–17°C) are expected. The flowers of this plant will grow up to 4½ feet (1.40m) tall in various soft colors. The leaves are not attractive, so plant foxtail lily among medium-tall perennials. The foliage can be hidden from sight by *Pelargonium* or *Gypsophila*, for example.

Dicentra spectabilis.

Erythronium (Dog-tooth violet)

The spotted leaves of the dog-tooth violet will remind you of the leaves of wild orchids. *Erythronium dens-canis* is usually supplied mixed in colors varying from pink to lilac. The plant will do best in humusy soil in half shadow. The

Erythronium tuolumnense 'Pagoda' flowers in April. The spotted leaves are attractive.

leaves appear in March, the flowers in April. *E. tuolumnense* is a slightly larger species, of which the variety 'Pagoda' is most often cultivated. The flowers are yellow.

Fritillaria meleagris.

Fritillaria (Crown imperial)

A majestic, old-fashioned plant for flower beds is *Fritillaria imperialis*, of which the varieties 'Rubra' (red), 'Lutea' (yellow), and 'Aurora' (orange-red) are most often cultivated. Plant the crown imperial in a warm spot, at least 10 inches (25cm) deep. The bulbs are known to repel moles. The light green leaves are beautiful even before flowering, but the 3-foot-tall (1m) flowers are indeed imperial. Equally tall, but more for the *Fritillaria* enthusiast, is *F. persica,* with

Fritillaria assyriaca.   Fritillaria imperialis *'Aurora'*.

small plum-colored bells and gray-green foliage. This April-bloomer grows 31 inches (80cm) tall.

Fritillaria meleagris (Checkered lily, snake's head lily)

Unlike the previous *Fritillaria*, this plant grows in moist to wet places to a height of 8 inches (20cm). The flowers are brownish and white, with darker spots.

Galanthus (Snowdrop)

To prevent dehydration, snowdrops should be planted rather deep in a location that is not too sunny. The most common is *Galanthus nivalis*, of which 'Flore Pleno' is a fully double snowdrop. *G.n.* 'Atkinsii' has larger flowers with a green spot. The old variety 'Lutescens' is marked with yellow on the inner petals. *G. elwesii* is the large-flowered snowdrop, blooming about two weeks earlier than the common snowdrop. *G. ikariae* has flower stalks of 8 to 12 inches (20 to 30cm).

Galanthus nivalis.

Galtonia

White bell-shaped flowers hang from a stem of up to 3 feet (1m) tall. *Galtonia candidans* is not hardy. Where winter temperatures hit 20°F (–6°), it is preferable to plant it in large flowerpots, which can be placed in a cool, dark room in winter. The plant flowers in August. In the garden, *Galtonia* can be planted in April and dug up in October.

Geranium tuberosum

The geranium requires a sunny, warm spot. The leaves remind one of the common perennial garden geraniums. From April to June this plant bears pink flowers.

Geranium tuberosum.

Galtonia candidans.

Gladanthera

This is a hybrid of the gladiolus and *Acidanthera*. The flowers resemble those of the gladiolus, the fragrance that of *Acidanthera*. The botanical curiosity originated in 1955 in New Zealand.

Gladiolus

Gladioli are too large to be used in a refined garden. The colors are very bright, too. The plants are suitable for the cut flower garden. Buy the bulbs with care, selecting pleasing colors, because a wild mixture of the bright colors will not be very harmonious. If you like the effect of mixed colors, leave out yellow and orange, and you will still achieve a certain peace. Plant the bulbs in April or May in well-mulched and fertilized soil, 4 inches (10cm) deep and 6 inches (15cm) apart. The flowering period is August. The flowers grow up to 5 feet (1.5m) tall, so plant them in a sheltered spot and give them support. By the end of September, the bulbs can be dug up. Store them in a dry place to prevent mold.

Gladiolus nanus

The bulbs of this hardy gladiolus can survive a cold winter. The flowers are smaller than those of the

Large-flowered gladiolus
'President de Gaulle'.

somewhat arching stem from which bell-shaped flowers hang on only one side, is *H. non-scripta* (syn. *Scilla non-scripta*). They are easy bulbs that will thrive in any moist type of soil.

Hyacinthus (Hyacinth)

The hyacinth is an excellent bulb for planting in beds and borders. Plant approximately 50 bulbs per square yard (m²) at 4 inches (10cm) deep. Store the bulbs at room temperature before planting. The flowering will decrease each year if you leave the bulbs in the soil; dig them up in July and store them in a warm place. The bulbs were popular as early as 1700, when enthusiasts paid enormous amounts of money for them, as much as $500 per bulb. It wasn't until the nineteenth century that hyacinths were planted in gardens. At one time, some two thousand different varieties were in cultivation, most of which have been lost. Still, the selection is vast. Some examples are listed below.

Name	Color	Flowering period
'Prins Hendrik'	light yellow	early
'Maria Christina'	apricot	early
'Mulberry Rose'	pink	early
'Carnegie'	white	early
'Delfts Blauw'	pale blue	early

cultivated gladioli, and are beautiful, soft shades of violet, pink, and white. They are suitable for the ornamental garden, in the border, or even the rock garden. This gladiolus resembles the wild species that grows naturally in mountain meadows in southern and eastern Europe: *G. communis,* a species 2 feet (60cm) tall with purple-red flowers. *G. carneus,* which originated in South Africa, is creamy-colored with purple spots. All these wild species flower in June/July and are hardy.

Gloriosa (Climbing lily)

This plant is suitable only for greenhouse culture. The plant can grow up to 10 feet (3m) tall. Cut it back in autumn. It is not a difficult plant, if the temperature is sufficiently warm at all times.

Hyacinthoides (syn. Scilla—English bluebell, Spanish bluebell)

H. hispanica (*Scilla hispanica*), the Spanish bluebell, is a good bulb to plant in large numbers among such creepers and ground covers as ivy. It flowers in June with large bunches of bright blue, pink, or white flowers 12 to 16 inches (30 to 40cm) tall. Slightly smaller, and with a

The hyacinths are in full bloom in the flower fields near Lisse, The Netherlands. The *bulbs are most suitable for flower pots and for forcing indoors.*

'Jan Bos'	red	early
'Lady Derby'	pink	late
'Ostara'	blue-purple	early

Page 343:
Gloriosa rothschildiana.

Hyacinthoides hispanica.

Incarvillea delavayi.

'Pink Pearl'	pink	early
'L'Innocence'	white	early
'Lord Balfour'	violet	late
'Fürst Bismarck'	pale blue	very early

Hymenocallis
See "Container Plants A to Z," page 389.

Incarvillea
This perennial needs a warm place in the sun. Do mulch it well in winter, and don't let it get too moist, or damage from freezing may result. When the first leaves appear, the flowers come up. The plant can be cultivated in pots with great success and can be forced for indoor enjoyment. *Incarvillea delavayi* bears bright pink, gloxinia-like flowers.

Ipheion (syn. *Triteleia*—Spring starflower)
Here is another small bulbous plant with blue flowers, this time with a delicate, pale silvery blue color. *I. uniflorum* (with one flower on every stem) never flowers very abundantly, but it flowers for a long period of time, providing a long season of interest, as long as from March to June. Put *Ipheion* in a sunny spot. The plant is suitable for edging.

Iris
There are spring-flowering irises (among which are some very early bloomers) and then there are the well-known tall summer-flowering iris that are splendid cut flowers.

Spring-flowering iris
By February *Iris reticulata* may already be in flower with blue or purple flowers. The plants grow only 8 inches (20cm) tall, but have the strength to grow straight up through the snow. Plant *I. reticulata* near a window so that you can enjoy it from indoors. The variety 'Harmony' has a beautiful bright blue color, as opposed to the species, which is a rather uninteresting violet. *I. danfordiae* resembles the latter with yellow flowers. Plant them in groups of at least 10 to make them sufficiently eye-catching. These low-growing iris are suitable for planting in the rock garden among short or prostrate perennials, and they are also nice in pots.

Summer-flowering iris
The so-called Dutch iris, a hybrid of various different iris, are splendid cut flowers and are recommended for the cut flower corner of the garden. These flowers with their long stems need support. These bulbs are sensitive to frost

and should be dug up in August, and stored at a temperature of 68°F (20°C).

Iris reticulata *'Harmony'*.

Ixia (Corn lily)

Ixia has nicely formed flowers that appear in June/July. They can be planted in autumn if they are sufficiently covered. Plant 3 inches (10cm) deep.

Ixiolirion

This is a little-known and underappreciated bulbous plant. The slim stem has gentian blue, lily-like flowers. The plant flowers in June and requires a sunny, dry location. The most well-known species is *I. tataricum* (syn. *I. ledebourii, I. pallassi),* which grows 12 inches (30cm) tall.

Leucojum (Snowflake)

The snowflake, *Leucojum vernum,* is often confused with the snowdrop. The snowflake has broader leaves and larger flowers and blooms later than the snowdrop. Give the bulbs a moist location, and plant them quickly to prevent dehydration. The spring snowflake (*L. aestivum*) flowers in May with hanging white bells on slightly longer stems. They are beautiful naturalized or in a naturalistic garden with good moisture, where flowers grow taller than the long grass. The variety 'Gravetye Giant' has even larger flowers than the common species.

Liatris

This plant is usually sold as a perennial. It is a good cut flower for a sunny spot. The most common species is *L. spicata*, which grows as tall as 2½ feet (80cm), depending on the type of soil (but the plants usually remain smaller). The flowers, which may be a light purple, through lavender to nearly white, bloom from the top down.

Leucojum aestivum.

Leucojum vernum.

August/September; do not plant too deep. The leaves will come up again before the winter, and should be protected from frost damage. Choose a large bulb at the nursery, and do not be disappointed if no flower appears the first year. Do not dig up the bulbs: They do not like to be disturbed. *L. martagon*, the Turk's cap lily, is one of the finest perennial lily species. They also do not like being transplanted; once planted, they will spread steadily.

Think of other lilies as summer bulbs to plant in spring and dug up in autumn. Store the bulbs in a cool, frost-free place during the winter. *L. tigrinum*, the tiger lily, and *L. speciosum*, of which there are a number of varieties, are very often used.

Montbretia
See *Crocosmia* (page 335).

Muscari (Grape hyacinth)
These are the most undemanding and least expensive bulbs. One disadvantage is that they produce a lot of foliage. For that reason, plant them between perennials that will overgrow them by May, so the ugly foliage is

Some botanical lily species can grow as tall as 6½ feet (2m).

Lilium (Lily)
As a rule, lilies are not fully hardy. Often cultivated as cut flowers in greenhouses, they should be planted very deep in the garden in humusy, friable soil. Cover them well in winter. *Lilium candidum*, the Madonna lily, is an exception as far as time and method of planting are concerned. Planting time is after flowering in

Liatris spicata.

hidden from view. Grape hyacinths usually flower in blue. *M. armeniacum* 'Blue Spike' has fully double flowers. *M. botryoides* has shorter foliage than *M. armeniacum*, with flowers in fuller bunches. *M.b.* 'Alba' is white and 'Carneum' is a fleshy pink. The tassel hyacinth, *Muscari comosum*, which grows up to 12 inches (30cm) tall and flowers in May/June, deserves mention. The most beautiful grape hyacinths are *M. latifolium* and *M. neglectum;* unfortunately, they are not available everywhere.

Narcissus (Daffodil)

The daffodil was popular with the ancient Greeks and Romans. The shape of the flowers determines narcissus classification. There are trumpet, large-cupped, small-cupped, double, and split-cupped daffodils, among others.

Of the tall narcissi, many varieties are sold in various color combinations of yellow, white, and orange. More than ten thousand species are listed. Examples of some classificiations with some notable varieties are listed below:

cyclamen-flowered narcissus	'February Gold'
	'Jack Snipe'
fully double narcissus	'Von Sion'
	'Texas'

Muscari armeniacum.

Muscari comosum.

Narcissus *'Ice Follies'*.

Narcissus triandus *'Thalia'*.

jonquil narcissus (with a strong fragrance, not very hardy)

large-cupped narcissus	'Carlton'
	'Fortune'
	'Ice Follies'
Narcissus jonquilla	'Sundial'
poet's narcissus	'Actaea'
polyanthus narcissus (not hardy, for indoor cultivation)
	'Paperwhite'
short-cupped narcissus	'Barrett Browning'
	'Birma'
triandrus narcissus	'Thalia'
trumpet narcissus	'Golden Harvest'

Some botanical species are suitable for the rock garden or at the front of the border. The plant least resembling a daffodil is *N. bulbocodium*, recently reclassified as *Corbularia*. *N. minor* also flowers in yellow. Both bloom in March, earlier than other narcissus.

Nerine

See "Container Plants A to Z," page 397.

Ornithogalum (Star of Bethlehem)

The largest and most beautiful is *O. nutans*, with green-white, torch-shaped flowers, on 12-inch-long (30cm) stems. Plant in sun or partial shade. The true star of Bethlehem, *O. umbellatum*, does well in shade, but produces more flowers in full sun; shorter, it bears starry, snowy-white flowers. Both are suitable for naturalizing. *O. thyrsoides* is less suitable for the garden. *O. arabicum* has the largest flowers.

Oxalis (Wood sorrel)

The pink-flowering *Oxalis adenophylla* can be planted in a warm and sunny location for good. In less-than-ideal places, it is better to dig up the bulbs every year. The species occurring most often are *O. adenophylla*, *O. deppeiu*, and *O. triangularis* with red leaves.

Puschkinia

This pale blue, early-flowering bulb is suitable for naturalizing in drier places, and will also do well in the rock garden and in flowerpots. This is a plant for every garden. The flowering period is March/April. Plant large numbers for a dramatic massing effect. The bulbs are inexpensive. *Puschkinia libanotica* 'Alba', 4 inches (10cm) tall like the species, has slimmer flower stalks.

Page 349: Daffodil 'Birma'.

Ornithogalum thyrsoides.

Scilla (see also Hyacinthoides)

As mentioned, sometimes changes in the scientific names of plants are required. With *Scilla*, the name has been changed so often that even professionals have difficulty keeping up. The taller scillas are now of the genus *Hyacinthoides* ("resembling the hyacinth"); the more delicate low-growing ones are still classified *Scilla*. A wonderful bulb for naturalizing is *Scilla*

Oxalis deppei.

siberica, which is suitable for planting in lawns. Plant them slightly deeper (3 inches/8cm) in a drier lawn. Moderately moist lawns are most suitable, preferably in partial shade. The earliest flowering is *S. tubergeniana*, which is very pale blue to white, with denser bunches of flowers. This plant comes into bloom as early as February, given frost-free weather. *S. peruviana* is expensive and frost-sensitive; in spite of its name, it comes from southern Europe and

Scilla siberica.

northern Africa, and flowers in June. Plant the bulbs on a warm, sheltered spot and cover them well in winter.

Tulipa (Tulip)

The ideal time for planting in most temperate climates is October or November. If you plant the bulbs much earlier, they will come up too early in spring and be susceptible to damage by frost. In somewhat warmer areas, you can still plant them at Christmas time. Plant them approximately 4 inches (10cm) apart. If you do not intend to dig the tulips up in summer and store

Oxalis adenophylla.

them, plant them deeper and mulch them with peat for winter. (Christmas tree branches make good garden protection.) The large-flowered tulip hybrids are separated into a number of main groups, with a seemingly unlimited number of varieties. Cultivated varieties change from year to year—new ones are added, and older ones are often taken out of commerce to make room for them. Therefore, it is important to take a look at the new catalogs from professional growers before buying tulips. You will then be able to select from varieties currently available, and note newcomers. The main groups of tulips for the garden are:

Single Early tulips	Single Late tulips
Double Early tulips	Double Late tulips
Triumph tulips	Cottage tulips
Lily-Flowered tulips	Parrot tulips
Darwin Hybrid tulips	

As a rule, tall tulips tend to flower late, when the perennials have acquired some height of their own. Early-flowering tulips are suitable for the perennial border, and late-flowering tulips can hold their own in separate flower beds. An unchanging group of tulips is *Tulipa* species, tulips found as they grow in nature. They are very suitable for naturalizing, for the rock garden or the small city garden. Plant them in a sunny, dry spot.

Scilla siberica.

Name	Color	Height	Flowering time
T. acuminata	red/yellow	20 inches (50cm)	April
T. aucherana	deep pink	2 inches (5cm)	April

Above: Darwin hybrid
'Apeldoorns Elite'.

Below: Lily-flowered tulip
'Aladdin'.

Above: Tulipa kaufmanniana
'Stresa'.

Below: Tulipa urumiensis.

Zephyranthus.

T. biflora	white/green	6–10 inches (15–25cm)	April
T. patens	red	4 inches (10cm)	May
T. clusiana	white/red	12 inches (30cm)	April/May
T. hageri	red	6 inches (15cm)	April
T. liniflora	scarlet	6 inches (15cm)	April/May
T. marjoletti	pale yellow/ pink rim	20 inches (50cm)	May
T. polychroma	white with yellow heart	3–4 inches (8–10cm)	April
T. praestans	red	10 inches (25cm)	April
T. pulchella 'Humilis'	violet/pink	6 inches (15cm)	February/ March
T. pulchella 'Violacea'	purple-pink	4 inches (10cm)	February/ March
T. sylvestris	yellow	10 inches (25cm)	April
T. tarda	yellow and white	4 inches (10cm)	April
T. turkestanica	white, yellow heart	10 inches (25cm)	March/April

T. urumiensis	yellow	4–6 inches (10–15cm)	April

Vallota
See "Container Plants A to Z," page 399.

Zephyranthes
See "Container Plants A to Z," page 399.

Vallota speciosa.

14 Water Plants A to Z

Anyone who intends to create a pond or a brook in the garden should realize that gardens abounding in water are not exactly easy to maintain. Patience and pleasure in the work are expected of the amateur gardener, who will be well rewarded for those efforts. What is more pleasant than a terrace near a pond or brook, with its variety of flora and fauna?

Looking over the pond in peace and quiet is well combined with a somewhat more critical intent, because with small ponds, in particular, care must be taken that water plants don't overgrow the water surface.

Japanese flag 'Walk in Beauty'.

And remember, insects and other animals will find your water garden as attractive as you do.

Submerged plants

Aponogeton distachyus   Water hawthorn
Ceratophyllum demersum   Hornwort

In the small garden, take into account the added dimension that reflection from your water garden can add.

Elodia canadensis   Water weed
Nuphar luteum   Yellow water lily
Nymphoides peltata   Yellow floating heart
Potamogeton   Pondweed
Ranunculus aquatilis   Water crowfoot

Floating plants

These plants do not set root at the bottom, and may move about in an open pond.

Bog bean.

Eichhornia crassipes	Water hyacinth
Hydrocharis morsus-ranae	Frog's bit
Lemna	Duckweed
Pistia stratiotes	Water lettuce
Salvinia natans	
Stratiotes aloides	Water aloe
Trapa natans	Trapa nut

Marsh plants

Alisma plantago aquatica	Water plantain

Butomus umbellatus	Flowering rush
Calla palustris	Water arum
Caltha palustris	Marsh marigold
Eriophorum angustifolium	Cotton grass
Euphorbia palustris	
Hippuris vulgaris	Mare's-tail
Iris kaempferi	Japanese iris
Lysichiton americanum	
Menyanthes trifoliata	Bog bean
Mimulus luteus	Water musk
Myosotis scorpiodes	Water forget-me-not
Veronica beccabunga	European brookline

Littoral plants

Most of these plants can camouflage the concrete or plastic of a pond lining. Some plants have sharp parts that puncture plastic, and these plants are better used on concrete.

Acorus calamus	Sweet flag
Butomus umbellatus	Flowering rush
Iris pseudacorus	Water flag
Mentha aquatica	Water mint

Nuphar luteum.

Water lilies are available in many colors. Size is critical: Find a water lily in good pro-portion to the size of the pond, to ensure that the water surface will not be covered completely.

Phragmites australis	Reed
Polygonum amphibium	Water smartweed
Pontederia cordata	Pickerel weed
Ranunculus lingua	
Sagittaria sagittifolia	Arrowhead
Sparganium erectum	Bur reed
Typha angustifolia	Narrow-leafed cattail
Typha latifolia	Common cattail

Plants for wet soil

These plants need not be near a pond; other wet or very moist spots can be suitable. For these plants, the amount of sun or shade is of great importance for good growth.

Astilboides	partial shade

Frog spawn can be an intriguing element in a naturalistic pond. The frogs lay their eggs very early in spring.

Brunnera macrophylla	shade
Cotula squalida	sun
Filipendula ulmaria	sun
Gunnera	sun
Hemerocallis	sun, partial shade
Hosta varieties	partial shade
Ligularia	sun
Lysimachia nummularia	sun
Lythrum salicaria	sun
Polygonum bistorta	sun
Primula	partial shade, shade
Thalictrum	sun, partial shade
Trollius	sun

Water Plants A to Z

Acorus (Sweet flag)

A. calamus grows 3 feet (1m) tall at the most and needs water 4 to 16 inches (10–40cm) deep. The variety 'Variegata' has leaves with yellow stripes.

Sparganium.

Lysimachia nummularia.

Alisma (Water plantain)

A. plantago-aquatica is slightly larger and looks more succulent than the common plantain we know as a weed. The flowers grow at most 5 feet (1.5m) tall, pyramid fashion, with horizontal flower stems. The plant is suitable for very large as well as very small water gardens. Water depth for water plantain may vary from virtually none to 16 inches (40cm).

Aponogeton

A. distachyus, the water hawthorn, can survive moderate winters if the water is so deep that the rootstock will not freeze. The plant has three periods of bloom, and bears white flowers. The floating leaves are beautiful.

Butomus (Flowering rush)

B. umbellatus is, in some countries, a protected plant for water of up to 20 inches (50cm) deep. The pink flower umbels are most beautiful in July, a pretty contrast to the grasslike foliage. Give the flowering rush a sunny spot.

Calla (Water arum)

This plant prefers partial shade. It needs water of up to 6 inches (15cm) deep, and bears white flowers in May/June.

Caltha (Marsh marigold)

The most striking littoral plant with yellow flowers in early spring is *C. palustris*. Be warned: Nurseries usually sell *Caltha* with dark yellow fully double flowers, *C. palustris* 'Plena'. For most water gardens, this is no improvement compared with the common species. *C. p.* 'Alba' has beautiful white flowers. *C. polypetala* occurs less often; this vigorous plant originates from Persia.

Aponogeton distachyos.

Marsh marigold.

Carex gracilis (Sedge grass)

This fine, grasslike plant has flower spikes like small cigars. The height of the plant is approximately 31 inches (80cm), in water up to 12 inches (30cm) deep. *C. pseudocyperus* is shorter, with hanging flower spikes.

Ceratophyllum (Hornwort)

This rampantly growing underwater plant has very fine leaves, but not very striking flowers, unlike *Ranunculus*

Comarum.

aquatilis. Hornwort and *R. aquatilis* can easily be confused.

Comarum palustre

In spite of the name, this is not a spectacular plant, though it is a sturdy plant for shallow waters. The red-brown flowers grow among the strawberry-like leaves. This is a quiet addition to the enthusiast's garden.

Eichhornia (Water hyacinth)

In tropical climates this plant grows so rampantly that ships can be hindered by them! Let these plants float in a trough with water or in a pool in the hothouse. They spread very effectively all by themselves. This temperamental plant remains appealing for its particularly nice blue-purple flowers.

Elodea (Wateweed)

The most important oxygenator for water gardens is *E. canadensis,* a submerged plant. This rather hardy plant has spread all over the world and grows rampantly; the plants should be cut back as necessary. Some fish favor *Elodea* as food.

Eriophorum (Cotton grass)

In spring *E. angustifolium* (cotton grass) and *E. latifolium* (cotton rush) are eye-catching for their fluffy balls. They need nutrition-poor conditions (they grow naturally in bogs), and for that reason are not suitable for most gardens. They can often be seen at botanical gardens.

Euphorbia

E. palustris flowers are green-yellow, like all other *Euphorbia.* The plant grows 3 feet (1m) tall at most, and is suitable for a sunny spot in water up to 8 inches (20cm) deep.

Filipendula (Meadowsweet)

Filipendula is a suitable plant for the very moist bank and shallow water of the pond. *F. ulmaria* has creamy white flowers, unspectacular but pleasant. The plant does well in sun and partial shade, but cannot grow with less sun than that.

Glyceria

Glyceria is a wild grass that grows 27½ inches (70cm) tall at most. The variegated *G. maxima* 'Variegata' is most often used. Water should be 0 to 8 inches (20cm) deep.

Page 359:
Comarum.

stems, in white, pale blue, or dark blue. *I. sibirica* needs a dry-to-moist location and should not stand in water.

Lysichiton

L. americanum has elliptical leaves and grows up to 3 feet (1m) tall. The plant blooms with modest yellow flowers in April and May. Plant *Lysichiton* in the bank at water level. Though it is sensitive to frost, this expensive plant is worth trying in a larger garden, or as a special element in a smaller garden. Less vigorous

than *L. americanum* is *L. camtschatcense*, which produces attractive white flowers.

Lotus

See *Nelumbo* (page 361).

Mentha

M. aquatica flowers like other mint species in the

Potentilla palustris.   Hottonia.   Hippurus vulgaris.

Hippuris (Mare's-tail)

H. vulgaris needs water 12 inches (30cm) deep, preferably in partial shade. It grows rampantly where its cultural requirements are satisfied. The segmented stems are attractive, the flowers are insignificant.

Hottonia (Water violet)

This evergreen plant has pink flowers and needs water 6 to 31½ inches (15 to 80cm) deep. The water violet can withstand shade. *Hottonia* is a fairly easily accomodated addition to the water garden.

Hydrocharis

Hydrocharis has attractive small, round, buoyant leaves. *H. morsus-ranae* bears white flowers in July/August. It is a freely floating plant that happily drifts over the water surface.

Iris (Flag)

Iris pseudacorus should stand in water 15 inches (40cm) deep at most. *I. kaempferi*, the Japanese flag that has blue, white, or pink flowers, is more a bog plant and slightly sensitive to frost. It blooms freely with large flowers in June/July. *I. sibirica* bears smaller flowers on long slim

herb garden, but grows in water of up to 15 inches (40cm) deep. The plant does not flower spectacularly, but gives off a pleasant fragrance when touched.

Menyanthes (Bog bean)

This plant has eye-catching foliage: a large cloverleaf, slightly leathery, and bluish-green in color. The white-pink flowers appear in May/June. The depth of the water should be 12 inches (30cm) at the most; the plant will do best in 8 to 10 inches (20 to 25cm).

Mimulus (Common monkey flower)

M. guttatus naturally grows in the shallow water of brooks, but can also be planted in slightly drier locations. The plant is yellow with brown spots. Garden hybrids are often orange or reddish-brown.

Myosotis (Water forget-me-not)

M. scorpioides flowers like the common forget-me-not, with blue flowers in May/June. Depth of the water should be 6 inches (15cm) at the most.

Nelumbo (Lotus)

N. nucifera cannot be cultivated outdoors in temperate climates. Avid water-gardeners cultivate them in tubs set in the warmest spot of the garden in summer. When the

Iris pseudacorus grows well planted on the banks of a stream or water garden.

plant dies back, put it in a more or less dry, not too cool, place to hibernate indoors. Do not put them outdoors too early. The flowers are pink or white. *Nelumbo* flowers are among the most dramatic and sought-after yellows, pinks, and creams.

The Japanese flag 'Time and Tide' improves any garden.

Lysichitum camtschatcensis.

N. 'Atropurpurea', dark carmine, 16 inches (40cm)

N. 'Attraction', dark red, 24 inches (60cm)

N. 'Aurora', pink-orange, 12 inches (30cm)

N. 'Cardinal', dark red interior, lighter outside, 27½ inches (70cm)

N. 'Charles de Meurville', wine red interior, lighter exterior, 31½ inches (80cm)

N. 'Chrysantha', apricot, 12 inches (30cm)

N. 'Colonel A.J. Welch', canary yellow, late, 31½ inches (80cm)

N. 'Colossa', flesh-colored to white, 27½ inches (70cm)

N. 'Comanche', yellowish, later darker, 20 inches (50cm)

N. 'Conqueror', dark red, 24 inches (60cm)

N. 'Ellisiana', bright red, later darker, 12 inches (30cm)

N. 'Formosa', peach pink, carmine center, 24 inches (60cm)

N. 'Gladstoniana', bright white, only for the largest ponds, 60 inches (150cm)

N. 'Gloriosa', striped exterior, red interior, 27½ inches (70cm)

N. 'Helvola', sulphur yellow, 8 inches (20cm)

N. 'Hermine', pure white, tulip-shaped, 27½ inches (70cm)

N. 'James Bridon', cherry red, good grower and bloomer, 24 inches (60cm)

N. 'Laydekeri Lilacea', lilac-pink with red dots, 12 inches (30cm)

Nuphar

The foliage of this plant reminds one of the water lily. The yellow flowers, which appear in May, do not have very large petals, and seem to remain buds although they are quite mature. The plant is suitable only for large water gardens, because the foliage takes up much of the water surface.

Nymphaea (Water lily)

Picture a water garden, and the first plant that comes to mind is probably a water lily. When choosing a water plant, choose an appropriate size of plant for your water garden. Not only are water lilies available in many colors, but in many sizes, too. Of the forty species, only a very few are hardy.

N. alba, the white water lily, grows in water 1½ to 6½ feet (50–200cm) deep. *N. tetragona*, still sold under the name *N. pygmaea*, grows in water 2 to 6 inches (5–15cm) deep. The plant is ideal for tub water gardens.

Hybrids

The numbers indicate the average depth of the water. The depth gives an indication of the size of the plant.

Fringed water lily with bog bean in the background.

N. 'Mme Wilfron Gonnere', pink, fully double, 20 inches (50cm)

N. 'Marliacea Carnea', bright pink, 27½ inches (70cm)

N. 'Marliacea Rosea', like the above, but darker, 35½ inches (90cm)

N. 'Maurice Laydeker', orange to red, 12 inches (30cm)

Nymphaea alba.

N. 'Moorei', yellow, marbled dark green leaves, 24 inches (60cm)

N. 'Newton', pink, flowers high above the water, 24 inches (60cm)

N. 'Richardsonii', white, richly flowering, 31½ inches (80cm)

N. 'Rose Arey', pink, 24 inches (60cm)

Nymphoides (Floating heart)

Nymphoides has small, floating water-lily–like leaves. It is an undemanding, somewhat ordinary plant that needs water 4 to 40 inches (10 to 100cm) deep. The yellow flowers appear between June and August. For small ponds, it may be preferable to choose a small water lily than this plant.

Phragmites (Reed)

The common reed, *P. australis*, is not frequently planted in water gardens. It should absolutely not be planted when plastic or rubber pool liners are used, as it will surely puncture them.

Pistia

P. stratiodes requires a warm, sunny spot. Store a few plants indoors over winter. They will soon grow out again in spring. The plant floats on the water.

Polygonum (Smartweed)

The name *P. amphibium* indicates that the plant will grow in both dry and wet locations. The foliage of this plant develops differently when growing in deeper water as opposed to soil, a characteristic shared by *Ranunculus*

Fringed water lily is a beautiful name for this enthusiastic plant, the leaves of which remind us of those of the water lily. After a few years, these plants may fill your water garden, and you will have to cut them back.

Do not plant reeds in pools with any of the softer liners, and do not plant bamboo nearby. The sharp ends of the roots will grow right through the liner.

aquaticus. This rampant grower bears pink flowers from July to October.

Pontederia

Pontederia cordata, pickerel weed, with its beautiful blue, hyacinthlike flowers, should be planted in every water garden. It is a very undemanding plant. If not

Pontederia cordata.

planted in full sun, and in water 8 to 16 inches (20 to 40cm) deep, it will bloom continuously from June to October. The leaves are attractive, too. Where it is happy, the plant will increase. The plant can be sensitive to frost.

Potamogeton (Pondweed)

The floating leaves are especially beautiful. The plant is suitable for moving water, a boon to water gardeners who have a stream. The following species are cultivated; the numbers indicate the depth of the water preferred by the species.

P. crispus	2 feet (60cm)
P. lucens	6½ feet (200cm)
P. natans	up to 3⅓ feet (100cm)
P. pectinatus	up to 5 feet (150cm)

Ranunculus (Crowfoot)

R. aquatilis strongly resembles *Ceratophyllum* in its submerged, fine foliage. If the water level drops, the plant will form light green, rounded leaves. The white flowers will set just above water level. *R. lingua* grows in shallow water of a depth of 12 to 16 inches (30 to 40cm); this simple and cheering water-plant, with its yellow flowers, more resembles the buttercups we know from meadows. Though not so flashy and brilliant as *Nelumbo* and some others, this is a reliable performer.

Arrowhead.

Sagittaria (Arrowhead)

This handsome plant produces white flowers with dark red centers between June and August. The arrowhead-shaped leaves sit above water level, and the plant is very

popular for this display of foliage. The plants are not as sturdily upright as some, but make a fine addition to a water garden collection.

Salvinia natans

Salvinia natans looks like duckweed, but has bigger leaves. These plants are preferable to the common duckweed, because they are easier to remove from the water.

Sparganium (Bur reed)

The beauty of this plant lies in the spiky fruits. The bur reed grows rampantly, and so is not suitable for small water gardens, which it might handily overpopulate. The plant is reedy in appearance. Plant it in water 4 to 20 inches (10 to 50cm) deep.

Stratiotes (Water aloe)

These charming, floating green plants of the water garden sink to the bottom in autumn, and they will float up again by themselves in spring. They require clear, still, deep water.

Trapa (Trapa nut)

This buoyant plant roots at the bottom of the pond and is suitable for small water gardens with a depth of 6 to

Never take Butomus umbellatus, *or any plant, from nature. Buy water plants in late spring, from mid-May on, for the best selection of stock.*

20 inches (15 to 50cm). *T. natans* has a beautiful autumn color. It requires a sunny spot.

Typha (Cattail)

These well-known reedy plants have large brown "cigars" instead of flower panicles. The plants are widespread in nature. The common cattail, *T. latifolia*, and the narrow-leafed cattail, *T. angustifolia*, are nice additions to the garden. Always plant *T. angustifolia* in small ponds; it remains smaller, and tends to grow less rampantly—and that calls for less upkeep. Even so, all cattails are spreaders. You can plant them in larger, sunken containers to hold them in check.

Veronica (Brookline)

Veronica blooms with the blue of forget-me-nots, and has fleshy leaves. This plant is suitable for moist or shaded places, and can also be grown in water.

15 Annuals and Biennials A to Z

Like all plants, annuals and biennials have specific characteristics of which you should make optimal use. They are undemanding plants, and often ideal for filling in empty spots in your garden. In the new garden, they provide excellent temporary solutions. In an established garden, they can extend the bloom period, and fill in gaps in the perennial border.

One of the nice elements of using annual plants in your garden is the speed with which everything happens; you sow one day, and after only a short while, the plants have matured and are blooming.

With the arrival of the first killing frost, the annuals die. With biennials you need a little more patience. Sow them at midsummer, when the busy spring season is behind you. In their first year, biennials form only leaves, most often in the shape of a rosette. In their second year, the plants start into growth early in spring and may come into bloom as early as May. After they finish blooming and have formed their seeds, they die.

Annual flower meadow.

Annuals to Grow against Walls and Fences

When you wish to camouflage an ugly wall or a boring fence, you needn't limit your choice to the true vines. Some annuals and biennials can also be of service here:

Cobaea	cathedral bells, cup-and-saucer vine
Convolvulus tricolor	dwarf morning glory
Eccremocarpus scaber	glory flower
Ipomoea purpurea	morning glory
Lathyrus odoratus	sweet pea
Thunbergia alata	black-eyed Susan
Tropaeolum	nasturtium

In the Victorian fashion, "bedding out" with annuals at Wisley Gardens, London. Paving needn't be reserved for paths and terraces; it can also serve to divide herbs in the herb garden or to emphasize the shape of a bed.

Annuals are also very suitable as border plants.

Children's Competitions

Hold a light-hearted competition in your neighborhood for children, and let them grow annuals on their own. Who can grow the largest, most beautiful, or tallest plant? It might call for some planning, but it is easy and rewarding, and a nice idea for an affordable children's party. The whole neighborhood profits when the plants bloom. And, you may inspire a life-long love of gardening. Give all the children a kit made up with seeds of:

Cucurbita pepo	ornamental gourd or pumpkin: for the largest fruit
Cucurbita pepo var. *longissima*	small gourd: for the longest fruit
Helianthus annuus	sunflower: for the tallest flower
Humulus scandens	Japanese hop: for the tallest plant
Kochia scoparia	summer cypress: for the largest plant

Annual Plants for Taking Cuttings

Chrysanthemum frutescens
Coleus
Felicia
Gazania
Heliotropium
Pelargonium

Gardening without a garden. This "hanging" garden is in Bath, England.

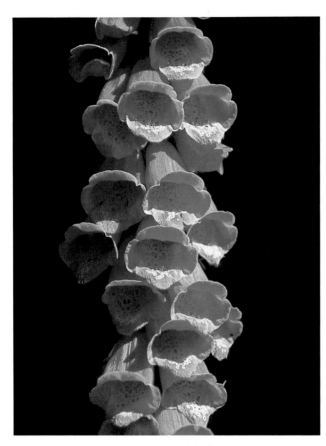

Digitalis.

"Spontaneous" Annuals and Biennials

"Spontaneous" annuals and biennials are plants that spontaneously start growing again unexpectedly. The following plants have the best chance of growing spontaneously:

Adonis aestivalis
Bellis perennis
Borago officinalis
Calendula officinalis
Centaurea cyanus
Digitalis purpurea
Impatiens glandulifera
Lobularia maritima
Papaver
Salvia viridis
Verbascum
Viola

Annuals for Arrangements

It often seems a waste to pick flowers from the garden just when they look their best. When laying out your

garden, think about whether you'll want to pick flowers for making arrangements. You can spread out plantings of those annuals suitable for picking in such a way that they are situated among other plants that you do not want to pick. That way, it will scarcely be noticeable when you pick some flowers. Especially during those summers when it is either too wet or too cold to sit outdoors often, you will still enjoy your annuals in flower arrangements. Some annuals recommended for cutting:

Arctotis	African daisy
Aster	
Calendula	pot marigold
Callistephus	China aster
Centaurea	cornflower
Chrysanthemum	annual chrysanthemum
Clarkia	
Cosmos	
Delphinium	larkspur
Gypsophila	baby's breath
Helianthus	sunflower
Lathyrus	sweet pea
Scabiosa	pincushion flower
Tagetes erecta	African or Aztec marigold
Zinnia	

Cleome spinosa, *spider plant.*

Verbena.

Annuals for Growing in Containers

These annuals bloom from mid-May through November, depending on the weather. Other plants that bloom for shorter periods can be planted with them. Remember the ornamental value of plants with decorative foliage.

Ageratum
Begonia semperflorens
Calceolaria
Cuphea
Fuchsia
Heliotropium
Impatiens
Lobelia
Lobularia
Pelargonium
Petunia
Salvia
Tagetes
Verbena

Annuals and Biennials for Drying

When sowing annuals, consider "everlastings," flowers you can enjoy dried. Harvest them on a warm, dry day. Hang them upside down in a dry, dark room with good circulation until dry and ready for arranging. Many everlastings are annuals:

Ammobium alatum	winged everlasting
Gomphrena	globe amaranth
Helichrysum	immortelle
Helipterum	strawflower
Limonium	sea lavender
Moluccella	bells of Ireland

Helichrysum.

Sowing

When you want to do your own sowing, consider these three questions:
- How many seeds are there in one gram of sowing seed?
- How long does it take for the seeds to germinate?
- How long can the seed be kept (in a dry, cool spot)?

Plant	Number of seeds per gram	Sprouting time (days)	Germination power (years)
Ageratum	7000	5	4
Antirrhinum	6000	20	3
Calendula	150	10	2
Callistephus	450	10	4
Cannabis	56	10–15	2–3
Centaurea cyanus	250	8–20	2–3
Chrysanthemum	aver. 500	5	2–3
Clarkia	3000	8–15	2
Cleome	4000	8–15	2
Cosmos	200	5	2–3
Dimorphotheca	860	15	2–3
Eschscholzia	500	5	1
Gazania	230	8–10	2
Gypsophila elegans	2500	15–20	1–2
Helianthus annuus	25	14	3–4
Impatiens balsamina	50	15–20	2–3
Kochia	14	15–20	2–3
Lathyrus	160	15–20	2–3
Limonium	400	15–20	1–2
Linum	28,000	7–15	3–4
Lobularia maritima	3000	5	3
Mesembryan-themum	4000	8–15	2–3
Nicotiana	6300	5–7	3
Nigella	400	8	2–3
Papaver rhoeas	9400	8–15	3–4
Petunia	9000	20	2–3
Phacelia	500	20	2–3
Phlox drummondii	500	20	2–3
Portulaca	10,000	20	2–3
Ricinus	2–4	15	2
Salvia splendens	350	15	1
Sanvitalia	1600	12–20	2
Tagetes erecta	250	8–15	3–4
Tagetes tenuifolia	1200	8–15	3–4
Tithonia	100	8–14	3
Tropaeolum	9	15–20	3–4
Zinnia elegans	120	5–10	3–5

CUT 1 LINE COL 1

Annuals and Biennials A to Z

Adonis (Pheasant's eye)
The pheasant's eye carries red flowers among fine foliage and fits in well with perennials in the flower border. The plant can be sown directly where it is to grow. *A. aestivalis* is annual; see also "Perennials A to Z," page 280.

Ageratum houstonianum (Flossflower)
This low-growing annual is entirely suitable for flower beds, where it is pretty at the front of the border. It makes a reliable edging, too. It usually blooms with blue flowers, but pink and white varieties also occur. The variety 'Schnittwunder' grows taller than *A. houstonianum*.

Agrostemma (Corn cockle)
This wild plant is known to grow, as the common name suggests, in corn fields. It is a good plant for annual flower meadows. *A. gracilis* prefers relatively dry soil in a location in full sun. Sow it directly where it is to grow, as it doesn't like being moved.

Antirrhinum majus.

Alonsoa

A. warscewiczii has small, red flowers and bright green foliage. You can start the plants indoors. Cut back the plant regularly to encourage vigorous growth; they grow to 2 feet (60cm) tall.

Alyssum

See *Lobularia* (page 380).

Amaranthus (Amaranth)

The annual amaranth grows as two varieties: *A. caudatus* (love-lies-bleeding) with red, pendant flower tassels, and the very brightly colored *A. cruentus*.

Ammobium alatum (Winged everlasting)

The plant blooms with small white flowers that look a bit like daisies, and is excellent for drying. Sow it in your cut-flowers corner; it is less suitable as a border plant. Provide a location with ample sun and soil that isn't too wet. The height of the plant is 2 feet (60cm).

Antirrhinum (Snapdragon)

Snapdragons bloom in various colors and grow to various heights. Plant the taller ones for cutting, and the shorter varieties as border flowers. Often the seeds is sold mixed. It is better to buy single colors and then mix

Begonia semperflorens *planted for edging. Canna and fuchsia*   *add to this lively mixture.*

them as you like. Start the plants indoors for earlier results, or sow them out in the garden where they are to grow.

Arctotis (African daisy)

Arctotis bears daisylike flowers in many colors. The plants grow to 2 feet (60cm). Start the plants indoors, then plant them out in the border, preferably where the soil is not very wet.

Begonia

It is preferable to buy plants, because sowing is successful only with high temperatures (over 70°F/21.1°C). The plants that are for sale as early as May are already in full bloom. You can find red-leafed plants as well as those with green foliage; both bear red, pink, or white flowers. (For information on tuberous begonias, see "Bulbous and Tuberous Plants A to Z," page 332.)

Bellis (Daisy)

These biennial daisies are available for sale in early spring. We commonly see the very large-flowered double type. The small-flowered pompon type looks a little more

Browallia.

natural. Keep an eye on your garden to keep them from spreading too much; the double daisies will appear everywhere in your lawn if you have not been careful, as more-or-less ordinary daisies, and this is probably not the effect you hope for.

Borago (Borage)
This plant is discussed under herbs (page 197). It is pretty planted among flowers in the border, and will spread spontaneously every year. Remove only the "excess" plants.

Brassica (Ornamental kale)
In autumn, most flower shops sell ornamental kale. They are suitable for growing in flower containers or for adding fall color and texture to borders in the garden. They can give a bare vegetable garden a nice appearance during the winter. B. oleracea 'Plumosa' comes in various colors. The plant is frost resistant.

Briza (Quaking grass)
This annual grass is suitable for using in dried arrangements. Sow the plant in your cut-flowers corner (in the ornamental garden it does not really look its best).

For other grasses, see "Grasses, Ferns, and Bamboos A to Z," page 400.

Browallia
Browallia is a thickset plant with campanulalike bellflowers. Until recently, this plant was considered a houseplant, but it does well as a border plant too. It can be sown early in the greenhouse.

Calceolaria (Slipper flower)
The golden flowers of this plant are smaller than those of numerous houseplants. The plants must be started indoors. The slipper flower is suitable for growing in containers.

Calendula (Pot marigold)
This old-fashioned garden plant blooms with yellow or orange, single or double flowers. Sow it directly where it is to grow. Chances are that the plants will spontaneously come up in the same place again next year. Calendula is good for repelling ants.

Callistephus (China aster)
Here is another old-fashioned border plant, which offers tall varieties for cutting and shorter varieties for borders. They are available with double and single flowers in all colors. Sow China aster in March/April in the greenhouse, or where they are to grow in the garden once the soil has warmed.

Centaurea cyanus.

Campanula (Bellflower)
C. medium is a biennial with very large, bell-shaped flowers on stems 3 feet (1m) tall. The flowers may be pink,

blue, or white. Sow at the beginning of June for flowers in the following year. Bell flowers may be propagated by division as well. It is necessary to cover the plant lightly during the winter to give it a good chance of survival. Shorter varieties are available, too.

Celosia (Cockscomb)

The cockscomb bears flowers in bright, neon colors. These are somewhat unnatural-looking plants. *C. cristata* has a rounded form; the "Plumosa" types are plume-shaped. Use them in a spot to which you want to draw attention. Use this plant judiciously, as the colors do not combine well with other plants.

Centaurea (Cornflower)

The annual cornflower, *C. cyanus*, can be bought as seed of mixed color, or you can select the color you want, with single or double flowers. The single blue flowers can be used for the annual flower meadow; the double flowers are better for the cutting garden. More appropriate, too, as a cut flower is *C. moschata* (mixed colors) with a silky sheen and bigger flowers.

Cheiranthus (Wallflower)

The biennial wallflower blooms in shades of orange, red, purple, yellow, or brown. Sow in June for a sea of flowers

Cheiranthus cheiri.

next year as early as April. They can be combined with other early-spring-blooming flowers, such as various bulbs.

Chrysanthemum (Summer marguerite, summer chrysanthemum)

C. segetum and *C. multicaule* are yellow. *C. coronarium* is yellow or white. *C. carinatum* is variegated. All varieties

Chrysanthemum segetum.

sow easily directly where they are to grow. *C. paludosum* and *C. parthenium* both bloom with small white flowers with yellow hearts and feature beautiful, thick growth. *C. frutescens* is propagated by cuttings rather than sowing. It is best to buy this plant in spring. This marguerite is sometimes cultivated as a standard on a different rootstock.

Clarkia

C. unguiculata can be sown directly where it is to grow. The plant is sold in mixed colors; the dark red, pink, violet, and white colors harmonize very well; this is one case where mixed seeds are not a problem.

Cleome spinosa (Spider plant)

This is an ideal plant. It is suitable for borders, as a flower for cutting—in short, you can put the plant anywhere you like in any kind of garden. The height at maturity is over 3 feet (1m). Start the plants indoors, then transplant the seedlings to a warm and sunny spot with good drainage.

Cobaea (Cup-and-saucer vine)

This creeper bears large bell-like flowers. The plants have to be started indoors, and should be planted out in the garden around mid-May when all danger of frost is past and the soil has warmed. The color of the bells is violet. Site the plants in a warm spot; they will not grow well during a cold summer.

Coleus (Flame nettle, painted leaves)

This plant can be sown as early as February/March. It is not the flowers, but the colorful leaves that give the plant

its ornamental value, sometimes with a riotous mixture of magenta, rust, scarlet, orange, cream, and shades of green. They look nice planted among annual flowers.

Convolvulus (Dwarf morning glory)

This annual creeper flowers in bright colors. Sow it directly where it is to grow.

Coreopsis

This plant looks like a perennial. The simple yellow flowers of *C. bigelovii* can be sown directly where they are to grow. Trim the plant back regularly; cutting coreopsis for flower arrangements will accomplish this. *C. tinctoria* is available in russet and yellow, growing to 1 to 3 feet (30cm to 1m) tall, depending on the variety. Do not plant *Coreopsis* in soil that is very wet, and provide some water during periods of drought.

Cosmos

This is an ideal plant for children. It can be sown directly where it is to grow. This excellent cut flower is handsome in the perennial border. The height of the plant varies from 3 to 5 feet (90cm to 150cm). The simple pink, white, or pink-red flowers are partly hidden by bright green, fine foliage. Plant cosmos in soil with good drainage.

Cucurbita (Ornamental gourd)

The ornamental gourd may be various colors and shapes: green, yellow, orange with dots or stripes, smooth or with warts; apple-, pear- or banana-shaped. You can never tell beforehand what the seeds will yield. Sow every seed separately in a pot indoors in April, and put them out after mid-May, once all danger of frost has passed. Give them enough space: the plants spread out over the ground and therefore need a large area to grow unrestricted. Beware of snails and slugs, and check the plants regularly.

Cuphea

It is preferable to buy plants, unless you have a greenhouse in which to start the seed and nurture the seedlings. These low-growing, thickset flowers bear small, bar-shaped red flowers. To be seen, they should be placed at the front of the border. The plant is also suitable for a rock garden.

Cynoglossum (Hound's tongue)

C. amabile, with veronica-like blue flowers, can be sown directly outdoors. Cut the flowers back in August when the bloom is almost past, in order to promote a second blooming.

Dianthus barbatus.

Dahlia

The low-growing varieties can be sown directly. This must be done as early as February (as long as there is no danger of frost), depending on where you live. It is preferable to start the plants indoors. Separate the corms at summer's end, and keep them for planting next year.

Delphinium (Larkspur)

The annual larkspur is a good cut flower and excellent for drying. The plants, which grow to a height of more than 3 feet (1m), are a nice addition to the perennial border to lengthen the blooming period. Seed mixtures may include hues of pink, violet, and blue, and the flowers may be single or double. Sow larkspur directly where it is to grow.

Dianthus (Sweet william)

Sweet william is a biennial. Sow the seeds in a seedbed in June, and move the young plants to their final home in October. There are various mixtures of colors, tall- and low-growing, in shades of red, violet, and white. All are *D. barbatus* hybrids. *D. chinensis* is an annual, usually red. This low-growing plant should be sown under glass;

Delphinium.

The old-fashioned Dianthus barbatus, *sweet william, with its silky flowers, is biennial.*

Digitalis.

Eccremocarpus (Glory flower)

This annual creeper (really a climbing shrub) should be sown in a hothouse, and for more than just this reason, is not suitable for the beginning gardener. It can be temperamental. Plant it on a sunny, warm spot. In a cold summer, the plant will be disappointing. The orange-red flowers look like those of the trumpet vine (*Campsis radicans*).

Eschscholtzia californica.

somewhat temperamental, it is not suitable for beginners. *Dianthus* prefer free-draining soil on the sandy side.

Digitalis (Foxglove)

Foxglove, a biennial, should be sown in June. In humusy soil, it will rise beautifully. In heavier, clayey soil, the plants may not germinate. This plant does well in sun, as well as in partial shade. Buy a package of mixed seeds, and rogue out any plants you do not want; after a number of years, you will have the best-looking foxgloves in your neighborhood, in the shades that please you best, whether they be pink, purple, mauve, yellow, or white.

Dimorphotheca (Cape marigold)

The cape marigold comes in orange-yellow just like the common marigold *Tagetes*. It requires a sunny, warm spot. The height at maturity is 1 foot (30cm). Sow it directly where it is to grow.

Dipsacus (Teasel)

Dipsacus is a biennial, sowing out spontaneously. It is a good butterfly plant, and a marvelous flower for drying. It grows to 7 feet (2m) tall.

Echium (Viper's bugloss)

There are more than thirty species, blooming in shades of red, pink, purple, blue, and white. *E. lycopsis* is an annual, bearing blue flowers that are most attractive to bees. The plant blooms in July and August, reaching a height of approximately 2 feet (60cm). It is best sown directly where it is to grow.

Felicia amelloides.   *Page 377:* Dipsacus fullonum.

Fuchsias come in many colors and forms.

Eschscholzia (California poppy)

This plant turns the deserts of California and Chile into blooming meadows. The seed is sold mixed and selected for color (orange). Let children sow the seed—it cannot fail. It will grow well in average soils, but is content in dry, poor soils, too.

Felicia (Blue daisy)

Buy *F. amelloides* as a plant, as growing it from seed is an extremely unreliable undertaking. Once it is established, you can take cuttings on your own to increase your stock.

Fuchsia

See "Container Plants A to Z," page 395.

Gazania (Treasure flower)

This plant bears daisylike flowers in bright, primary colors. Give *Gazania* a dry, warm, sunny spot. The flowers open when there is enough sunlight. The plant as such is not a very pretty sight, but the flowers definitely make up for this small shortcoming with their cheery appearance.

Godetia (Satin flower)

This plant deserves more attention than it seems to get. The flowers bloom in shades like those of sweet william (*Dianthus*, see above). The seed can be sown directly where it is to grow.

Gomphrena (Globe amaranth)

The globe amaranth is an excellent drying flower for the cut-flower garden. As a border plant, it may go unnoticed. It is best to start globe amaranth indoors, then plant it out when the weather is warmer. Harvest the flowers when they have fully opened, as they will not open farther once cut.

Gypsophila (Baby's breath)

Baby's breath is a good plant to weave among other plants in the flower border, and it is frequently used to fill out flower arrangements. The tiny white flowers soften the brighter colors of other plants, mediating less fortunate color combinations. It does not make much of a statement on its own. Sow seed directly where the plants are to grow. *Gypsophila* can be transplanted with success.

Helianthus annuus.

Helianthus (Sunflower)

There are tall and short varieties, flowers double and simple, and colors that range from yellow to reddish brown. The tallest sunflowers grow from the seed commonly used for bird seed. (See also "Children's Competitions," page 367).

Helichrysum (Immortelle)

This is the most famous flower for drying. The plants

Helichrysum.

bloom in all colors, and there are tall as well as short varieties. Harvest the flowers when they have just opened; harvested too late, the flowers will fall apart after drying.

Heliotropium (Heliotrope)

The heliotrope is a beauty that can be used for many purposes. Sow early indoors if you like, but it is preferable to buy plants. You can take cuttings to increase your stock. The violet-red color of the flowers is almost fluorescent. The plants slow their growth a little in cool summers; be sure to give them a warm spot. Do not confuse *H. arborescens* with the 7-foot-tall (2m) *H. peruvianum.*

Helipterum (Strawflower)

H. manglesii is a strawflower variety with single pink or white flowers. This plant can be sown directly where it is to grow in the cutting garden; it fits in well with other annuals and perennials, too. *H. roseum* has larger flowers of the same colors.

Hesperis (Dame's rocket)

The pink or white *H. matronalis* is a biennial. This plant requires a nutritious soil. Sow the seed in partial shade in June. The plant reaches a height of 3 feet (1m) the second year. Like honeysuckle, *Hesperis* has a strong fragrance at night, which attracts moths.

Humulus (Japanese hop)

When an eyesore in the garden needs to be covered, it is a good plan to start hop indoors and plant it out in May for the quickest remedy. Even so, direct sowing produces impressive results, too—the plant will grow to a height of 17 feet (5m) the same summer. The flowers and fruits are not particularly noticeable; the ornamental value is in the foliage.

Impatiens (Balsam, impatiens)

One of the most well-known border plants is the impatiens. It is also an excellent plant for containers, all the more so because it can grow well in shade. Give all members of this family lots of water; even out in the garden, impatiens may need extra water regularly. In full sun, a little water deprivation will make the plants wilt quickly. The plants with light pink and white flowers grow much larger than the red and violet ones, something to bear in mind when you plant mixed colors. *I. balsamina* is a thickset plant up to 1 foot (30cm) tall, many with double flowers. The giant balsam, *I.*

Lathyrus *in the cutting-flower corner. Give it something to climb on. For the tall-growing* *varieties, bamboo is suitable; for the shorter ones, stakes will suffice.*

glandulifera, is often considered a weed. This plant is a spreader but the superfluous plants can be pulled up easily.

Ipomoea (Morning glory)

The morning glory is an excellent vine for sheltered, warm spots. The plant can fill a small greenhouse during the summer. Big blue flowers appear between July and September. Start plants indoors for earlier flowering.

Kochia (Summer cypress)

K. scoparia, with its columnar habit, can provide a nice accent in the flower border. The plant grows to a height of 3 feet (1m) and looks like a small conifer. The light green foliage turns a beautiful red in autumn. Summer cypress is perfectly suited for symmetrical plantings.

Lagurus (Hare's-tail grass)

The annual hare's-tail grass is one of the nicest of the ornamental grasses. Sow it directly where it is to grow, in April. The plant can be dried. It reaches a height of 1 foot (30cm) and is striking planted between other annuals. For other grasses, see "Grasses, Ferns, and Bamboos A to Z," page 400.

Lathyrus (Sweet pea)

Lathyrus blooms in all colors, and there are tall and short varieties. The tall ones need something to climb on; short varieties can be planted in the perennial border. Let children sow the sweet pea; they always germinate and grow. It is a good idea to soak the seed before planting. If you need to protect the plants when they are young from birds, string black thread between the plants.

Lavatera

The annual *L. trimestris* is one of the most striking annual plants. The large pink flowers always look good. *Lavatera* can grow to 5 feet (1.5m). It is an easy plant that can be sown directly where it is to grow. *Lavatera* has a long blooming period.

Lobelia

The lobelia is a popular border plant, but sowing it yourself is not very easy. It is better to buy plants. Some grow in bush form and are sold as "erect" lobelias; others are more pendant. Lobelias bloom in sky blue, violet-blue, or white. They can be grown in containers or in the border.

Lobularia (Sweet alyssum)

This border plant is easy to sow. If you sow the plant at various times, you'll lengthen the period of bloom. Cutting back before the plant forms seed ensures a quick repeat bloom.

Lunaria annua.

Lunaria **(Honesty, money plant, moonwort, satin flower)**

The biennial honesty is an early bloomer in the colors purple and white. It grows to about 2½ feet (75cm). The flat white fruiting stems can be used in dried arrangements. Once sown, the plant will grow spontaneously in later years.

Lupinus **(Lupine)**

L. *hartwegii* is the annual lupine, which blooms in various colors. *L. luteus*, which bears yellow flowers, is sometimes used as a "green manure" crop in commercial agriculture. The perennial lupine is easily sown.

Malope **(Mallow-wort)**

This member of the malva family is a guaranteed success. *M. trifida* has a long blooming period, with pink or white flowers. Give the plant room to grow to 3 feet (1m).

Matricaria

This chamomile-like plant resembles *Chrysanthemum parthenium*, and combines well with it. The thickset plants are loaded with rounded flowers. The plant reaches 1 to 1½ feet (30 to 45cm).

Lupinus lutens.

Lobelia is suitable for growing in containers.

Matthiola incana.

Mattholia (Stock)

Stock, the biennial, is not suitable for beginners. The annual plant is a bit easier, but should be started in the greenhouse in order to have the plants bloom in June.

Mesembryantheumum

This flower needs the warmest location and fullest sun exposure. The flowers open only in the sunshine. Give

Mesembryanthemum.

the plants a dry spot in order to prevent them from rotting. The bright colors—shades of red, pink, occasionally yellow, and white—often don't really harmonize with others in the garden. Try planting them in a separate area, perhaps in the rock garden. Clearly, this is not the most easily accomodated garden plant. Consider growing it in a container.

Mirabilis (Four-o'clock plant)

The four-o'clock plant blooms in colors repulsive to many gardeners (just like *Celosia*), but children adore them. Four-o'clock plants have to be started in a warm spot. Give the plants, which grow to 3 feet (1m) tall, a warm, sunny spot in moist soil; dehydration causes early death. The blossoms open in late afternoon on sunny days, hence the common name.

Moluccella (Bells of Ireland)

The green flowers (actually, the flower bracts) are indeed bell-shaped. They fit well in every border, and are beautiful in flower arrangements; if the stems are placed horizontally in the bouquet, the tips will curl up within a day. The plant grows 3 feet (1m) tall.

Myosotis (Forget-me-not)

Sow this biennial directly in the garden, in a spot that does not receive too much sun, in June or July. In suitably moist soil, *Myosotis* will spread every year. There are varieties of different heights. Use the shorter varieties for naturalizing; they bloom with white, blue, or pink flowers.

Nemesia

Nemesia blooms in various colors. The seed can be sown directly where it is to grow. A disadvantage is that the bloom period ends early in the summer, especially when the plants grow in too dry a location. They require full sun.

Nicandra physalodes *is easy to sow. You can see from the flowers that the plant belongs to the potato family; the calyx looks like those of the Chinese lantern, but is green.*

Nicandra

N. physalodes (see Physalis, to which it is related, under "Perennials A to Z," page 306) is sown for its ornamental value when dried.

Nicotiana (Flowering tobacco)

This annual is easy to sow, but plants can be purchased, too. The plant is excellent to take over where bulbs leave off, and it also looks nice among perennials in the border. The N. × sanderae 'Lime Green' combines well with all kinds of other plants. Flowering tobacco blooms from July to September.

Nigella (Love-in-a-mist)

Love-in-a-mist is a favorite among horticulturists, for so many attractive qualities are combined into one plant: It can be sown directly in the garden; the seed is easily harvested; the plant can be sown by children; the flower colors harmonize with many other plants; and it is a good dried flower. Nigella damascena can be sold as mixed colors. Gardeners are short-changed with such mixtures.

Choose the Nigella best for your garden:

Nigella damascena 'Albion', white, 2 feet (60cm)
N. d. 'Mulberry Rose', 2 feet (60cm)

Geranium *does not look at all like* Pelargonium. *This is a garden geranium.*

N. hispanica, deep purple blue with purple center, the largest flowers
N. d. 'Oxford Blue', 2½ feet (75cm)
N. sativa, white or pale blue flowers. The seeds are strongly aromatic, nice in sachets.

Oenothera (Evening primrose)

As an annual, this yellow flower blooms in late summer; as a biennial sown in July, it blooms earlier with bigger flowers. The plants have a delicate appearance. O. biennis grows to about 3 feet (1m tall).

Papaver (Poppy)

Be careful when making your purchase, because there are annual and biennial varieties. See also "Perennials A to Z," page 305. P. nudicaule is biennial. Sow directly where it is to grow in July. The plant blooms the following year in soft shades of yellow, white, pink, and red. P. rhoeas is annual, the Flander or field poppy, of which various varieties are available in nice colors; the original color is red. The opium poppy is P. somniferum. This tall plant with its soft pink color looks nice

By letting Pelargonium
"hibernate," you may have   *bushes up to 7 feet (2m) tall.*

among perennials in the border. This is true for the single as well as the double poppies. Some varieties of this last group are:

P. 'Black Paeony'	velvety dark brown-red
P. 'Cream Paeony'	cream
P. 'Purple Paeony'	bright purple
P. 'Red Paeony'	bright red
P. 'Scarlet Paeony'	scarlet

Poppies are difficult to transplant because of their fragile roots; therefore, sow them where they are to grow, but not too close together. You can sow sequentially from one package of seeds, some fifteen days apart, to lengthen the blooming period.

Pelargonium (Geranium)

Pelargonium is the scientific name for the plant we commonly call "geranium." Usually, geraniums are grown from cuttings. This yields the most beautiful flowers. Geraniums from cuttings are a bit more expensive than sown plants, but they are worth the money. Inexpensive geraniums are nearly always sown, and such plants are suitable only for the flower borders in the garden; the plants from cuttings are better for growing in containers. You can sow the seed yourself in January in a warm place. The so-called Austrian geraniums become very large, with small flowers. They don't look great when you buy them, but grow into the most beautiful plants with a little fertilizer.

Penstemon (Beard tongue)

Penstemon is one of the most beautiful annuals, but it is certainly not the easiest one. Sow as early as March in a warm location. The foxglove-like flowers combine well with perennials in the flower border.

Perilla

Like *Coleus*, this plant is grown for its foliage. *P. frutescens* 'Atropurpurea', with its dark brown-red leaves, can soften a border that is a bit too colorful.

Petunia

Petunias come in an astonishing number of varieties, though there are usually only a few types for sale at the local garden center. You can choose from pink, white, red, purple, blue, and even striped, flowers. You can also buy mixed seed packages; start these in a warm seedbed and later select the suitable colors when planting them out in the garden. These are very undemanding annuals, little effort for the color impact.

Phacelia

This easy-to-sow plant is attractive to bees. *Phacelia* can be sown up to the end of June for bloom in late summer. The blue-flowered plants are ideal for filling gaps in the garden. Sow *P. tanacetifolia* directly where it is to grow.

Phlox

The perennial phlox is rather tall; annual phlox grows only to a height of 1 foot (30cm). Sow in a cold frame and plant out around mid-May. Phlox flowers in all bright colors. Depending on your climate and the growing conditions you can offer your plants, you may find your phlox is troubled by mildew. Avoid working in your garden during wet weather, so as to lessen the chance of spreading mildew.

Polygonum

There are creepers, perennials, and weedy plants, too. *P. capitatum* is not much like these. A ground cover with tiny pink flowers, it is ideal for the rock garden, as a border plant, and to grow in a container, spilling softly over the edges.

Polygonum capitatum.

Portulaca (Moss rose)

P. grandiflora will grow under the same conditions as *Mesembryanthemum*: sunny and dry. The plants bloom in bright colors. Here again, consider growing the plants in containers outdoors.

Ricinus (Castor bean)

This ornamental plant has big green or red leaves. *R. communis* reaches a height of 6 feet (2m). This plant is a poisonous plant—see also page 124.

Salvia

Salvia do not all look alike. Most important are the following:

Salvia sclarea (Clary)

This biennial has large, softly hairy leaves and flower stems up to 3 feet (1m). Soft pink or lilac flowers appear. Sow it in May, and give the plants enough space when planting them out.

S. splendens (Scarlet sage)

This annual is the famously fire-red salvia. Nowadays, we see more orange-red colors, which is a shame, because

Salvia sclarea.

Salvia splendens *with* Canna indica. *In the middle of this nineteenth-century–style bed* *stands* Phormium tenax *'Variegata'.*

the true red ones of days gone by were more beautiful. These salvia make a bold statement all by themselves.

S. patens (Gentian sage)

The gentian sage is usually grown as an annual. Bring the plant indoors for the winter; give it little water. The most beautiful variety, with unsurpassed blue color, is *S. p.* 'Cambridge Blue', which grows up to 2 feet (60cm) tall. The cultivar 'Alba' offers white flowers. Some cultivars reach 3 feet (1m) in height.

S. viridis

The leaves of this taller salvia have ornamental value. This annual blooms in the colors red, pink, and white. It may also be found as *S. horminum*.

Salvia horminum.

S. farinacea

This annual blooms with dark blue flowers. This taller variety is the best cutting flower of all the salvias. The flower buds appear dusted (farina = meal, mildew), and this is the right variety for a blue-gray border. In arrangements it is especially pretty with reds and pinks.

Sanvitalia

Plant *Sanvitalia* for a miniature sunflower in your garden. This creeping plant is relatively easy to direct sow; avoid very wet soil. It is a good ground cover for the rock garden, and a nice edging plant.

Senecio

Senecio is biennial, but is almost always grown as an annual. The plant with the gray foliage is *S. cineraria*, dusty miller. Gray makes all the colors of other plants look prettier. Sometimes these plants survive a mild winter; then, the following year, they will grow to almost 2 feet (60cm) tall and bloom with small yellow flowers.

Statice

S. sinuatum and *S. suworowii* are good drying flowers. The latter is also suitable for planting in the border.

Sanvitalia.

Tagetes patula.

Tagetes (Marigold)

This is one of the most frequently planted annuals, but it is not the most beautiful. Marigolds are thought to help fight off rose pests. Try planting some between the roses for prevention once every few years. The most suitable marigold for this purpose are the small-flowered single varieties. All marigolds are easy to sow. Start them in a cold frame or indoors for early bloom. In addition to all the many shades of yellow and gold, there are now white marigold varieties.

Tagetes erecta (African marigold)

The African marigold is the largest of the marigolds, growing to 3 feet (1m) in height with very large flowers. Today, we see many varieties with such large flowers as these on shorter plants. It is useless to argue about taste, but one might wonder whether the proportions were given sufficient thought.

T. patula (French marigold)

This small marigold usually has many-rayed flowers in orange or yellow, and some with both brown and yellow.

Tagetes *seems to help keep roses healthy. The rose here is* 'La France', *the first tea hybrid rose from 1868.*

Verbascum.

T. tenuifolia (Signet marigold)

Of the signet marigold, get to know the varieties 'Lemon Gem' and 'Golden Gem'. These are single-flowered, natural-looking marigolds, the most elegant for all their simplicity.

Thunbergia (Black-eyed Susan vine)

This vine bears orange-yellow flowers with black centers, and grows to about 5 feet (1½m). The plant is suitable for growing in containers (they do well in window boxes in warmer climates), and can even be grown indoors. Sow it in a warm place in March.

Tropaeolum (Nasturtium)

The beautiful round leaves are exceptional. The single and double, short and tall nasturtium is often seen in old-fashioned gardens. Nasturtiums spread even when the soil has not been worked very well. The flowers bloom in shades of gold, yellow, orange, orange-red, and even pink tones. They can be purchased in mixed colors and by single color. You can harvest the seeds of your most beautiful specimen and sow them a year later. *T. peregrinum*, the canary creeper, looks very different, with a somewhat tangled manner of growing.

Verbascum (Mullein)

This biennial grows well in poor soil, even soil that is dry and limy, and full of stones or pebbles. The tall (2 to 4 feet/60 to 120 cm) flower spikes tower over low foliage.

Verbena (Vervain)

V. bipinnatifida and *V. canadensis* are ideal plants for growing both in containers and borders. They can grow quite large, but no taller than 1½ feet (45cm). *V. bonariensis* (syn. *V. patagonica*) is a tall plant (maximum 5 feet/1½m) with small flowers. Plant this throughout your border for a united look, to bring the whole picture together. Plant it in somewhat dry soil; the fallen seeds will probably germinate and grow the next year.

Viola (Pansy)

The large-flowered *Viola* are biennials and should be sown in July. Plant them out early in the year in order to enjoy them for as long as possible. It is possible to plant the pansies out in the autumn, but they'll need protection; when it freezes, covering them up with spruce branches is enough for a mild winter, depending on where you live.

Zinnia

It is easier to buy plants than to sow zinnias. This is a good cutting flower, but the flowers sometimes drown in summer rain, and rot. Their brilliant, jeweltone colors and large-petaled heads, whether they be double or merely single, are always attention grabbers.

Verbena bippinatifida *used as a ground cover beneath a* standard Plumbago.

16 Container Plants A to Z

Gardening in containers has become very popular in the last few years. In many gardens, containers, are arranged on the terrace, and balconies turn into "hanging gardens" in miniature with a profusion of containers.

Pink Brugmansia.

Plants in containers are a boon to the gardener with little time. Often they need to be brought indoors over winter, and the same plants may enliven the garden the following summer without the gardener having to replant. The choice of container is almost without limit, from large to small, contemporary to old-fashioned. Moreover, containers may be constructed of wonderfully diverse materials: pottery, iron, aluminum, wood, marble, plastic. Even an old whiskey barrel can become an eye-catcher when filled with blooming flowers.

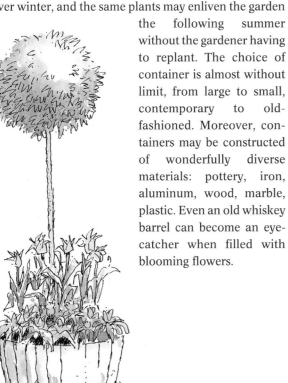

Bulbous Plants for Container Culture

Certain kinds of bulbs are particularly suitable for a spot on or near the terrace during the summer. Let them overwinter in a dark, frost-free place such as the garage, the basement, or even the attic.
Suitable plants include:

Agapanthus
Crinum
Eucharis
Eucomis
Hippeastrum
Hymenocallis
Nerine
Vallota
Zephyranthes

Containers arranged on a terrace or along a path can complement and contrast with plantings in the garden.

Where do "Container" Plants Come From?

The plants that we place outdoors for the summer usually are native to countries with warm climates. They will not survive harsh winters when they are not protected.

Geographic area	Plant
Mediterranean:	*Olea*
	Nerium
	Phoenix
South Africa (the Cape):	*Pelargonium*
	Plumbago
	almost all bulbous plants
Asia:	*Citrus*
	Camellia
South America:	*Datura*
	Fuchsia
	cactus varieties
New Zealand:	*Phormium*
	Leptospermum
Australia:	*Callistemon*
	Eucalyptus

Container Plants A to Z

Agapanthus

With its violet-blue, funnel-shaped flowers on 3-foot-tall (1m) stems, *Agapanthus* is one of the most popular container plants. It blooms in August, but the small, light green leaves are attractive all summer. An often-heard complaint is that the plants bloom hardly, or not at all. You can promote bloom by overwintering the plant at a low temperature, in a frost-free location, which may be dark. *Agapanthus* requires little in the way of upkeep. Repot the plant once every couple of years, taking care not to damage the succulent roots. There are dwarf varieties available, if a smaller plant is to your liking.

Agapanthus.

Agave

The agave comes originally from North America, but now is a familiar sight in all the tropical and subtropical areas in the world. Some varieties are used to feed cattle, others yield the fiber to make sisal hemp.

The agave is easy to grow in a sunny location. The plant prefers to overwinter in a light spot, with temperatures above freezing. The plant can't withstand frost.

Increase your stock by removing young plants from the mother plant when you are repotting, and place them in their own containers. Protect them from near-freezing temperatures, and they will perform for you.

Bougainvillea

This old-fashioned houseplant is almost exclusively seen today grown as a container plant. In a large container, this plant can reach a height of 7 feet (2m). Place it in full sun in summer, and in a frost-free, cool spot in winter. The leaves will fall off, but the plant will grow new ones in the summer. Growing new plants from cuttings is difficult; the soil has to be warm, at least 77°F (25C°), and high humidity is desirable. It is not the small white flowers that give the plant its beauty, but the colorful bracts—purple, pink, red, yellow, and white (the most common is purple)—that truly command attention. These are the beauties we admire in so many tropical lands.

Brugmansia (Angel's trumpet)

The most famous is *B. suaveolens*, which blooms in white, pink, or yellow. This plant has large, hanging flowers with a sweet, heavy fragrance—a very dramatic combination. The flowers are indeed trumpet-shaped. The plant cannot withstand frost. The woody plants can be cut in autumn and placed indoors. The temperatures should not drop below 40°F (4.4C°). Give *Brugmansia* a lot of fertilizer and water.

An advantage of pots is that they can easily be taken indoors during the winter. Earthenware pots must not be left out in cold weather, because they won't endure frost. When the water in the pot freezes, the pot will break.

Yellow Brugmansia.

Containers large and small need a hole in the bottom so excess water can drain. Pots without one (or more) drainage holes should have a layer of pot shards on the bottom.

Calla
See *Zantedeschia* (below).

Callistemon (Bottlebrush)
This plant, which grows as a shrub or small trees, blooms with remarkable red flowers. *Callistemon* can withstand temperatures as low as 28°F (–2.2°C).

Camellia
You can drink tea made from camellia leaves; these leaves come from *Camellia sinensis*. When we speak of the common camellia, we mean *C. japonica*. In recent years, horticulturists have tried to breed more frost-proof plants. The species can survive temperatures to 50°F (10°C), but the new container plants can now stand some frost.

The camellia desires acid soil, and should not be placed in full sun. This evergreen plant can stay outdoors, provided you don't forget to bring it in during periods of frost. Camellias really are not garden plants, except in warmer climates.

Canna indica (Indian shot)
Indian shot was a popular Victorian plant. It blooms with red, orange, yellow, or bicolored flowers. The red plants grow the tallest: 7 feet (2m).

There could scarcely be more noticeable flowers. The blooming period is from June to late autumn. New, shorter varieties are offered as houseplants. Give them rich, humusy soil, which makes it easier to clean the soil from the rhizomes in the autumn. Save the rhizomes in peat moss over winter to prevent dehydration, at a temperature of 50°F (10°C). Move them to warmer quarters early in the spring, to presprout them, and then plant them in pots (or outdoors, in warm areas) in June, when the soil has warmed. Nowadays, the plants are sold selected by color; they used to be sold by variety name only, with such names as 'Alphonse Bouvier', 'Baron de Richter', 'J. B. van der Schoot', and 'King Humbert' (the plant was a favorite in European countries).

If you leave the plants in pots over the summer, give them sufficient water. A sunny, warm spot is preferred by this semitropical plant.

Citrus (Orange, lemon)
This is the preeminent container plant. Louis XIV imprisoned his Minister Fouquet out of jealousy over Fouquet's beautiful gardens; all the citrus plants from

Canna *'Lucifer'*.

Fouquet's garden (Château Vaux-le-Vicomte) were transferred to Versailles. The genus *Citrus* (which includes lemons, oranges, and grapefruits) can withstand very cool temperatures over winter, but they prefer not to have frost. Put them on a warm spot in the sun during the summer. If you wish to sow *Citrus*, you may have success with grapefruit. It will take many years before

Page 393:
Canna indica.

Clivia.

fruits appear. You can grow beautiful trees regardless of whether they bear fruit; whether pollination will occur, though, is not a sure thing.

Clivia

Clivia used to be grown exclusively in temperate and colder climates as a houseplant, but it makes a satisfactory container plant. Put it outdoors with the protection of some shade during the summer, and in a cool room during the winter. Their ideal winter temperature indoors is 65°F (18.3°C). With this treatment, the plants will bloom in late summer and early spring (February). *Clivia* flowers, which are good-sized, may be red, red/white, or orange.

Crinum

This bulbous plant can overwinter in the greenhouse; the tropical varieties need to "hibernate" in relative warmth. *C.* × *powellii*, with its amaryllislike flowers, is suitable as a container plant. *Crinum* plants bloom in shades of red, through pink tones, to white.

Datura

See *Brugmansia* (page 391).

Eucalyptus

In Australia, at least five hundred eucalyptus varieties are grown. Although the plants are trees in their home country, they can be grown as shrubs in containers, with pruning. The most famous is *E. gunnii*, with remarkable blue-gray foliage, and which can withstand temperatures as low as 24°F (−4.4°C). Almost all other varieties must overwinter in a frost-free location.

Eucharis

E. grandiflora requires a warm spot, but not in full sun. The plant should overwinter in a warm place as well. Give it the highest humidity possible.

Eucomis (Pineapple lily)

It is not the yellow-green color of the foliage, but the shape of the flower that makes the plant attractive. Make sure the big bulbs are not left to overwinter in too cool a location. Give them a warm spot in partial shade during the summer.

Ficus (Fig)

Figs can be grown in containers, but can also overwinter in the garden in a suitably warm spot, climate permitting. They can withstand temperatures as low as 19°F (−7.2°C).

Eucomis bicolor.

Eucomis bicolor.

A nice container plant is *F. pumila*, creeping fig. This plant does not bloom, but the flat, rounded leaves are very graceful in combination with other plants or in the background. This is generally considered a tropical plant, but it can withstand some cold. It grows slowly when young. Put the plant in a warm spot in partial shade during the summer. Be careful of dehydration. The *Ficus* we know as houseplants in temperate climates are usually not suitable for placing outdoors.

Fuchsia

Fuchsia blooms in a thousand shapes and colors. The flowers may be single or double, in color combinations quietly handsome or loudly exuberant. There are clubs for fuchsia lovers around the world, and they hold annual exhibitions. *F. procumbens* is a nice hanging plant with rounded leaves. More difficult to obtain is *F. arborescens*, tree fuchsia, on which the flowers grow directly from the stem; this plant reaches a maximum height of 25 feet (7½m).

Keep fuchsias in a frost-free, but cool, location. If you do not have such a place available to you, it is better to opt for *F. magellanica*, a fuschia that will endure a little frost. In the garden, the plant freezes to the ground, but

it will start growing again. When placed indoors during periods of frost, the bush may reach a height of 7 feet (2m). This is the hardiest fuchsia.

Gardenia

This plant bears waxy, white, richly scented flowers and requires an acid soil, just like the camellia. It should overwinter at a temperature between 40 and 70°F (4.4 and 21.1°C). Put the plant in a warm spot in partial shade during the summer.

Heliotropium (Heliotrope)

The large flower's cymes are of an almost neon violet color during the entire summer. The plant may be kept for a long time. The flower stems turn somewhat woody, after which the plant can be shaped into a standard, and grown to a height of 3 feet (1m). Overwinter the plants at temperatures between 50 and 60°F (10 and 15.6°C).

Hibiscus

The Syrian hibiscus is discussed with the shrubs (page 247). The Chinese hibiscus, *H. rosa-sinensis,* actually grows too large for the windowsill. Horticulturists therefore apply substances in order to limit the growth.

Fuchsias are very popular, suitable for containers and   *also for hanging baskets.*

Hippeastrum *'Zenith'*.

The white Ismene festalis.

The plants that are treated this way are not suitable as container plants. In order for the plants to grow well, and to make them suitable as container plants, they must be trimmed and the roots cleaned. Plant them in fresh potting mixture, and set in a warm, humid location. They will then be able to grow into large shrubs, a beautiful sight on your terrace. Prune in early spring. Do not overwinter them at temperatures below 50°F (10°C).

Hippeastrum (Amaryllis)

This winter bloomer can live through the summer in shade on your terrace. Bring it indoors in October, and put it away in a dry location until the first flower stem appears. Then, start watering again. By mid-May, with reliably warm weather, the plant can be moved outdoors. If you do not have a green thumb, you can buy a new bulb every year in November/December.

Ismene

This bulbous plant should not overwinter in too cool a location. The bulbs can be left in the soil in the container.

Lantana (Shrub verbena)

Overwinter this plant between 40 to 50°F (4.4 to 10°C). An overnight frost will cause leaf-drop, but the plants will start growing again. With careful pruning, you can create a very pretty standard of *Lantana*. The best known is *L. camara*, with reddish or yellowish flowers.

Laurus (Laurel)

This small tree is often seen as a standard, pruned into a round shape. The plant can withstand night frost well, but it prefers to overwinter at temperatures between 40 and 50°F (4.4 to 10°C).

Hippeastrum *'Red Lion'*.

Lantana camara *can be planted out in the garden, depending on the climate; it is a good container plant.*

Leptospermum

L. scoparium is a broomlike shrub, and can endure little frost. Make sure that the plant is never dehydrated. You can cut it back directly after blooming. This New Zealand plant offers varieties with single and double flowers. *L.s.* 'Nanum' is a dwarf variety.

Nerine

This excellent cut flower bears flowers that may be light blue, pink, or white; it looks a little like *Agapanthus*. Culturally, it is similar to *Agapanthus*, too, though it prefers temperatures a little higher. The plant doesn't withstand frost. The bulbs of this bulbous plant can overwinter in soil or potting mixture.

Nerium (Oleander)

The ancient Greeks and the Romans grew oleanders. Although the plant can withstand some frost, it is best to overwinter at temperatures between 50 and 60°F (10 and 15.6°C). You can cut the plants back in June, and they will bloom the following year. Check the plants regularly on the underside of the leaves for scale; if the infestation

is small, you can easily remove the scale with your thumbnail. See also under poisonous plants for oleander (page 124).

Olea (Olive)

The olive is an easy plant to grow. It can endure a little frost, but it is safer to let it overwinter indoors. It is difficult to grow plants from cuttings; it is better to buy a small plant. *O. europaea* is the most common.

Passiflora (Passionflower)

The passionflower can be bought for indoor as well as for outdoor enjoyment. There are many types and varieties. The hardiest one is *P. caerulea* with green-white sepals and a purple-blue corona. For a pure white variety, choose 'Constance Elliott'. This passionflower is the only one that can withstand some frost. It is easy to raise this fast grower in a container. In the garden, older plants can withstand some frost if they are situated in a sheltered location.

Phormium (New Zealand flax)

This old-fashioned garden plant is returning to popularity. The long, basal, sword-shaped leaves seemingly rise from the soil. It usually does not bloom; the ornamental value lies in the foliage. The plant can

Nerine sarniensis.

Nerine bowdenii *blooms in beautiful Persian pink.*

Punica (Pomegranate)

This ancient shrub can withstand temperatures as low as 25°F (−3.9°C). The plant has red flowers and bears edible, multiseeded fruits. Hybrid varieties in culture have orange or white flowers.

Poncirus trifoliata.

endure frost, but it is better to grow it in containers. Numerous varieties are available. *P. tenax* with its dark blue-green leaf can reach a height of 7 feet (2m). There are red-leafed and gold- and silver-variegated varieties.

Pittosporum

This evergreen shrub is originally from New Zealand. A number of varieties are in culture; all can withstand a minimum temperature of 25°F (−3.9°C). *Pittosporum* is one of the easiest plants to grow in a container.

Plumbago (Leadwort)

This shrub with its long, weak leaves can endure temperatures as low as 32°F (0°C), but it is better to let it overwinter at temperatures between 40 and 60°F (4.4 and 15.6°C).

The racemes of flowers that appear in late summer are a beautiful sky blue or white.

Poncirus

This bush looks very much like a lemon tree. *P. trifoliatia* can usually overwinter in a sheltered garden. As a standard, it makes a handsome sight in a container.

Rosmarinus (Rosemary)

This popular herb usually freezes to the ground in the garden, but it can endure considerable frost. Growing it as a container plant has the advantage that you can harvest leaves for kitchen use very easily during the winter. The plant will grow into a bush, but can be trained into a standard.

Solanum

Solanum is of the same family as the potato and tomato. For container culture, two varieties can be recommended particularly: *S. jasminoides*, with white flowers, and *S. crispum*, with blue flowers. Of the latter, 'Glasnevin' bears the biggest and most beautiful flowers. This plant can, however, withstand little frost. *S. jasminoides* can usually overwinter well in a sheltered patio garden, but must be considered as a container plant in cooler climates.

Sparmannia (Indoor linden)

What is true for *Clivia* is also true for *Sparmannia*: Our living rooms today are too warm for overwintering. Winter temperatures should be between 40 and 50°F (4.4

and 10°C). Put the plant outdoors around mid-May, when the weather is reliably warm, in a spot that is not too windy. During hot summers the plant can suffer badly from white fly; moving the plant to a breezier spot will help.

Strelitzia (Bird-of-paradise)

This plant belongs to the banana family. If you buy a large plant directly from a specialty nursery, you can cut bird-of-paradise flowers for arrangements; they are very expensive at florist shops, and this may be the most economical way to obtain them. You have to buy a large plant for this, because otherwise you have a long wait for flowers, as the plant grows slowly. Overwinter *Strelitzia* in a cool spot (40°F/4.4°C) or indoors. Put the plant in full sun during the summer.

Vallota

This bulbous plant is not hardy, and should overwinter in a cool, frost-free location. It appreciates a moist—not wet—soil. The amaryllislike flowers appear in August/September.

Viburnum

The evergreen *Viburnum tinus* has small, oval, dark green, shiny leaves. The plant can stay outdoors during mild winters if planted in a sheltered spot. It is better to bring the plant indoors during harsh winters; the foliage may otherwise take on a rather beaten appearance. Cold temperatures promote blooming, so do not overwinter in a warm room. *V.t.* 'Variegatum' has variegated foliage; 'Purpureum' has red foliage. The plant blooms with white flowers; 'Eva' produces pink flowers.

Zantedeschia aethiopica.

Yucca

As a container plant, *Y. aloifolia*, with very narrow, sharply pointed leaves, is recommended. This plant withstands temperatures as low 28°F (−2.2°C)—rather surprising for such an exotic-looking specimen.

Zantedeschia (Calla lily)

This old-fashioned houseplant likes a cool spot (up to 60°F/15.6°C) during the winter. Outdoors during the summer, place it in a warm spot in the shade. This plant was considered a houseplant years ago because people lived in cool rooms. Now that we have turned the heat up a bit higher, and central heating ensures constant warmth, this plant is no longer happy as a houseplant. It makes a better container plant today. Overwinter the plant in an unheated attic or frost-free garage. Give the calla lily lots of water. *Z. aethiopica* bears white, pink, or yellow flowers.

Zephyranthes

Zephyranthes is an early-summer bloomer. This bulbous plant, belonging to the amaryllis family, should overwinter in a cool, frost-free place.

Many hanging pots do not have drainage holes in the bottom. Do not give them too much water if that is the case, as excess water will remain in the pot.

17 Grasses, Ferns, and Bamboos A to Z

If any plants were often misunderstood, it is this group. Many people think grasses are weedy, that ferns are gloomy (or that they can be grown only as house-plants), and that bamboos look bare and dead most of the time. Yet all of these plants can be beautiful additions to your garden.

Grasses are far more varied than most people think, and today a garden without an ornamental grass variety of one kind or another would be a pity. Ferns give an air of tranquillity, and bamboos can add a graceful, even rarefied, exotic, or even tropical effect.

Asplenium ruta-muraria.

Achnatherum

A. brachytricha is a grass for full sun. It reaches a height of about 4 feet (1¼m). In the late summer, the dewdrops hang gracefully from the tips of the plume-shaped blooms.

Adiantum (Maidenhair fern)

Maidenhair fern is often grown as a houseplant. A number of varieties are suitable for the garden. *A. pedatum* is a bright, light green, and reaches a height of almost 1 foot (30cm). *A.p.* 'Japonicum' grows taller, with red leaves.

Agropyron (Wheatgrass)

A. pubiflorum is a grass with a beautiful blue color. The plant, native to New Zealand, has light blue spikes and grows about 2 feet (62cm) tall.

Alopecurus (Foxtail)

This grass is often seen by the side of the road. The flower spikes can be dried, and they are also beautiful in fresh arrangements of meadow flowers. *A. pratensis* 'Aureovariegatus' has a beautiful yellow-variegated leaf.

Arundinaria

A. muriliae, a medium-size bamboo, is suitable for forming a hedgerow. The stalks become a gray-blue. Like all bamboos, the plant can be grown in full sun and partial shade. It grows about 8 feet (2½m) tall.

Asplenium (Spleenwort)

Spleenwort is usually grown as a houseplant, but there are some fine species for the garden. *Asplenium* needs moist, humusy soil in shade. It must be covered up well during the winter. Try *A. ruta-muraria*, wall rue, against the northern side of a wall.

Athyrium

One of the most common garden ferns is *A. filix-femina*, the lady fern. This large fern dies back in the winter. It grows a little over 3 feet (1m) tall. This is one of the easiest ferns; it will grow in any type of soil, provided it is planted in partial or full shade.

Avena (Blue oat grass)

See *Helictrotrichon* (page 404).

Blechnum (Hard fern)

Deer fern, *B. spicant*, is a low-growing, dark green plant, a good ground cover for the deepest shade in the garden. *Blechnum* can be recognized by the clearly different sterile (without spores) green leaves and the fertile leaves that are completely brown from the spores that cover them. This evergreen fern remains short. *B. penna-marina* has a finer leaf and needs good protection from frost.

Briza (Quaking grass)

B. media is an annual grass that is often grown for drying. The plant is suitable for the cut-flower corner of the garden. The panicles tremble in a charming way when disturbed.

Bromus

B. lanceolatus is grown as an annual for dried bouquets. This rather hairy plant with its thick, small spikes will reach a height of 1½ feet (45cm).

C. acutiflora is one of the most beautiful ornamental grasses, beautiful even during winter because the flower

The flower spike of Carex.

spikes remain on the plant after blooming until spring. The height of the plant is about 5 feet (1½m).

Carex (Sedge)

Sedges are grasslike plants that thrive in soil that is not too dry, in full sun or partial shade. The height of most varieties reaches no more than 1½ feet (45cm). An exception to this generalization is *C. pendula*, which grows to 3 feet (1m). As early as May, the long-blooming stalks have reached their height and gracefully hang over.

Ceterach (Rusty-back fern)

C. officinarum grows on old walls in the shade, for a very romantic effect.

Cortaderia (Pampas grass)

The pampas grass (*C. selloana*) usually has white plumes. The flower stalk reaches a height of 10 feet (3m). The pampas grass with pinkish plumes grows up to 7 feet (2m), but is even more sensitive to frost than the white one. You can give the best frost protection by planting *Cortaderia* in a dry spot; remember, it is the combination of wet and cold that is deathly to so

Ceterach officinarum, *the rusty-back fern.*

many plants. Wrap it in burlap for winter protection and spread leaves around the plant. In spring, cut pampas grass to about 3 inches (8cm) above the ground; you'll need to "trim" the clumps with a saw or even a sharp ax as pruning shears won't be heavy enough. *C.s.* 'Pumila' is a richly flowering, white dwarf variety.

Cyrtomium (Japanese holly fern)

C. falcatum, with its shiny, dark green leaf, and *C. fortunei,* with its dull green leaf, can be grown in a cool spot in the house, or in a relatively warm spot in the garden. They can grow in deep shade, and need, like almost all ferns, lots of moisture. The Japanese holly fern is a good container plant for a shady spot.

Cyrtonium falcatum, *the Japanese holly fern.*

Cystopteris (Bladder fern)

C. bulbiferum grows 1½ feet (45cm) tall, has light green fronds and forms bulblets. *C. fragilis* is much smaller.

Deschampsia (Tufted hair grass)

This plant can be recognized by the small twists in the stalks of the flower plumes. *D. caespitosa* is a plant for full sun, but it will grow in some shade. The dark green foliage is pretty.

Dicksonia (Tree fern)

The vast majority of tree ferns are tropical plants. An exception is the New Zealand native *D. antarctica,* which can stand up to a little frost. The plant is suitable for a greenhouse heated only during very cold weather. The tree fern can be grown as a container plant. The ferns are very valuable, selling commonly for as much as $500.

Dryopteris (Wood fern, shield fern, buckler fern)

These are cluttered-looking ferns for a woodland area at the back of the garden. *Dryopteris* can grow in the deepest shade, just like *Asarum europaeum* and *Symphytum grandiflorum.*

Equisetum (Horsetail)

This primitive plant multiplies mainly by underground rhizomes. *E. telmateia,* a handsome plant, can not often be found; it has beautiful light green foliage and reaches a height of 3 feet (1m). It is suitable for moist, shady places. *E. arvensis* is an annoying weed that we can often see growing by the side of the road. Weeding will eradicate it.

Erianthus (Plume grass)

E. ravennae is a grass that forms a large, wide tuft. The plant does not bloom in cooler areas. The plant can grow to a spectacular height of 7 feet (2m), making a dramatic statement.

Festuca (Fescue)

F. ovina var. *glauca,* of which various varieties exist, has a blue-green color. The thick tufts grow to a maximum height of 1 foot (30cm). This plant is suitable for filling up bare spots in a border, and it also looks nice in the rock or heather garden. *F. filiformis* has very fine, bronze-green leaves and reaches a height of 1 foot (30cm). The

Page 403: Cortaderia selloana *(syn.* Gynerium argenteum)*, pampas grass, develops plumes that can reach a height up to 10 feet (3m). The variety 'Pumila' is shorter.*

Equisetum *is closely related to* Hippuris. *See the water plants* *chapter (page 360) for more information .*

somewhat taller *F. amethystina* is fine-leafed with purple-green spikelets. Plant in full sun; the grass blooms between May and July and is handsome in combination with red-foliaged garden neighbors. *F. gigantea*, the giant fescue, has fresh green foliage and grows up to 4 feet (1⅓m).

Glyceria (Manna-grass)

G. maxima 'Variegata' is a grass for a moist location. The plant has a slightly pink hue in spring and autumn, and is striped a fresh-looking white and yellow during the summer.

Gymnocarpium (Oak fern)

This small fern has fine overlapping foliage. The plant is not evergreen, so plant it where it won't receive lots of attention when it is not at its best. It grows to a height of 1 foot (30cm).

Helictrotrichon (syn. Avena–Blue oat grass)

H. sempervirens is a grass 2½ feet tall (75cm) with blue-green leaves. The plant is suitable for dunes or other sandy soil in full sun.

Holcus (Velvet grass)

The ordinary velvet grass is a weed that can occur in neglected lawns. *H. mollis* 'Albovariegatus' is attractive, with a white-variegated leaf. The plant grows to over 1 foot (30cm) tall, and will grow in full sun or partial shade.

Koeleria (Blue hairgrass)

K. glauca is a famous variety with blue-gray foliage, and grows to a height of nearly 2 feet (60cm). The flower spikes appear in June and July. The plant is suitable for drier soil.

Luzula (Wood rush)

This evergreen grassy plant is often used as a ground cover in shade. *L. nivea* has silver leaves with a white bloom, and reaches a maximum height of a little over 2 feet (60cm). The shorter *L. sylvatica* can be used for the same purpose. See also *Carex pendula*, above, which likes the same growing conditions.

Matteuccia (Ostrich fern)

M. struthiopteris holds its light green foliage in a vase shape. The plant spreads underground vigorously, so do not buy too many of this plant—it multiplies by itself. The ostrich fern can grow under wet conditions. The fern dies back, but the fertile leaves with their spores stand up straight during the winter, something interesting to see in the garden when all else is quiet.

Miscanthus (Silver grass, maiden grass)

Miscanthus is sometimes incorrectly sold as bamboo. This ornamental grass dies back every year, then grows again each summer to a height of 10 feet (3m). Many varieties exist of *M. sinensis*. The silvery gray flower spikes appear in late summer. Even though the plant dies back in the winter, this plant is suitable to forming hedgerows.

Molinia (Moor grass, Indian grass)

The moor grass grows naturally as a companion to heather. Give the plant poor, sandy soil. It will grow in wet or dry soil. *M. caerulea* 'Variegata' has striped creamy yellow foliage and reaches a height of 2 feet (60cm). *M. litoralis* grows much taller, the variety 'Fontäne' looks gorgeous all by itself, and the variety 'Transparant' is beautiful in the flower border.

Onoclea (Sensitive fern)

O. sensibilis is a fine fern for moist growing conditions. The foliage is light green. Do not plant it in the path of

Heather and Pennisetum.

wind. It prefers partial shade near the water's edge; the leaves dehydrate quickly. True to its common name, *Onoclea* needs some tender, loving care. This fern is not quite hardy; cover it with leaves to help protect it.

Osmunda (Flowering fern)
O. regalis, royal fern, can grow to an imposing, regal height of 7 feet (2m) when the growing conditions are favorable. It does not usually grow taller than 4 feet (1⅓m), however. This is one of the best ferns to grow by itself as a specimen. The variety 'Cristata' has crested tips and gives a waved effect. *O. cinnamomea*, the cinnamon fern, remains shorter, as does *O. claytoniana*, interrupted fern. Plant in a humusy, moist soil in good—not too deep—shade.

Panicum (Switch grass)
P. virgatum is a perennial, but not completely hardy. It is better to avoid disappointment and think of this species as an annual. The plant will reach 3 feet (1m), with loose, thin plumes. *P. violaceum*, an annual, grows nearly 2 feet (60cm) and has pendant plumes that hang gracefully.

Pellaea
P. rotundifolia, button fern, is an elegant fern from New Zealand. It is grown in temperate climates almost exclusively as a houseplant, but can withstand a little frost. This evergreen fern is most suitable as ground cover in the hobby greenhouse.

Pennisetum
There are many varieties of this plant, and some of these are perennials. *P. alopecuroides* (syn. *P. compresse-taceum*) grows up to 3 feet (1m) tall with soft, long flower spikes. The 1½-foot-tall (45cm) *P. villosum* has gray-green "hairy" foliage. The flower spikes form in August and remain on the plant for a long time. Provide a sunny, rather moist spot. *Pennisetum* is excellent for drying, nice in arrangements, and handsome by itself.

Phalaris (Ribbon grass)
P. canariensis, canary grass, not only provides bird seed, but can also be dried for "everlasting" bouquets. The flowers of this annual plant are the most attractive part. *Phalaris* is suitable for the cut-flower corner and in an annual flower meadow. *P. arundinacea* is a perennial plant that grows up to 4 feet (1⅓m). The variety 'Picta' has striped leaves; the flower spikes of this plant are suitable for fresh arrangements, and the leaves themselves make a striking inclusion, for an unexpected and graceful look.

Phyllitis scolopendrium,
the hart's-tongue fern.

Phyllitis (Hart's-tongue fern)

One of the few ferns that does not have a feathered leaf is *P. scolopendrium*. The light green fronds stand up straight to a height of 1 foot (30cm). The plant prefers moist growing conditions. *Phyllitis* is suitable for a rock garden with limy soil. There are varieties with crested, wavy, or forked fronds.

Phyllostachys (Bamboo)

There are a number of varieties available, tall, evergreen plants with dark green foliage. *P. aureosulcata* is a straight plant with green stalks. The stems zigzag at the bottom. *P. bambusoides* is suitable only for the largest gardens, with its shining green leaves. This plant spreads vigorously and grows, like the above-mentioned variety, to about 20 feet (6m). The most well known is *P. nigra*, black bamboo, with black-spotted or completely black stalks.

Pleioblastus

P. pymaeus does not spread and is suitable as a ground cover. It is a bamboo for sun and partial shade, and grows to a height of 1½ feet (45cm). *P. viridistratus* has yellow-gold striped leaves. The color of the leaf is at its best when the plant grows in full sun.

Polypodium (Common polypody)

P. vulgare is a small evergreen fern that grows well in limy soil. It is a good plant to grow on roof tiles, when provided with enough moisture. (Roofs of houses under trees can be entirely covered with this fern.) In moist forests, the plant also grows in trees. It stays quite green during the winter.

Polystichum (Shield fern)

This fern family includes evergreen varieties, most of which have dark green, shiny foliage. The most well known is *P. setiferum*, hedge fern. After a few years, this fern forms a stalk. The plant grown most often is *P. setiferum* 'Herrenhausen', which at maturity has a diameter of 3 feet (1m). *P. aculeatum*, 3 feet (1m) tall, is a good fern for deep shade.

Pseudosasa (Bamboo)

Pseudosasa, with its unusual good looks, makes a good specimen plant. *P. japonica* (syn. *Arundinaria japonica*) grows with striking, onionlike bulges on the stalks. The leaves grow horizontally at a sharp angle from the stalks.

Pteridium (Bracken fern)

P. aquilinum grows to a height of about 5 feet (1½m), with large, single fronds. Do not try to harvest the plant from nature; it will always be a disappointment, never growing again. The bracken fern sends out long rhizomes that are hard to get rid of, once the fern has become established.

Sasa (Bamboo)

S. palmata is a good bamboo species that can reach a height of 7 feet (2m). The plant has a broader leaf than other bamboos, and spreads quickly; give it enough space.

Semiarundinaria

S. fastuosa is a columnar bamboo. The plant grows between 14 and 20 feet (4 and 6m) tall.

Sinarundinaria

S. nitida is a fine-leafed bamboo with dark branches. This 10-foot-tall (3m), rising variety has black-purple stalks. It will grow in full sun and partial shade. The height can make if tricky to plant in combinations.

Stipa (Feather grass, needle grass)

Gray-green foliage and 4-foot (1⅕m) plumes are the hallmark of *S. gigantea*. The plumes remain on the plant from June to August.

Thelypteris

T. palustris is a fresh green, small fern for swamplike growing conditions, something few enough garden plants seem to care for. The plant can also grow in sun. It reaches a height of 4 feet (1⅕m).

18 Acid-Loving Plants A to Z

Every plant has a preference as to soil, and it is wise to acquaint yourself with plants' needs. A plant that thrives in sandy soil will not thrive in clayey soil, and it may even die.

O ne of the factors that may help you determine which plants to grow in your garden is the pH value—that is, the relative acidity—of your garden soil. In the average garden, the pH varies from 4 to 8. A value of approximately 7 is neutral; 4 is on the acid side, 8 is limey, or alkaline. Soil so acid that it measures a value of less than 4, or so alkaline that it is over 8, will be problematic for most plants.

Rhododendrons bloom in many colors, including bright ones.

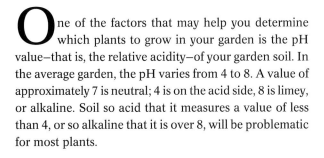

The large-flowered rhododendrons bloom in *more colors than most garden centers can offer.*

Most acid soils have a pH between 5.6 and 7.4, and most alkaline soils have a pH over 7.5. The pH value of the soil in your garden is not a thing fixed forever, though. You can change the soil acidity in your garden by adding organic or commercial fertilizer. Your garden soil changes without your interference, too. Precipitation, and the dissolved elements and compounds the precipitation contains, can break down the organic components of the soil. The natural decomposition of such debris as leaves and pine needles have an effect, too.Plants have ideal acid-alkaline values, an acidity at which they grow best. It is a good idea, therefore, to let your plant selection be guided by the natural acidity of the soil in your garden. Berries and apples, for example, do very well in acid soil, while stone fruits such as apricots, cherries, and prunes do much better on an alkaline soil. Many cultivated plants require a soil with a pH value higher than 6.2.

Most soils have a tendency to become more acid after a while. You can prevent this by adding lime fertilizer. Soils that are too alkaline, or basic, can made more acid by the addition of acid fertilizer, sulphates, and super-phosphates. The pH of sandy soil varies, so you shouldn't add enormous quantities of pH-altering amendments. Clayey soil, on the other hand, needs large amounts of

lime or peat moss in order to change the acid value. How do you know what your soil "needs"?

You can have the pH of your garden professionally gauged, but there is a simple do-it-yourself trick that can help you determine whether your soil is suitable for acid-loving plants. When you pour vinegar over a small amount of soil, it will foam if it is basic. That tells you that acid-loving plants would be a poor choice for this soil. You can get an idea of your garden soil pH by looking at the plants that grow there "spontaneously." In acid soil you will find, among others, sedges, hosta, and the blueberry. In neutral soil, you find *Anthemis*, and in basic soils you find white clover. It doesn't

In a sheltered border, in front of a south-facing wall, you can experiment with plants that do not stand up to frost well.

Keep in mind that plants tend to suffer from soil that is too wet in winter. This rock garden is in Oxford, England.

pay to install plants in soil that naturally is far from their preferred condition. It is better to select plants appropriate to the conditions you can provide. Changing pH several degrees is neither permanent nor uncomplicated.

Acid-Loving Plants for Heather and Conifer Gardens

The plants in this chapter all need acid soil (soil with a pH value of about 4.5).

The following plants grow well in acid soil and are harmonious additions and pretty accents to heather and conifer gardens:
Amelanchier lamarckii
Betula pendula
Cytisus scoparius

A cultivated heath garden, with large areas planted with a single variety.

Heath garden in Edinburgh, Scotland.

Genista anglica
Ilex varieties
Myrica gale
Ulex europaeus

A number of perennials that are suitable for the heather garden (not all are acid-loving) include:
Antennaria
Armeria
Astilbe chinensis 'Pumila'
Cotula squalida
Gentiana
Primula
Pulsatilla
Sedum

Dwarf conifers for the smallest gardens:
Abies balsamea 'Nana'
Chamaecyparis obtusa 'Nana Gracilis'
Cryptomeria japonica 'Globosa Nana'
Juniperus squamata 'Blue Star'
Picea abies 'Gregoryana'
Picea abies 'Little Gem'
Picea abies 'Nidiformis'
Picea abies 'Repens'
Platycladus orientalis

Acid-Loving Plants A to Z

Acer
Acer palmatum, the cutleaf Japanese maple, is pretty especially by the water's edge, in combination with other plants in the heather garden. The deeply cut foliage has a somewhat fernlike appearance. Also see "Shrubs A to Z," page 235. Many varieties offer fine fall color.

Andromeda (Bog rosemary)
Andromeda japonica is now classified under the family of *Pieris. A. polifolia* (syn. *A. rosmarinifolia*) in itself may be not a beautiful shrub, but it bears beautiful large, pink flowers. If you plant it in combination with heather or blueberry, the ugly growth is invisible, and the blossoms get all the attention. This very hardy plant grows extremely slowly, so the gardener must be patient.

Arbutus (Manzanita, strawberry tree)
See "Shrubs A to Z," page 236.

Arctostaphylos (Bearberry, manzanita)
This is a large group of woody plants, most of them native to North America. With two exceptions, *Arctostaphylos* can't withstand frost, so select your shrub varieties accordingly. *A. nevadensis*, from California, is a shrub with tangled growth, and blooms with white to pink flowers in April. *A. uva-ursi* (syn. *Arbutus uva-ursi*), from Scandinavia, is commonly planted. Known as bearberry, this is a creeping evergreen shrub that makes an excellent ground cover. It produces large red berries. Plant it out in the garden when the soil has warmed and there is no danger of frost. See also "Shrubs A to Z," page 236.

Calluna (Heather)
Heather is suitable for sandy and lime-free peaty soil. It

Acer japonicum, the Japanese maple, may have red or green leaves.

blooms from August to September in most cases; some varieties continue to bloom until November. For a long-blooming heather garden, plant a combination of heather varieties that will flower in succession throughout the season, together with other blooming shrubs. Do not forget to plant some shrubs that are not evergreen, so you can mark the change of the seasons. With only heather and conifer plantings, the garden has virtually the same appearance throughout the year, and though it may be pretty, you may find it monotonous. You miss the opportunity to look forward to spring, with all its exciting changes.

Listed below are some recommended *Calluna* varieties. The blooming period is indicated by month.

Calluna.

Cultivated variety	Color	Height	Characteristics	Months of bloom
'Alba Dumosa'	white	16 in (40cm)	spreading	7–8
'Alba Erecta'	white	20 in (50cm)	bright green	8–9
'Alba Plena'	white	16 in (40cm)	spreading	8–10
'Alba Rigida'	white	6 in (15cm)	low-spreading	8–9
'Alportii'	purple	28 in (70cm)	rising	8–9
'Aurea'	purple-pink	16 in (40cm)	leaf golden	7–9
'Barnett Anley'	purple	20 in (50cm)	wide	8–9
'Beoley Gold'	white	16 in (40cm)	pure yellow	8–9
'Carmen'	purple-red	18 in (45cm)	wide, rising	8–9
'Cramond'	pink	20 in (50cm)	wide, rising	9–11
'Cuprea'	purple	18 in (45cm)	bronze	8–9
'C. W. Nix'	red	31½ in (80cm)	rising	8–9
'Dainty Bess'	pink	4 in (10cm)	blue-gray	8–10
'Darkness'	purple-pink	16 in (40cm)	rising	8–9
'Egelantissima'	white	21½ in (55cm)	gray-green leaf	9–12
'Flore Pleno'	pink	18 in (45cm)	wide, rising	9–10
'Golden Carpet'	pink	4 in (10cm)	golden	8–9
'Golden Feather'	purple	12 in (30cm)	bronze-yellow	8–9
'Gold Haze'	white	20 in (50cm)	bright yellow	8–9
'Hammondii'	white	24 in (60cm)	dark, rising	8–9
'H. E. Beale'	pink	24 in (60cm)	cut flower	8–11
'J. H. Hamilton'	dark pink	10 in (25cm)	low-spreading	8–9
'Long White'	white	28 in (70cm)	rising	9–10
'Peter Sparkes'	pink	24 in (60cm)	cut flower	9–11
'Ralph Pernell'	purple	24 in (60cm)	rising	8–9
'Robert Chapman'	purple-pink	16 in (40cm)	wide, rising	8–9
'Silver Queen'	mauve	18 in (45cm)	gray leaf	8–9
'Sister Anne'	lilac	4 in (10cm)	gray-green leaf	8–9
'Sunset'	purple-pink	12 in (30cm)	bronze leaf	8–9
'Tenuis'	pink	12 in (30cm)	wide	7–11
'Tib'	purple	16 in (40cm)	rising	6–10
'Underwoodii'	purple	18 in (45cm)	rising	10–11

Camellia

Varieties that can withstand temperatures as low as 20°F (–6.6°C) are more expensive than the regular varieties, which are suitable only as container plants. *Camellia sinensis* yields the leaves for tea; *C. japonica* and its hybrids are ornamental plants. Mulch the plants well during harsh winters. The roots must not freeze; it is best to move plants in pots indoors.

Cornus (Bunchberry)

The ground cover *Cornus* varieties such as *C. suecica* and *C. canadensis* like lime-free soil and are suitable plants for the heather garden. They bloom with white flowers. The plant grows 6 inches (15cm) tall.

Daboecia (Saint Dabeoc's heath)

This is a plant that doesn't endure frost well, but it is favored because it bears much larger flowers than the tree heath. The evergreen plant looks like a low bush with urn-shaped flowers. It blooms from June to September. Of the species *D. cantabrica*, the following cultivated varieties exist:

'Alba'	white
'Atropurpurea'	purple-pink
'Bicolor'	purple, white, white with purple stripes

Rhododendron catawbiense *'Grandiflora'*.

'Cinderella'	light pink to white
'Praegerae'	dark pink, tender
'William Buchanan'	crimson

Daphne

D. cneorum is a dwarf bush. The fragrant pink flowers appear in April/May. There are numerous varieties: 'Alba', with white flowers; 'Eximia', with larger flowers; and 'Variegata', with cream borders on the leaves. See also under "Shrubs A to Z," page 242.

Empetrum (Crowberry)

Empetrum is a good ground cover with shiny, dark green foliage. The unassuming flowers bloom in early spring, followed by black berries.

Enkianthus

E. campanulatus is a rising shrub that can reach a height of 17 feet (5m). The shrub blooms with urn-shaped, pink-striped flowers in May. Another attractive characteristic of this plant is that it displays a beautiful autumn color, for a striking display two seasons out of four.

Erica (Heath)

The common heath has striking little pendant flowers. The colors are more noticeable than those of *Calluna*. The common heath blooms in autumn; tree heath varies more in its bloom period. Perhaps the most famous heath is *E.* × *darleyensis*, which blooms in pink and white during the first four months of the year. This heath is the one most suitable for containers. For sheltered gardens, *E. arborea*, the true tree heath, is suitable. This plant blooms from March to May and can reach a height of 7 feet (2m). Give it protection during harsh winters.

Other varieties of *Erica* include:

Erica carnea (Spring heath, snow heather)

Cultivar	Color	Height	Characteristics	Months of bloom
'Aurea'	purple-pink	8 in (20cm)	yellow leaf	2–4
'Cecilia M. Beale'	white	8 in (20cm)		11–3
'Foxhollow Fairy'	pink	8 in (20cm)	yellow-green leaf	1–3
'Heathwood'	purple-pink	10 in (25cm)	bright green leaf	3–4
'James Backhouse'	purple-pink	10 in (25cm)	bright green leaf	2–4
'King George'	purple-pink	6 in (15cm)		12–3
'Loughrigg'	purplish pink	8 in (20cm)	bronze leaf	2–4
'Myreton Ruby'	wine red	8 in (20cm)		3–4
'Pink Spangles'	pink-red	10 in (25cm)	wide and loose	3–4
'Praecox Rubra'	purple-red	8 in (20cm)	spreading	12–3
'Rosy Gem'	pink-red	8 in (20cm)		2–4
'Ruby Glow'	purple-pink	8 in (20cm)		11–4
'Snow Queen'	white	6 in (15cm)		1–3
'Springwood Pink'	light pink	8 in (20cm)	creeping	1–3
'Springwood White'	white	8 in (20cm)	creeping	1–3
'Thomas Kingscote'	purple-pink	8 in (20cm)		3–4
'Vivelli'	carmine	8 in (20cm)	bronze leaf	12–4
'Winter Beauty'	dark purple-pink	6 in (15cm)	compact	12–3

Erica cinerea (Bell heather, twisted heath)

Cultivar	Color	Height	Characteristics	Months of bloom
'Alba'	white	10 in (25cm)	wide-growing	7–8
'Alba Minor'	white	6 in (15cm)	compact	7–10
'Atropurpurea'	dark purple	8 in (20cm)		8–9
'Atrorubens'	deep pink	10 in (25cm)		7–10
'C. D. Eason'	bright red	12 in (30cm)	dark leaf	6–9
'Cevennes'	pink	10 in (25cm)	rising	7–10
'Coccinea'	carmine	8 in (20cm)	creeping	6–9
'Domino'	white	10 in (25cm)	brown flowers	7–9
'Eden Valley'	lilac-white	6 in (15cm)	dwarf	7–9
'Golden Drop'	purple-pink	6 in (15cm)	bronze leaf	7–8
'Golden Hue'	lilac	14 in (35cm)	yellow leaf	7–8
'G. Osmond'	lilac	12 in (30cm)	rising	7–9
'Katinka'	dark purple	12 in (30cm)	rising	6–10
'Mrs. Dill'	bright red	6 in (15cm)		6–8
'Pallas'	purple	14 in (35cm)	wide, rising	6–9
'Pink Ice'	soft pink	6 in (15cm)	compact	6–9
'P. S. Patrick'	purple	12 in (30cm)		8–9
'Pygmaea'	pink-red	6 in (15cm)	creeping	6–8
'Rosea'	bright pink	10 in (25cm)	compact	7–8
'Velvet Night'	dark purple	12 in (30cm)		7–8

Rhododendron japonicum.

Erica tetralix (Cross-leaved heath, bog heather)

Cultivar	Color	Height	Characteristics	Months of bloom
'Alba'	white	10 in (25cm)	gray-green leaf	6–8
'Alba Praecox'	white	10 in (25cm)	gray-green leaf	6–8
'Con. Underwood'	carmine	14 in (35cm)	gray-green leaf	7–9
'Daphne Underwood'	salmon	8 in (20cm)	weak grower	6–8
'Helma'	pink	12 in (30cm)	rising	7–8
'Hookstone Pink'	salmon	10 in (25cm)	gray-green leaf	6–10
'Ken Underwood'	carmine	10 in (25cm)	gray leaf	6–10
'L. E. Underwood'	apricot	10 in (25cm)	rising straight	6–10
'Pink Star'	mauve-pink	6 in (15cm)	low and wide	6–9

Erica vagans (Cornish heath)

Cultivar	Color	Height	Characteristics	Months of Bloom
'Alba'	white	16 in. (40cm)	wide, rising	7–9
'D. Hornibrook'	red	14 in. (35cm)		7–10
'Grandiflora'	soft pink	24 in (60cm)		8–10
'Holden Pink'	pink	14 in (35cm)	wide, rising	8–10
'Lyonesse'	white	14 in (35cm)	yellow helmet buds	8–10'
'Mrs. F. D. Maxwell'	red	14 in (35cm)	compact	7–10
'Nana'	creamy white	10 in (25cm)	compact	8–10
'Pyrenees Pink'	salmon	14 in (35cm)	red helmet buds	8–10
'St. Keverne'	salmon	14 in (35cm)	compact	8–10
'Valerie Proudley'	white	8 in (20cm)	wide, rising	8–10

Reflected in the water, this rhododendron offers the viewer twice the pleasure (Rhododendron catawbiense 'Grandiflora').

Gaultheria

Two species of *Gaultheria* are of particular note, but they do not look alike: *G. shallon*, salal, and *G. procumbens*, wintergreen. The first reaches 3 feet (1m) and produces black berries. The latter is an evergreen ground cover and has red berries.

Kalmia (Laurel)

This shade-loving evergreen shrub bears purplish, light to dark pink or white flowers. *K. angustifolia*, known variously aas sheep laurel, lambkill, and dwarf laurel, is narrow and rising. *K. poliifolia* is shorter, and its best feature is its beautiful flowers. *Kalmia* ranges from fairly to moderately hardy.

Ledum

L. groenlandicum, Labrador tea, is an evergreen bush with white flowers. The height of this plant is 3 feet (1m). The variety 'Compacta' has a more compact habit. *L. palustre* (wild rosemary) and *L. glandulosum* are less common; give these plants a moist location. *Ledum* blooms in May/June.

Leucothoe

This evergreen shrub blooms with white flowers in May and June, which is the same time that *Ledum* blooms. *Leucothoe fontanesiana*, drooping leucothoe or fetter bush, has somewhat arching branches, and is moderately hardy. The foliage of the plant is bronze during the winter. The plant can be grown in shade as well as in the sun.

Pernettya

See "Shrubs A to Z," page 253.

Phyllodoce (Mountain heather)

This evergreen shrub must be covered well during the winter in order to prevent frost damage. *P. aleutica* blooms with white flowers; the flowers of *P. breweri* are purple-pink.

Pieris

See "Shrubs A to Z," page 253.

Rhododendron

An enormous number of rhododendrons are suitable for the garden. An overview follows, with plants selected for color and other characteristics. In principle, the rhododendron is a beautiful plant that can bloom spectacularly in May/June, but you should take into account that many of the plants can grow very large. Not only will their height be considerable, but their width, too, may present problems for the space they take up in your garden. The rhododendron is excellent for large gardens, and can make a generous statement in the landscape. The first chart lists larger rhododendrons; the second chart, smaller ones.

Large-flowered, evergreen, mature height more than 7 feet (2m)

Pink flowers	Height
'Albert Schweitzer'	7–14 ft. (2-4¼ m)
'Ammerland'	7 ft. (2m)
'Anna Rose Whitney'	14 ft. (4¼ m)
'Arthur Bedford'	14 ft. (4¼ m)
'Cheer'	7 ft. (2m)
'Christmas Cheer'	7 ft. (2m)
'Concorde'	7–14 ft. (2-4¼ m)
'Constanze'	7–14 ft. (2-4¼ m)
'English Roseum'	14 ft. (4¼ m)
'Furnival's Daughter'	7–14 ft. (2-4¼ m)
'Hazel'	7 ft. (2m)
'Helen Johnson'	7–14 ft. (2-4¼ m)
'Karin Seleger'	7 ft. (2m)
'Kokardia'	7–14 ft. (2-4¼ m)
'Lem's Monarch'	7–14 ft. (2-4¼ m)
'Melpomene'	7 ft. (2m)
'Memoir'	7 ft. (2m)
'Mrs. Charles Pearson'	7–14 ft. (2-4¼ m)
'Omega'	14 ft. (4¼ m)
'Pink Pearl'	14 ft. (4¼ m)
'Rocket'	14 ft. (4¼ m)
'Sugar Pink'	7–14 ft. (2-4¼ m)

'Trude Webster'	7–14 ft. (2–4¼m)
'Van'	14 ft. (4¼m)
'Van der Hoop'	14 ft. (4¼m)

Newly planted rhododendrons need shade. When the plants are older, the full strength of the sun is less harmful to them.

Purple/lilac/violet flowers

'Black Spot'	7 ft. (2m)
'Bluebell'	14 ft. (4¼m)
'Blue Jay'	7–14 ft. (2–4¼m)
'Boursault'	14 ft. (4¼m)
'Carola'	14 ft. (4¼m)
'Catawbiense Grandiflorum'	14 ft. (4¼m)
'Dorothy Amateis'	14 ft. (4¼m)
'Eva'	7–14 ft. (2–4¼m)
'Fastuosum Plenum'	14 ft. (4¼m)
'Hildegard'	7–10 ft. (2–3m)
'Hoppy'	7 ft. (2m)
'Humboldt'	7–14 ft. (2–4¼m)
'Lee's Best Purple'	7–14 ft. (2–4¼m)
'Leopold'	7–14 ft. (2–4¼m)
'Mrs. P. D. Williams'	7 ft. (2m)
'Nathalie'	7–14 ft. (2–4¼m)
'Nicholas'	7–14 ft. (2–4¼m)
'Nigrescens'	7 ft. (2m)
'Polarnacht'	7–14 ft. (2–4¼m)
'Purple Splendour'	7 ft. (2m)
'Rasputin'	7 ft. (2m)
'Windsor Lad'	7 ft. (2m)

Red flowers

'Betsie Balcom'	7 ft. (2m)
'Britannia'	7–14 ft. (2–4¼m)
'Caractacus'	14 ft. (4¼m)
'Crossroads'	7 ft. (2m)
'Cynthia'	14 ft. (4¼m)
'Fascination'	7 ft. (2m)
'General Eisenhower'	7–14 ft. (2–4¼m)
'Giganteum'	14 ft. (4¼m)
'Handsworth Scarlet'	7 ft. (2m)
'Johnny Bender'	7–14 ft. (2–4¼m)
'Lee's Scarlet'	7–14 ft. (2–4¼m)
'Nicoline'	7–14 ft. (2–4¼m)
'Nova Zembla'	14 ft. (4¼m)
'Old Port'	7–14 ft. (2–4¼m)
'Oratorium'	7 ft. (2m)
'Sammetglut'	7–14 ft. (2–4¼m)
'Taurus'	7–14 ft. (2–4¼m)
'Thunderstorm'	7–14 ft. (2–4¼m)
'Wilgens Ruby'	7–14 ft. (2–4¼m)

White flowers

'Argosy'	14 ft. (4¼m)
'Aurora'	14 ft. (4¼m)
'Bismarck'	7 ft. (2m)
'Catawbiense Album'	14 ft. (4¼m)
'Euterpe'	7 ft. (2m)
'Helena'	7–14 ft. (2–4¼m)
'Hyperion'	7–14 ft. (2–4¼m)
'Mme. Masson'	7–14 ft. (2–4¼m)
'Mrs. Lindsay Smith'	14 ft. (4¼m)
'Multimaculatum'	7–14 ft. (2–4¼m)
'Rothenburg'	7ft. (2m)
'Schneebukett'	7–14 ft. (2–4¼m)

Yellow flowers

'Bernstein'	7–14 ft. (2–4¼m)
'Diana'	7–14 ft. (2–4¼m)
'Fred Hamilton'	14 ft. (4¼m)
'Goldica'	7 ft. (2m)
'Silvia'	7 ft. (2m)
'Trompenburg'	7 ft. (2m)
'Virginia Richards'	7–14 ft. (2–4¼m)

Evergreen, mature height less than 7 feet (2m)

Red flowers — Height

'Abentglut'	2 ft. (60cm)
'Abentrot'	2 ft. (60cm)
'Aksel Olsen'	2 ft. (60cm)
'Bad Eilsen'	3 ft. (1m)
'Bambola'	5 ft. (1½m)
'Bengal'	3 ft. (1m)
'Better Half'	3 ft. (1m)
'Buketta'	3 ft. (1m)
'Burning Love'	3 ft. (1m)
'Cheyenne'	3 ft. (1m)
'China Boy'	5 ft. (1½m)
'Dido'	3 ft. (1m)
'Elizabeth'	3 ft. (1m)
'Fascination'	3 ft. (1m)
'Fandango'	3 ft. (1m)
'Flora's Boy'	3 ft. (1m)
'Friedrich Deuss'	3 ft. (1m)
'Frülingstraum'	3 ft. (1m)
'Juwel'	3 ft. (1m)
'Little Ben'	2 ft. (60cm)
'Lucy Brand'	3 ft. (1m)
'Mannheim'	3 ft. (1m)
'Monica'	3 ft. (1m)
'Peekabo'	2 ft. (60cm)
'Red Bewlls'	3 ft. (1m)
'Royston Red'	3 ft. (1m)

'Scarlett Wonder'	3 ft. (1m)
'Thomsang'	3 ft. (1m)
'Titian Beauty'	5 ft. (1½m)
'Venetian Chimes'	5 ft. (1½m)

Dark red flowers

'Antje'	6 ft. (13/4m)
'Arthur Osborne'	3 ft. (1m)
'Carmen'	2 ft. (60cm)
'Impi'	6 ft. (1¾m)
'Oporto'	3 ft. (1m)

White flowers

'Blewburry'	6 ft. (1¾m)
'Edelweiss'	3 ft. (1m)
'Emanuela'	6 ft. (1¾m)
'Hultschin'	6 ft. (1¾m)
'Ken Janeck'	3 ft. (1m)
'Lamentosa'	6 ft. (1¾m)
'Olympic Lady'	6 ft. (13/4m)
'Partyglanz'	3 ft. (1m)
'Pook'	3 ft. (1m)
'Schlaraffia'	6 ft. (1¾m)
'Schneekrone'	6 ft. (1¾m)
'Silberwolke'	3 ft. (1m)
'Tibet'	3 ft. (1m)
'Yaku Angel'	2 ft. (60cm)

Yellow flowers

'Balinda'	6 ft. (1¾m)
'Breslau'	6 ft. (1¾m)
'Ehrengold'	3 ft. (1m)
'Goldbuckett'	6 ft. (1¾m)
'Graf Lennart'	3 ft. (1m)
'Haida Gold'	6 ft. (1¾m)
'Hotei'	6 ft. (1¾m)
'Lachsgold'	6 ft. (1¾m)
'Libelle'	6 ft. (1¾m)
'Marietta'	6 ft. (1¾m)
'Moonstone'	3 ft. (1m)
'Nippon'	3 ft. (1m)
'Primula'	6 ft. (1¾m)
'Volker'	3 ft. (1m)

Light pink flowers

'Andre'	6 ft. (1¾m)
'Apfelblüte'	6 ft. (1¾m)
'April Glow'	6 ft. (1¾m)
'Bajazzo'	3 ft. (1m)
'Bow Bells'	3 ft. (1m)
'Brigitte'	6 ft. (1¾m)

'Doc'	6 ft. (1¾m)			*Japanese azalea*, Rhododen-	
'Harmony'	6 ft. (1¾m)			dron japonicum.	
'Hydon Ball'	6 ft. (1¾m)				
'Kantilene'	6 ft. (1¾m)		'Georg Stipp'	6 ft. (1¾m)	
'Lumina'	6 ft. (1¾m)		'Hallelujah'	6 ft. (1¾m)	
'Mancando'	6 ft. (1¾m)		'Himalaya Stern'	6 ft. (1¾m)	
'Oberschlesien'	6 ft. (1¾m)		'Honingen'	6 ft. (1¾m)	
'Oudijk's Sensation'	6 ft. (1¾m)		'Hydon Dawn'	6 ft. (1¾m)	
'Rijneveld'	6 ft. (1¾m)		'Idomeneo'	6 ft. (1¾m)	
			'Julischka'	6 ft. (1¾m)	
Dark pink flowers			'Karin'	6 ft. (1¾m)	
'Anuschka'	6 ft. (1¾m)		'Kimberley'	6 ft. (1¾m)	
'Diadem'	6 ft. (1¾m)		'Largo'	3 ft. (1m)	
'Don Giovanni'	6 ft. (1¾m)		'May Glow'	6 ft. (1¾m)	
'Kantate'	6 ft. (1¾m)		'Monika'	6 ft. (1¾m)	
'Linda'	6 ft. (1¾m)		'Papageno'	6 ft. (1¾m)	
			'Pink Cherub'	6 ft. (1¾m)	
Pink flowers			'Pink Pebble'	3 ft. (1m)	
'Bad Zwischenahn'	6 ft. (1¾m)		'Polaris'	3 ft. (1m)	
'Bashful'	6 ft. (1¾m)		'Psyche'	6 ft. (1¾m)	
'Berliner Liebe'	6 ft. (1¾m)		'Rendez Vous'	6 ft. (1¾m)	
'Claudine'	6 ft. (1¾m)		'Rosa Perle'	6 ft. (1¾m)	
'Daniela'	6 ft. (1¾m)		'Rose Point'	2 ft. (60cm)	
'Dormouse'	6 ft. (1¾m)		'Rosita'	6 ft. (1¾m)	
'Evelyn'	6 ft. (1¾m)		'Santana'	6 ft. (1¾m)	
'Frülingsanfang'	6 ft. (1¾m)		'Silver Sixpence'	6 ft. (1¾m)	

Rhododendron japonicum
(syn. Azalea mollis*)*.

'Super Star'	6 ft. (1¾m)
'Winsome'	6 ft. (1¾m)

Lilac-pink flowers

'Belona'	6 ft. (1¾m)
'Bleurettia'	6 ft. (1¾m)
'Caroline Allbrook'	6 ft. (1¾m)
'Kalinka'	6 ft. (1¾m)
'Roselyn'	6 ft. (1¾m)
'Tatjana'	6 ft. (1¾m)

Deciduous Rhododendrons

Usually these rhododendrons are called azaleas. This group includes the large-flowered *Rhododendron japonicum* (syn. *Azalea mollis*) and the beautiful Knaphill/Exbury azaleas.

Deciduous Rhododendrons

Yellow flowers, sometimes with white	*Height*
'Adriaan Koster'	12 ft. (3⅔m)
'Buttercup'	12 ft. (3⅔m)
'Chevalier de Realli'	6 ft. (1¾m)
'Comte de Gomer'	12 ft. (3⅔m)
'Evening Glow'	12 ft. (3⅔m)
'Golden Eagle'	6 ft. (1¾m)
'Golden Sunset'	12 ft. (3⅔m)
'Graciosa'	6 ft. (1¾m)
'Klondyke'	6 ft. (1¾m)
'Persil'	10 ft. (3m)
'Sun Chariot'	6 ft. (1¾m)
'T. J. Seidel'	12 ft. (3⅔m)

White flowers

'Ballerina'	6 ft. (1¾m)
'Silver Slipper'	12 ft. (3⅔m)

Red flowers

'Fanal'	12 ft. (3⅔m)
'Feuerball'	12 ft. (3⅔m)
'Feuerwerk'	12 ft. (3⅔m)
'Radiant'	12 ft. (3⅔m)
'Willem Hardijzer'	12 ft. (3⅔m)

Orange flowers

'Babeuff'	12 ft. (3⅔m)
'Christopher Wren'	12 ft. (3⅔m)
'Goldflamme'	12 ft. (3⅔m)
'Mrs. Norman Luff'	12 ft. (3⅔m)
'Royal Command'	12 ft. (3⅔m)
'Tunis'	12 ft. (3⅔m)

Evergreen Azaleas

These can withstand some frost, but must be planted in a sheltered spot, preferably in partial shade. Wind can be desiccating, so you may wish to provide a windbreak. Strong winter sun can be harmful.

Evergreen Azaleas

White flowers	*Height*
'Adonis'	1½ft. (45cm)
'Bernina'	6 ft. (1¾m)
'Everest'	3 ft. (1m)
'Gumpo White'	1 ft. (30cm)
'Helen Curtis'	1½ft. (45cm)
'Luzi'	3 ft. (1m)
'Marie's Choice'	1½ ft. (45cm)
'Noordtiana'	3 ft. (1m)
'Palestrina'	3 ft. (1m)
'Schneeglanz'	5 ft. (1½m)
'Schneewitchen'	3 ft. (1m)
'White Lady'	1½ ft. (45cm)

Red flowers

'Aladdin'	3 ft. (1m)
'Brunella'	1½ ft. (45cm)
'Florida'	1½ ft. (45cm)
'Galathea'	3 ft. (1m)
'Hino-Crimson'	1½ft. (45cm)
'Mme. van Hecke'	1½ ft. (45cm)
'Red Pimpernel'	1½ft. (45cm)
'Rubinstern'	3 ft. (1m)
'Vuyks Scarlet'	3 ft. (1m)

Various rhododendrons. This picture shows clearly that rhododendrons need a lot of space, especially when you want to combine different colors.

Pink flowers

'Allotria'	1½ ft. (45cm)
'Anne Frank'	3 ft. (1m)
'Chippewa'	1½ft. (45cm)
'Double Beauty'	3 ft. (1m)
'Favourite'	3 ft. (1m)
'Girards Rose'	1½ ft. (45cm)
'Little Princess'	1 ft. (30cm)
'Mme. Boussear'	3 ft. (1m)
'Rosalind'	3 ft. (1m)
'Silvester'	1½ ft. (45cm)
'Vida Brown'	1 ft. (30cm)

Orange flowers

'Addy Wery'	3 ft. (1m)
'Ageeth'	3 ft. (1m)
'Nordlicht'	1½ ft. (45cm)
'Orange Beauty'	3 ft. (1m)
'Orange Favourite'	3 ft. (1m)
'Satchiko'	1½ ft. (45cm)
'Signalglühen'	3 ft. (1m)

Purple/lilac flowers

'Amoena'	2½ft. (75cm)
'Arendsii'	3 ft. (1m)
'Beethoven'	3 ft. (1m)
'Fumiko'	1 ft. (30cm)
'Ledicanense'	1½ ft. (45cm)
'Purple Splendour'	3 ft. (1m)
'Purple Triumph'	3 ft. (1m)
'Yuka'	1½ft. (45cm)

Skimmia

There are male as well as female *Skimmia* plants. A male plant is needed in order for berries to be produced. The greatest charm the plants have to offer is at the budding stage. The flowers remain in bud all winter. The leathery foliage remains a beautiful, dark green in partial or full shade. Never plant *Skimmia* in full sun. *S. japonica* reaches over 3 feet (1m) tall; *S. × foremanii* reaches 2½ feet (75cm).

Ulex

See "Shrubs A to Z," page 258.

Vaccinium (Blueberry, bilberry, whortleberry)

V. vitis-idaea is an evergreen shrub with leathery foliage; it grows 1 foot (30cm) tall. Red fruits appear in fall.
V. myrtillus is the blueberry. *V. macrocarpon* (syn. *Oxycoccus macrocarpus*), the cranberry from North America, is a low-growing, mat-forming plant with large red, edible fruits. The high-bush blueberry, *V. corymbosum*, is perfectly suited to large heather gardens.

Viburnum

V. tinus is a shrub especially suitable for the heather garden. Give this evergreen plant a sheltered location. It will bear pinkish white flowers early in spring. Just as with *Skimmia*, the flower buds remain on the shrub all winter. These buds are nearly as pretty as the flowers themselves.

Zenobia

Z. pulverulenta (syn. *Andromeda pulverulenta*) is a semi-evergreen shrub of irregular form. The white, bell-shaped flowers appear in May/June. The foliage is leathery.

19 A Few Garden Designs

Because the conditions of each garden are unique, each garden needs its own planting plans. The ultimate success of any garden design lies in the satisfaction of the garden owner. One person may desire many perennials in a certain color combination, while another person may prefer annuals or a more naturalistic appearance altogether. Hedgerows can be enjoyed neatly cut, or left loose and natural, depending on the likes and dislikes of the owner of the garden.

I t is a good thing that people have such different tastes. That way, no two gardens are precisely alike. There is something different to be enjoyed in every garden. The garden designs discussed in this chapter are all different. You can copy one completely if you like, or you can "borrow" parts of them for your garden. The designs have one thing in common: In each case, a house was the starting point; for most gardeners, much of the year is spent looking at the garden from indoors. Nothing obliges you to follow a design, or even part of it, by the way. The designs that follow are meant to be an inspiration.

This garden was designed for a house that was built in 1912.

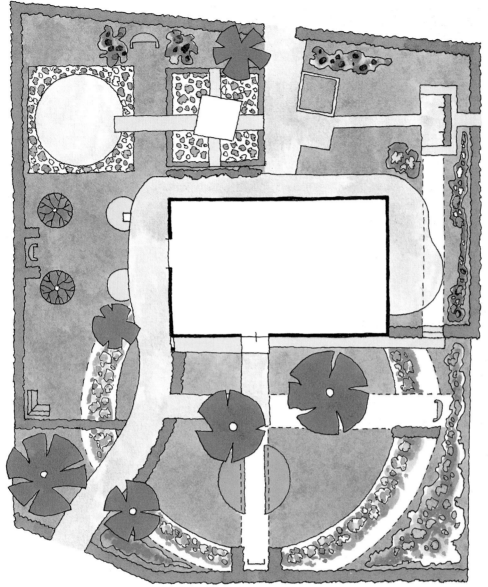

When you move to a property that was once a farm, you usually have a lot of room. This garden, which was used exclusively as lawn, has been adapted completely to the wishes of the new owner, yet is still in keeping with the character of the house.

The Garden of a House from the Early Twentieth Century

Characteristics

The gardens of houses from this period are characterized by rigid, geometrical lines. Often there is a sunken garden, with colorful flowers and many stairs. The garden axes are in line with the house. In the case of this particular property, the owners look along the garden axes from the porch and from one of the common rooms to the end of the garden.

The Assignment

There must be room for children to play, and for a henhouse and poultry run. The owners want an old-fashioned orchard with high-stemmed fruit trees, and a part of the garden set aside as a cutting garden. The vegetables could grow in a central position. In short: The owners want a garden that can be enjoyed by the whole family.

The Design

The children were considered in the design, as well as the fact that the house might serve another purpose in the future. The house remains surrounded by a lawn; the dotted lines indicate the principle lines of sight. The children have room to play now, but "their" lawn can be changed easily into a flower garden later, which will create an even greater sense of harmony. The henhouse has a central position. Opposite is a garden bench. The sides of the henhouse can be covered with vines. A cut flower corner at the back of the garden would be a waste; the flowers deserve to be seen. They are placed alongside the longest axis. At the end of this axis, another bench could be placed; from there, one would enjoy a beautiful view. The fruit trees are in the back, behind a hedge–a kind of secret garden that offers a peaceful place to read quietly under the trees. The large middle section is cleared for vegetables. The vegetable garden can be planted with an eye for color and form, and it can also be outlined with a hedge such as *Buxus*. The center could be punctuated by a large rounded plant, a sundial, or even a circular garden bench (provided with an umbrella for shade in the summertime). In the beginning of this century, a near-riot of colors could be used together, as the rigid form typical of the day holds the picture together. The garden bench could be quite big, especially if surrounded by a growing taxus hedgerow. All the paths are 7 feet (2m) wide, a width that would be comfortable even in a smaller garden; this width allows two people to walk through the garden side by side. Gravel can be used in paving the paths to keep costs down. Later, if the owners desire it, another paving material could be chosen to replace the gravel.

The narrow area for the henhouse is filled with perennials, in all colors. The garden owner can use a statue, neoclassical or modern, to punctuate a view or the crossing of the major garden axes. A flower urn of the period when the house was built would be a good alternative. In front of the hedge, there is another small path, to make it easy to cut the hedges and maintain them during the growing season.

The Garden of an Old Farm

Characteristics

Traditional farm gardens are characterized by simple patterns–circles and squares. They have much in common with what are known as "cottage" gardens, with hedges, and full of colorful flowers. Vegetables and herbs take pride of place in the happy confusion of plants. Before a garden is designed, a decision must be made: whether to involve the surrounding landscape in the garden.

The Assignment

The owners of this farm want to really make use of their garden, with many inviting spots to sit, and they wanted a design appropriate to the original function of the old farmhouse. Both owners work away from home, so the garden mustn't require lots of time to maintain. It was decided to plant the garden with many herbs and perennials, as well as some flowering shrubs, a mixture the owners hoped would achieve the pretty, jumbled effect of the cottage garden style.

The Design

The rather ordinary "front" door is at the side of the house. In order to give the door a central position, a

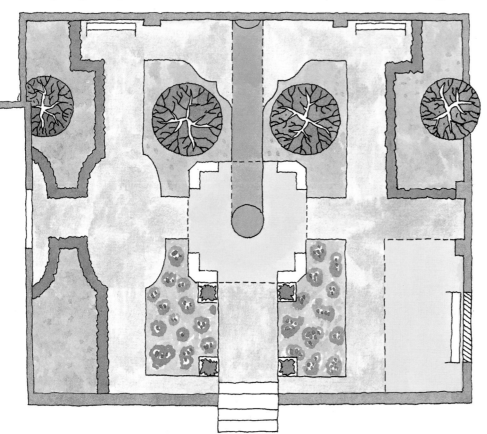

City gardens–especially in new suburbs–are usually characterized by straight lines. The layout of the garden can either attempt to soften this linearity, or emphasize it, depending on the wishes of the owners. City houses can be very old, so remember the rule that the garden style must agree with the style of the house. That has been achieved with this rococo garden.

round border was created with this door as the center. The existing trees have been left alone. The square garden shed (indicated in brown in the drawing) in the back garden is not in line with the house, and so a similar asymmetry was repeated in the "renaissance" border, filled with herbs. The large, round terrace in the corner is surrounded by flowers for cutting. In the future, a tree could be planted in the middle of this. A central window at the back of the house looks out on a beautiful view of the meadows behind the garden. The view axes extend from one corner of the garden to the other, the view attenuated, making a walk in this average-size garden very pleasant. Try to establish view axes in your own garden; position a bench, flower container, or other attractive object as punctuation at the end of an axis.

The hedgerows in a farm garden should not be made of taxus, a plant poisonous to animals. A row of privet, beech, or hornbeam is a better choice. Fruit trees are characteristic of this type of garden, preferably high-stemmed trees. The grass under the trees does not have to be cut every week; a slightly unkempt garden is in keeping with the look of a farm. (Don't let the grass go for too long, though, or it will be more difficult to cut and you may be faced with the job of raking it all.) Modern plastic garden furniture does not go well with a farm garden, nor does teak English furniture. Wooden furniture of a more rustic style requires a bit of paint in this case, preferably in a color that has been used on the woodwork of the house. The

paths do not have to be paved with costly paving materials–simple pebbles will do. A number of layers of pebbles makes refilling the paths a rare task.

The lines of this garden are in character with the ideals and practice of an old-fashioned farm garden: simple, consisting of such plain geometric shapes as circles and squares. If more time for maintenance is available later on, rounded *Buxus* could be placed to accent the corners of the squares. This would add a slightly formal element, but the upkeep wouldn't be terribly taxing. In a simple design, a varied mixture of flowers can work nicely; for an even quieter look, you can plant only one variety, such as hosta, where the larger plants are shown, or *Aubrieta* with low-growing perennials behind them. A general rule of thumb: The simpler the design, the greater the variety, and the more numerous the colors of plants the garden can manage successfully.

A City Garden

Characteristics

This city garden belongs to a house circa 1750, designed in the rococo style. This type of garden allows for slight asymmetry; it needn't be as strictly regular as a garden styled after the Renaissance fashion, for example. The scrolls and flourishes that are the hallmarks of rococo can be created in patterns of *Buxus*.

The Assignment

The owners want the garden (30 by 30 feet/9 by 9 meters) to seem inviting. It will nevertheless have to keep some formality in its lines, to be compatible with the house. The garden design must be compatible with the look of this eighteenth-century structure.

The owners like to entertain, and therefore want to be able to sit in the garden with lots of guests. Maintenance of the garden mustn't be very complicated. The owners want to hide an ugly view of buildings in the background. Water or a small pond is wanted to create soothing sounds in order to screen the noise of traffic, for this garden is both at the side of a busy road and near the train tracks.

The Design

Taking the windows of the house as a cue, three garden axes have been created, two of which lead to garden benches. The middle one leads to the center of the garden, where there is a small bower over a sunken area. Four benches mark the center of the garden and create a convivial sitting area. On the back wall is a lion-head fountain that "spits" water; running water is an important element in the city garden, as it helps keep down the sound of voices and traffic. The sound of running water is soothing, too, and somehow always makes a garden seen larger. Four slim English oaks (*Quercus robur* 'Fastigiata'), which grow very tall, solve the problem of hiding the ugly buildings.

The green spots on the design represent *Taxus baccata*. These shrubs can be trimmed horizontally to a height of, for example, 2 feet (60cm). The middle areas are full of flowers, which, although less than consistent with the style of the house, provide the color the owners want in their garden. The paths are paved with gravel, the terrace on the right front with cobblestone. When the garden is full of people, the gravel path around the terrace can be included as part of the terrace by the addition of chairs. Around the garden, the walls are covered with vines, making this young garden look green and full of bloom. Perennial honeysuckle (*Lonicera japonica* 'Halliana') has been included.

In the winter, a city garden (or any garden, for that matter) must look attractive from the house. A sheltered garden offers a comfortable place to sit early in the year, when the sun's first rays aren't very strong and the trees haven't yet leafed out. Hedges, low walls, fencing, and other structures can function as windbreaks, while lending structure and atmosphere.

The ideal furniture for a rococo garden is of cast iron. Some of the furniture can stay in the garden during the winter; cast iron can endure all sorts of weather, provided it is well maintained. (You must treat it with care; cast iron breaks easily.)

A Backyard Garden for a Detached House

Characteristics

Modern materials may be used in a garden for a new house. For this garden, a contemporary design with lots of water, wide paths and view axes, and large terraces was selected. The owner of this garden did not want any flower borders, preferring the controlled look of green in many shades.

The Assignment

The owner is a garden lover who wants a great variety of plants, ponds, and enough pavement in order to be able to reach his plants easily. Enthusiasm for different sorts of plants meant lots of variety. The lines of the garden have to fit in with the architecture of the house.

The Design

Very wide paths create a feeling of peace and quiet in this garden. The path connects to the terrace near the house. Wide paths look narrower– a sort of trompe l'oeil– if they are sunken; in this case, they were sunk more than half a foot (15cm). Where the paths intersect, there is a rectangular trellis as tall as it is wide. A bare trellis or arch always looks too tall; a feeling of the right proportions has to "grow in" with the developing plants. Symmetry lends an air of harmony, which is necessary in this case, because a large variety of perennials was desired. The lawn with its triangular pond is bordered with *Rosa* 'The Fairy', a richly blooming, low-growing, double pink rose. The hedges, planted in straight lines from the windows of the living room, do not limit the view from the window, but do give depth to the garden. In the small back garden, there is enough room for growing vegetables, and there is a compost heap in the corner. Two large trees have been used: a *Liquidambar styraciflua* and a *Gleditsia triacanthos* 'Sunburst'. The first was selected for its beautiful autumn color, and the second for its beautiful yellow, fine foliage that give the terrace a sunny appearance. In a simple design as for this modern back yard, it is easy to spade up portions of the lawn for plants whenever the owner desires. If the time available for maintenance is a concern when a garden is being designed, it is a good idea to install fewer plants; then, as time allows in the future, the owners can exchange lawn for other plants as they like.

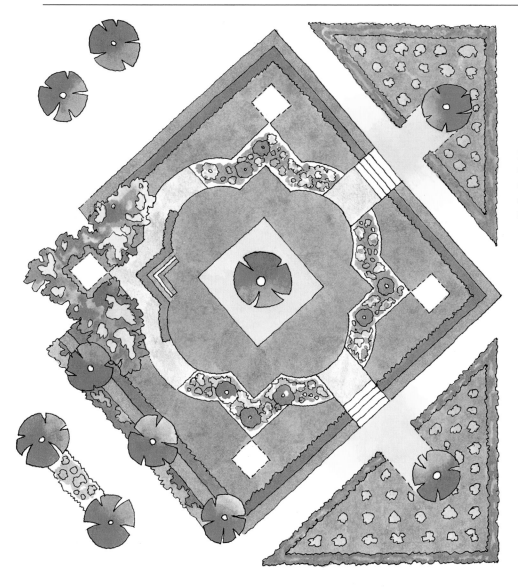

With a design such as this, you can fill in the shapes with all kinds of plants, not only annuals, or a combination of annuals and biennials, but with herbs and vegetables, too.

A Square Turn-of-the-Century Garden

Characteristics

At the turn of the century, gardens often had a symmetric layout, based on circles, squares, or a combination of the two. These shapes could be "filled" with all kinds of colorful flowers. The squares were often depressed or sunken, and sloping grades were planted with flowers as well.

The Assignment

The style of garden should be in harmony with that of the house. Cheering flowers and a place to sit in the shade were desired by the owners, and a wall for sedums and other rock garden plants.

The Design

The layout consists of squares, sunk 2 feet (60cm) and surrounded by a low wall on which rock garden plants can be grown. Directly across from the stairs, there are trees and a comfortable bench. The triangles are surrounded by tall hedges, and the interior portion is planted simply with snowberry (*Symphoricarpos*). The snowberry can be trimmed flat for rigid form, but that would cut away most of the pretty white berries; for berries, leave the shrubs untrimmed. The tree in the center of the garden requires a tree bench, which will fit well into the period of the garden design. The layout is symmetrical, but at the left of the design, a hedge has been planted to follow the pattern of the flower bedding. This hedge serves as a background for the corner bench. (Always give a garden bench a background. Nobody likes to sit on a bench in completely open space; the next time you visit a city park, you will notice that no one sits on exposed garden benches out in the middle of the lawn.) And with a backdrop, a bench becomes more noticeable, more of a garden accent.

The tree in the middle can be left out of the design if a nice lawn for play is wanted; here, it provides shade and a place for the eye to rest. The white areas can be made into little pools, or pillars could be set there for vines to cover; the options for these four accent points are virtually unlimited. Even a vegetable garden with a pleasing shape could be added to this basic design if the owners are inclined to plant one.

A Long, Narrow Garden for a Detached House

Characteristics

Long view axes are directed toward the windows and doors of the house, providing handsome views from indoors looking out, and integrating the house with its

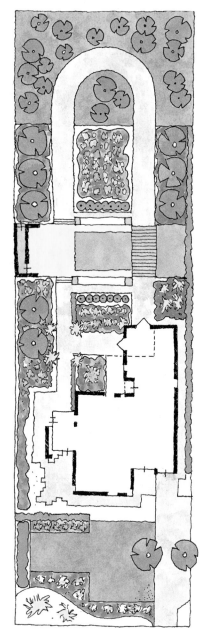

At first, when the property was bare, it seemed impossible to fill in such a long and narrow garden effectively. From the drawing, however, it appears that a garden with such a restrictive shape can be filled with imagination and fancy.

setting when viewed from the garden. The garden is straight, with wide paths and a simple design. There is quite a lot of pavement, and little lawn. There are no flower borders.

The Assignment

The owners, both of whom work away from the home, want a garden with lots of privacy, and one that needs relatively little upkeep. They want a gazebo and a pool, many fruit trees, and a vegetable garden. The result is a quiet garden with a modern design.

The Design

In order to keep the maintenance to a minimum, the back portion of this long garden has been planted with trees. While effectively defining the limits of the garden, they are not very demanding of time. The view axes continue into this little forest. (It would be a shame to close off a part of this garden from view.) It is pleasant to sit by the pool, and so the gazebo has been built nearby. When looking over a garden plan, turn it around and look at it from another point of view once in a while, because you see quite a different picture. Look from the gazebo over the pool. Whenever there is a natural difference in grade, it is a nice opportunity to create a little waterfall in a water garden or naturalistic pond. On both sides of this pool are pillars for vines, and the view through them makes the garden seem larger. Usually terraces for sitting are situated adjacent to the house. Try placing a bench in a different spot for a change, as in this design, where it is near the gazebo. You have your choice of sun or shade, a pleasant advantage, and it is nice to look toward the house rather than away from it. The vegetable garden is near the kitchen; a well-maintained kitchen garden can be a beautiful thing. The location is practical, especially handy for visits to the vegetable patch in wet weather. The terrace at the front is screened by a hedgerow in such a way that passersby cannot see from the roadside, but the person sitting on the terrace can see visitors as soon as they enter the driveway. On the road side of the hedge are perennials all around the house for a cheerful look. Along the perimeter of the garden are tall hedgerows and flowering shrubs, interplanted with evergreen shrubs that ensure some privacy in the winter. For easy maintenance, ivy is used as a ground cover. Ivy grows under shrubs so well that few weeds will grow there.

The terrace near the gazebo is lowered. All parts of the garden can be reached with a wheelbarrow by using a bridge over the waterfall. Ask yourself whether the garden has to be accessible for wheelchair users, too.

20 Garden Ornaments

Garden ornaments have recently become fashionable again. There is much from which to choose: statues; garden seats; arches; urns, pots, and other containers in all shapes, sizes, colors, and materials; fencing; and trelliswork. Many objects that once had a purely practical function are now used as garden ornaments. Consider, for example, the way old wheelbarrows and drying racks are used. Garden owners can use their imaginations and creativity when it comes to garden ornaments, because there are only a few rules.

A garden urn of cast iron in baroque surroundings.

The choice of decorative objects and materials sold at garden centers is enormous, but the prices are often high. It is often worth having a go at it yourself.

A garden bench of cast iron in the rococo style. The detailed photograph of the back shows how beautifully the bench is made.

be successful. Usually, it is desirable to avoid as much as possible throwing together styles of different periods. A landscape architect would not go to the trouble of finding a nineteenth-century fence only to place it in the garden of an eighteenth-century house.

For the same reason—to avoid an unsuccessful mixture of periods and styles—we must be careful when combining objects and styles from different cultures. Venetian gardens are attractive with their charming bird cages. Such a particular ornament as this, and especially one evocative of a certain place, shouldn't thoughtlessly be added to gardens in very different circumstances. There is nothing wrong with bringing your canary out into the garden once in a while, but it wouldn't do to try to imitate a Venetian garden in a suburban setting.

Placement, Size, and Color

The placement of decorative objects in the garden is critical. One natural spot for such an object is at the far end of a view along a major garden axis. This makes one want to walk toward the object, even if it is in an out-of-the-way spot in the garden. The object acts as a focal

A garden urn from the baroque period, with a dwarf Kenilworth ivy at its base, is a handsome ornament at an intersection of two paths.

Chains have been attached to a simple nineteenth-century post, creating a fence.

With old wood properly painted, tin, stones, or concrete, you can create almost anything you like. With the help of the photographs in this chapter, you will get an idea of the possibilities.

Period and Place

In days gone by, more so than it seems today, functional objects such as foot-scrapers and fences were made to be beautiful as well as useful. A lot of ornamental wrought iron took the form of gates, arches, garden seats and so on. Pavilions, water basins, balustrades, and pagodas were built for gardens purely because they were a pretty sight.

Landscape architecture and garden ornamentation have taken on different styles at different times. The style of a building is usually a good indication of the period in which it was built, and this can be said of garden style, too. Of course, styles can be imitated long after they were initially fashionable, and this must be done with care to

A "spy" on the wall gives a nice view from the room into the garden.

Old children's toys have been a favorite of collectors for years. Strangely enough, we do not see them much in gardens.

change enormously, and if you don't like the ornaments later, you're stuck with them. When the plants are grown, you will better be able to judge how adding new elements might improve your garden.

When gardens were enjoyed by only the wealthy, garden benches, balustrades, gates, and the like were designed individually for the particular garden in question. Today, you can buy almost anything you might need ready-made. From store-bought ironware, you can create your own fence or arch. This is a lot less expensive than purchasing factory models from a garden center.

Old Is "In"

When you picture garden statuary, the figures that come to mind may well be neoclassical. You'll want to consider using a modern statue, created by a contemporary artist, if you have a new house. It is often thought that statuary and other ornaments are very expensive, but that isn't always the case, especially when you go to the trouble of looking for unknown or young artists.

You will be amazed by what other people throw away. Garden furniture from the fifties or the sixties, picked up by the garbage man a few years ago, today can be bought-again—for rather a lot of money—fresh from the factory. Garden ornaments that were fashionable forty years ago today are objects desired by many people. What someone throws away as junk might be the perfect addition to your garden.

point and makes the garden seem larger. The object focuses attention to the use of space, and it detracts attention from less beautiful areas of the garden. An object to use as a focal point might be a chair or garden bench, a statue, a children's swing, or a large earthenware planter. The size of the ornament should be in good proportion to the width of the view axes. A dainty bird bath that rests on the ground would be lost in a vast expanse of lawn, but what a pretty accent it would make in a little bed of ivy by the terrace. The ornament, whether it be art or a planter, should be an inconspicuous color if it is large, and a conspicuous, even attention-getting, color if it is somewhat small. You can make a garden ornament seem bigger by placing a trellis or mirror behind it.

Plants and Objects

Take the growth of nearby plants into account when you place statues and other art objects in the garden. Any object looks too large in a newly planted garden. Do not buy lots of art objects or other ornaments for your garden during the first two years, because your garden will

Through this metal archway, a veranda can be seen in the background. This is a very clear example of a view axis.

Materials and Combinations

Be consistent in the materials you use in your garden. A limited "palette" of materials, for example, concrete and glass, or wood and natural-looking stones, is best. Avoid bringing a little bit of everything into your garden.Wood may be the easiest material for the handyman (often the garden owner) to work with, but it does not fit well with the modern architecture of a house. A concrete statue or garden vase does not look its best when set on wooden planking, rather than stone. Take note of ornamentation you admire in private and public gardens you visit.

Clay

Flower pots of brick-red pottery have been used in gardens for thousands of years. These pots are often called terra-cotta pots, the name for fired clay pottery from the south of Europe, and which literally means "baked earth." The thickness and durability of the pot and the temperature to which it was fired determine how it will stand up to freezing temperatures. A glaze can make the pot stronger. Use only pots that can endure freezing temperatures for plants that overwinter outdoors. Always

ensure that excess water can drain from the pot; putting a shard or two at the bottom of the pot over the drainage hole, and setting the pot up above the ground by resting it on small stones will help. If the pots sit on the ground, be sure water can drain away from them during the winter. Make sure the pots cannot be blown over by strong gusts of wind.

For use in the garden, obtain large pots with a diameter greater than 18 inches (45cm). They won't fall over easily, and you won't have to water them as frequently. Smaller pots easily go unnoticed in a garden; with one large pot you achieve an effect greater than with ten small pots.

A flower pot that is placed in shade will soon turn green with algal growth. It is better not to clean the pot when this happens. The green pots look even better in the surrounding garden than the orangey-red ones. After a couple of years, a layer of moss will appear if you are fortunate, imparting an evocative sense of permanence.

Sandstone

Sandstone and limestone are soft types of stone that are used frequently in the making of statuary. The ability of such statuary to survive freezing weather undamaged varies greatly, depending on the hardness and porosity of the stone. In the winter, most garden statues can be left outdoors as long as they are wrapped up to stay dry. Special mats were once used for this purpose, but plastic works well, as long as the statues are dry before they are wrapped. Soft stone varieties will quickly develop a mossy growth.

The dwarf Kenilworth ivy (Cymbalaria muralis) is at home with old garden urns, and blooms all summer.

Page 431:
 A Spanish oil urn. It is better not to plant in vases and bowls not meant for this use originally.

This terra-cotta container is from Egypt. The pottery is very porous and must be placed indoors during the winter.

Concrete is not pretty when it is new, but after a couple of years, after the acids in the concrete have been neutralized, the first lichens start to grow in all kinds of colors, even if the object is placed in full sun. Garden statues of concrete are usually not very pretty; air bubbles in the casting can blur details in the statue. In England, a sort of artificial stone is much used. It is not a cast material, but rather is pushed into a desired shape manually. The contours of objects made of artificial stone are always clean.

In England, they make great use of concrete edging, particularly pretty when it is designed as the so-called roped edge. This gives a formal, finished look to a flower bed, and crisp definition to the perimeter of lawns. It serves to enhance any unusual or elaborate shape a bed, greensward, or reflecting pool might have, and it can border a path paved with any of many different materials.

Wood

Depending on how it is applied, and the type selected, wood can look unsurprisingly natural in the garden. As garden furniture it may have a rustic or elegant appearance, old-fashioned or up-to-the-minute. Wood can be treated chemically to last a long time outdoors without rotting. These chemicals are toxic, however. The use of wood planking is discouraged, as wood becomes slippery, especially in shade. For garden benches, hardwood varieties are often used, and especially teak, because this

You can encourage and speed up this growth by painting buttermilk or yogurt over the statue, which creates an excellent culture medium for mosses. (This trick works on rocks in your water garden, too.)

Concrete

Concrete is used today in the making of garden ornaments, but it has been around for a while. During the last century, concrete was used in parks and public and private gardens. Concrete was fashioned into artificial hollow trees with stairs built into the trunk, and once mosses grew thickly, these trunks couldn't be distinguished from the trunks of real trees. Today, concrete is more likely to be used for birdbaths, statues, and wall fountains.

If you have a contemporary-style garden, look through the catalog of a supplier of concrete ornamentation. Ready-made pieces in various sizes and shapes are available. If you need a water sluice, for example, for your water garden, factory-produced gutters (perhaps designed for another use entirely) might serve this purpose very well.

Terra-cotta rhubarb pots are ornamental in the garden, and practical, too.

does not weigh much and is relatively flexible. The natural oils in the wood make it water repellent, without additional treatment. A grey patina, a silvery glow, develops that only heightens the beauty of the object. Other hardwood varieties are also used, but they may be heavier, last less long, show cracks soon, or warp. Nowadays, almost all hardwood is sold as plantation wood, meaning that it is farmed, rather than harvested irresponsibly from nature. Checking this, however, is almost impossible for the individual.

If you want to be sure that your garden ornaments aren't constructed of endangered or rare wood, buy (or build) a bench of ordinary, softer wood. If you maintain it well with paint or a protective stain, the bench can last you a lifetime, especially if it is stored indoors during the winter. (In the old days, people always took the trouble

A wooden tree bench has to be built on the site. Once constructed, it remains in its place for good.

of storing chairs, tables, benches, and umbrellas in a sheltered place.)

Small trees and handsome shrubs are often planted in wooden barrels or planters. Versailles-style planters, for example, seem once again to be for sale everywhere.

This cast-iron bootjack has the shape of a snail.

This decoy goose, once used in hunting, is a jewel in the garden pond. Winter frost enhances its beauty.

Cast-iron stools are very heavy,   best.
so leave them where they work

With a simple handtruck, large planters can be transported easily around the garden.

Unpainted wooden garden walls and stockade fences of ordinary wood varieties are not pretty. They usually look better when painted in the colors of the house, to help them look as though they "belong."

Cast Iron

Cast iron was once an extremely popular material for fences, gates, garden seats, urns, pillars, steps, and an endless number of other ornaments. The nineteenth century was virtually a festival of cast iron. Only the surface of cast iron turns rusty; internally, the cast iron is almost always sound, even when the surface has rusted. Cast iron can withstand long periods of neglect, not that neglect is recommended. Maintenance can be limited to a bit of paint once in a while. Nowadays, all kinds of cast-iron objects are for sale: replicas of antique urns, foot scrapers, door knockers, lanterns in all different styles. You'll find everything from Victoriana to modern art. Remember, select ornaments that are appropriate with the look of the house. Treat cast-iron objects with care; the material is easy to break, and difficult to weld.

Wrought Iron

Wrought iron lends itself to innumerable applications. Wrought-iron objects are often pieced together (welded) from many small round or flat shapes. Unlike cast iron, wrought iron rusts in layers, and this undermines the structural integrity of the object. To help keep it from rusting, it should be galvanized, or maintained regularly. It is softer than cast iron.

These Empire-style chairs,   graceful, additional flourish of
made of wrought iron, have a   cast iron.

Zinc

Zinc is a cheap and flexible material. A zinc roof is perfect for a garden shed. Zinc is a nice alternative to corrugated iron or asphalt; it gives a much more romantic look than roofing shingles. The shine of new zinc disappears within a couple of months, leaving a sophisticated, matte surface.

Wrought iron fences have to be   order to prevent them from
maintained well with paint in   rusting.

Bronze

Bronze was very popular in the nineteenth century as a material for artworks for the garden. Unlike copper, bronze takes a long time to change color. Bronze is an expensive material, but for a central position in the garden, a bronze ornament may be just the thing. Bronze will last for generations, and can be a shrewd investment that increases in value. In the winter, bronze ornaments can stay outdoors. They don't require special treatment—no wrapping or building of removable shelters. Again, when you have small ornament, highlight it by backing it with a mirror, hedge, or trellis, or surround it on three sides with glass. Or, you might grow a sort of "stage set" or showcase for it of a small-leaved, evergreen hedge shrub.

Lead

Lead was used for garden ornamentation in ancient times. Marble statues were copied in lead, a material that can withstand freezing temperatures. During the baroque period, lead ornaments were treated with nitric acid to make them white, giving them a stronger resemblance to the marble statues and urns they imitated. Lead becomes a beautiful silver-gray, and requires no maintenance.

A wooden gazebo in the shape of a Turkish tent, from the beginning of this century.

Natural Ornaments

Plants trimmed into shapes—hedges, cubes, topiary, foliage corridors, rounds, and so on, are inexpensive ornaments that you create to your own specifications. You do need some imagination for such projects, to visualize the final result, which may take years. Plants that are excellent for trimming into shapes are *Buxus* and taxus, but the evergreen *Lonicera nitida* can also be trimmed into (slightly more irregular) shapes. *Carpinus betulus* 'Fastigiata' can be shaped into straight, tall columns. Geometric shapes such as cubes, globes, columns, and pyramids are easy for the beginner. Bears, peacocks, and other popular shapes for topiary require considerable knowledge and experience. Few horticulturists specialize in topiary. Beautiful niches can be trimmed into hedges, to accommodate statues or garden seats. Try to create harmony between the ornament and its surroundings; the only thought you want the viewer to have is how perfect the object in question looks in its place.

21 Practical Gardening Tips

When you are preparing to lay out a new garden, or to redesign an existing one, you have the fun of researching the possibilities in gardening books and magazines. Looking at all those gorgeous photographs can be instructive, and it is such fun.

However, not everything can be learned from magazines. Many things about gardening become clear only in practice. Listed below are some of these facts and details, based on the practical experiences of other gardeners. When it comes to gardening, doing is learning. Turn to this chapter whenever you need the wisdom of experience!

Weeds and Other Unwanted Vegetation

Algae and Moss on Stone and Brick

You can remove the vegetative growth by scrubbing with water and a stiff, outdoor broom. Walkways and terraces should be maintained well, scrubbed once a week in summer; be especially vigilant about areas in shade. A newer (and faster) method of cleaning is the high-pressure sprayer. With this method, the growth stays clear for some time, but you are using a great deal of water rather than your own elbow grease, a renewable resource!

Weeding

For removing weeds, you need a sharp hoe. A hoe, though it appears to have only a small blade, will allow you to weed a good-sized area in almost no time at all. In addition to this, because you work a hoe from an upright position, there is less strain on your back. The best time to weed is in the morning. The weeds are hoed up out of the soil and have a whole day to dry out, so that it is easy to remove them at the day's end. You must weed carefully when colder weather approaches; when you loosen the top layer of soil, chances improve that the soil will freeze. (The upper layer gives off heat when loosened.)

Regular weeding is the best method of control. It is critical to stay ahead of weeds! You don't want them to have a chance to mature and propagate, so you must stop them in their tracks, before they produce runners, or seed, for example. Certainly you can weed by hand ("grubbing"), but the right tool makes the job less onerous. Weeding a plot for the first time is different from maintaining a planted garden. Use a hoe where the plants are not too close together. But in areas where they are very close, weeding by hand or hand-held cultivator is the solution.

Plants in Containers and Pots

Planting

Use a prepared potting mixture when planting in containers. When you use garden soil, or potting mixture in which another plant has grown, you may spread disease to the newly potted plant. When you buy a packaged mixture, you know exactly what you are getting. Every newly potted plant deserves the best start you can give it, in sterile, balanced potting mixture. Another reason not to use soil from the garden: It will not retain enough water, causing the plants in the pots to dry out.

The Shape of Containers

Never put plants in containers that are narrow at the top. Removing the plant later to a larger container will not be possible, because the roots won't fit out through the narrow top because they will have grown and spread out. A container with straight sides is fine, and flaring sides just make transplanting that much easier.

Container Size

Instead of many small pots, plant two large ones and position them symmetrically, whether indoors, on a terrace or flanking an entrance, or out in the garden. The effect has much more impact. Little containers tend to get lost in the garden, even when clustered on a garden wall.

Sowing, New Plants, and Compost

Labeling

Plant labels from nurseries usually become illegible after some time outdoors, erased by sun and rain. In order to remember which plant you put where, you can make your own weather-resistant labels. Write the plant names on plastic labels with a pencil, first rubbing the label with some fine sandpaper before writing. The plant names will be legible for a long time because the graphite of the pencil works into the roughened label surface. Alternatively, wax pencils are fairly durable, but they run the risk of smudging.

Birds and Cats

Right after sowing, chances are that birds and cats will be after your seeds. In order to keep them away, place chicken wire over the area to be protected. Fruit, too, is popular with birds. You can protect trees, bushes, and smaller plants by covering them with chicken wire or netting. Nets have the disadvantage that they sometimes rest directly on the plant they cover, so the birds can still reach the fruit. (See also under "Herbs, Fruits, and Vegetables" in this chapter, page 444.) A solution for protecting very small plants is discarded nylon stockings, which will be strong enough to thwart the birds, yet soft enough not to damage the plants, which will still be able to grow, pushing the nylon as they do.

Compost

To help provide oxygen for your compost heap, start building the heap on branches and straw. As the compost heap builds, you must alternate layers of the various kinds of waste.

About every 8 inches (20cm), add some lime and, if possible, some garden soil. The compost heap should be kept moist. As it decomposes, it will shrink. To speed up the decomposition, it is useful to "turn" the heap, using a pitchfork or shovel to move the lower layers up on top. Do not put cooked food or any greasy materials on the heap, because this attracts vermin.

Today, many people separate their household waste, keeping "green" waste apart from recyclable glass and plastic, and from incinerables and those materials that go to the landfill. With a little patience, this green waste, added to garden waste in the compost heap, turns into compost, or "gardener's gold." Do not locate the compost heap too close to the house; it attracts insects. You can choose from many different models of the commercially available compost bins, if you prefer.

winds for any length of time. Cover exposed roots with a moist cloth when you are transplanting. Rehydrate roots that seem dry in a bucket of water immediately before you plant them. It is best not to plant out in the garden on very hot, cloudless days.

Bulbs and Tubers

Types of Soil

Clayey soil will remain cold and wet for a long time. You don't want to plant or sow in wet soil. Clay is often full of lime and contains many nutrients. It is particularly suitable for fruit trees and cabbage varieties.

Sandy soil is usually poor in nutrients and the organic substances that give it water retention. Therefore, it dries out quickly. The soil will improve when you add organic compost and peat moss. Because sandy soil is dry and warms quickly, you can start sowing and planting early.

Peaty soil does not dehydrate quickly because of the high humus content. This soil has the ability to retain water. Peaty soil is acid, containing little lime. Rhododendrons, azaleas, and heathers thrive in peaty soil. You can improve the lime level by applying lime every winter.

Loam is a mixture of sand and clay. It is ideal garden soil.

Nutrients

Adding compost, manure, leaf mold, and peat moss to soil improves the humus level. Humus is decomposed plant and animal material. It is rich in nutrients and holds moisture. Some soil types naturally contain many nutrients, but in other cases, nutrients should be added, whether they be organic or inorganic. The use of inorganic soil amendments exclusively is not good, because the humus in the soil will become depleted, and with that, the beneficial organisms, including bacteria, will disappear from the soil.

Replanting

You may notice, when transplanting, that the roots of some plants are very long. It won't damage the plant to cut a piece off, because the roots will recover quickly. However, never leave bare roots exposed to sun or drying

Planting Bulbs

After planting bulbs, it is a good idea to cover them with chicken wire to protect them from hungry predators. Birds and mammals won't be able to get at them, and the plants will simply grow up through the wire. When the bulbs start growing, mulch them with some compost, or dried or well-rotted manure.

Planting Depth

A rule of thumb: Plant bulbs (or tubers) at a depth equal to twice the diameter of the bulb. A tulip bulb 2 inches (5cm) across is thus planted at a depth of 4 inches (10cm). It is always best to follow the instructions on any packaging for the bulbs.

Saving Bulbs

Brush away any soil, and spread the bulbs (or tubers) out in a cool, dark place with good air circulation to dry a bit. Then put them in a box, or hang them in a mesh bag, in a dry, dark, cool, but frost-free place.

Replanting Bulbs

Some bulbs that have been forced for indoor enjoyment can be planted outdoors, weather permitting. This can often be done successfully with hyacinths, crocuses, and daffodils. Tulip bulbs are worthless after forcing, and hyacinths and crocuses forced with their roots in water (rather than having been precooled and placed to grow in a potting mixture) often have no chances of survival, either.

Annuals and Biennials

Selecting Annuals

If you want to buy summer-flowering annual plants in the summer, don't pick the plants with the most flowers. They will suffer most from the change from greenhouse to your garden or terrace.

Flowering Annuals

A garden of summer bloom is a beautiful sight—when your plants bloom well. Flowering plants need phosphorus, lime, and little nitrogen. (Too much nitrogen promotes foliage growth at the expense of flowers.)

Annual Plants

When you buy annuals—and this is also true for vegetables and herbs—and you want to put them in the ground, you first must make sure that they are fully hydrated. Most plants are rather dry when you buy them, so give them the water they need to get over the shock of being transplanted. Put the plant in a bucket or sinkful of water. You can tell that the roots are full when air bubbles stop rising. Make sure that the soil you plant them in is moist enough, because otherwise it will wick moisture away from the newly transplanted plants. Finally, water in your newly planted plants well.

Biennials

Biennial plants are sown before the summer, the year before they are to bloom. In May you can sow, for example, hollyhock and foxglove. Other plants such as the daisy, wallflower, and forget-me-not can be sown in July.

The best place for biennials is a sunny spot in moist soil. Cut the plants back right after they bloom. This prevents them from forming seeds. Some plants can spread very efficiently through their seeds; be especially careful with honesty, mullein, foxglove, and giant hogweed. You want your biennials to put their energy into growing strong and handsome, not into reproduction.

Sowing

You can sow annuals yourself. You can choose between two methods: starting the plants indoors and later planting them out in the garden, or sowing them outdoors right away. When you start plants in seed trays or individual peat pots indoors, you have the advantage of being able to sow earlier, and enjoy earlier flowering. The earlier you sow, the further along the plants will be when

they are planted outdoors. The critical factors when starting seed indoors are temperature and light. For germination, most seeds do not need light. As soon as the seedlings are visible, they need lots of light.

If you opt for sowing directly in the garden, begin with the sturdier varieties such as sunflower, marigold, aster, and nasturtium. Seeds that are sown outdoors often bloom quite late. You can begin sowing outdoors in April or May, depending on your climate.

Jam Jars As Hothouses

Never throw old jars away, but use them as little garden bell jars to protect young seedlings. Glass keeps the interior warmer and moister.

Creepers and Vines

Location

You can plant creepers and vines against a bare wall, at the base of an arch or trellis, or fence. The most common creeper is ivy, a sturdy, reliably green plant that grows quickly and is suitable for use as a ground cover, too. Ivy remains green in winter. The plant grows well in shady spots, even those with dry soil. *Clematis vitalba*, a woody climber, can also be recommended. This extremely fast-growing plant can overgrow everything in its path, so give it enough space. The flowers are white. Creepers have suckers, rootlets, petioles (leaf stalks), or tendrils in order to climb, but some creepers are sprawlers that cannot climb. They need support, for example, by tying.

Creepers can be planted in flower pots on the terrace or balcony. For annual creepers, it is best to use an oblong flower container. For such plants as rambler roses and honeysuckles, a larger container is needed, for these plants grow in size appreciably as they mature.

A Rose Arch As Niche

Rose arches and trellises can be placed against a wall, forming an attractive niche. This creates a nice spot for an urn, flowering plant, or garden statuary. If there is no wall, you can create a "back" to the niche by stretching gauze or all-weather fabric across the arch from top to bottom.

Twining Plants

There are left-winding and right-winding plants. Examples of left-winding plants are the string bean, black-eyed Susan, and the true morning glory. (See also under *Wisteria*, in the chapter "Climbing Plants A to Z," page 325.) Often, creepers are planted against a wall, but this is not always a suitable place. The soil near the foundation may be quite limey, and it is usually quite dry. If you still want to grow the plant here, do not set it right up against the wall. Make a wide planting hole, and fill it with good soil, amended with potting mixture and/or compost.

The Rock Garden

The Right Spot

Rock garden plants are best planted in late spring, so that there is no risk of freezing. Spreading gravel between the plants not only gives a naturalistic effect, but it has advantages. Rainwater will not stand in it, nor will the soil dry out quickly; weeds will be discouraged, and there will not be as many snails or slugs. A number of rock garden plants grow very well in shade. Elevating rock garden plants by tucking them among stones makes for excellent drainage; if the roots are waterlogged, chances are they will rot. If you can't situate your rock garden plants among rocks, it is a good idea to construct a drainage layer of small stones and pebbles under the area to be planted. After a while, these stones may work their way down into the soil, and you may need to apply a new layer. Rock garden plants root quite deeply, so tearing out a plant without harming it may prove difficult. It is important that you decide on the right place for a plant before planting it.

Rock garden plants are usually more upset by excess water than by frost. Sensitive plants can be protected with a glass plate or cloches (or discarded jam jars), if cold is a concern. Given their sensitivity to excess water, it is better to water them a little every day after a dry period than to drown them in lots of water all at once. When watering the smallest and the least established of your plants, use a rose head for a fine shower from the watering can.

Perennials, Ferns, and Hedges

Flowering Perennials

You can extend the bloom of some perennials by cutting them back about 1 foot (30cm), trimming the stalks somewhat irregularly all over the plant. The trimmed stalks will branch off and form new flower buds. If the plants are ugly after blooming, cut off the ugly portions close to the ground; depending on the type of plant, this may encourage a burst of fresh growet if it is early enough in the season.

Filling In

You can place some annuals in any bare spots between the perennials. It is best to do this in June, which gives the perennials enough time to show they are not going to perform as you would like them to. This ensures that there will be no ugly empty spots, whether because the perennial plants are young, have suffered frost damage, or stopped blooming too early.

Planting Perennials

Perennials are sometimes weak-stemmed or grow so tall that they need extra support. You can tie them gently to stakes, positioned close enough to support the plant without pulling it, but not embedded in its roots. A number of perennials do not like nutritious, humusy soil, preferring instead a soil mixed with sand or pebbles. Give your perennials enough water when you plant them. This is especially necessary in spring. It is best to moisten the soil before you start planting or sowing.

Newly transplanted plants require a lot of water—not a little bit every day, but a lot every week. Plant your perennials the proper distance apart; this is important for good development later.

Fern Varieties

There are ferns that do not reach even 1 foot (30cm), and there are ferns that grow more than 3 feet (1m) tall. Ferns can thrive in rather dark gardens, but there are ferns that do better in sunny, dry spots. Most ferns prefer a shady location.

Some fern varieties of note:

Ostrich fern
The young leaves unfold in spring. In the winter, the spur leaves stand up straight, while the fronds die back.

Glade fern
This fern is well suited to shady locations with a humusy, moist soil.

Oak fern
Holds its dark green leaves, and likes soil with a lot of humus.

Cutting Hedges

Most people tend to trim hedges farther back at the bottom than at the top, yet that is the opposite of what the hedge needs. Always leave the base a bit wider, so sunlight reaches the bottom branches unimpeded by overhanging upper growth. This is more attractive, too, for the hedge looks securely grounded, not top-heavy.

correct　　　　　　*not ideal*　　　　　　*incorrect*

Roses

Roses

Roses are lovely in the garden, and they can thrive on patios, terraces, and balconies, too. Use a large enough container and fill it with the proper potting mixture. If the container is too small, the rose will not grow and bloom properly.

Roses must be pruned regularly. Polyanthus roses, large-flowered, and miniature roses will bloom longer. There is, of course, no use in trimming flowers that bloom only once a season in hopes of repeat bloom.

Pruning

The best time to prune roses is March. Much earlier than that, and you run the risk of damage from cold temperatures. Pruning later results in late growth. Rambler roses that bloom only once are best pruned immediately after flowering, in June/July. Prune back hard any rose that isn't growing well. Compost is essential for roses.

Heathers

Soil

Heathers grow best in soil that is rich in humus and lime. If you don't naturally have the desirable growing conditions, it will be quite difficult to make the soil right. A tremendous amount of garden peat is needed. Make sure to buy a peaty soil mixture, because peat dust decomposes quickly.

The peat moss should be mixed into the topsoil with a shovel of sharp (builder's) sand. A heath garden in clayey soil is a difficult proposition, because clay is poor in lime. Heather does not grow in shade, but prefers full sun. The plants benefit from some compost once in a while. When the foliage turns yellow, there is too much lime in the soil, which makes it impossible for the plants to absorb the nutrients they need.

Limy Soils

Some varieties, such as *Erica carnea* and *E. × darleyensis*,

can grow in a somewhat limy soil. These varieties bloom in winter. It is best to plant heathers in fall or, even better, in spring. During winter it is too cold for the plants to form roots.

Planting

Do not set the plants too shallow. It is better to set these plants too deep than too shallow. If the plants are not deep enough, they will dry out, and then die. A sufficiently moisture-retentive environment is essential.

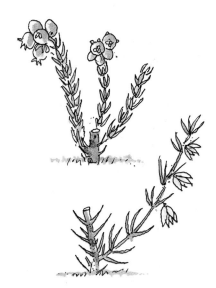

Pruning

Heather must be trimmed every year. Plants that bloom in summer or autumn should be pruned in March/April. Plants that bloom in winter and spring must be trimmed right after blooming. Pruning may be done manually, or with pruning scissors. You must prune by cutting twig by twig.

Water in the Garden

Algae

Algal growth is quite a problem in the water garden. An exploding algae population is unsightly, and unhealthy. Too much algae results from too many nutrients in the water.

There may be various causes:
- the water is not deep enough, which makes the temperature too high
- there are not enough submerged (oxygenating) plants
- too many leaves from nearby trees have fallen into the water
- there are too many fish

A Fountain

A small fountain in your pond is amusing, but it also serves a purpose. It oxygenates the water. For floating water plants, however, moving water is less hospitable.

Biological Balance

A healthy biological balance in a pond is not easy to achieve. The most important elements are the depth of the water and the type of plants. Slowly fill the pond with water. If there is enough water in it, you can start planting waterside plants and water plants, but you must wait a while for the fish.

A Small Garden with a Pond?

Dig a long trench across your garden—this will form your pond. Put a grid over the trench. Now the "trench" has a double function: walking path and water in the same spot. You can create a small water garden in a hobby greenhouse, using a grid; this is an excellent way to make good use of the available space.

A Pond with a Liner

For laying out a pond with a liner, first place a hard concrete bottom layer in the middle of the pond. Then place the liner. Now you have the ability to place an art object or flower container in the middle of the pond, where it is fully supported. Even a heavy container, planted with water plants, won't tilt or slip, because it is resting on the level bottom.

Making Your Own Pond

You can make your own pond with a special thick liner (0.02–0.04 inch thick), a type meant to last at least ten years. This gives you the ability to shape your water

garden any way you like. A concrete pond will last a lifetime, and a hard, preformed liner will age well, too.

Too shallow a pond will be too hot in the summer and freeze in the winter. Make sure there are no sharp or hard objects in the ground when you start working with flexible lining material. It is easy to buy too small a prefabricated pool, because once in the ground they look smaller than in the store. Give your new pond a professional finish by arranging flagstone or other paving material around the edges. This will make the edges of the pond less noticeable.

Lawns

Maintenance

A healthy lawn is a beautiful sight, but it does require some maintenance. When the lawn turns yellow, the cause may be the presence of grubs. Dandelions, which have deep tap roots, can become troublesome weeds; cut these plants out regularly before they can proliferate.

Troubles with Fies?

Plant a walnut tree (*Juglans*) in the lawn. You will not be bothered by flies under this tree.

Herbs, Fruits, and Vegetables

Herb or Weed?

Sometimes it is hard to distinguish herbs from weeds in the garden. One way to solve this problem: Take a large or small pot, depending on the size of the herbs you want to plant–and cut out the bottom. Set the pot in the garden, allowing the rim to stick up a little bit so that you can see it easily. Plant the herb in the pot. Everything that grows around the pot is weed, and you can now remove it without fear of tearing up your new little plants.

The Strawberry Plant

A strawberry plant 3 or 4 years old loses its vigor. It produces fewer and smaller fruits. Do not plant strawberries in the same place again and again; this will make them more prone to disease. Do not set the plants too deep in the soil, or too shallow. Compost has an

undesirable effect: The plants grow lush foliage, while the fruit seems more prone to rot. Compost is not suitable for strawberries. However, a mulch of straw between the plants conserves moisture and results in cleaner fruit.

The Blue Grape

The fast-growing blue grape is an ideal climber for a wall or arch. If you would like to harvest grapes, you should not only prune regularly, but also "pinch" the plant regularly during the summer, removing the young shoots developing in the leaf axils. You want to encourage vertical growth, for good height.

Bird Nets

Check daily whether birds are caught in your nets, so you can free them. It is preferable to choose white, conspicuous nets, which the birds can see and try to

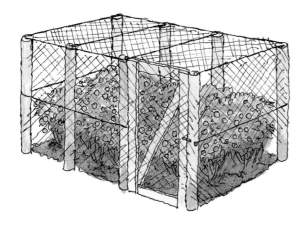

avoid. (Heavy black thread doesn't really give them fair warning.) An alternative is the fruit cage, tall enough so you can stand up straight in it.

Sowing Seed
The ideal soil for herbs is sandy soil with good humus content. Herbs that do not transplant very well are better sown directly where they are to grow, whether in the garden or in containers. If you want to start the plants indoors, place the containers in a place that receives good light, preferably on a windowsill. Sow herb seed shallowly, in a loose mixture. Then press the seed gently into the mixture, and cover with a thin layer of sand. Remember that germinating seed needs a constant lever of good humidity in order to work its magic. Many herbs grow best in full sun, among them anise, rosemary, marjoram, thyme, and lavender.

Potatoes
Potatoes are affected by many diseases. Therefore, it is better to buy new seed potatoes every year. In spring the potatoes start shooting; they should not start running until March. The potatoes should be kept in a dark place at a temperature of 60–70°F (15.6–21.1°C). In April you can plant the potatoes, about 18 inches (45cm) apart. When the potatoes grow above the ground, they will turn green. The green spots

are somewhat poisonous, containing solanine. Prevent the production of this undesirable substance by adding soil as needed to cover the potatoes and shield them from sunlight.

Potatoes and Frost
Potatoes are very sensitive to frost. Once frozen, a potato becomes soft and mushy. If the plants grow above ground too early and frost is expected, cover them with soil to provide a blanket of insulation as needed to prevent freezing.

Cucumber
You can grow cucumbers in shallow pans or in any flat container. Well-rotted horse manure is good for cucumbers. When four true leaves are formed on a seedling, pinch the plant to encourage lateral growth. Provide sufficient water and good air circulation during the summer. The cucumbers that rest on the soil (virtually all of them, if they are growing on the "ground") will become dirty. If you place black plastic mulch over the soil, it will not dehydrate, weeds won't be able to grow, and the cucumbers will be cleaner.

The Vegetable Garden
Vegetables need lots of sunlight, every bit as much as you can give them, so do not lay out a vegetable garden in shade; partial shade is not ideal, either. Consider carefully how many crops and how much of each to sow, and when.

Natural Placemats
When you eat in the garden on warm summer nights, the table can be set in style. Bring the garden right up onto the table, and let your imagination take flight. Use a fern frond or ivy leaf as a coaster for wine glasses. Your guests will be delighted to see large leaves as placemats. You might use rushes, ornamental grasses, or the like for a table runner, and hollowed out vegetables are charming flower vases.

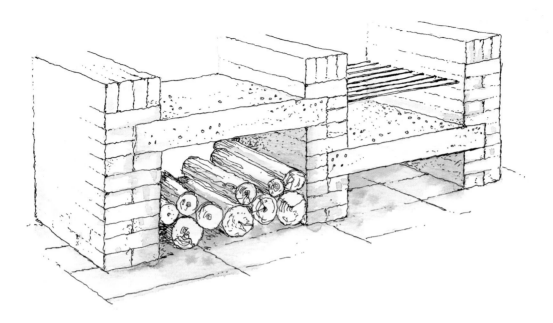

The Barbecue

If you enjoy cooking out in the garden, a permanent barbecue is useful. The drawing above depicts a practical design that is easy to construct: There is a storage area for wood—or bags of charcoal—to keep it dry and close at hand, and above this, a place for platters and bowls. The barbecue can be cleaned very easily: the ashes are simply swept away, and if necessary you can point the garden hose at it once in a while. The grill can be bought ready-made.

Homemade Toys

With some leftover wood you can make all kinds of garden toys. This seesaw is suitable for small children because it is not very tall, and it can be set up over soft ground. For the sandbox, you will want to construct a cover. When the children have outgrown the sandbox, use the spot for the compost heap or, covered with a sheet of glass or heavy plastic, as a small cold-frame greenhouse.

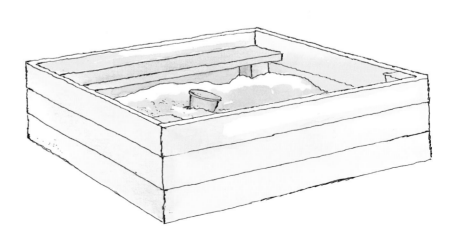

22 Terms

When you embark on gardening, you need to learn about many kinds of plants, all with their own cultural requirements. And in learning about the plants that interest you, you must also learn to understand what the horticulturist, the landscape architect, and the botanist are talking about. Their language is replete with names and terms that are not always understood by the beginner. Here are the most frequently occurring:

Acclimatize
Become accustomed to different, especially less favorable, climatic circumstances.

Acid soil
Strictly speaking, soil with a pH value of less than 7; in practice, soils with a pH value between 6 and 8 are considered "neutral."

Airing
Opening of windows, in order to lower the temperature and humidity in greenhouses and rooms where plants overwinter or are dormant.

Alkaline soil
Strictly speaking, soil with a pH value greater than 7. See "Acid soil," above.

Allée
Lane lined with trees or hedgerows on both sides.

Alpine
A plant native to high-altitude habitats; from mountainous, or alpine, regions.

Alternate
The arrangement in which a single leaf grows from each node on a stem.

Alternating growth
A system by which the same type of plant is not grown on the same place for two or more years. This system is applied in order not to exhaust the soil.

The onion is a fine example of a bulbous plant, with tunics that are clearly visible.

Annual plant
Plant with a life cycle of one season.

Apex
The terminus or tip, often the growing point.

Arboretum
A place where trees and shrubs are cultivated for scientific and educational purposes.

Aromatic
Said of a plant that is fragrant in all its parts except the flowers.

Assortment
Various sorts.

Author's name
The author's name is the name of the person who gave the plant its scientific name, for example the abbreviation L. for Linnaeus (1707–1778), written next to the scientific name of the plant.

Basal
Said of leaves that emerge from the base of the stem.

Bedding plant

Collective term for many annual or biennial plants that can be grown effectively in flower beds.

Biennial plant

Plant with a growth cycle of two years; does not bloom the first year. Foliage develops in a rosette.

Border

Border bed, bedding of undefined width, usually planted with perennials.

Bosquet

Planting of trees, surrounded by tall hedges (from the French, "grove").

Botanical

(Of plants): as found in nature, not improved.

Botrytus

Fungus disease, often of seedlings.

Bract

A multireduced leaf at the base of the flower stalk; picture the "flower" of Arum. The poinsettia has insignificant flowers, but the bright red, pink, or white bracts make the plant very attractive.

Bulbil

The tiny bulb that develops from the "parent" bulb; a single bulb may produce more than one bulbil at any given time.

Bud

Undeveloped flower.

Bulb

A subterranean, specialized thickening of the stem, with fleshy leaflike scales.

Calyx

Collectively, the sepals.

Cane

A woody stem that is pliable.

Canker

Fungus that causes deformation, especially in fruit trees.

Cascade

Water stairs.

Fasciation (band-forming) is a phenomenon that often occurs in plants. The well-known band-willow, Salix sachalinensis *'Sekka' is propagated by taking cuttings, thanks to this concrescence. Here, fasciation of the flower stalk of the foxglove.*

Coat-hook

Said of an incorrectly pruned branch; a stump was left behind on which a coat could be hung.

Columnar

Shaped like a column; fastigate trees are columnar.

Compound leaf

A leaf composed of two or more leaflets.

Conifer

Literally: bearing cones. Many evergreen trees and shrubs are conifers.

Conservatory

Room attached to the house (usually the living room), unheated, as a transition between house and garden, with seating during the summer. It is not specifically

Grass path.

intended for plants, but is often used for overwintering them. The word may be used to mean greenhouse.

Container-grown
A plant raised solely in a pot rather than out in the garden.

Container plant
A plant grown in a pot, that can't withstand winter outdoors, and that can be grown as a houseplant. Plants such as *Clivia* and *Zantedeschia*, that once were grown only as houseplants, are now counted among the container plants, because our houses today are too warm for them in winter. Garden plants that can stay outdoors in the warmer parts of the United States have to overwinter indoors in the colder parts. The plants are usually from the subtropics.

Corm
A bulblike portion of subterranean stem, as of a crocus, that has vegetative, propagative function.

Cottage style
Of the old farm-house style, thickly planted with flowers and little lawn.

Cormel
The tiny corm that develops from the "parent" corm.

Creeper
Plant that grows up a support by twining its branches around it.

Cultivar
Cultivated variety or breed; the cultivar name is always written with a capital letter and between single quote marks. See also "Variety," page 454.

Cutting
A piece of plant without roots, taken from one plant to propagate another. The cutting is potted as a new plant when it has developed roots of its own.

Deciduous
A plant that sheds its leaves seasonally.

Dioecious
Having male and female flowers on separate plants; for pollination, two plants of different sexes are required.

Dried plant in an herbarium from 1884.

Division
The separation of a plant into two or more pieces as means of asexual propagation, with the intention that each piece will produce a new plant.

Diurnal
Said of those flowers that open their petals only during daylight.

Ecology
The science occupied with the study of the relation between living things and their environment.

Endemic
In nature occurring only in a certain place or country.

Espalier
A ligneous plant, usually a fruit tree, trained to grow in two dimensions against a flat trellis.

Evergreen
A plant that holds green foliage from one growth cycle to the next.

Fan
Trimming form that is often applied to peach trees.

Fasciation
Band-forming, spontaneous concrescence.

Fastigiate
The outline of a plant wherein the branches grow erect from and continue to grow close to the stem, or trunk.

Fertile
Some ferns, such as *Blechnum*, have both fertile and sterile leaves. The fertile leaf has enormous numbers of spores. The inner flowers of *Viburnum opulus* are fertile, the outer flowers are sterile.

The tuber of Anemone blanda.

Flora
All plant life.

Flora forgery
Sowing plants in natural or seminatural locations, for example, in nature preserves and at roadsides, where the plants would not occur naturally.

Foliage bench
Garden seat topped with a trellislike structure on which creepers grow.

Folly
Frivolous or incidental construction, a romantic ornament in the garden.

Garden mirror
Garden ornament in the shape of a convex mirror.

Garden peat
Frozen black peat moss: peat moss from the lower layer, which can be used for gardening only after being frozen.

Germinate
To sprout, as of seeds.

Grafting
Inserting a piece of one plant into another plant so that they will grow together as a single plant, combining the desirable qualities of both. The root portion is called the "stock."

Grass path
Grass instead of pavement. Suitable for paths where not many people walk during the winter.

Green fertilizer
Growing a plant in order to turn it over in the soil as a fertilizer. Some plants used for this purpose are: clover, *Vicia*, *Phacelia*, and lupine. Most plants are sown in the winter and dug under in the early spring. Also known as "green manure."

Habit
The appearance or form of a plant.

Habitat
Natural growing environment or type of environment where a plant grows wild.

Ha-ha
A deep trench made invisible in the landscape when seen

One person may consider daisies in the lawn a weed.   *Someone else may like them and leave them there.*

from the garden, intended to keep livestock on a property.

Half stem
A tree with a short trunk; the branches start at a height between 2 and 3 feet (60–100cm).

Hardiness
The relative ability of plants to survive and thrive after prolonged exposure to freezing temperatures.

Herbaceous
Said of a plant that has no woody portions growing above ground.

High stem
A tree with a moderately tall trunk; the branches start at a height of 7 feet (2m).

Humus
Plant material in the soil that is decomposing. Humus is spongy, odorless, and dark in color. It is water retentive.

Pinetum: collection of coniferous trees.

Hybrid

The botanical result of breeding two (or more) species or genera.

Landscape architect

Designer of gardens, not necessarily the one who arranges the planting. A landscape architect is often not a horticulture specialist.

Lateral

Emerging from or on the side.

Lenticel

Opening in the bark of ligneous plants; a tree can often be identified by the shape of the lenticel.

Microclimate

The temperature range, degree of wind, humidity, and sun exposure in a small area.

Midrib

Of foliage, the central vein.

Monocyte

Single-cotyledonous, herblike plant belonging to the family of grasses and orchids.

Mulch

A soil covering that may be organic or inorganic, and that may be intended to impede the growth of weeds, conserve moisture in the soil, maintain even soil temperatures, and/or improve the nutrient content of the soil.

Native

Indigenous to a specific area, not introduced artificially.

Natural fertilizer

Organic fertilizer such as stable manure or compost.

Node

The point from which leaves arise on a stem.

Opposite

The arrangement in which two leaves grow from each node on a stem.

Orangery

A growing area, indoors or out, specifically for citrus trees growing in large containers.

Organic fertilizer

Manure.

Parasite

Organism that lives at the expense of another organism, without immediately killing the host organism: Without the host, the parasite does not thrive.

Patio

Paved courtyard or inner garden surrounded by walls, or a terrace.

Peat dust

Also peat mull: the partially decayed upper layer of peat moor.

Peat pot

Peat moss, sometimes combined with additional soil amendments, compressed into the shape of a little pot, for sowing seed indoors; an advantage to the peat pot is that the fragile seedling can be transferred to the garden, peat pot and all, so the roots continue to grow undisturbed.

Axis in a nursery garden.

Perennial plant

Herbaceous plant (nonwoody) that will thrive for an indefinite number of years, dying to the ground in the autumn, and growing again in spring.

Petiole

A leaf stalk.

Pinetum

Collection of living coniferous trees.

Plant breeder's rights

Patent for plants as determined in the treaty of Paris (1961).

Porch

A covering attached to the house, with at least one open side. A porch may surround the house or adjoin one side of it only.

Portico

Covered gallery, often at the terminal point of the main garden axis; a frequent feature of baroque gardens.

Potting mixture

An artificial mixture usually containing peat moss, with a desirable pH value; commercial potting mixtures often include inert materials such as vermiculite, for good drainage.

Pricking out

Transplanting seedlings to larger quarters; it is often necessary to prick out twice.

Prickle

Thorny protrusion of the upper tissue layer of a branch, cane, or twig; roses and brambles have prickles. See also "Thorn."

Propagate

The production of new plants by sexual or asexual means.

Prostrate

Creeping; growing close to, and usually lying on, the soil.

Raised bed

Raised beds, in which an area for growing is elevated or built up, came into use at the beginning of the twentieth century. A raised border in the garden appears larger, and raised beds enjoy excellent drainage.

Rambler

Ramblers are climbing roses with flexible canes, most of which grow from the base of the plant. The canes of ramblers can reach considerable length.

Resistance

Resistant plant strains are less susceptible to certain diseases.

Rhizome

Underground portion of the stem.

Rosarium

Garden of assorted roses.

Rosette

A wreathlike arrangement of leaves at the base of main stem, especially frequent in biennials, but also occurring in some perennials.

Shrub

Woody, relatively low-growing plant, that produces several to many branches, not one main trunk, from the base.

Sterile

Nonfertile; see also "Fertile."

Stolon

A stem that grows along or just under the soil surface, and which sends down roots that produce new plants.

Strain

See "Cultivar."

Stratify

Keeping seed in moist sand or peat at a low temperature for a period of time, in order to create conditions favorable to germination.

Suckers

Straight, usually vertically growing branches, usually said of shrubs and fruit trees. When the rootstock of a grafted plant, such as a rose, starts to send up stems or branches, these undesirable growths are called "suckers."

Symbiosis

The mutually beneficial growing together of two organisms, for example, of a plant and a fungus. The beech lives in symbiosis with the soil fungi; without the fungi, it grows less vigorously.

Synonym

An unofficial, but commonly used, botanical name (abbreviated "syn.").

Terrace

Level section of sloping ground or lawn. Also: paved area in the garden, usually adjoining the house, where one can sit.

Thorn

Ligneous, sharply pointed growth of a branch or leaf; acacias and hawthorns have thorns. See also "Prickle."

Topiary

Trimming or shaping of plants into desired forms, usually of taxus and *Buxus*. Topiary may be trimmed freehand or by following a template; the plant may also be grown on a frame.

Trellis

Ornamental support, usually constructed of wood, for creepers.

Trompe l'oeil

Optical illusion.

Tuber

Thickened subterranean structure that stores food for the plant.

Unisexual

Said of a flower that has either stamens only or pistils only.

Variegated

Said of foliage that is striped, edged, spotted, or otherwise marked in a color other than green.

Variety

Unlike "cultivated variety" or "cultivar," this is a naturally occurring subdivision of a species. The name of the variety is always written in lower-case letters, without quotation marks, to distinguish it clearly from a cultivar name.

Vegetation

The growth; the vegetation may be rich while the flora in the same place is poor. For example, a lawn has rich vegetation with poor flora. The reverse is also possible: Poor vegetation may include rich flora (little growth, but many kinds of plants).

Gazebo in the style of a Turkish tent.

Vista
Unobstructed view axis.

Wall greenhouse
An attached or "lean-to" greenhouse that uses one wall of the house for one of its long sides. See also "Conservatory," "Porch," and "Winter garden."

Weed
Any plant growing where it is not wanted.

Whorl
An aggregate of leaves or flowers, three or more, growing in a circle around the stem at any single node.

Winter garden
Built-in (or partially built-in) greenhouse attached to the house, providing a location for ornamental plants and places to sit.

Index

A

D

H

I

J

K

L

M

T

Acknowledgments

Many thanks to the photographers and companies that have provided their stock images:

Arboretum Kalmthout, Kalmthout: pages 75 above, 214, 222 middle below, 224, 263, 269 below

E.A. Barentsz, Oosterbeek: pages 17 below, 35 below, 75 below, 172 below, 234 above, 300 above, 306 above, 309 below, 319, 376 below, jacket

mevr. Bax, Lunteren: pages 160 below, 230 right above and below

G. v.d. Berg-Noordijke, Noordwijk: pages 15 below, 51 above, 69 above, 105 below, 118, 125 below, 139 left above, 148 above, 160 right above, 161 below, 165 above, 167, 176, 179, 180, 251, 295 above, 342 below, 382 below, 395 above, 448

Black & Decker Nederland BV, Etten-Leur: pages 87, 97, 98 below, 101 below

De Boer Steffen, Rijswijk: pages 100 above and middle, 101 above, 407 below

W.M.Th.J. de Brouwer, Den Haag: pages 45, 46 middle, 50 below, 62 above, 64 below, 107 below, 122 middle and below, pages 162 right above, 198 above, 225, 229, 231, 235 left below, 236 below, 240 left below, 244 below, 249, 255 below, 256 above, 258 above, 270 left above, 279, 280 above, 284 above, 296 above, 354 left above, 357, 360 below, 364 left below, 369 above, 372 above, 376 left above, 383, 385 above, 386 below, jacket

dhr. Buys, Apeldoorn: pages 15 left above, 25 below, 26 above, 30, 31, 33, 40 below, 44, 48 middle and below, 53 below, 56, 57 below, 60 above, 61 below, 65, 66, 70, 71, 73, 74, 78 above, 80, 90 below, 91, 92, 93, 94 above and right below, 95 below, 106, 108 above, 111, 115 above, 117, 127, 139 below, 158, 163 below, 185, 216 below, 218 above, 222 above, 226 below, 232, 235 above, 238 below, 242 above, 243, 245 above, 248 above, 250 below, 255 above, 256 below, 257, 258 below, 259 above, 261 below, 262, 270 below, 272 middle, 274 below, 275, 277, 282 above, 284 below, 285, 286, 288 above, 289, 290 below, 291, 292 below, 294 below, 299 above, 301 above and left below, 302, 304, 306 below, 307 below, 308, 309 above, 310 below, 311 above, 312 below, 313, 315, 317 above, 318, 346 right below, 355, 356 below, 359, 361 above, 362 below, 363 below, 364 above and right below, 365, 372 below, 381 below, 451, jacket

M. Claessen, Peer Wijchmaal, België: pages 40 left above, 41, 42, 43, 46 below, 47 below, 49 above, 57 above, 58, 60 below, 68 above, 77, 187, 211 left above, 213

D. Croockewit, Amsterdam: pages 52 left above and below, 54 above

J. Dieker, Doetinchem: pages 19 above, 51 below, 140 right above

Foto P.C. Driedijk, Bergen op Zoom: pages 47 above, 94 left below, 108 below, 121 below, 128, 178, 218 below, 240 right below, 260 below, 296 below, 312 above, 323, 369 below, 370, 373 below, 374, 376 right above, 379, 387 above, 410, 418, 447

I. Elias, Chaam: page 156 below

A.H. Hekkelman, Bennekom: pages 149, 234 below, 237, 244 above, 246 below, 398 right above

W. van der Helm, Spijkenisse: pages 69 below, 115 below, 316 above

O. van Heusden, Druten: pages 17 middle, 20 above, 21 below, 22, 72, 112 below, 120, 233 below, 247 below, 287 below, 288 below, 298 below, 300 middle, 307 below, 310 above, 356 above and middle, 358 below, 360 above and middle, 405

F. Hoefnagels Natuurfotografie, Asten: pages 59 below, 81, 82, 83, 84, 85, 102 above and middle, 103, 104, 105 above, 112 left above, 114 below, 121 above, 123, 124 below, 125 above, 126, 132 left below, 135, 136, 137, 138, 159, 162 left above, 163 above, 183, 184, 186, 189, 191 below, 193, 196, 197, 198 below, 199, 200, 201, 221, 226 above, 228, 238 above, 240 above, 241 below, 245 below, 246 above, 250 above, 252, 253, 254 above, 261 above, 264, 265, 267, 268, 269 above, 272 above, 273, 274 above, 276, 294 above, 303, 311 below, 326 below, 337, 354 middle, 377, 382 above, 385 below, 400 below, 402, 406, 407 left above, 408, 409, 415, 419, 449

M. Hop, Groningen: pages 16, 37, 40 right above, 241 above, 287 above, 299 below

Internationaal Bloembollen Centrum, Hillegom: pages 326 above, 327, 328, 329, 330, 331, 332, 333, 334, 335, 336, 338 left above, 339 above, 340, 341, 342 above, 343, 344, 345, 346 above and left below, 347, 348, 349, 350, 351, 352, 353, 389 left above, 390

middle, 392 middle, 393, 394 below, 396, 397 below, 398 left above, 399 above, 450 right above, jacket

Intertool BV, Roden: pages 96, 98 above, 99, 100 below

mevr. Kalkhoven, Apeldoorn: pages 18, 19 below, 20 below, 29, 34, 48 above, 50 above, 53 above, 63 above, 113 below, 124 above, 130 left below, 134, 146, 157 above, 164 below, 166 below, 172 middle, 188, 190, 191 above, 192 above, 212 above, 215, 217, 219 above, 223, 226 middle, 227, 233 above, 254 below, 259 below, 271, 281, 358 above, 363 above, 368 above, 380 below, 381 above, 384, 411, 414

R.E. Kresner, Zoetermeer: pages 164 above, 169, 171, 174, 175, 177, 182 middle

KTM, Leens: pages 366 middle, 378 below, 386 above, 388 below

C.M. Meuzelaar, Gorinchem: pages 32, 63 below, 67, 235 right below, 367 below

F. Meijer, Landgraaf: pages 25 above, 35 right above, 38, 39, 266, 413

dhr. Moerheim, Ouderkerk a/d Amstel: pages 141, 142, 144 below

K. Noordhuis, Leens: pages 8, 9, 10, 11, 12, 13, 14, 17 left above, 21 above, 23, 24, 26 below, 27, 28, 36, 49 below, 54 middle and below, 61 above, 68 below, 78 below, 112 middle, 114 above, 116, 130 above and right below, 131, 140 left above, 144 above, 145 below, 147, 148 below, 151, 155, 156 above, 157 below, 160 left above, 168, 170, 195, 212 below, 216 above, 219 below, 230 left above, 236 above, 247 above, 280 below, 282 below, 283, 290 above, 292 above, 293, 316 below, 317 below, 325, 339 below, 362 above, 368 below, 375, 387 below, 388 above, 389 right above, 391 below, 394 left above, 395 below, 397 above, 401, 404, 417, 420, 427, 428, 429, 430, 431, 432, 433, 434, 435, 436, 450 left above

Nijboer-Diepenheim, Veere: jacket

A. Nijdam-Dijkstra, Ravenswoud: pages 52 middle, 153, 248 below, 297, 382 middle

B. Roorda-Fables, Heemstede: pages 55, 102 below

W. Stegeman, Ommen: pages 95 above, jacket

S.W.T. Tolboom, Didam: pages 62 below, 79, 107 above, 143, 305 below, 366 below, 380 above

H. Ufkes-Knip, Zutphen: pages 390 above, 391 above, 392 above, title page

J. Uiterwijk, Beetsterzwaag: pages 129, 132 right below, 165 below, 192 middle, 242 middle, 320 above, 321

F. Verasdonck, Groningen: pages 202, 203, 204, 205, 206, 207, 208, 209, 210, 211 right above, 239, 314, 366 above, 455

G. Verswijver, Hoevenen, België: pages 270 right above, 295 middle and below, 298 above and middle, 301 right below, 305 above and middle, 354 below, 361 below

G. v.d. Weide, Doornspijk: pages 88, 89, 90 above, 113 above, 119, 122 above, 132, 133, 139 right above, 140 below, 145 above, 161 above, 166 above, 173, 182 above, 193 below, 194, 260 above, 320 below, 338 middle and below, 367 above, 371, 378 above, 399, 400 above, 403, 407 right and above, 452, 453, half-title page